Google Maps
Power Tools for
Maximizing the API

About the Author

Evangelos Petroutsos has an M.Sc. degree in Computer Engineering from the University of California, Santa Barbara, and has worked for universities such as UCSB and the California Institute of Technology. Evangelos is fascinated with geography and was among the early users of ARC/INFO. For over two decades, he has been involved in the design and implementation of mainstream business software and has authored many books and numerous articles on programming topics. He is experienced with spatial databases and GIS, and has implemented map-enabled sites based on Google Maps since version 2 of the API. He is currently involved in a GIS project for a gas utility company.

About the Technical Editor

Dr. Simon Monk (Preston, UK) has a degree in Cybernetics and Computer Science and a Ph.D. in Software Engineering. Simon spent several years as an academic before he returned to industry, cofounding the mobile software company Momote Ltd.

Simon is now a full-time author and has published books with both McGraw-Hill Education and O'Reilly. His books include three in the McGraw-Hill Education Evil Genius series as well as books on .Net Gadgeteer and IOIO. He has also authored *Hacking Electronics* and coauthored the third edition of *Practical Electronics for Inventors*. His most successful recent books are *Programming Raspberry Pi: Getting Started with Python* and *Programming Arduino: Getting Started with Sketches*, both with McGraw-Hill Education.

Google Maps
Power Tools for Maximizing the API

Evangelos Petroutsos

New York   Chicago   San Francisco   Athens
London   Madrid   Mexico City   Milan
New Delhi   Singapore   Sydney   Toronto

Cataloging-in-Publication Data is on file with the Library of Congress

Google Maps: Power Tools for Maximizing the API

1 2 3 4 5 6 7 8 9 0   DOC DOC   1 0 9 8 7 6 5 4

ISBN   978-0-07-182302-9
MHID   0-07-182302-6

Sponsoring Editor
Brandi Shailer

Editorial Supervisor
Patty Mon

Project Manager
Sapna Rastogi,
Cenveo® Publisher Services

Acquisitions Coordinator
Amanda Russell

Technical Editor
Simon Monk

Copy Editor
Nancy Rapoport

Proofreader
Susie Elkind

Indexer
Ted Laux

Production Supervisor
James Kussow

Composition
Cenveo Publisher Services

Illustration
Cenveo Publisher Services

Art Director, Cover
Jeff Weeks

Cover Designer
Jeff Weeks

To the loving memory of my mother

Contents at a Glance

Contents

Acknowledgments

I would like to start by thanking my friends George, Charles, and Gregory for their encouragement during the process of writing this book, from its initial ideas to the early reviews of the chapters and the sample applications. They've all contributed to this book in important ways. I would also like to thank friends and colleagues who took the time to look into selected topics and make suggestions.

I especially want to thank Simon Monk for reading the manuscript twice and spotting blatant errors and inaccuracies. Given his background in cybernetics and computer science, Simon brought to this project an unconventional view of the text.

Special thanks to the talented people at McGraw-Hill Education: the acquisitions editor, Brandi Shailer, who has followed every step of the process and handled the entire project, including delays and unexpected changes, with grace; Amanda Russell, who has kept us all in step by controlling new, edited, and revised chapters; the copyeditor, Nancy Rapoport, for scrutinizing every sentence of the manuscript; the proofreader, Susie Elkind; Ted Laux for preparing the index; and everyone else who has contributed their expertise and talent.

Introduction

Why This Book?

This book is the result of my interest in geography and applied math, and over two decades of experience in software development. With the introduction of Google Maps and the support of spatial data by SQL Server, I was able to combine both disciplines and work on challenging and interesting projects, including map-enabled web sites for hotel bookings, reports with spatial features, and the layout of a large gas pipe network on the map. I decided to write this book because I felt I had practical information to share that would be useful to many developers interested in all aspects of map-enabled applications, and also because it would be fun to write. And fun it was, indeed. I have been fascinated with Geographical Information Systems since my first encounter with satellite images: the first commercially available Landsat images in the late 1980s. These were low resolution images that we could view and process on bulky monitors through a command line interface.

Geographical Information Systems are based on spatial data, but span a very broad spectrum of activities and incorporate many diverse technologies: from large databases and complex queries, to advanced user interfaces and elaborate reports, and to the development of web services and JavaScript client applications. I hope that all readers will find in this book some useful information and programming techniques, ranging from KML to spatial databases, practical JavaScript techniques for creating highly interactive applications at the client and, most importantly, interesting sample applications that you can use as the starting point for building custom applications to address your specific requirements.

Who Should Read This Book

This book is addressed to developers who wish to incorporate maps in their applications, both in Windows and web applications. Even if you plan to add a spatial "touch" to a typical business application, this book will help you. After all, everything happens somewhere. The Google Maps API was designed to be used on the web and most of the sample applications included in this book are web pages driven by embedded scripts written in JavaScript. You will, however, learn how to use the API from within .NET languages to build very specialized and highly interactive desktop applications with embedded maps.

Regardless of the format of the application, all mapping applications are based on scripts that interact with the map. These scripts are written in JavaScript and are executed in the context of the browser. Programming mapping operations is nothing more than manipulating the objects of the Google Maps API, something that takes place from within a script at the client, and JavaScript is the only language that can be executed by all browsers. (Microsoft's TypeScript is in the makings, but it's not yet available.) This book is about programming the Google Maps API with JavaScript.

Of course, only learning the language and the objects of the API won't help you build map-enabled applications. The best way to master a new field or technology is to work with sample applications you like, or sample applications that are somehow related to a project you have in mind, so that you won't start building your own applications from scratch. Many of the sample applications included in this book are not trivial. You will find complete applications with many of the features you would like to include in a custom application. I also created large sets of data to help readers see how their application will behave with a reasonably sized data set. Apart from the data I borrowed from third parties, I developed an application to trace features on the map and reuse their geocoordinates, the Map Traces application, which is included in the book's support material.

This book isn't about creating web pages with embedded maps and identifying points of interest with markers. You will learn how to program advanced operations, such as annotating your embedded maps with labels and shapes, and exporting your annotations to KML files and even inserting your annotations in a spatial database, among other operations. This book will also show you how to develop highly interactive applications that allow users to draw on the map, enable your client applications to request data through web services, and visualize masses of data on the map. It will also show you how to animate items on the map to create visualizations that combine the spatial and temporal components of certain data sets (events that happen at specific locations at specific times). You will also learn in this book how to embed Google maps in desktop applications to combine the richness of the Windows interface with the unique features of the API.

What This Book Covers

Like most computer books, this one starts with an overview of the technology it covers. The first chapter is about maps and the challenges of producing maps. Then it continues with the basic objects of the API and moves on to fairly advanced topics. Typical computer book readers are not totally unfamiliar with the subject and they often read selected chapters. The book was written with this in mind and it contains references to related topics in other chapters, whenever needed. You can read the book cover to cover, or read about the topics you're interested in.

The book assumes some familiarity with programming at large, but JavaScript is not a prerequisite for reading it. It includes two chapters on JavaScript as it's applied in the sample applications because the book is addressed not only to seasoned web developers, but also to web designers and developers who may not be familiar with JavaScript. The scripts used in the sample applications are well documented, and you will be able to easily follow the code.

To make the book as useful as possible, I've included chapters that address different and diverse aspects of Google Maps, including a thorough explanation of geodesic features, techniques for handling many points of interest on a map, how to discover geo-coordinates from physical addresses with the Geocoding API, how to request instructions for driving from one location to another with the Directions API, and more.

How to Use This Book

The book doesn't simply explain the objects exposed by the Google Maps API; it covers many aspects of developing map-enabled applications. I have tried to include interesting applications that you can use as starting points for highly specialized custom applications.

To make the most of this book, you should open the sample applications and follow the code, as explained in the text. You will find in the text suggestions for extending the sample applications by adding more features to them. Visit www.mhprofessional.com, search for 0071823026, and then select View Product Details to download code and additional content for this book.

How Is This Book Organized?

The book's first chapter is an introduction to cartography: the science of generating maps. Understanding the basics of cartography will help you understand the seemingly "odd" look of the world according to Google Maps. You will also learn how latitudes and longitudes are used to identify any location on the globe, and you will be introduced to the shortcomings of projecting a round planet onto a flat surface. This chapter also serves as a very gentle introduction to the API. In the second chapter, you learn how to create web pages that contain maps and how to perform basic tasks on the maps, such as adding markers to identify points of interest.

The following two chapters are an introduction to JavaScript. These two chapters are meant to explain the basics of JavaScript to people who wish to program the API but are new to JavaScript. The two chapters do not contain a general introduction to JavaScript; instead, they address the basics of the language and the advanced topics that are used in the sample applications later in the book.

Starting with Chapter 5, you learn how to embed Google maps in your web pages. Chapter 5 is an overview of the objects exposed by the API: Such objects are the geo-coordinates of a location, the markers, even the map itself. The objects of the API are the map's programmable entities, and each object exposes very specific functionality through properties and methods. After reading Chapter 5, you'll able to embed maps in your web pages and customize the map's appearance.

Chapter 6 deals with desktop applications: how to embed the web page with the map in a Windows desktop application and how to control the map from within a .NET language. This chapter discusses how to control the map from within your .NET application by tapping into the client script.

Over the next few chapters, you will learn how to annotate maps. In Chapter 7, you learn how to create markers that identify points of interest and place them on a map. You also learn how to associate the bubble windows with additional information about the markers and how to handle multiple markers on a map. In Chapter 8, you will learn how to place shapes (such as lines, circles, and polygons) on a map.

Chapter 9 explores techniques for annotating maps interactively. In this chapter, you learn how to write an interactive application for editing shapes on top of the map, using the map's features as guides. The techniques discussed in this chapter will come in very handy in building highly interactive mapping applications. The same techniques will be used in Chapter 12 to build a mapping application with rich GIS features.

Chapter 10 is a detailed presentation of the API's geodesic features. In this chapter, you will see the difference between drawing lines and shapes on a flat map versus drawing the same items on a sphere. You will also learn about the geometry library of the Google Maps API, which contains methods for performing complex geometric calculations on the sphere. If you're not familiar with map projections, you should read this chapter.

Annotating maps is one of the mainstream activities for any mapping application, but you need a mechanism to store the annotations to an external file. In Chapter 11, you learn about KML, a format for describing spatial data. KML files can be rendered on top of Google maps with a single line of code. You can also share KML files that describe spatial features with other users, who will be able to open them on top of a Google map.

In Chapter 12 you will combine many of the topics presented in earlier chapters to develop a mapping application with GIS features. You learn the basics of designing an interactive GIS application on top of Google maps. You will actually build both a web and a desktop application with very similar features. This application will allow you to draw shapes on top of the map and add custom attributes to these shapes. You will also see interesting techniques for selecting a shape on the map and editing it.

Chapter 13 takes the topic of persisting spatial data one step further. In this chapter, you learn how to store spatial data to a database that supports spatial features, such as SQL Server, and also how to perform queries based on spatial criteria, such as the distance between locations, or locations within the bounds of a state or county.

Chapter 14 returns to a basic topic, that of manipulating markers on a map. This chapter discusses techniques for handling maps with too many markers. The following chapter is an introduction to web services, which enable client applications to request specific data from a remote server as needed. Being able to call web services in your script will help you minimize the amount of data included in the script.

Chapter 16 deals with the topic of annotating maps. In this chapter, you learn how to annotate maps with labels and even images, as markers are not always the best method of identifying points of interest. You will also see how to generate HTML pages with annotated maps as stand-alone pages and serve them to clients as needed.

Chapter 17 deals with two map-related APIs, the Directions API and the Geocoding API, which allow you to request instructions for getting from one place to another, and retrieve the geo-coordinates of a physical address, respectively. You learn how to use the Directions API from within web pages and display the suggested routes on the map, but also how to retrieve the directions returned by the service from within a desktop application.

The last three chapters of the book deal with presenting data on the map. In Chapter 18, you will find techniques for identifying locations on the map with shapes as an alternative to markers. When the number of data points increases to a point that you can't represent each one of them on the map, you can create a unique type of graph known as a heatmap, which translates the distribution on the data items with a color gradient. The last two chapters deal with moving items, or items that evolve with time on the map. In these two chapters, you will see how to visualize both the spatial and the temporal dimensions of your data with animation.

CHAPTER 1

Introduction to Maps and the Google API

Google is a company that, more than any other, shapes the way we use computers today. No scientific discovery, new technology, or space mission has had as much impact in our daily lives as the Google Search service. Need information on "anything"? Just google it. Another service from Google that has become a household term is Google Maps, a technology that added a spatial dimension to everything. Google Maps is much more than a digital map; third parties are adding all types of information on the map and new creative applications based on Google Maps surface every day.

All events have two basic dimensions: a *temporal dimension* (when it took place) and a *spatial dimension* (where it took place). Google Maps is the tool that helps you visualize the spatial dimension of an event. Besides data with an obvious spatial component, such as temperatures and city populations, even simple business data such as sales have a spatial component, as the two basic attributes of an invoice are its date and the customer's address. Even the simplest hotel booking applications provide a lot of functionality through Google Maps; the IP addresses hitting a specific site can also be easily tied to a location, and the list is endless. And then there are the GIS systems (Geographical Information Systems) that associate data of all types with geographical locations.

Up until now, the spatial dimension has been overlooked because there were no tools to easily explore the world. Not anymore. With Google Maps, you can see the earth at a glance, get an overview of your neighborhood, and view everything on our small planet in place. Everyone has seen photos of the Eiffel Tower in Paris or the Elizabeth Tower in London. But with Google Maps, you can view the monument in place. You can actually see what it looks like from the street level and drive around it.

Google Maps is also changing the way people look at the world. You can personalize the map by identifying the features you're interested in, explore cities you will never visit, plan your trips before getting there, and document them when you return. It's an amazing service and it comes for free to all (7 billion) of us. With Google Maps, you can create your own personalized maps of your neighborhood and the places you love to visit. All this is available to you on a variety of devices, including tablets and phones, and soon to your glasses.

In addition to the basic services of Google Maps (and Google Earth, for that matter) available directly from Google, numerous applications make use of this technology to add value to plain maps. Close to one million sites are built on top of Google Maps and these sites attract users with special interests. While most of these sites rely on the built-in functionality of Google Maps, many sites add value to Google Maps by embedding useful data and operations on the map. These sites are applications built on top of Google Maps using the Google Maps API, similar to the applications you will build in the course of this book. If you want to know how other developers exploit Google Maps, visit Google Maps Mania at http://googlemapsmania.blogspot.com. The site reviews third party sites that rely on Google's mapping technology.

Building Map-Driven Applications

Because readers of this book are more than familiar with Google Maps (every computer user is), this chapter starts with the basic ingredients of a map-driven application: an application that incorporates a Google map and allows users to interact with it in ways that go beyond mere zoom or drag operations. A map-driven application is a web page that contains HTML and some JavaScript code. The HTML content of the page takes care of the appearance of the page and, at the very least, contains a placeholder for the map. The script is responsible for rendering the map in its placeholder and enabling users to interact with the map. The script can be very simple, or very lengthy, depending on the complexity of the interaction model.

To better understand how Google Maps works, you need to understand the architecture of a map-driven web page. To display a map on your page, you set aside a segment of the page where the map will be displayed (or use the entire page for this purpose). You also download a program—let's call it the application—which is executed at the client. The client is your computer; it's your browser, to be precise, because the application runs in the context of the browser. The application at the client is responsible for the interaction between the user and the map. Every time the user drags the map, or zooms in and out, the application calculates the coordinates of the part of the world that should appear on the user's browser, requests it from a server, and renders it on the page. Google Maps is a client server application that uses the client computer to intercept the user's actions, and the server to retrieve the information required by the client on the fly.

The map is stored on powerful servers located around the world and every time a user requests a new map, an image is transmitted from one of these servers to the client. If you consider the number of people using Google Maps around the world, the size of the world, and the zoom levels, you will soon realize that serving all the users is an extreme challenge. Yet maps are downloaded to clients very quickly. To simplify the process of transmitting the requested maps to its clients, Google uses map tiles. The global map is broken into small squares and the client application requests only the tiles required to generate the map requested by the user. It's imperative that the servers provide the information needed at the client and no more.

The Map Tiles

Google's maps are digital and, as such, their content changes depending on the zoom level. As you zoom into the map, more and more information becomes available on the map. At the globe or continent level, you see just countries and then again not all of them. As you zoom in, you start seeing large cities and highways, then smaller cities and local roads, all the way down to your backyard or a Buddha monument somewhere in Asia that you will never see in real life. Google doesn't maintain a single map with all the details. Instead, it maintains different maps for different zoom levels, and maps at different zoom levels have different content.

To organize all these views, Google breaks up its maps into tiles and each tile is an image of 256 by 256 pixels. The size of the map at the client determines the number of tiles that must be downloaded from the Google servers. Even if the map is displayed in a 256×256 pixel section of the page, the user may center it anywhere and, as a result, multiple tiles may have to be transmitted to the client for a map that's no larger than a tile. At zoom level 1, the entire globe fits into a single tile, and when you view this tile there are no labels on the map—just the continents and the oceans (and the ice of the Arctic and Antarctic circles). This tile fits easily on most monitors and it's repeated sideways to cover the segment of the page devoted to the map. When you zoom in to level 2, you switch to a different map that displays the continent labels. The entire map is made up of four tiles, each one being an image with 256×256 pixels. The map contains twice as much information in either direction, or 2×2 tiles. Zoom in again and you'll see the names of the largest countries. This time the map is made up of 4×4 tiles, or sixteen tiles, and this process continues. At zoom level 10, the map is made up of 1024×1024 or one mega tiles. At this zoom level, Google keeps as many tiles as there are bytes in a megabyte! And you're still at level 10. At zoom level 20, there are $2^{20} \times 2^{20}$ tiles. That is 1,099,511,627,776 tiles—one trillion is a large number of bytes even for a typical server. Here we're talking about tiles, or $256 \times 256 = 65,536$ pixels. Multiply this by the number of tiles and try to read out the number. It's an incredible amount of information, all stored at Google's servers.

The tiles are generated from raw data and are stored in a format that can be modified. As the raw information changes, the tiles are updated. And then there are satellite and aerial views of large parts of the world, also stored as tiles. It goes without saying that all information is duplicated along numerous servers, which explains why Google Maps is never down and also why Google servers respond so fast.

NOTE It's no wonder Google is investing into clean energy alternatives because running all these servers with electricity generated from fossil fuels translates into tons of CO_2 per hour. There are no figures for Google Maps, but an estimate provided by Google for the energy cost of a single Google search is 0.2 grams of CO_2. There's no direct link between the two services, but the footprint of Google's services on the environment is not negligible. After all, Google is serving more users than any other company. Currently, Google uses renewable energy sources to power 34 percent of its operations, and this trend will continue.

In addition to storing huge volumes of data for the needs of its mapping operations, Google has to maintain this information. There are many people in many countries that actually maintain the Google Maps. New information is added on a daily basis as features are modified and as new data becomes available. The world is not static: New roads are built every day, new building are erected, and so on. The satellite images do not always correspond to the latest features on the ground. If you place a pool or a guest house in your backyard, it will be a while before you can see it in Google Maps, but eventually you will see it. And we're not counting the street view images, which include images in the Antarctic Circle.

How Tiles Are Organized

At each zoom level, the entire map is made up of X tiles horizontally and Y tiles vertically. The titles are numbered by the zoom level and their X and Y index. The application running at the client calculates the three indices of the tiles required to display the requested map and retrieves the appropriate tiles from the server. The tile that contains the entire globe has the coordinates 0/0/0: At the first zoom level, there's only one tile. At the next zoom level, this tile is broken into four tiles, two for the Northern Hemisphere and two for the Southern Hemisphere. The first coordinate is 1 for all four tiles (it's the zoom level). The second coordinate is 0 for the Eastern Hemisphere and 1 for the Western Hemisphere, and the third coordinate is 0 for the Northern Hemisphere and 1 for the Southern Hemisphere. So the coordinates of all four tiles at zoom level 1 are

```
Z=1/X=0/Y=0,
Z=1/X=1/Y=0,
Z=1/X=0/Y=1 and
Z=1/X=1/Y=1
```

This process continues until the maximum zoom level is reached and at each level the number of tiles is doubled in each direction. This isn't the type of information that will help you design mapping applications, and you will never have to request tiles from within your script. It always feels good, however, to demystify some technology, especially when it's based on simple principles.

You may use this information if you plan to substitute the background of the map with your own image. You obviously can't create a better map of the earth, but you can use any other image as the background. The following site demonstrates this technique and it explains how it was done (the site was built with version 2 of the API and hasn't yet been upgraded to version 3): http://forevermore.net/articles/photo-zoom/.

This site uses the interface of Google Maps to enable users to navigate through an extremely large image with the zoom and drag operations used by Google Maps. The author of the photo-zoom site broke up the image into tiles and serves it as the background of Google Maps.

You can use Google's documentation at the following URL to research the use of custom images as map backgrounds:

```
https://developers.google.com/maps/documentation/javascript/
maptypes?hl=pl#ImageMapTypes.
```

The sample application provided by Google demonstrates how the surface of the moon is displayed in Google Moon. Google Moon is based on the same technology as Google Maps, but it uses different tiles and there's no roadmap view for the moon (not yet). As you will read in the documentation, the individual tiles are requested with a URL like the following:

```
http://mw1.google.com/mw-planetary/lunar/lunarmaps_v1/clem_bw/Z/X/Y.jpg
```

where Z is the zoom level, X the x-coordinate and Y is the y-coordinate of the desired tile. This URL isn't going to work if you substitute values for the X, Y, and Z parameters. It must be called from within the application. However, it's possible to create your own background for Google Maps by creating the tiles that make up the entire image at all (or selected) zoom levels and naming them appropriately.

By the way, this tile-naming scheme is not unique to Google Maps. All services that provide map backgrounds, including Bing Maps, use the same technique because it's simple and it works very well.

Cartography 101

Google provides maps by combining the tiles that have been prepared and stored at their servers. But where did the information come from? To make the most of Google Maps, you need to understand how maps are constructed. Even though Google has taken care of this step for you and provides a global map with all the detail you may need, you should be aware of the process of map production, mainly because there are inherent limitations— some very serious limitations, actually.

The science of map making is known as *cartography*. To some extent, it's also an art, although the creative part of cartography is in the decline with so much aid from satellites. To appreciate cartography, think of it as the science, or practice, of mapping a round planet onto a flat surface, be it a computer screen or a printed map. People have been fascinated by the vastness of the planet and have tried to document the world since they started traveling. Figure 1-1 shows the map of Ptolemy dating back to the second century. This map depicts the "known world" at the time: the countries around the Mediterranean and the Indian Ocean. Figure 1-2 shows the same area in Google Maps. This part of the world hasn't changed over the last 2,000 years, but the cartography techniques have surely evolved.

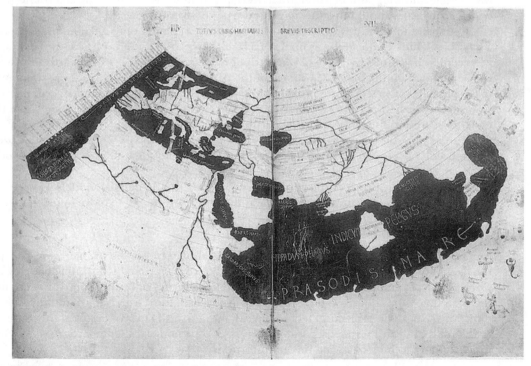

Figure 1-1   The world according to Ptolemy (courtesy of Wikipedia)

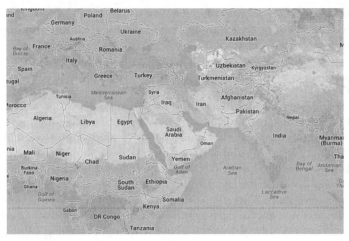

Figure 1-2 The same part of the world according to Google

The goal of cartography is to project the features of a round planet onto a flat surface, which is the map. To put it simply, there's no way to "unfold" the surface of the earth on a flat surface. It's like trying to lay the peels of an orange on a flat surface (between two glasses, for example). Parts of it will be squashed together, and parts of it will come apart. Conversely, you can't wrap a printed page around a sphere; no matter how you go about it, the paper will wrinkle and there will be substantial overlaps. In short, you can't project a round planet on a flat surface without introducing various types of distortion.

To transfer the features from the surface of a round planet onto a flat map, we perform a *projection*. Think of the globe as made of a semitransparent material and a source of light in its center. If you place a piece of white paper near this globe, part of the earth's surface will be mapped on the paper. If you orient the paper correctly, you will end up with a map that is partially correct. Features near the center of the map are depicted more accurately than features away from the center (assuming that the center of the map is the point where the paper is nearest to the globe). This map can be considered accurate for a small area. For other areas you would have to use different maps. Even though you will end up with dozens, or hundreds, of (mostly) accurate maps, you won't be able to stitch them together to produce a large map.

There are many projection techniques, all based on mathematical models. Google Maps uses the Mercator projection, so this is the only projection we will explore in this book.

The Mercator Projection

Can we project the entire globe on a flat surface? The answer is yes, as long as we accept the fact that no projection is perfect. There are different types of errors introduced by each projection type, and no single projection minimizes all types of errors. Some projections preserve shapes but not sizes; other projections preserve local sizes but not distances or directions. No single projection technique can minimize all types of errors at the same time, and that's why there's a separate category of projections, called *compromise projections*, which attempt to hit a balanced mix of distortions.

The projection used by Google Maps is the Mercator projection. Proposed by the Dutch cartographer Gerardus Mercator in 1569, the Mercator projection has become the standard projection for nautical maps and remains quite popular even today. Over the years, maps based on Mercator's projection have become very popular. The maps in basic geography books use this projection and the wall maps at school also used the Mercator projection. As a result, we've learned to accept gross inaccuracies, such as Greenland appearing as large as Africa while, in reality, Greenland is only a small fraction of Africa. On the positive side, the Mercator projection yields a rectangular map and turns parallels and meridians (the vertical and horizontal circles going around the globe) into straight lines, as shown in Figures 1-6 and 1-7 later in this chapter. This is the very feature that made the Mercator maps so useful to sailors.

Mercator devised this map construction technique to assist sailors. The name of his map was "new and augmented description of Earth corrected for the use of sailors." It's clear that Mercator's map was designed to assist sailing, which was a risky business at the time. Moreover, the word "corrected" indicates that he was aware of the errors introduced by his projection technique.

Performing the Projection

The Mercator projection is a cylindrical projection: It's produced by wrapping a cylinder around the globe so that it touches the globe at the equator. The features on the globe are projected on the cylinder by lines that start at the center of the globe, pass through the specific feature, and extend to the surface of the cylinder. After projecting all the features on the cylinder, you unfold the cylinder and you have a flat map.

To understand the way Mercator projected the earth on a map and the distortions introduced by this projection, consider the following explanation, which was suggested by Edward Wright in the seventeenth century, almost a century after Mercator proposed his technique. Imagine that the earth is a balloon and the features you're interested in are drawn on the surface of the balloon. Place this balloon into a hollow cylinder so that the balloon simply touches the inside of the cylinder. The points of the balloon that touch the cylinder form a circle that divides the balloon in two halves. This circle is the equator by convention. Since the balloon is a perfect sphere, any circle that divides it into two hemispheres is an equator and there's an infinity of equators you can draw on a sphere.

Now imagine that the balloon expands inside the cylinder and the features drawn on the balloon's surface are imprinted on the inside surface of the cylinder. As the balloon is inflated, more and more of its surface touches the cylinder's surface. No matter how much the balloon is expanded, however, the two poles will never touch the cylinder. This explains why you'll never see the two poles on a conventional map. All maps show parts of the polar circles, but never the two poles, because the poles can't be projected on the cylinder wrapped around the equator. Features near the equator will touch the surface early, before the balloon is substantially inflated, and these are the features that are mapped with very little distortion. Features far from the equator will touch the cylinder's surface only after the balloon has been inflated substantially.

There are variations to reduce the errors of the Mercator projection. The part of the sphere with the least distortion is the part that touches the cylinder on which the globe is projected. This is the part of the world on and near the equator. As you move from the equator toward either of the poles, the distortion becomes more and more significant. The type of distortion introduced by the Mercator projection changes the size of large shapes. This explains why Greenland appears to be larger than Australia on Google maps, while in reality it's much smaller.

To minimize the distortion, cartographers can make the cylinder smaller than the equator so that part of the earth lies outside the cylinder. This part is also projected on the equator with the same math, but it's projected from a different direction. With this projection there are two zones of minimal distortion and they're above and below the equator, where the cylinder cuts through the surface of the earth. The advantage of this projection, known as *secant projection*, is that the distortion starts above and below the equator and the usable part of the map extends a bit further to the north and a bit further to the south. If you consider that most of the population lives in a zone to the north of the equator, the most populated part of the world is depicted more accurately.

Why the Mercator Projection

The next question is, of course, why has Google used a practically ancient projection for its maps? Google Maps is a service for viewing small parts of the world, not an accurate depiction of the globe. When you zoom down to your neighborhood, the map should match the satellite view. The Mercator projection doesn't change small shapes. Even if it does, it does so in a uniform manner, which is quite acceptable. The important point to keep in mind is that Google Maps treats the earth as a perfect sphere and that the global view of the map is not very accurate near the poles. Open Google Maps at zoom level 1 and you will see most of the Arctic and Antarctic circles, but not the poles themselves. The Mercator projection is practically useless at latitudes over 70 degrees in either direction. The most northern tip of Finland is at latitude 71 degrees. In the opposite direction, the most southern tip of Chile is at –55 degrees (or 55 degrees south). The parts of the world that are of interest to most of us are well within the range of the Mercator projection.

Figure 1-3 is borrowed from Chapter 10 and demonstrates the type of distortion introduced by the Mercator projection. All the circles you see in the figure have the same radius, but they're drawn at different parallels. The sizes of the circles are getting larger the further away from the equator. The pattern shown in the figure is known as Tissot Indicatrix and is discussed in detail in Chapter 10.

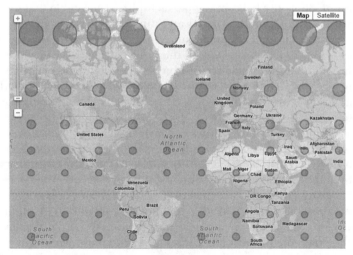

Figure 1-3   This pattern of equal radii circles repeated at constant latitude/longitude values shows how shapes are distorted far from the equator.

Google Earth to the Rescue

Is there an optimal projection technique? As far as Google Maps go, the answer is no, because the projection process will inevitably distort the map. One might claim that the best maps should be shaped like shells: If you could carry with you maps printed on curved surfaces, you'd have a much more accurate view of the world. While carrying such maps is out of the question for most practical purposes, the digital era has made non-flat maps a reality. Welcome to Google Earth. Google Earth displays the earth as-is on the monitor and it doesn't introduce the usual distortions resulting from the projection process. The monitor is still flat, but what you see in Google Earth is a round planet. When you zoom in deeply enough, the visible area is so small that it's practically flat. Viewing details on Google Earth is like projecting a small part of the earth on a flat surface without distortion. As you zoom out, you see the earth in its true shape, not a flattened version of it. When more elaborate 3D viewing techniques become widely available, flat maps will become as antiquated as the Ptolemy map, and Google Maps will be a thing of the past.

If you install Google Earth, you will be able to see any part of the world without distortion. If you place yourself right over Greenland and Australia, you will be able to compare their sizes, because you're seeing them in their true scale, as shown in Figure 1-4. The problem with Google Earth, however, is that you can't view the entire globe at once. On Google Maps, you can view both islands on the same map, but you can't compare their sizes.

Compare the relative sizes of Greenland and Australia in Google Earth and in Google Maps, shown in Figures 1-4 and 1-5. Google Earth doesn't introduce any distortion to the shapes in its center, but you can view only a small percentage of the planet at the time.

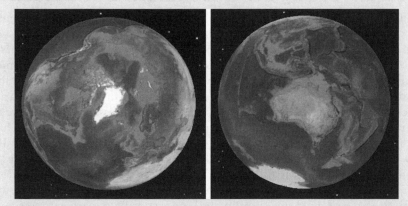

Figure 1-4   On Google Earth, you can compare the sizes of Australia and Greenland, even though you can't view both islands at once.

(continued)

Figure 1-5   Google Maps distorts heavily the shapes far from the equator.

A Global Addressing Scheme: Parallels and Meridians

Another important question that has to be answered before attempting to make a map is how we identify a point on the earth's surface. On the plane, we always use two axes: the horizontal (or X) axis and the vertical (or Y) axis. Any point on this plane is identified by its horizontal and vertical displacements from the origin. The two displacements are the point's coordinates, and by convention we list first the horizontal and then the vertical coordinate. The origin is where the two axes meet. The units along the two axes may correspond to actual, meaningful values, but this isn't necessary. The purpose of coordinates is to uniquely identify each point on the plane. Of course, if the coordinates have meaningful units, they're much more useful in that they allow us to compare distances. If the plane is a map of a town, or the blueprint of a building, then the units on the two axes are units of length, such as meters or feet.

To identify locations on the surface of the earth, we use two coordinates, which are known as *geo-coordinates* or *geo-spatial* coordinates. These coordinates are expressed in degrees because the earth's equator is a perfect circle (as far as Google Maps is concerned, of course) and, as such, it spans 360 degrees. Any circle on the surface of the earth parallel to the equator also spans 360 degrees, even though it's smaller than the equator and as you approach the poles these circles are very small. Instead of the two displacements we use on the plane, on the sphere we use two circles to identify the location of a point on the surface of the sphere. One of the circles is parallel to the equator and goes through the point in question, and the other one goes through the two poles and the same point. The two circles are perpendicular to one another. (Two circles are perpendicular to one another when the planes on which they lie are perpendicular to one another.)

Figure 1-6 shows a location on the earth and the two circles that identify this location on the sphere. One of them goes through the specific location and the two poles. All circles that go through the two poles are called *meridians*. The origin of this circle is the equator and angles to the north are positive angles from 0 to 90 degrees (the North Pole is at 90 degrees), while angles to the south of the equator are negative values from 0 to –90 (the South Pole is at –90 degrees). The second circle is parallel to the equator. All circles parallel to the equator are called *parallels*. The two angles that identify every point on the surface of the sphere are called *latitude* and *longitude*. The point's longitude is the angle between the prime meridian and the meridian going through the point (λ). The point's latitude is the angle between the equator and the parallel going through the same point (φ).

We also need to define a starting point on each circle, from where we'll measure the angles. The origin for the parallels is the equator: Each parallel is defined by its distance from the equator in degrees. The distance of a parallel from the equator is the angle formed by a radius that extends from the center of the earth to the equator and another radius that extends from the center of the earth to the specific parallel. However, there's no apparent origin for the meridians, so an origin has been defined arbitrarily. The first meridian, known as the *prime meridian*, is the meridian that goes through the two poles and through the Royal Observatory in Greenwich near London. If you rotate the prime meridian around its north-south axis, it will cover the entire sphere, and it will yield all other meridians. The equator can't produce the other parallels by rotation. Figure 1-7 shows the locations of the equator and the prime meridian on the map. In the figure, which was produced by Google Earth, you see two important parallels: They're the parallels at 23.5 and -23.5 degrees (or 23.5 degrees north and south) and they're known as the Tropic of Cancer (north) and the Tropic of Capricorn (south), respectively. The zone inside the two tropics is the part of the

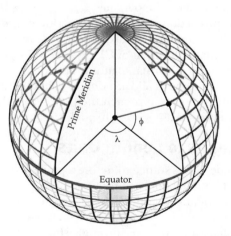

Figure 1-6   Identifying a location on the globe with latitude (φ) and longitude (λ) value.

Figure 1-7   The prime meridian, equator, and a few meridians and parallels on the globe

earth that gets directly under the sun. The position of the earth directly under the sun is the location nearest to the sun and it changes as the earth rotates. No location outside this zone ever gets directly under the sun.

Imagine a plane that slices the earth in two halves along the equator. Move this plane north or south and keep it parallel to the equator's plane at all times. The intersection of this plane with the globe yields the parallels.

On the Mercator projection, parallels and meridians are converted into straight lines, which is an extremely convenient feature. It was, at least, extremely convenient to sailors for centuries, before the deployment of GPS (Geographical Positioning System) satellites. Figure 1-8 shows some lines of constant latitude and longitude on Google Maps. The distance between meridians is the same at all latitudes and all longitudes. The distance between parallels becomes larger as they approach the poles, even though all parallels are spaced 10 degrees apart. The darker line going through Congo is the equator.

Converting Angles to Length Units

Latitude and longitude values suffice to define a point on a sphere, regardless of the size of the sphere; you would use the same values to define a point on a marble ball, or on the sun. The two values represent angles and they're adequate to identify any point on the sphere. They can also be translated to distances on the surface of the earth. The API treats the earth as a perfect sphere and so a specific angle should present a specific distance on the surface of the earth. On the equator, each degree corresponds to approximately 69 miles

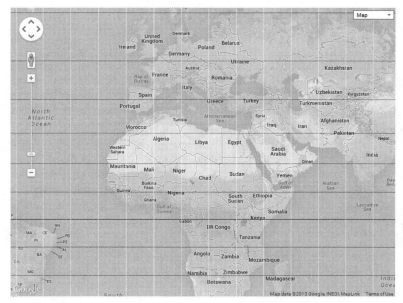

Figure 1-8   Parallels and meridians are mapped into straight lines under the Mercator projection.

and here's why. The equator is a full circle spanning 360 degrees and its circumference is
2 * π * R where R is the earth's radius. A good approximation of the earth's radius is
3,960 miles, or 6,371 kilometers. The circumference of the equator is 24,881 miles and
corresponds to a full circle. The distance on the surface of the earth that corresponds to
1 degree is 1/ 360th of the circumference: 24,881/360, or 69.11 miles.

If you perform the same calculations along a meridian, the result will always be the
same. If you perform the same calculations on a parallel other than the equator, the result
will be smaller because the parallels are not equal. The parallels become smaller as you
move away from the equator. One degree of longitude is 69.11 miles on the equator and it
shrinks to zero at the poles. At a latitude of 45 degrees, the circumference of the parallel is
2 * π * R * cos(λ) or 19,060 miles (λ being the latitude). If you divide this by 360,
the distance on the surface of the earth corresponding to 1 degree of longitude at the
specific latitude is 52.95 miles. You realize that the use of units of length to express
coordinates on the sphere is out of the question. The angles are the only alternative and
work nicely all over the globe. Angles are often used to specify distances because an angle
of 1 degree is always the same, regardless of where it's projected on the earth's surface.

Longitude and latitude angles are expressed as decimal angles. Latitude values are
measured from the equator and they go from –90 to 90 with positive angles corresponding
to points in the Northern Hemisphere and negative values corresponding to points in the
Southern Hemisphere. Longitude values are measured from the prime meridian and they
go from 0 to 180 in the Eastern Hemisphere (east of the prime meridian) and from 0 to
–180 in the Western Hemisphere (west of the prime meridian). The Latitudes Longitudes
application (see Figure 1-9) shows the coordinates of any location on the globe. Just click to

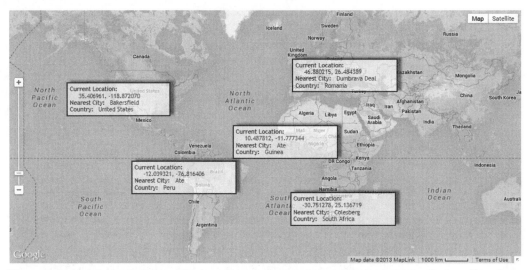

Figure 1-9 Use the Latitudes Longitudes web page to experiment with the geo-coordinates of locations around the globe.

place a label with the current location's coordinates on the map. To delete a label, simply click it. The label also contains the nearest city (if available) and the country you clicked.

A slightly different notation uses positive numbers and a suffix to identify the hemisphere. This notation uses positive values for western longitudes and southern latitudes and the suffix E (for East), W (for West), N (for North), and S (for South). The coordinates of the city Ate in Peru can be written as (−12.039321, −76.816406) or as (12.039321W, 76.816404S). This notation of coordinate specification is called *decimal degrees* because it uses fractional degrees.

The Degrees-Minutes-Seconds System

Another common method of expressing angles is the degrees, minutes, and seconds notation (DMS units). If you look up the geo-coordinates of LAX, for example, many sites list it as 33°56′33″N 118°24′29″W. The first part of this expression is the latitude and the second part is the longitude, and each coordinate is expressed in degrees, minutes, and seconds. It's very similar to decimal degrees, only minutes are 1/60 of a degree and seconds are 1/60 of a minute.

Let's demonstrate the process of converting latitude/longitude values into DMS notation with an example. The geo-coordinates of the Eiffel Tower in decimal degrees are (48.8582, 2.2945). The integer part of the angle corresponds to degrees and doesn't change. The 0.8582 degrees of latitude are 60 * 0.8582, or 51.492 minutes. The integer part of this value is the number of minutes of latitude. The fractional part, 0.492 minutes, corresponds to 60 * 0.492, or 29.52 seconds. So the 48.8582 degrees of latitude correspond to 48 degrees, 51 minutes, and 29.52 seconds. The coordinates in the DMS system are written with the N/S qualifier for the latitude values (depending on whether they lie in the northern or Southern Hemisphere) and the W/E qualifier for the longitude value. The coordinates of the Eiffel Tower in the DMS system are written as 48°51′29.5″N, 2°17′40.2″E.

The Google Maps API uses decimal degrees, so if you have the DMS coordinates of a point, here's how you will calculate the decimal degrees value. This time, let's use the coordinates of the Statue of Liberty in New York: 40°41′21″N 74°2′40″W. Because the longitude value lies in the Western Hemisphere, it will have a negative sign in the decimal degrees system. The degree values remain as they are. The 41 minutes of latitude are 41/60 or 0.6833 degrees, and the 21 seconds are 21/(60 * 60) or 0.0058 degrees. The latitude value of the monument's coordinates is 40 degrees and 0.6833 + 0.0058, or 40.6891 degrees. With similar calculations, the longitude value is 74.0444W, or –74.0444. The coordinates of the Statue of Liberty in DMS notation are 40°41′21″N 74°2′40″W and in decimal degrees notation they are (40.6891, –74.0444).

The Google Maps API

You know how to identify any point on the surface of the earth and you have a good understanding of the projection process and the distortions it produces. To exploit Google Maps, you must familiarize yourself with a component that Google developed for you, and you can reuse it in your pages to add mapping features to them. The functionality of Google Maps is made available to developers through an Application Programmer's Interface (API), a specification of how an application exposes its functionality through methods and properties to other applications. The Google Maps API is a set of objects that represent the programmable entities of the map. These objects are the Map object that represents the map itself; the Marker object, which represents the markers you place on the map to identify points of interest; the InfoWindow object, which represents the popup window displayed when users click a marker; and many more. These objects provide their own properties and methods, which allow you to access their functionality from within the code and manipulate the map, and they constitute the Google Maps API: the tools for programming the map.

Using the Google Maps API

Because not all readers are familiar with APIs, let's look at some very basic examples to understand how an API works and how it exposes the functionality of an application. In a way, an API is the software equivalent of a user interface: Just as users can access the functionality of an interactive application through its user interface, applications can access the functionality of a service such as Google Maps and manipulate it through a set of "commands." These commands are functions that the external application can call to manipulate Google Maps. To zoom into a Google map, you can click the zoom-in button on the map's visual interface, To do the same programmatically, you can call the setZoom() method of the Google Maps API, this time using the application's programming interface.

To use the API, as you will see in the following chapter, you must insert a special JavaScript program in your page. This program is a script and it is available from Google for free; it contains the implementation of the API. The script contains the google.maps library and all objects for manipulating maps are implemented in this library.

To create a new map on the page, you must use the following statement to create a new Map object:

```
var myMap = new google.maps.Map(. . .);
```

This statement creates a new map on the page. The ellipsis indicates the arguments you pass to the constructor; they're discussed in detail in the following chapter. They specify where on the page to place the map and the initial properties of the map. To understand the role of the API, just keep in mind that the preceding statement embeds a map on the current page and stores a reference to it in the myMap variable. To manipulate the map, you manipulate the myMap variable's properties and call its methods. To change the current zoom level from within your code, for example, you must call the setZoom() method of the myMap variable as follows:

```
myMap.setZoom(12);
```

Let's say that you have embedded a map on a web page, and that the map is referenced in your code by the myMap variable. You can manipulate the map by calling its methods. You can also place items on the map, such as markers. To place a marker on the map, you must create a Marker object and specify the marker's location and title.

To specify a point in Google Maps, you must create a LatLng object passing its coordinates as arguments:

```
RomeLocation = new google.maps.LatLng(41.9, 12,5);
```

The values in the parentheses are the latitude and longitude values that identify the point on the globe. The variable RomeLocation represents the location of Rome on the globe. You can use this variable to place a marker to identify Rome on the map, to calculate the distance of Rome from any other location represented by another LatLng object, or to center the map on Rome.

To place a marker on Rome, you must create a new Marker object with a statement like the following:

```
var marker = new google.maps.Marker({
    position: RomeLocation,
    title: 'Rome',
    map: myMap);
```

The basic attributes of the Marker have a name and a value. The attributes are set by name and their values follow the name and a colon. One of the attributes is the position of the marker, which is a LatLng object. The title attribute is the marker's title, and the map attribute determines the map on which the marker will be placed.

The LatLng object can also be used with the *geometry* library (also available from Google) to calculate the distance between any two points. First, you create two LatLng objects to represent two locations, as in the following:

```
var P1 = new google.maps.LatLng(32.89680099, -97.03800201);
var P2 = new google.maps.LatLng(39.78279877, 116.3880005);
```

The P1 variable corresponds to Dallas and the P2 variable corresponds to Beijing. To find out the distance between them, call the computeDistanceBetween() method, passing the two points as arguments:

```
google.maps.geometry.spherical.computeDistanceBetween(P1, P2);
```

Don't try to figure out how to use these examples in your scripts yet; they were included here as an overview of how the API is used to produce useful results. All the objects and methods shown in this section are discussed in detail later in this book.

Embedding a map in your HTML page is almost trivial and so is the placement of markers on the map to identify points of interest. Later in this book, you learn how to place more items on the map, such as lines and shapes. To make a mapping application really unique, however, you must enable users to interact with it in a friendly and productive manner. A good portion of this book is dedicated to this type of interaction, which is based on events. The API allows you to react to various events, such as the click of the mouse, or the dragging of the map itself, and you can design a highly interactive map by programming the map's events. In Chapter 9, you learn how to let users draw on the map with the mouse by exploiting the click event. Users can draw shapes based on the underlying map's features, and these shapes can be the outlines of landmarks (lakes, properties, airports, administrative borders, land usage, and so on). In addition to the basic Google Maps API, there are auxiliary APIs that rely on this API. The geometry library, discussed in Chapter 10, allows you to perform basic calculations with the map's features, and you have already seen an example of the computeDistanceBetween() method of the geometry library. You can use this library to calculate the length of a route or the area covered by a shape you have drawn on the map. The visualization library, which is discussed in Chapter 18, enables you to create graphs for visualizing large sets of data on the map. The graph you see in Figure 1-10, known as a heatmap, corresponds to the distribution of the airports around the world.

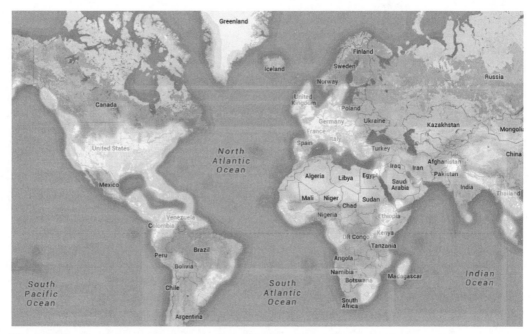

Figure 1-10   Displaying a very large number of items on the globe as a heat map graph

There are so many airports that it's practically impossible to view them as individual markers on the map. The heatmap represents the density of the airports around the globe as a gradient: Areas with many airports correspond to brighter colors in the figure. The black and white version of the printed image doesn't do justice to the heatmap. You can open the original image, which is included in the chapter's support material, to see the colors of the gradient. Or you can double-click the file Heatmap.html in the folder with this chapter's support material, to view the heatmap in full color.

Summary

Google Maps are based on a projection of the globe onto a flat surface. The projection used by Google Maps is the oldest one, the Mercator projection, which was designed more than three centuries ago. The Mercator projection introduces some substantial distortions, especially as you move toward the poles, but it has advantages that outweigh its shortcomings, including the fact that the Mercator projection is a rectangular one and that the meridians are transformed into straight lines.

You're ready to start exploring the Google Maps API, and in the following chapter, you learn how to embed a map in a web page.

2 Designing Web Pages with Embedded Maps

It's time now to look at the process of generating web pages with embedded maps: HTML pages with a special component where a map is displayed. You can make this special component large enough to cover the entire page. Or, you can reserve some space on the page to place controls that will enable users to interact with the map. You can even fill your page with the map and place the controls you need for your application's interface on top of the map.

As far as the "special" mapping component, it's there for you to use it, courtesy of Google. Google has done all the work for you. Not only do they offer you the map, but they also provide the programming tools to control the map from within your application. All it takes is a little JavaScript code. Or a lot of JavaScript code, depending on how far you want to go.

In this chapter, you're going to build your first web page with an embedded Google map and learn how to design web pages for hosting maps. Instead of jumping directly into the details of the necessary script, let's start by reviewing the structure of a typical web page for the benefit of readers who aren't familiar with web pages.

The Structure of a Web Page

A web page consists of three parts:

- **The HTML code that describes the page's static content**   The text and multimedia items on the page, as well as the various controls that allow users to interact with the page.

- **The CSS section that contains styles to be applied to the various page elements**
  The same elements can be formatted in the HTML statements that generate these elements, but it's a much better practice to create named formats (styles) and apply them to multiple elements.

- **The JavaScript section that contains code**   The program that enables users to interact with the page in a direct manner.

HTML was designed to be interactive from the ground up. The hyperlinks on the page are the most basic method of interacting with a web page: You click a hyperlink and you're taken to another page of the same site, or a page of a totally different site. This type of interaction was very important and it made the Web so popular. For today's standards, however, this is hardly the interaction you're looking for in a web page. The next level of interactivity allows users to enter data on a web page, click a button to submit the data to the server, and get back another page. Imagine a page that allows users to enter latitude and longitude values and submits these values to a remote server. An application on the remote server converts the coordinates to a physical address (a process known as *geocoding*) and returns a new page to the client. This type of application involves a trip to the remote server and displays the results on a new page, which is generated at the server. The interaction isn't instant because no code is executed at the client (except for some rudimentary data validation code). Everything takes place at the server. This was a "more" interactive Web, but still very far from what today's users are expecting from a web application.

Today's web applications use JavaScript to perform all kinds of operations at the client. It's very easy to design a web page with a Google map and two boxes where users can enter geo-coordinates. When they press a button, the map is panned to the new location without a trip to the server. You can also use JavaScript to perform geocoding. The process of converting geo-coordinates to physical addresses (or the reserve process) is too complicated to be performed at the client, but you can use JavaScript to contact a Google service that performs the calculations and get back just the physical address, instead of a new page. The introduction of JavaScript enabled developers to design web pages that behave like applications and perform all kinds of calculations and data validation at the client. The latest generation of web applications uses JavaScript to retrieve data and update parts of the interface without having to rely on a server that supplies a totally new page every time a selection is made on a form.

HTML is a language for describing the placement and format of the various items that make up the page. These items are text, images, tables, multimedia and, yes, maps. An HTML page contains mostly text and other visible elements, as well as "commands" that control how the text will appear on the page. These "commands" are called tags; they're special keywords embedded in a pair of angle brackets and they come in pairs (the opening and closing tag). The command takes effect for the part of the page between the opening and closing tag. The `<b>` tag, which turns on the bold attribute of the text, is a good simple tag example. The closing tag `</b>` turns off the bold attribute. Another tag you'll use with every page in this book is the `<div>` tag, which denotes a section of the page. Using the `style` attribute of the `<div>` tag, you can specify the size and position of this section on the page. The map you place on a web page always appears on a `<div>` element. You can create a fixed-size `<div>` element, or a `<div>` element that fills the entire page, so that the map is resized when the user resizes the browser's window.

The following is the structure of a typical script-enabled web page:

```
<html>
  <head>
    <style>
      enter your style definitions here
    </style>
    <script type="text/javascript">
      enter your script here
    </script>
```

```
   </head>
   <body>
     enter your HTML code here
   </body>
</html>
```

The page has two major sections—the head and the body sections—and they're delimited with the appropriate tags. The page's script is contained in the head section of the page along with the style definitions. The script section contains code written in JavaScript that manipulates the contents of the page.

Reacting to Events

Let's see some JavaScript in action. Start by creating a panel on the page, where the current date and time will appear and a button that will actually populate this panel. The panel is a `<div>` element and the button is inserted on the page with an `<input>` element. Here's the HTML code that must appear in the page's `<body>` section:

```
<body>
  <input type="button" value="Show time" onclick="showDate()">
  <span id="date" style="border: 1px solid black; width: 200px"></span>
</body>
```

Notice that you can't insert a date into the web page when it's created, or even when it's requested, because the page may reside on a server in Hong Kong and be opened by a client in New York. The client expects to see the local time, not the Hong Kong time. To display the correct date and time at the client, you must provide a short program that will be executed at the client and display the local time. In the button's definition, you must insert the attribute `onclick` and set it to the name of the function, the `showDate()` function, which will display the current date. The function's definition must be placed in the `<script>` section, as follows:

```
function showDate() {
   var dateTimeDiv = document.getElementById("date")
   dateTimeDiv.innerHTML = Date();
}
```

The code does two things that are typical in a script: It retrieves an element on the page, in this case the `<div>` element, and sets one of its properties. The `dateTimeDiv` is a local variable, which references the element whose `id` attribute is `date`. Any element that you wish to control from within your script must have an `id` attribute; this attribute is passed as an argument to the `getElementById()` method. The `getElementById()` method is a method of the `document` object, which represents the page that contains the script. The `document` object exposes the elements that make up the document being displayed, and is also known as the Document Object Model (DOM). DOM is a hierarchy of objects that make up an HTML document, including its script. You can even manipulate the page's script through the DOM!

You can use the DOM to not only retrieve elements of the page, but also to manipulate them. For example, you can create new elements on the page, or even add a new code segment to the page's script. In Chapter 7, you will see this technique in action, but let's continue with the exploration of the more basic features of a web page.

The dateTimeDiv variable represents a <div> element on the page, and the <div> element's basic property is the innerHTML property, which represents the contents of the element. Typically, you place formatted text on <div> elements. The <div> element is a section of the page that holds anything that could appear in an HTML page: text, images, tables, and the map, of course. In this example, you'll print the current date and time on the <div> element.

The following is the listing of the entire page (see the JavaScript Demo 1.html file in this chapter's support material).

```
<html>
  <head>
    <script>
      function showDate() {
        var dateTimeDiv = document.getElementById("date")
        dateTimeDiv.innerHTML = Date();
      }
    </script>
  </head>
  <body>
    <input type="button" value="Show time" onclick="showDate()">
    <span id="date" style="border: 1px solid black; width: 180px"></span>
  </body>
</html>
```

This is how JavaScript typically interacts with the page's elements. A function is invoked in response to an event, such as the click of the mouse, the press of a key, the drag of the map, and so on. Any keyboard or mouse action that can be detected by an element on the page fires an event. To react to an event, you must assign the name of a function that handles the event to the appropriate attribute of an element on the page. The event onclick is fired when the user clicks an element (usually a button); the event onkeypress is fired when the user presses a key while the corresponding element has the focus, and so on. The functions that handle specific events are called *event listeners* and this model of coding applications is referred to as *event-driven*. There's not a monolithic segment of code that handles the interaction with the user. Instead, scripts are made up of isolated functions (the event listeners), which are invoked automatically when users initiate certain actions (events) on certain controls.

One of the most common operations performed with maps is the drag operation, and the map itself fires the dragstart, dragend, and drag events. As you will see in Chapter 5, the dragstart and dragend events are fired when the operation starts and ends, respectively, while the drag event is fired continuously while the map is being dragged.

Another common usage of JavaScript is to manipulate the style of the various elements on the page. Let's assume that the amount field is where users are supposed to enter a monetary amount. If the amount is negative, the field should be colored red, otherwise black. The event you must program this time is the keyup event of the field. The following HTML segment displays an input box that reacts to the keyup event:

```
<input id="amount" type="text" size="10" value=""
       style="text-align:right" onkeyup="colorField()">
```

This statement creates an input box long enough to accept up to ten characters. The `text-align` attribute tells the control to align its text right (all numbers should be right-aligned in their fields). The last attribute tells the JavaScript engine to call the `colorField()` function every time a key is released. The definition of the `colorField()` function, which changes the color of the text on the control, is shown next (the function renders positive numbers in black color and negative numbers in red color):

```
function colorField() {
    if (parseFloat(document.getElementById("amount").value) < 0) {
        document.getElementById("amount").style.color="#ff0000"
    }
    else {
        document.getElementById("amount").style.color="#000000"
    }
    return true;
}
```

First, you define the action that will trigger the function. Then, in the function, you request one of the page's elements, the *amount* element, and change its `color` attribute. The code examines the value of the *amount* field after it converts it to a numeric value. If this value is negative, it retrieves the *amount* element and changes its style by setting the `color` attribute to the hexadecimal value of the red color. By the way, colors are represented as hexadecimal values with two bytes per color component. The first two bytes correspond to the red component of the color, the following two bytes correspond to the green component, and the last two bytes correspond to the blue component. Each hexadecimal digit has a value in the range 0 - 9, A - F. The preceding sample application is the `JavaScript Demo 2.html` file, included in this chapter's support material.

The key point to take away from this discussion is that JavaScript is a language that enables the HTML page to interact with the user at the client: No trips to the server are required. All elements on an HTML page have an `id` attribute, which is a unique identifier; the `getElementById()` method can retrieve any element by its `id` attribute. Then the script can manipulate its content and style through the properties exposed by the element.

This book is at least 90 percent about scripts and less than ten percent about HTML. Designing elaborate HTML pages is probably more difficult than writing JavaScript code because there are no visual HTML designers. Yes, there are many programs to help you design web pages visually, but unless you understand how HTML is structured and the role of tables in placing the sections of a document on a HTML page, you won't go far with visual tools.

The sample applications in this book use straightforward, easy-to-understand HTML code. Some interesting pages that use non-trivial HTML code will be explained in the course of the book, but the focus is on JavaScript and how you will use it to manipulate the objects of the Google Maps API. And you're going to start right away by building a simple HTML page with a Google map.

Adding a Map to Your Page

To display a Google map on your page, you need to reserve an area on the page where the map will be displayed. This area is defined as a <div> element and it usually takes up most of the page. Here's the body of a typical web page with a placeholder for a map:

```
<body>
  <div id="map_canvas" style="width:800px; height:500px"></div>
</body>
```

As you can see, the <div> element has an id attribute, which you will use in your script to reference the element where the map will be displayed. The style of this element is defined in-line: The style definition is embedded in the declaration of the <div> element. You don't need to use a separate style for this element because it's unique on the page. The <div> element is set to fixed dimensions, specified in pixels.

To make the map fill the entire page, set the width and height attributes to 100 percent, as shown here:

```
<body>
  <div id="map_canvas" style="width:100%; height:100%"></div>
</body>
```

To display the map in the <div> element, you must first embed a script in your page. Insert the following line in the page's <head> section:

```
<script type="text/javascript"
src="http://maps.google.com/maps/api/js?sensor=false"></script>
```

The <script> tag tells the application to download the script from the maps.google.com server. This script contains the code that interacts with a Google server to display the map: Every time a user drags the map or zooms out, new tiles must be downloaded from the remote server and rendered on the page. It's this script's responsibility to detect the changes in the map's bounds and request the new tiles.

New tiles are also requested when the user zooms into the map. The map isn't simply blown up because different zoom levels are constructed with their own tiles, which contain different information. When you center the map on Santa Barbara and look at it at the state level, you will see only the city name and a couple of landmarks. The Google server transmits only information that can be displayed on the map. As you zoom in, the script requests new tiles that cover a smaller area, but with additional information.

So far, your page's code should look like the following:

```
<html>
  <head>
    <script type="text/javascript"
            src="http://maps.google.com/maps/api/js?sensor=false">
    </script>
  </head>
  <body>
    <div id="map_canvas"
```

```
        style="width:100%; height:100%; border: 2px solid darkgreen">
    </div>
  </body>
</html>
```

Do not open this page in your browser yet because it's not quite ready to produce a map. You need a script to initiate the map and this script is pretty standardized. Add the following function to the <script> section of the page:

Listing 2-1
All map-enabled
web pages must
contain a script to
set up and render
the map.

```
function initialize() {
    var latlng = new google.maps.LatLng(34.4126213,-119.8483640);
    var settings = {
          zoom: 15,
          center: latlng,
          mapTypeId: google.maps.MapTypeId.ROADMAP
    };
    var map = new google.maps.Map(
            document.getElementById("map_canvas"), settings);
}
```

The initialize() function displays the map in the area reserved for this purpose, and it's pretty much the same for all applications. You can specify a few more attributes for the map, or use different settings, but the basic outline of the function remains the same.

The name of the function can be anything, but this is the name you will find in most examples. The initialize() function will not be activated on its own; you need to call it after the page has been loaded. The <body> tag recognizes the attribute onload, which must be set to the name of a function that will be executed as soon as the page is loaded:

```
onload = "initialize()"
```

Listing 2-2 is the listing of a simple map-enabled web page including the script.

Listing 2-2
A typical
web page for
displaying a map

```
<html>
  <head>
    <script type="text/javascript"
            src="http://maps.google.com/maps/api/js?sensor=false">
    </script>
    <script type="text/javascript">
      function initialize() {
        var latlng = new google.maps.LatLng(34.4126213,-119.8483640);
        var settings = {
              zoom: 15,
              center: latlng,
              mapTypeId: google.maps.MapTypeId.ROADMAP
        };
        var map = new google.maps.Map(
                    document.getElementById("map_canvas"), settings);
      }
    </script>
  </head>
<body onload="initialize()">
```

```
    <div id="map_canvas"
        style="width:100%; height:100%; border: 2px solid darkgreen">
    </div>
  </body>
</html>
```

Enter the entire listing in a text file (use Notepad for this) and save it to a file with the extension html. Or, you can open the Simplest Map Page.html file in this chapter's support material. Figure 2-1 shows the page's contents in Notepad, and Figure 2-2 shows the page in Internet Explorer. To open the page in your default browser, just double-click the HTML file's name.

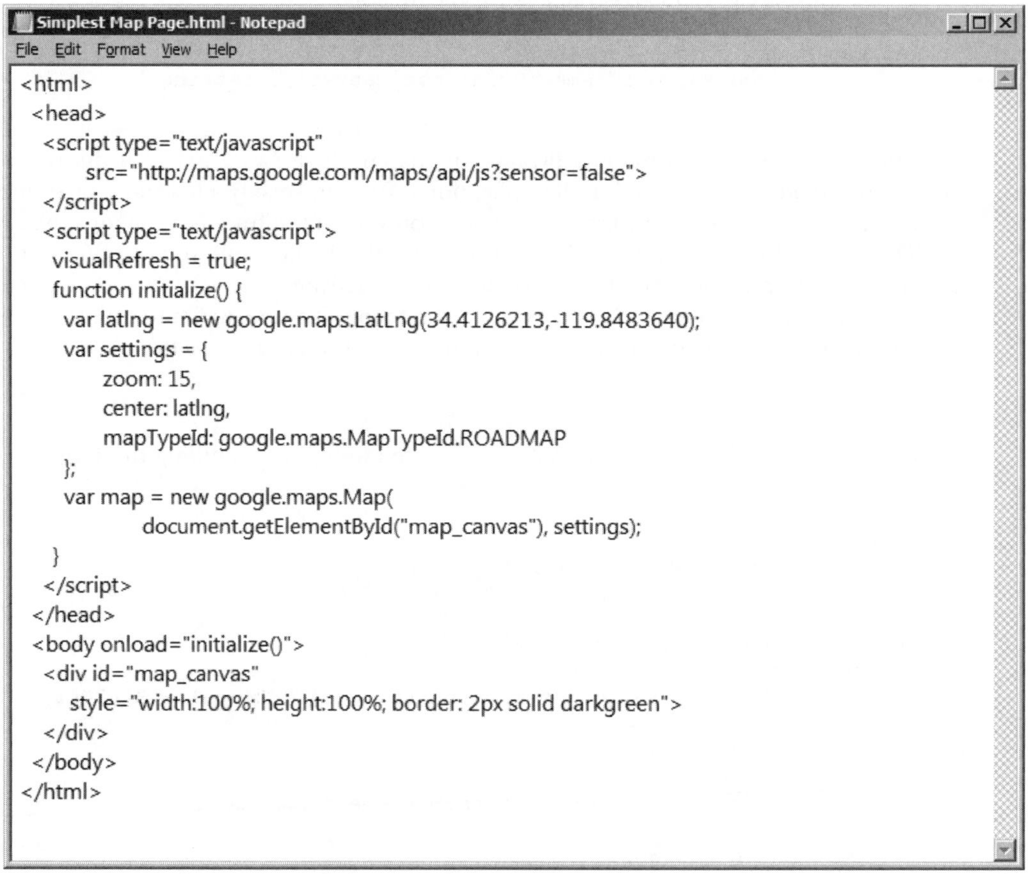

```
Simplest Map Page.html - Notepad                              _ |□| x|
File  Edit  Format  View  Help
<html>
 <head>
  <script type="text/javascript"
       src="http://maps.google.com/maps/api/js?sensor=false">
  </script>
  <script type="text/javascript">
   visualRefresh = true;
   function initialize() {
    var latlng = new google.maps.LatLng(34.4126213,-119.8483640);
    var settings = {
        zoom: 15,
        center: latlng,
        mapTypeId: google.maps.MapTypeId.ROADMAP
    };
    var map = new google.maps.Map(
            document.getElementById("map_canvas"), settings);
   }
  </script>
 </head>
 <body onload="initialize()">
  <div id="map_canvas"
     style="width:100%; height:100%; border: 2px solid darkgreen">
  </div>
 </body>
</html>
```

Figure 2-1 Preparing the Simplest Map Page.html with your favorite text editor (Notepad is not recommended, but it will do.)

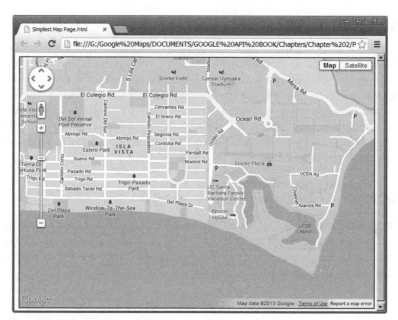

Figure 2-2   The `Simplest Map Page.html` page rendered in the browser.

Is Notepad the Editor of Choice?

You used Notepad to create your first mapping application. Is this the best editor for the job? There are many tools you can use in its place, and Notepad++ is a much better choice. Seriously, though, there are many tools for generating web pages and the best of them come with two components: a visual editor to generate web pages and a JavaScript editor that helps with the syntax of the script. The short answer to the question is that there are visual editors for web page designers, JavaScript editors for developers, and some tools like Visual Studio/WebMatrix that do both. If you're a web designer, continue using your favorite web page designer, copy the HTML code this tool produces, and paste it into a plain text editor. Then type the script to complete the page.

Visual Studio Express 2013 for Web is a free tool for developing web applications, but it runs on the Windows platform only. You can use it to edit both HTLM and JavaScript files and ignore its (many) extra features if you don't care about full scale Web development. It also includes a visual HTML editor. If you prefer the Macintosh platform, TextMate is a good choice, and so is Aptana. If you're a Java developer and you're using Eclipse, make sure you have installed the Web Page Editor component. You can also install Aptana as a plugin for Eclipse.

All HTML pages for this book were created manually and make little use of style sheets so that you can edit them easily. You can replace the HTML section of a page with your own HTML code and, as long as you use the same IDs for the various elements, the script should work without any modifications.

Map Localization

By default, the names of the features on the map are displayed in the system's default language. These names include names of countries, cities, monuments, and other map features, as well as copyright notices, the text on the controls, and even the directions when you request instructions for getting from one place to another. If this isn't what you want for your application, you can request that the strings on the map appear in any other language. To change the default language, add the `language` parameter to the Google Maps script, as in the following example, which requests that all names appear in Japanese and produces the map shown in Figure 2-3:

```
<script type="text/javascript"
  src="https://maps.googleapis.com/maps/api/js?sensor=false&language=ja">
```

Use this parameter for web sites that run behind a firewall, or are limited to a very specific audience. For publicly accessible sites, stick with the default option. To see the complete list of language codes, visit https://spreadsheets.google.com/pub?key=p9pdwsai2 hDMsLkXsoM05KQ&gid=1.

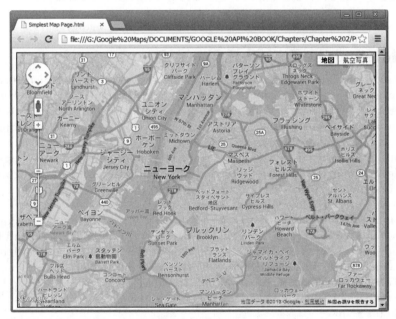

Figure 2-3   The map of Manhattan with Japanese labels

By default, the Google Maps API is geared for the U.S. market and it's biased toward users in this country. You can request different tiles for your application to overwrite the default behavior with the `region` parameter. This parameter doesn't affect the language of the text on the map, but it affects the results of geocoding operations. When you search for "Athens," for example, the first match will be Athens, TX. If the map's region is set to "gr" (Greece), then the first match will be Athens, Greece. For a list of region codes, visit http://www.iana.org/assignments/language-subtag-registry/language-subtag-registry.

Zooming with the Mouse

An alternative method to zoom into the desired area of a map is to draw a rectangle with the mouse around the feature you're interested in while holding down one of the control keys (SHIFT, CTRL, or ALT). This operation is known as *drag zoom* and it's implemented by a script, which isn't part of the Google Maps API and you must include it in your script with the following statement (which in your script should appear on a single line):

```
<script type="text/javascript"
      src="http://google-maps-utility-library-
          v3.googlecode.com/svn/trunk/keydragzoom/
          src/keydragzoom.js">
</script>
```

To activate the drag zoom feature for a specific map, call the `enableKeyDragZoom()` method, as shown here. This statement usually appears in the `initialize()` function:

```
map.enableKeyDragZoom();
```

The `enableKeyDragZoom()` method accepts as an argument an array with parameters, which primarily affect the appearance of the selection square. The properties you can pass to the `enableKeyDragZoom()` method are as follows:

- **key** The key property is a string that specifies the hot key to be held down for the drag zoom: SHIFT, CONTROL, or ALT. The default value of the `key` property is SHIFT.

- **boxStyle** This property is a CSS object that determines the style of the border that marks the area to be zoomed. The default style is

  ```
  {border: 'thin solid #FF0000'}
  ```

  Border widths can be specified in pixels, or with the following descriptive strings: `thin`, `medium`, and `thick`.

- **paneStyle** This property is another CSS object that determines the style of the area within the zoom border (the rectangle that overlays the map during a drag zoom operation). The default is

  ```
  {backgroundColor: 'white', opacity: 0.0, cursor: 'crosshair'}
  ```

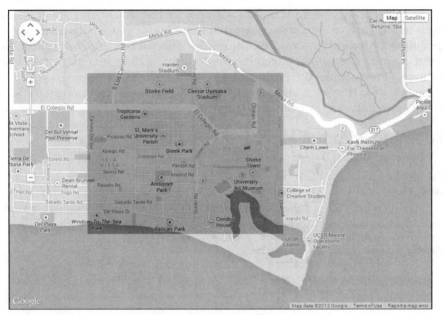

Figure 2-4 The drag-and-zoom feature in action; both the selection pane and its border are customized.

Note that the attributes of the paneStyle property are passed as an array of key-value pairs, just like the attributes of the enableKeyDragZoom() method. The following is a typical call to the enableKeyDragZoom() method:

```
map.enableKeyDragZoom({
     key: "shift",
     boxStyle: {
          border: "2px dashed black", backgroundColor: "red", opacity: 0.5
     },
     paneStyle: {
          backgroundColor: "gray", opacity: 0.2
     }
});
```

You can open the KeyDragZoom.html page in this chapter's support material to see an example of the drag zoom features. Figure 2-4 shows the sample page during a drag zoom operation.

The Map's Controls

By default, several controls are placed on the map to help users pan and zoom into the area they're interested in. You can control the appearance of these controls, or even remove them entirely from the map, depending on your application's specific requirements. The items you can't remove from the map are the Google logo at the lower-left corner of the map and the map's copyright messages at the lower-right corner.

It's doubtful that there are users who aren't familiar with Google Map's visual interface, but it should be mentioned here that the exact appearance of the controls on the map depend on the size of the map. When the map is too narrow for the Zoom control to fit on the map, the Zoom control is reduced to a narrow control with a plus and a minus button, without the bar between them. It's a good idea to test your web pages not only on various devices, but also on screens of widely different sizes.

The map controls are discussed in detail in Chapter 5, but the following sections provide an overview.

The Scale Control

This control is optional and it's not displayed by default. If you turn it on, it will appear in the lower-right corner of the map. To turn the visibility of this control on or off, set the `scaleControl` option to `true` or `false` in the map's options:

```
var options = {
    zoom: 15, center: latlng, mapTypeId: google.maps.MapTypeId.ROADMAP,
    scaleControl: true
};
```

The first line contains the mandatory properties; you can't set the optional attributes and skip any of the mandatory ones.

The Navigation Controls

The most important control is the navigation control that appears on the left of the map and allows users to zoom in and out, as well as to pan the map. There are four navigational controls: Pan, Zoom, Street View, and Rotate. The Street View control is the Pegman icon that allows you to switch to a street level view of the map. To change views, just drag this icon and drop it on the map to see the area from the street level: What you see is a sequence of stitched pictures taken at ground level. When you switch to Street View, the Pan control is replaced by a compass wheel, which allows you to select a direction to look at.

The Rotate control switches the Street View into 45 degrees imagery, when available. When such images do not exist, the Rotate control doesn't appear.

To manipulate the visibility of the navigational controls, use the following options:

```
panControl: true/false
zoomControl: true/false
mapTypeControl: true/false
scaleControl: true/false
streetViewControl: true/false
```

The OverviewMap Control

This control, which is disabled by default, displays a small map with a larger area in the main map's lower-right corner. The overview map is centered at the same location as the main map. Figure 2-5 shows a simple map with the OverviewMap control enabled (it's the `OverviewMap` `.html` sample page). Notice that the corresponding area shown in the original map is outlined.

To turn this feature on, specify the following option:

```
overviewMapControl: true
```

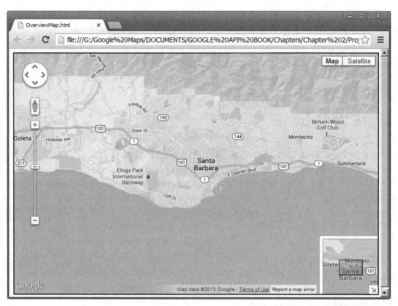

Figure 2-5 The small map in the lower-right corner is an overview of the larger area around the main map.

The MapType Control

This control allows users to set the map type: Map view or Satellite view. Both views have two options. When the map type is set to Map view, you can turn the terrain on or off. When terrain is on, you see the elevation of the various features, most notably the mountains. When the terrain option is off, you see only the administrative boundaries and feature locations, without the elevation shading. Likewise, in Satellite view, you can turn the labels on or off.

Adding Markers to the Map

Embedding a Google map in a web page is straightforward. The challenge is to add value to this map by placing useful information on it, as well as providing more elaborate interfaces that will enable users to interact with the map. Before ending this chapter, let's explore briefly a very basic feature of Google Maps: the placement of markers on a map. Markers are discussed in detail in Chapter 7 of the book, but first let's explore the basic statements for identifying points of interest with markers. It takes just a single statement with several parameters to place a marker on the map.

Just like the map is a new instance of the Map object, markers are new instances of the Marker object. Both objects are part of the google.map library, which was imported to your page's script with the <script> directive. If you think about it, all the information that's really required to place a marker on the form is the marker's location. In addition, a marker should also have a title, which is the description displayed on a small window as you hover the mouse over the marker. The Marker object's constructor accepts three arguments, the position and title arguments, and a variable that references the map to which it belongs.

To place a marker at the location of the Space Needle monument, start by creating a `LatLng` object that represents the location of the marker.

```
var poi = new google.maps.LatLng(34.4126,-119.8483);
```

Then create a new instance of the `Marker` object with the following statement:

```
var marker = new google.maps.Marker({position: poi, map: map, title: "Space
Needle"});
```

The sample page, `Space Needle.html`, displays the area in the vicinity of the Space Needle monument and a marker at the location of the monument, as shown in Figure 2-6.

You're already seeing the pattern of typical scripts that manipulate maps: The various items you can place on the map are represented by objects, which you must initialize in your code with the new keyword. The new keyword creates a new instance of an object and the type of the object determines its function on the map. All objects related to maps are provided by the script you download from Google. `LatLng` and `Marker` are two objects that represent locations and markers, respectively, and you can create as many variables of each type to identify points of interest on the map as needed.

Figure 2-6   A map of the Space Needle area with a marker

A Useful Template for Mapping Pages

One of the common themes you will encounter as you design web pages to host your maps is the separation of the browser window into multiple sections. Maps usually take up most of the window, but you need to control the size of the map and ensure that there's enough space for the other elements on the page. A common pattern is to keep the size of the other elements fixed on the page and allow the map to grow or shrink as the browser window is resized. Figure 2-7 shows a web page with three sections: a title, an auxiliary pane on the left for displaying map-related data, and a map. The page was created with the Demo Map.html file. The data pane of this example contains driving directions for getting from the address specified in the box to the location of the marker on the map. To retrieve the directions, enter an address and press ENTER. Presumably, the marker identifies a point of interest on the map. You could use the data pane to display additional information about this feature, a list of nearby monuments, room prices (if this were a hotel), or anything you can think of.

Displaying the driving directions isn't a trivial topic; it's discussed in Chapter 17, but the functionality was included in the sample project to make it more interesting (as opposed to filling the data pane with some Latin text). The width of the column with the data pane is fixed and all remaining space is allocated to the map. The title bar takes up the entire width of the page. You can place a footer section with a fixed height that also takes the entire width of the page.

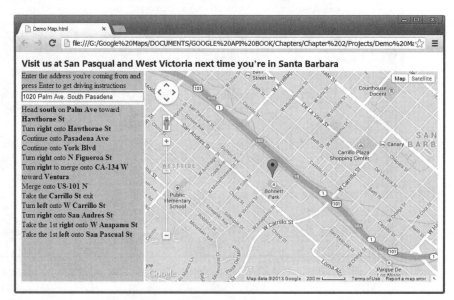

Figure 2-7   A basic web page with three sections for displaying a map and related data with a spatial component

Designing the Demo Map Page

The design of the Demo Map.html page is based on tables. The page is made up of a table with two rows and two columns, and the column on the right spans all rows. Listing 2-3 shows the HTML code with the page's content.

Listing 2-3
The HTML part of
the Demo Map
.html web page

```html
<body style="height: 95%" onload="initialize()">
  <table width='100%' height='100%'>
    <tr>
      <td colspan="2">
        <span style="color: darkblue; font-family: 'Segoe UI';
          font-size: larger; font-weight: 500; font-weight: bolder;">
        Visit us at San Pasqual and West Victoria next time
        you're in Santa Barbara</span>
      </td>
    </tr>
    <tr>
      <td width='30%'>
        <div style=' background-color: lightgray;
            font-family: 'Segoe UI';
            font-size: small; font-weight: 150; '>
        Enter the address you're coming from
        and press Enter to get driving instructions</div>
        <input id='origin' type='text' size='40'
            style="width:100%" onkeypress="getDirections(event)"
            value='1020 Palm Ave. South Pasadena'>
      </td>
      <td rowspan="3">
        <div id='map_canvas'
            style='height: 100%; width: 100%'>
        </div>
      </td>
    </tr>
    <tr>
      <td height='93%'>
        <div id='instructions'
            style='height: 100%; background-color: lightgray'>
      </td>
    </tr>
  </table>
</body>
```

The initialize() function contains the usual code for displaying the map, plus a few statements to place a marker on the map:

```js
function initialize() {
   var settings = {
        zoom: 15, center: latlng,
        mapTypeId: google.maps.MapTypeId.ROADMAP,
        scaleControl: true, overviewMapControl: true
   };
   var map = new google.maps.Map(
```

```
                        document.getElementById("map_canvas"), settings);
        marker = new google.maps.Marker({
                        position: latlng, title: 'Here we are!', map: map});
}
```

Note the attribute onkeypress of the <input> tag in the page's body. This tag corresponds to the input box where users are expected to enter their address. The onkeypress attribute tells the script which function to call when the user presses a key while the input box has the focus:

```
onkeypress='getDirections(event)'
```

The getDirections() function requests the driving instructions between the two points (the address entered by the user and the point of interest identified with the marker on the map). The function reacts only to the ENTER key; when any other key is pressed while the input box at the top has the focus, the function simply exits. In Chapter 17, you learn how to request driving instructions between any two locations using Google's Directions service. The result is then displayed on the data pane with the printInstructions() method. You can look up the code of the getDirections() and printInstructions() functions, or wait to read about the Directions service in Chapter 17. Here's just the if statement that causes the getDirections() function to react to the ENTER key:

```
function getDirections(e) {
  if (e && e.keyCode == 13) {
    // statements to contact Google's Directions service,
    // get driving directions and print them.
  }
}
```

As you will find out if you open the sample page, the two panes are resized automatically as the browser window is resized. The table takes up the entire page, because its width and height attributes are set to 100%. The browser resizes the two panes proportionally and users can't change this behavior. If you're already thinking about resizable panes, you should explore a jQuery component at http://api.jqueryui.com/resizable/.

Placing Multiple Maps on the Page

In Chapter 5, we discuss the Multiple Maps application, which is shown in Figure 2-8. This page contains three maps, all of which are centered at the same location and show the selected area at a different magnification each. The small map at the lower-right corner shows an overview of a larger area, like a state or country. The main map is a basic roadmap of a very specific area (the Santa Barbara airport) and the small map at the upper-right corner is a small detail in satellite view. The three maps remain synchronized: You can scroll any map and the other two will be updated automatically. To keep the maps synchronized, you need to write some JavaScript code, which is discussed in Chapter 5. Here, we're going to look at the page's body that contains the HTML code.

The page shown in Figure 2-8 was generated by the HTML fragment shown in Listing 2-4. The page's body is filled with a <div> element whose *height* attribute is set to cover the

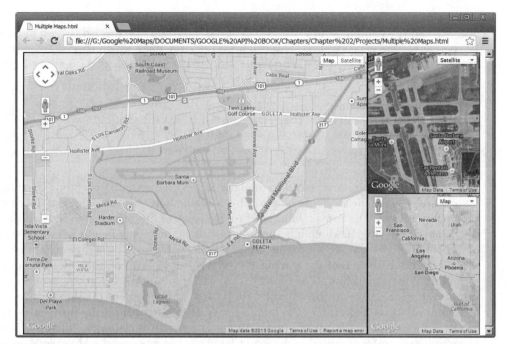

Figure 2-8   The Multiple Maps web page contains three synchronized maps.

entire page height (100%). This setting ensures that the `<div>` is resized every time the user changes the size of the browser's window.

Listing 2-4
Placing three
different maps on
the same page

```
<body style="height: 100%" onload="initialize()">
  <div style="height: 100%; background-color:'green; margin: 0px'">
    <table style="width:100%; height:100%">
      <tr style="height:100%">
        <td rowspan="2" style="width: 75%; height: 100%">
          <div id="map1" style="border: 2px solid black; height:100%;
                width: 100%; padding: 0px; margin: 0px">
          </div>
        </td>
        <td >
          <div id="map2"  style="border: 1px solid black; height: 50%;
                padding: 0px; margin: 0px">
          </div>
          <div id="map3"  style="border: 1px solid black; height :50%;
                padding: 0px; margin: 0px">
          </div>
        </td>
      </tr>
    </table>
  </div>
</body>
```

The outer <div> element contains a table with one row and two columns: The first cell takes up two rows and its width is set to 75 percent of the table's width (which in turn is 100 percent of the page's width). This cell hosts the large map, which covers the entire height of the page and 75 percent of the available width). The following <td> definition places the <div> element with the large map in its cell:

```
<td rowspan="2" style="width: 75%; height: 100%">
  <div id="map1" style="border: 2px solid black; height:100%;
          width: 100%; padding: 0px; margin: 0px">
  </div>
</td>
```

The other two maps are placed in the same <td> element, and each one has a height set to 50 percent of the available height. The available height is the height of the row to which they belong. The row's height is set to 100 percent of the available height, which is the height of the table to which it belongs. And, finally, the table's height is set to 100 percent of its container's height. To set the height of a table, you must also set the height of its container, and the height of the container's container, and so on up to the height of the body.

You can open the Multiple Maps project to experiment with the arrangement of the various <div> controls on the page and their sizes. The version of the sample application included with this chapter doesn't contain the code to synchronize the three maps (you can drag them independently of one another). The synchronization technique is based on JavaScript code and is discussed in detail in Chapter 5. For now, use the Multiple Maps project to experiment with the placement of three panes on the page.

Initializing the Maps on the Page

The maps are displayed in their containers from within the initialize() function's code as usual. Instead of creating a single instance of the Map object, you must create three distinct instances of the Map object and assign them to different variables. The code in the initialize() function starts by setting up a variable that represents the location of the center point for all three maps, and another variable with the initial settings of the maps:

```
var latlng = new google.maps.LatLng(34.4126213,-119.8483640);
var settings = {
        zoom: 14,
        center: latlng,
        mapTypeId: google.maps.MapTypeId.ROADMAP
        };
```

The settings apply to all three maps: They're centered at some location at University of California, Santa Barbara; the initial zoom is 14, and the type for all maps is ROADMAP.

Then the code creates three variables to represent the three maps, all with the same settings:

```
var map1 = new google.maps.Map(
               document.getElementById("map1"), settings);
var map2 = new google.maps.Map(
               document.getElementById("map2"), settings);
map2.setOptions({zoom: 16, mapTypeId: google.maps.MapTypeId.SATELLITE });
var map3 = new google.maps.Map(
               document.getElementById("map3"), settings);
map3.setZoom(4);
```

The variables `map1`, `map2`, and `map3` represent the three maps on the page. To manipulate the maps, you must use the corresponding variable. This application uses the same initial zoom and the same type for all three maps because all three `Map` objects use the same settings. After creating each instance of the `Map` object, the script calls the `setZoom()` method to set the zoom level of the two smaller maps and the `setOptions()` method to set the type of the upper one. There are individual methods for setting each property, but if you want to set multiple properties you should use the `setOptions()` method, which accepts as argument an array of property names and values. The curly brackets indicate objects in JavaScript, and in the case of this example, the argument is a custom object with two properties separated by a semicolon. Each property has a name and a value, and these items are separated by a comma. In short, the following call to the `setOptions()` method:

```
map2.setOptions({zoom: 16, mapTypeId: google.maps.MapTypeId.SATELLITE });
```

is equivalent to calling the `setZoom()` and `setMapTypeId()` methods:

```
map2.setZoom(16);
map2.setMapTypeId(google.maps.MapTypeId.SATELLITE);
```

The `Map` object provides a number of methods that you can use to control its appearance from within your script. The `getZoom()` method, for example, returns the current zoom level, while the `getCenter()` and `setCenter()` methods retrieve and set the map's center point, respectively. In effect, the `setCenter()` method allows you to pan the map from within your script. The `Map` object's methods are discussed in detail in Chapter 5.

Customizing the Map's Appearance

Another interesting page design for mapping applications is shown in Figure 2-9 and it's borrowed from Chapter 5. The Customized Map application, which is discussed in detail

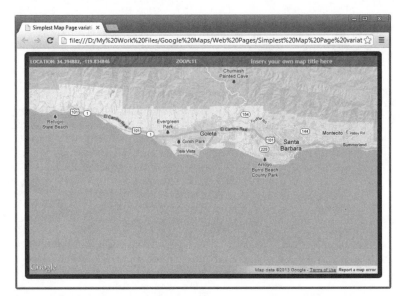

Figure 2-9   A web page with a customized map

in Chapter 5, places HTML elements on top of a "minimal" map; moreover, the `<div>` element that contains the map has rounded corners. Note that there are no controls on the map; users can zoom in and out by double-clicking the two mouse buttons and drag it with the mouse.

Summary

Embedding a Google map into a web page is a straightforward process: You reserve some space on the page for the map, a `<div>` element to be exact, and place an instance of the `Map` object in it. To display the map, you need to import a script from Google's site with the `<script>` directive and write a simple function that's called when the page has finished loading. Balancing the map's placeholder and the other elements of the page requires HTML skills, and you can use your favorite visual tools to design the page.

The map includes quite a bit of functionality as is, and in the course of this book, you will learn how to write unique applications on top of the map. The scripts that manipulate the maps on your web pages are written in JavaScript, so before you start exploring the Google Maps API, let's go over JavaScript's main features.

CHAPTER 3

Web Page Scripting: An Introduction to JavaScript

The Google Maps API is a JavaScript library that exposes all the functionality required to embed a map in a HTML page and manipulate the map from within the page's script. The API exposes its functionality through a number of objects, including the Map object that represents the map on the page, the Marker object that represents the markers you place on the map, and many more. To take advantage of the API, you must provide scripts that manipulate the objects exposed by the API and these scripts must be written in JavaScript. This is not a limitation of the API; JavaScript is the only language that runs in the context of the browser and it's supported by all browsers. The API itself is written in JavaScript so that you can include it in your scripts.

For the sake of readers who are not familiar with JavaScript, I explore the JavaScript programming language in this and the following chapter. If you're familiar with JavaScript, you can skip the two chapters and start your exploration of the objects of the Google Maps API in Chapter 5. If you're familiar with other high-level languages, you can still skip the chapters covering JavaScript and return to them to look up a specific feature or the syntax of a specific method. The two chapters on JavaScript were written to help readers program the Google Maps API and they do not cover the language end to end.

What Is JavaScript?

JavaScript deserves the title of the most popular programming language, primarily because it's the only language that can be used in web pages and be executed in the browser. As such, it runs on PCs, tablets, and smartphones. JavaScript, however, is not a "proper" programming language; it belongs to a special category of languages known as *scripting languages*. A scripting language is a lightweight programming language that does anything any typical programming language does, but has no visible interface and interacts with the user through the interface of the application that hosts it. When used with web pages, JavaScript interacts with the user through the web page displayed in the user's browser. The most important aspect of JavaScript is that it's supported by all browsers and the latest trend in application development is HTML5 and JavaScript.

Actually, there are three functions that allow scripts to interact with the user: the `alert()` function, which displays a message to the user; the `prompt()` function, which prompts the user for a value; and the `confirm()` function, which requests the user's confirmation to proceed. Figure 3-1 shows the three dialog boxes displayed by these functions and the statements that produced them.

To interact with the user in a friendlier manner, JavaScript must use the controls on the web page to which it belongs. The web page exposes the `document` object, which represents the page being displayed. One of the `document` object's methods is the `getElementById()` property, which retrieves an HTML element on the page by its ID. Let's say that the web page contains an input box whose `id` property is `user_Name`. The input box can be placed on the page with a statement like the following:

```
<input type="text" size="20" id="user_Name">
```

You can read the value entered by the user on this element with a statement like the following in your script:

```
document.getElementById("user_Name").value;
```

Conversely, you can change the contents of this element by assigning a value to the same expression:

```
document.getElementById("user_Name").value = "Joe Doe";
```

These statements appear in a function that's called when a certain event takes place, usually the click of a mouse or a hyperlink. The `document` object is a complex object that exposes a lot of functionality. It even allows you to create new elements on the page and/or hide existing ones by manipulating their `visibility` property.

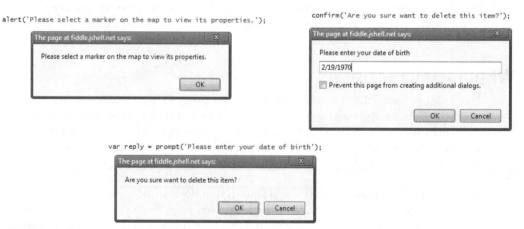

Figure 3-1 On its own, JavaScript can interact with the user with these three dialog boxes.

How to Test JavaScript Code

A script in an HTML page must be embedded in a pair of `<script>` and `</script>` tags, which usually appear in the page's `<head>` or `<body>` section. Here's the simplest script you can write:

```
<script>
  alert("My first script!");
</script>
```

To test this script, create a new text file with the extension .html and place the following code in it. The very first line is optional, but strongly recommended; it indicates an HTML 5 page.

```
<!DOCTYPE html>
<html>
  <head>
    <script type="text/javascript">
      alert("Welcome to JavaScript");
    </script>
  </head>
  <body>
    <h1>Javascript Tests</h1>
  </body>
</html>
```

Then, locate the file in your drive and double-click its name. As long as the file's extension is .html, it will be opened in your browser and you will see the alert box.

If you don't want to have to create HTML files all the time, you can use an online JavaScript editor, such as JSFIDDLE. Direct your browser to http://jsfiddle.net/ and you will see a page with four empty panes, as shown in Figure 3-2. The panes aren't empty in the figure, but when you first open the JSFIDDLE page, they will be.

Resize the four panes as you wish and for the time being ignore the HTML and CSS panes. Enter some JavaScript code in the JavaScript pane:

```
alert("Welcome to JavaScript");
var name = prompt("Please provide your name");
document.write("Welcome to JavaScript " + name);
```

JSFIDDLE will display a warning to the effect that you shouldn't be using the `document` `.write()` method (as shown in the Figure), but go ahead and use it. After all, you're only testing your code. Then, click the Run button to execute the script. Initially, you will see a welcome dialog box produced by the `alert()` function, and then you'll be prompted for your name. As soon as you enter your name and click OK to close the dialog box, a message appears on the output page. Testing simple scripts is easy with JSFIDDLE, and the code segments you write in JSFIDDLE are usually referred to as "fiddles." It's not the only online JavaScript editor, but it's a very popular one along with the Tryit Editor of w3schools (www .w3schools.com/jsref/tryit.asp).

Figure 3-2 The JSFIDDLE online web page editor

JSFIDDLE and Google Maps

To create a web page with a Google map in JSFIDDLE, you must import Google's script into your custom script. To do so, follow this procedure:

1. Click the External Resources header in the left pane to see an input box. Enter the following string in this box: https://maps.googleapis.com/maps/api/js?&sensor=false&dummy=js.

   The additional dummy parameter will be ignored when the request is transmitted to Google's servers, but you need to specify it to fool JSFIDDLE into thinking that it's loading a resource with the extension .js.

2. Then, click the button with the plus icon next to the input box. This adds the Google Maps API script to your page, and you can access its objects from within your script.

3. Insert the HTML code that creates the placeholder for your map in the HTML pane and the usual `initialize()` function in the JavaScript pane.

4. Finally, click the Run link at the top to view your page in the output window.

Figure 3-3 shows a fiddle with a web page that contains a Google map.

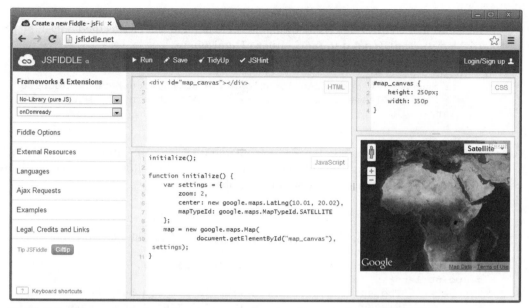

Figure 3-3   A page displaying a Google map designed and tested with the JSFIDDLE online editor

You enter your page's HTML code in the HTML pane, and you enter the style definitions for your page in the CSS pane. In effect, you can use JSFIDDLE to build complete HTML pages with scripts and test them. For the purposes of this chapter, you simply enter JavaScript code in the JavaScript pane and execute it.

JavaScript's Basic Syntax

Like any other language, JavaScript has its own basic rules and you must live by them. The first rule is that JavaScript is case-sensitive. Once you have declared the variable *age*, you can no longer refer to it as *Age* or *AGE*. It's absolutely valid, however (but certainly not recommended), to create three different variables named age, Age, and AGE.

Blocks of statements in JavaScript are enclosed in a pair of curly brackets. Any group of statements that must be treated as a unit should appear in a pair of curly brackets. A function's body as well as the body of an `if` statement is also enclosed in a pair of curly brackets. The `initialize()` function, for example, was declared as follows:

```
function initialize() {
    // statements to display the map on the page
}
```

All the statements that make up the `initialize()` function are embedded in a pair of curly brackets following the function name. In effect, the curly brackets delimit a segment of code that should be treated as a unit.

The following code segment demonstrates the use of the `if` statement. The block of statements in the curly brackets following the `if` statement will be executed only if the `point` variable represents a point in the Southern Hemisphere:

```
if (point.lat < 0) {
    var msg = "The specified location lies in the southern hemisphere" +
            "Please click somewhere in the northern hemisphere! ";
    alert(msg);
}
```

The `point` variable represents a location and it exposes the latitude (property `lat`) and longitude (property `lng`) of the specific location. The following statement will create a variable that represents a location on the globe:

```
var point = new google.maps.LatLng(-32.403, 23.10);
```

The brackets are not required if the block is made up of a single statement:

```
var point = new google.maps.LatLng(-32.403, 23.10);
if (point.lat < 0)
        alert("The specified location lies in the southern hemisphere" +
                "Please click somewhere in the northern hemisphere! ");
```

The call to the `alert()` function is a single statement, even though it's broken into two lines to fit on the printed page, so the brackets are optional and were omitted.

Statements in JavaScript are separated by a new line character, or by a semicolon (or both). If each statement appears in its own line, then you don't have to use semicolons. You can place multiple statements on the same line, in which case you must separate them with a semicolon. Most developers, however, use semicolons at the end of each and every statement, even when semicolons are not required. The reason for this is that some obscure statements (you won't find any of them in this book) do require the use of semicolons, so many developers use semicolons with JavaScript routinely. Others don't. Most published JavaScript code segments use semicolons at the end of each statement, and the sample code in this book follows this practice. If you miss a few semicolons, however, it's good to know that the JavaScript engine will still figure out where each statement ends.

As with any language, you can make your script more readable by inserting comments explaining the code. Comments are ignored by JavaScript and they're meant for people reading the code. You can embed comments anywhere in a script as long as you prepend them with two slashes (//). Everything that follows the two slashes on the same line is considered to be a comment and ignored by the JavaScript engine:

```
var NY = new google.map.Lng(40.7142, -74.0064);   // NY City coordinates
```

Note that you can't insert another statement after a comment; everything to the right of the two slashes is considered a comment. It's also possible—and quite common actually—to insert comments in their own line:

```
// NY City coordinates
var NY = new google.map.Lng(40.7142, -74.0064);
```

You can also create multiline comments. To insert comments that extend over multiple lines, begin the comments with the characters /* and end them with the same two characters in reverse order: */.

```
/*
     The following point is the geo-location of New York City
     Obtained from Wikipedia.
     Relevant link: http://en.wikipedia.org/wiki/New_City,_New_York
*/
var NY = new google.map.Lng(40.7142, -74.0064);
```

With these basic rules in mind, let's start our exploration of the JavaScript language.

Variables and Data Types

The most important aspect of any language is the set of data types it supports. JavaScript supports the three basic data types supported by most languages: *numbers, text,* and *dates.* In addition, it supports the *Boolean* data type (true/false values), and two special values, the null and undefined values. All numbers should be represented as 64-bit double precision values, but different JavaScript implementations store integer values differently.

Variables are created with the var keyword followed by the name of the variable. The var keyword declares the variable: It tells JavaScript to set aside a variable by that name. Variable names should begin with a letter or one of the two characters: $ (dollar sign) and _ (underscore). The remaining characters can be letters, numbers, and the two symbols mentioned. The letters can be any Unicode character; you can create variable names in any language. Just make sure that the variable name doesn't begin with a number.

In the following statements, age is the variable name and 25 is its value:

```
var age
age = 25;
```

You can also combine the declaration and assignment steps into a single statement:

```
var age = 25;
```

You need not specify a variable's type when you declare it. In fact, you can't specify a type for your variables; JavaScript determines the best type for any variable based on its content. You can also use the same variable to store values of different data types in the course of the application. For example, you can assign a numeric value to a variable so that you can use it in numeric calculations, and then assign a string to the same variable and print it:

```
var age = 25;
... other statements ...
age = "Twenty five"
```

JavaScript infers the variable's type from its value at run time and this can simplify the code a lot. When you add two variables, for example, JavaScript will calculate their sum if they're both numeric types:

```
var v1 = 3, v2 = 7;
alert(v1 + v2);
```

The result is 10. Now change the value of the second variable to a string with the same value, as shown here:

```
var v1 = 3, v2 = "7";
alert(v1 + v2);
```

JavaScript will concatenate them, because the second one is a string. The result this time will be the string 37. JavaScript figured out that it can't add the two values numerically; it can only concatenate them as strings. The plus operator has a dual role: It adds numbers and concatenates text.

Let's introduce a third variable. What do you think will be the result of the following statement?

```
alert(3 + 7 + "5")
```

JavaScript processes expressions from left to right. It will add 3 to 7 and reduce the expression to `10 + "5"`. Now it has to add a number and a string, and it will perform a concatenation. The result will be the string "105". The evaluation of the preceding expression was mentioned here to help you understand a little better how JavaScript evaluates expressions, but you should never use such statements.

By the way, JavaScript doesn't require that variables be declared before they're used. If you assign a value to a variable that hasn't been declared, a new variable will be created on the spot. If you attempt to evaluate an expression that contains a variable that hasn't been declared, however, a run-time error will occur.

`null` and `undefined` are two special values and they usually confuse beginners. When you attempt to access a variable that doesn't exist, JavaScript will return the value `undefined`: it means it can't even locate the variable. The `null` value, on the other hand, means that the variable has no value. We frequently set a variable to `null` to indicate that it has not been assigned a value yet. If you misspell property or variable name in your code, JavaScript will generate the "undefined variable" error at run time.

Arithmetic Operations

JavaScript supports all arithmetic operators (+ and – for addition/subtraction, * for multiplication, / for division, % for modulus division) and two unary operators: the ++ to increase a numeric value by one, and the - - operator to decrease a numeric value by one. The following are all valid statements for arithmetic operations:

```
var a = 3;
var b = 6;
var c;
c = a + b;
c++;
```

The last statement increases the value of c by one and is equivalent to the following:

```
c = c + 1;
```

The + operator can also be applied to variables that hold text, in which case it concatenates them and produces a new longer string. If you attempt to add a string and a numeric value, the result is always a string.

The equals (=) symbol is the assignment operator: it assigns the value that appears to its right to the variable to its left. The left part of an assignment operator is always a variable that accepts the value. The right part can be a literal (a number or string), but it can also be an expression. In this case, JavaScript evaluates the expression and then assigns it to the variable. It can also be a function that returns a value. As you recall from the preceding chapter, the `Map` object's `getZoom()` method returns the current zoom level of the map, which is an integer. The following statement stores the current zoom level to a variable:

```
var zoomLevel = map.getZoom();
```

The assignment operator can be combined with any of the arithmetic operators, as in the following example:

```
zoomLevel += 3;
```

The last statement adds the value shown to the right of the `+=` operator to the value of the `zoomLevel` variable and stores the result to the same variable. The `+=` operator is a shortcut for this statement:

```
zoomLevel = zoomLevel + 3;
```

The `*=` operator works in the exact same manner, only instead of adding the value to the variable, it multiplies the variable by the specified value.

The `zoomLevel` variable is not associated in any way with the map, of course. To change the map's magnification level, you must call the `setZoom()` method, passing the updated `zoomLevel` variable as an argument:

```
map.setZoom(zoomLevel);
```

You can also combine the two statements into a single one:

```
map.setZoom(map.getZoom() + 3);
```

Note that `getZoom()` is a method and not a variable, and an expression like `map .getZoom()++` is absolutely meaningless.

Math Operations

Typical applications do not involve more than basic arithmetic, but JavaScript supports many mathematical and trigonometric functions, which are contained in the Math library. Mapping applications are an exception and they may involve some serious math (you will see some non-trivial math calculations later in this book). The Math library exposes the following functions.

Function	Description
abs(v)	Returns the absolute value of the numeric value *v*.
acos(x)	Returns the arc that corresponds to a cosine of *x* in radians.
asin(x)	Returns the arc that corresponds to a sine of *x* in radians.
atan(x)	Returns the arc that corresponds to a tangent of *x* in radians.
atan2(y,x)	Returns the arc that corresponds to a tangent of the quotient of its arguments.
ceil(v)	Returns the value of the argument *v* rounded to the nearest larger integer. The name of the function comes from "ceiling" and the ceiling of 3.1 is 4, while the ceiling of –3.1 is –3.
cos(x)	Returns the cosine of *x*. The arguments *x* must be specified in radians.
exp(x)	Returns the value of *e* raised to the power *x*.
floor(v)	Returns of the argument *v* rounded to the nearest smaller integer. The floor of 4.1 is 3, while the floor of –3.1 is –4. It's equivalent to the ceil() function, but it rounds in the opposite direction.
log(x)	Returns the natural logarithm (base *e*) of *x*.
max(x,y,z,...)	Returns the largest number from its list of numeric arguments.
min(x,y,z,...)	Returns the smallest number from its list of numeric arguments.
pow(x,y)	Returns the value of *x* to the power of *y*.
random()	Returns a random number between 0 and 1.
round(x)	Rounds *x* to the nearest integer. The function round(3.1) returns 3 and the function round(3.9) returns 4. The value that lies halfway between two integers in rounded to the next larger integer.
sin(x)	Returns the sine of *x*. The argument *x* must be specified in radians.
sqrt(x)	Returns the square root of *x*.
tan(x)	Returns the tangent of *x*. The argument *x* must be specified in radians.

In addition to the functions, the Math library provides a few common mathematical constants, which are here.

Constant	Description
Math.E	The base of natural logarithms *e* (2.718281828 approximately)
Math.PI	The famous Greek π (3.14159 approximately)
Math.SQRT2	The square root of 2
Math.SQRT1_2	The square root of 1/2
Math.LN2	The natural logarithm of 2
Math.LN10	The natural logarithm of 10
Math.LOG2E	The 2-base logarithm of *e*
Math.LOG10E	The 10-base logarithm of *e*

The following methods, finally, allow you to convert numeric values to different formats.

Function	Description
`toExponential(n)`	Converts a number into an exponential notation
`toFixed(n)`	Formats a double value with *n* decimal digits
`toPrecision(n)`	Formats a number with *n* decimal digits
`toString()`	Converts a number to a string
`valueOf()`	Returns the numeric value of a string that represents a number

Working with Text

Variables that store text are called strings (from "character strings") and the text is always embedded in single or double quotes (as long as you use the same quote). The reason for allowing two different delimiters in strings is that you may have to embed the delimiters themselves in your text. Notice the following two assignments:

```
var str1 = 'JavaScript is a "scripting" language'
var str2 = "JavaScript's variables are objects"
```

You can still use single quotes to delimit some text that contains the same character, as long as you escape the single quote with the \ character in front of it:

```
var str2 = 'JavaScript\'s variables are objects'
```

If you don't escape the single quote in the text, JavaScript will think it has reached the end of the string and will attempt to interpret the rest of the string as code, which will result in an error. In most cases, you will get the "unterminated string" error.

The same escape character can be used to produce special characters in JavaScript. These special characters are \t for a tab, \n for new line, and \r for a carriage return.

Text Manipulation Methods

Even though what computers do best is calculations, typical applications contain many more statements that manipulate text than statements to perform math calculations, and it's no surprise that all languages come with a large set of methods for manipulating text.

The `string` object exposes a number of methods for manipulating text. It also exposes a property, the `length` property, which returns the length of a string. To call the `length` property, append its name to the name of a variable that stores text using the period as a separator:

```
var txt = "What a wonderful language";
var len = txt.length;
```

Two of the simpler methods are `toLowerCase()` and `toUpperCase()`, which return the string they're applied to in lowercase or uppercase, respectively:

```
txt.toLowerCase();  // returns the string 'WHAT A WONDERFUL LANGUAGE'
txt.toUpperCase();  // returns the string 'what a wonderful language'
```

The following sections describe the most commonly used methods of the `string` object.

`indexOf(string), lastIndexOf(string)`   The `indexOf()` method accepts a character or a string as an argument and returns the location of the first instance of its argument in the string to which it's applied. The index of the first character in the string is 0, not 1. The following expressions both return 4:

```
"JavaScript".indexOf("S")
```

and

```
"JavaScript".indexOf("Script")
```

The `lastIndexOf()` method is similar, but it searches from the end of the string. If you search for the last index of the character "a" in the string "JavaScript," it will return the value 3 (the zero-based position of the last "a" in the string).

NOTE The `indexOf()` and `lastIndexOf()` methods perform case-sensitive searches. To perform case-insensitive searches, convert both strings to upper- or lowercase:

```
"JavaScript".toUpperCase().indexOf("script".toUpperCase())
```

Using the string "SCRIPT" in the place of the expression "script".toUpperCase() would make the code a bit simpler. If you decide to replace the literal "script" with a variable, however, you have to use the method toUpperCase(). This odd expression was included in the example to demonstrate the flexibility of objects. The string methods apply not only to text variables, but also to text literals.

`charAt(position)`   The `charAt()` method accepts an integer value as an argument and returns the character at that location. The following expression will return "S":

```
"JavaScript".charAt(4)
```

`replace(string_to_replace, replacement_string)`   The `replace()` method accepts two arguments: the string to be replaced and the string to be replaced with. The `replacement_string` replaces all instances of `string_to_replace`. The following statement changes all instances of "blue" in the `instructions` variable to "red":

```
instructions = instructions.replace("blue", "red")
```

The rest of the string remains the same. Note that the preceding statement will also replace the "blue" in "blueberries."

The `replace()` method's first argument can be a regular expression, so you can replace patterns instead of plain text, but regular expressions aren't discussed in this book. For readers familiar with regular expression syntax, here's a simple example. The following expression replaces all e-mail addresses with a dummy string to mask personal data from the text:

```
var txt = "Please use my personal email address, " +
          "which is person@domain.ext, for your inquiries";
```

```
document.write("ORIGINAL STRING<br/>");
document.write(txt + "<br/>");
document.write("MODIFIED STRING<br/>");
document.write ( txt.replace(/\S+@\S+\.\S+/, "XXXX") );
```

If you execute the preceding statements, they will generate the following output:

```
ORIGINAL STRING
Please use my personal email address,
which is person@domain.ext, for your inquiries.
MODIFIED STRING
Please use my personal email address, which is XXXX for your inquiries.
```

The expression /\S+@\S+\.\S+/ is a regular expression, which is a pattern matching mechanism. Instead of a literal, it matches all valid e-mail addresses in the text (segments of the text that start with a word, followed by the @ symbol, then another word, a period, and then yet another word). The first and last characters in the example delimit the regular expression. As you can see in the example, it's not a perfect regular expression because it treated the comma following the e-mail address as part of the match. A regular expression for catching all valid e-mail addresses in the text is much longer (you can Google it), but this simple regular expression gives you an idea of the enormous flexibility you can embed in your scripts by means of regular expressions.

search(string)   The search() method searches a long string for a specific string, specified by its argument, and returns its position within the larger string, or –1 if the specified substring doesn't occur in the longer string. It's quite similar to the indexOf() method, only the search() method's argument can be a regular expression to locate patterns of text. Like the indexOf() method, the search() method performs case-sensitive comparisons.

split(delimiter)   The split() method splits a large string into smaller ones using its argument as delimiter. If you have a list of comma-delimited values, you can generate an array with the numeric values with a single call to the split() method:

```
var txtValues ="32.2, -41.9, 9.2"
var values = txtValues.split(",")
```

The values variable is an array (arrays are variables that store multiple values and are discussed shortly) with the values 32.2, –41.9, and 9.2.

substr(start, count) and substring(start, end)   Both methods return part of a string. The substr() method returns a number of characters starting at a specific location in the string, and its syntax is

```
substr(start_index, count)
```

where start_index is the index of the first character to be selected and count is the number of characters to be selected. The substring() method does the same, but it accepts different arguments: the indices of the first and last characters to be selected. The syntax of the `substring()` method is

```
substring(start_index, end_index)
```

The expressions:

```
"JavaScript".substr(0, 4)
```

and

```
"JavaScript".substr(4, 6)
```

will return the strings "Java" and "Script," respectively.

`toLowerCase()`, `toUpperCase()`   These two methods convert the string into lower- and uppercase, respectively.

Working with Dates

Another very important set of statements in any language deals with dates. Dates in JavaScript are stored internally as the number of milliseconds since January 1, 1970. Dates prior to this one are presented by negative values. To specify a date value, use a string that represents a date and pass it as an argument to the `parse()` method of the `Date` object. The following statements will generate valid date values:

```
var d1 = Date.parse("February 13, 2015");
var d2 = Date.parse("2/13/2015");
var d3 = Date.parse("Friday, February 13, 2015");
```

All three variables represent the same date. If you display the value of any of these variables with the statement:

```
alert(d1);
```

you'll get a number like 1,423,778,400,000, which is the number of milliseconds from January 1, 1970 to the specified date. To display an actual date, you must create a new `Date` object from this number, and then call its `toDateString()` method:

```
alert((new Date(d2)).toDateString());
```

This statement produces a date like "Fri Feb 13 2015."

The following methods of the `Date` object allow you to manipulate dates in JavaScript:

Function	Descriptions
`getDate()`	Returns the day of the month (an integer value in the range 1–31)
`getDay()`	Returns the day of the week (an integer value in the range 0–6)
`getFullYear()`	Returns the year (a four-digit integer value)
`getHours()`	Returns the hour (an integer in the range 0–23)
`getMilliseconds()`	Returns the milliseconds (0 through 999)
`getMinutes()`	Returns the minutes (0–59)
`getMonth()`	Returns the month (an integer value in the range 0–11)
`getSeconds()`	Returns the seconds (0–59)
`getTime()`	Returns the number of milliseconds since midnight Jan 1, 1970
`getTimezoneOffset()`	Returns the time difference between UTC time and local time, in minutes
`parse()`	Parses a date string and returns the number of milliseconds since midnight of January 1, 1970
`setDate()`	Sets the day of the month of a date object
`setFullYear()`	Sets the year (four digits) of a date object
`setHours()`	Sets the hour of a date object
`setMilliseconds()`	Sets the milliseconds of a date object
`setMinutes()`	Set the minutes of a date object
`setMonth()`	Sets the month of a date object
`setSeconds()`	Sets the seconds of a date object
`setTime()`	Sets a date and time by adding or subtracting a specified number of milliseconds to/from midnight January 1, 1970
`toDateString()`	Converts the date portion of a `Date` object into a readable string
`toISOString()`	Returns the date as a string, using the ISO standard
`toJSON()`	Returns the date as a string, formatted as a JSON date
`toLocaleDateString()`	Returns the date portion of a `Date` object as a string, taking into consideration the user's locale
`toLocaleTimeString()`	Returns the time portion of a `Date` object as a string, taking into consideration the user's locale
`toLocaleString()`	Converts a `Date` object to a string, taking into consideration the user's locale
`toString()`	Converts a `Date` object to a string
`toTimeString()`	Converts the time portion of a `Date` object to a string
`toUTCString()`	Converts a `Date` object to a string, according to universal time
`UTC()`	Returns the number of milliseconds in a date string since midnight of January 1, 1970, according to universal time
`valueOf()`	Returns the primitive value of a `Date` object

In addition to the get...() and set...() methods, which use the client computer's date and time, there are the getUTC...() and setUTC...() methods, which use UTC date and time.

Control Flow Statements

Control flow statements are a central part of any programming language; they allow applications to take a different course of action, or execute a number of statements repeatedly, depending on a condition. All control flow statements are based on conditions: When the condition is true, the code executes a block of statements. When the condition is false, an alternate block of statements is executed. JavaScript supports two categories of statements that control the flow of the script: the if statement, which executes or skips a block of statements depending on the outcome of a comparison, and two looping statements, the for and while statements, which execute a block of statements repeatedly.

Conditional Statements

JavaScript, like nearly all languages, provides the if statement, which allows your code to take a different path depending on the outcome of a comparison. Some languages use variations of the if statement with different names (ifTrue, for example), but most modern languages use the if keyword for the conditional statement. There are three variations of the if statement:

- **if statement**   Executes a code block only if the specified condition is true
- **if...else statement**   Executes a code block if the specified condition is true and another block if the condition is false
- **if...else if...else statement**   Selects one of many blocks of code to be executed based on consecutive comparisons
- **switch statement**   Executes one of many code blocks depending on the outcome of a single comparison

The if Statement

The if statement evaluates a logical expression and if the result is true, it executes the associated code block. Otherwise, program execution continues with the statement following the code block associated with the statement. The syntax of the if statement is quite simple:

```
if (condition) {
    // code block to be executed
  }
```

and here's a trivial example:

```
var part = "Northern hemisphere";
if (location.lat < 0) {
   part = "Southern hemisphere";
 }
```

The syntax of the `if...else` statement is identical, but it contains the `else` keyword followed by the code block that will be executed if the condition is false. Here's an alternate way to code the same operation:

```
var part;
if (location.lat < 0) {
    part = "Southern hemisphere";
}
else {
    part = "Northern hemisphere";
}
```

Because each clause of the `if` structure contains a single statement, the curly brackets aren't mandatory:

```
var part;
if (location.lat < 0)
    part = "Southern hemisphere";
else
    part = "Northern hemisphere";
```

(The semicolons aren't mandatory either, but as mentioned earlier, all statements in this book's code samples are terminated with a semicolon.) The following example uses nested `if` statements to handle three cases:

```
var part;
if (location.lat < 0)
    part = "Southern hemisphere";
else if (location.lat > 0)
    part = "Northern hemisphere";
else
    part = "Right on the equator! ";
```

Logical Expressions

The expressions evaluated by the conditional statements must return a true/false value; you can use the following operators to compare values:

==	Equal to
!=	Not equal to
===	Strictly equal to
<	less than
<=	less than or equal to
>	larger than
=>	larger than or equal to

You can also combine multiple comparisons with the following logical operators:

&&	Logical and
||	Logical or

The following expression evaluates to true if the variable a exists and it's smaller than 8:

```
if (a != undefined && a < 8) {
    // block of statements
  }
```

The difference between the equals and strictly equals operators is that the equal to operator compares values, but the strictly equal to operator compares values and types. The comparison 3 == "3" evaluates to true, but the expression 3 === "3" evaluates to false because the first value is a number and the second one is a string. Their values match, but not their types.

Why don't we simply compare the two variables in the preceding if statement? The following comparison may cause a run-time error:

```
if (a < 8) {

    // statements

}
```

The problem with this statement is that it will fail if the a variable hasn't been declared. The correct statement makes sure the variable exists before attempting to use its value. If the variable hasn't been declared yet, the expression will evaluate to false.

The switch Statement

The switch statement is just an alternative to multiple nested if statements. Use the switch statement to select one of many blocks of code to be executed.

```
switch(expression)
  {
 case "value 1":
   // code block to be executed if value is "value 1"
   break;
 case "value 2":
   // code block to be executed in value is "value 2"
   break;
 default:
  // code block to be executed for all other values
  }
```

This is how it works: First the expression in the parentheses following the statement name is evaluated. This is not a logical expression; the result of the evaluation can be a number, a string, even a date. Then, the result of the evaluation is compared with the values of each case in the structure. If there is a match, the block of code associated with that case is executed. The break statement isn't mandatory. If all cases are not mutually exclusive, then the expression evaluated at the top may match multiple cases.

You can also combine multiple values in the same case clause. The following script calculates the days in every month and handles three groups of months: the months with

31 days, the months with 30 days, and February. To calculate the number of days in February, the code examines the year, and if it's a leap year, February has 29 days, otherwise 28.

```
var year = 2008;
var month = 2;
var days;
switch (month) {
    case 1: case 3: case 5: case 7:
    case 8: case 10: case 12:
        days = 31;
        break;
    case 4: case 6: case 9: case 11:
        days = 30;
        break;
    case 2:
        switch (year % 4) {
            case 0:
                days = 29; break;
            default:
                days = 28;
        }
}
alert(days);
```

Note the use of the `break` statement. The `switch` statement may encounter multiple cases that meet the criteria. If you want to exit the `switch` statement after the first matching case has been executed, use the `break` statement. The cases in this example are mutually exclusive and the `break` statement is not required. It's a good practice, though, to break out of a switch statement as soon as possible to avoid unnecessary comparisons.

Looping Statements

Another common flow control structure in programming is the loop. Quite often, you want to repeat the same process over a large set of data, once for each data point. In these cases, you use a loop to iterate through the data. JavaScript provides two different statements for looping. If the number of iterations is known ahead of time, you use the `for` loop. If the number of iterations is not known beforehand, such as when you iterate through data points read from a remote service, you use a logical expression to end the iteration process. In these cases, you use a `while` loop. And there are, of course, variations on these loops.

The `for` Loop

The `for` loop has the following syntax:

```
for (statement 1; statement 2; statement 3)
    {
      // code block to be executed
    }
```

`statement 1` is executed before the loop starts and this is where you initialize the variable that will act as a counter for the loop. `statement 2` defines the condition for repeating the loop, and it's usually the maximum value that the counter can reach. `statement 3` is executed after each iteration of the loop. It's actually simpler than this description implies. Here's the `for` statement that iterates through the elements of the array `months`:

```
var months =
        ["January", "February", "March", "April", "May", "June",
         "July", "August", "September", "October", "November", "December" ];
var msg = '';
for (var month = 0; month < 12; month++)
    {
        msg += month + '.    ' + months[month] + '\n';
    }
alert(msg);
```

This code segment displays the month names prefixed by their number in a dialog box. To check it out, you can paste it in the JavaScript pane of JSFIDDLE as is and click the Run button. The first statement in the parentheses following the `for` keyword sets the counter, which is the `month` variable, to its initial value. The name of this variable can be any variable name. Following this, the next statement defines when the loop will terminate. It actually defines the condition that must be true for the loop to continue. In the case of the example, the counter must be less than 12. The last statement in the parentheses increases the value of the counter variable by one, so that the loop handles a different month each time.

Instead of hardcoding the value 12 in your code, you can implement the loop as follows:

```
for (var month = 0; month < months.length; month++) {
    msg += month + '.    ' + months[month] + '\n';
}
```

JavaScript allows you to write totally distorted code by moving the statements qualifying the `for` statement outside the loop:

```
var month=0, count = months.length;
for (; month < count; month++) {
    msg += month + '.    ' + months[month] + '\n';
}
```

There are developers who think this is clean code (they're probably old hardcore C++ developers). Writing obscure looking code just because you can does not make you a good programmer. Quite the opposite in fact.

You can even omit the statement that tells the loop whether to repeat the loop or not, by embedding this logic into the loop's body:

```
var month=0, count = months.length;
for (; ; month++) {
    if (month == count) break;
    msg += month + '.    ' + months[month] + '\n';
}
```

The code segment shown here uses the `break` statement to break out of the loop after the number of iterations has been exhausted.

The last statement in the parentheses usually increments (or decrements) the counter variable, but you can skip even this statement and perform the operation in the loop's body. However, you can't skip the semicolons.

The `for in` Loop

A variation of the `for` loop allows you to iterate through the elements of an array or through the properties of an object (objects are discussed in detail in the following chapter). Here's an alternate form of the `for` statement to loop through the elements of an array:

```
var months = ['January', 'February', . . . ., 'December']
for (m in months) {
    // process month months[m]
}
```

If the variable specified in the `for in` loop is an object, the loop will iterate through the properties of the object. Even though objects are discussed in the following chapter, here's a simple example that demonstrates this use of the `for in` loop:

```
var poi = {"place": "SpaceNeedle",
           "location": new google.maps.LatLng(47.62, -122.34),
           "state":"Washington"};
var txt = '';
for (p in poi) {
    txt=txt + p + ' >> ' + poi[p] + '\n';
}
document.write(txt);
```

This loop will store in the `txt` variable the values of the properties of the `poi` object; these values are the name of the point of interest and its coordinates. The preceding code segment generates the following output:

```
place >> SpaceNeedle
location >> (47.62, -122.340000003)
state >> Washington
```

The extra decimal digits were introduced by the internal representation of the longitude value. The specified value can't be represented exactly as a binary value, so JavaScript introduced some extra decimal digits.

The `while` Loop

The `while` loop repeats a code block when a condition is true, similar to the `for` loop, but there's no counter variable and there's no need to know the number of iterations ahead of time. The structure of the `while` loop is as follows:

```
while (condition)  {
    // statements to be executed
}
```

Here's how you can iterate through the elements of the months array with a while loop:

```
var months = ["January", "February", "March", "April", "May", "June",
              "July", "August", "September", "October", "November", "December"];
var month = 0;
var msg = "";
while (months[month]) {
   msg += month + ".   " + months[month] + "\n";
```

```
    month++;
}
alert(msg);
```

Why is the expression `months[i]` true, and when does it become false? This expression returns a value that's not undefined as long as the index value corresponds to an item in the array. When the variable *i* becomes 12, the element `months[12]` will return the value `undefined`, which is treated as a `false` value.

The do...while Loop

The `while` loop tests the condition at the beginning of the loop. If the condition is initially false, the loop's body won't be executed at all. There are situations where you want the loop to be executed at least once, and this is when you use the do...while variation. The do... while loop executes the code block and then tests the condition. Then it keeps executing the code block for as long as the condition is true. The following is the structure of this loop:

```
do {
   // statements to be executed
}
while (condition);
```

The following loop keeps prompting the user for numeric values and adds them. To stop the loop, the user must enter the value 0 (or nothing):

```
var sum = 0, number = 0;
do
    {
        number = prompt("Please enter another value");
        sum += parseFloat(number);
    }
    while (number != 0);
alert('The sum of the values you entered is: ' + sum);
```

Functions

Functions are groups of statements that are executed frequently, so they are put together to form a unit of code that can be called by name. A function has a name and it's followed by a block of code in curly brackets. The following function displays the map's center coordinates and the current zoom level, and it may be used in several parts of an application. Instead of repeating the same statements all over the script, you can package them as a function and use the function name just like the built-in functions. Assuming that the page contains two `<div>` elements named "coordinates" and "zoom," the following function displays the relevant data on these two elements:

```
function showMapData() {
    document.getElementById("coordinates").innerHTML =
                    'Map centered at: ' + map.getCenter();
    document.getElementById("zoom").innerHTML =
                    'Current zoom level: ' + map.getZoom();
}
```

Every time you need to display the map's data on the two auxiliary elements, you can call the showMapData() function as if it were a built-in JavaScript function.

The showMapData() function is a very simple function that extracts the data it requires from the Map object and displays it on the two elements. Most functions accept arguments, which are the values on which the function's code acts. Let's consider a function that sets the map's center and zoom level:

```
function centerMap(lat, lon, zm) {
    map.setCenter(new google.maps.LatLng(lat, lon));
    map.setZoom(zm);
}
```

The centerMap() function accepts three arguments: the coordinates of a location and a zoom level. The function's code centers the map at the specified location and changes the zoom level. To reposition the map from any place in your script, you can call the centerMap() function as follows, as if it were one of JavaScript's built-in functions:

```
centerMap(82.75, -109.55, 8);
```

Instead of passing the two coordinates as numeric values to the function, you can rewrite the function so that it accepts a LatLng object as an argument. Here's the revised centerMap() function:

```
function centerMap(latlng, zm) {
    map.setCenter(latlng);
    map.setZoom(zm);
}
```

This function should be called slightly differently:

```
centerMap(new google.maps.LatLng(82.75, -109.55), 8);
```

Finally, if you want to pan the map but not change its zoom level, call the centerMap() function as follows:

```
centerMap(new google.maps.LatLng(82.75, -109.55), map.getZoom());
```

Figure 3-4 shows a short script in JSFIDDLE that demonstrates the centerMap() custom function. In the same figure, you will see an odd statement: zm = zm * 1. The prompt() function returns a string, but the zoom factor must be an integer value. By multiplying the zm variable by 1, you force it to become a numeric value without affecting its value. You could use the parseInteger() method, too, but the technique shown here is a quick and dirty method to convert strings to numbers.

Earlier in this chapter, you wrote a few statements to calculate the number of days in a given month. If you need this functionality in your code, you should implement a function that accepts the month and year and returns the number of days in the month. By packaging

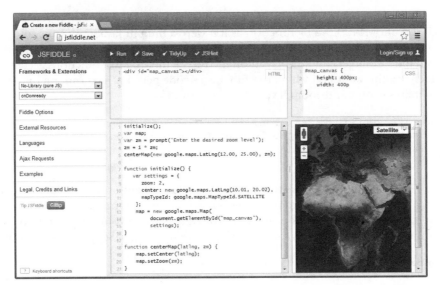

Figure 3-4 Exercising the centerMap() function with JSFIDDLE

the code you have already tested in a function, you can reuse it in your script by calling the function with the appropriate arguments every time. Here's the daysInMonth() function:

```
function daysInMonth(month, year) {
    var days;
    switch (month) {
      case 1: case 3: case 5: case 7:
      case 8: case 10: case 12:
          days = 31;
          break;
      case 4: case 6: case 9: case 11:
          days = 30;
          break;
      case 2:
          switch (year % 4) {
              case 0:
                  days = 29; break;
              default:
                  days = 28;
          }
    }
return days;
}
```

To test the new function call it as:

```
alert(daysInMonth(3, 2004));
```

Place this statement followed by the definition of the function in the JavaScript window of JSFIDDLE and run the code.

Arrays

In practice, data come in sets rather than isolated values. To store multiple data in a single variable, you use arrays. Arrays are variables with multiple values and you access the individual values with an index. The following statements create an array and store three values in it:

```
var cities[];
cities[0]="Greensboro";
cities[1]="High Point";
cities[2]="Durham";
```

The first element is at position 0 of the array, the second element at position 1, and so on. The numbers following the array name in square brackets are the indices that specify the order of the value you want to set, or read, in the array.

It's also possible to assign values to the elements of an array in the same statement that declares the array with an array initializer:

```
var cities[]=["Greensboro", "High Point", "Durham"];
```

The following is another notation to declare an empty array variable, and it's totally equivalent to the one used in the preceding sample code:

```
var cities = new Array();
```

Because the values are embedded in a pair of square brackets, JavaScript knows it's an array and you can omit the brackets following the array name:

```
var cities=["Greensboro", "High Point", "Durham"];
```

Array values can be objects. The following statement initializes an array with the coordinates of the same three cities:

```
var geoCities = [new google.maps.LatLng(36.0725, -79.7922),
                 new google.maps.LatLng(35.9556, -80.0056),
                 new google.maps.LatLng(35.9939, -78.8989)];
```

An object is any data type other than the basic ones (numbers, strings, dates, and the special values). While the basic data types are built into the language, objects are imported into the script. When you include an external script (such as the script for Google Maps) in your own script, the objects defined in the external script become available to your code. You already know one of the objects exposed by the Google Maps API, the LatLng object, which represents a point on the earth's surface. If you attempt to create a new google .maps.LatLng object without importing the appropriate script from Google, a run-time error will occur when you attempt to create a variable of the LatLng type. If you insert the <script> statement that references the Google script, which contains the definition of the LatLng object, then this and a host of other objects become available to your script.

Not only can arrays store objects, but they can store objects of different types. The following array contains numbers, strings, and custom objects:

```
var earthquake = [7.6, new google.maps.LatLng(10.811, 126.63800000000003),
                 "Philippine Islands region"];
```

The `earthquake` array stores the earthquake's magnitude (a numeric value), its location (a `LatLng` object), and the region (a string value). Things can get even better with arrays: If you declare multiple arrays, each one containing an earthquake's data, you can create an array in which each item is an array! Assuming that you have created three array variables to represent earthquakes, you can store all of them in a new array:

```
var earthquakes = [earthquake1, earthquake2, earthquake3];
```

The three variables that make up the `earthquakes` array are themselves arrays and they contain elements of different data types.

Array Properties and Methods

Arrays provide a number of properties and methods you can use to manipulate their contents. The number of elements in an array is the array's length and you can request the count of the elements with the *length* property. The expression:

```
cities.length
```

returns an integer, which is the number of items or elements in the array to which it's applied. The index of the first element is 0, and the index of the last element in the array is the length of the array minus 1.

If you add a new element to the `cities` array, its index should be 3. If you skip this index or you intentionally specify the value of an element with a higher index, the ones in-between will be left blank. It's totally valid to add an element at index 4. The fourth element, whose index is 3, will be blank. If you execute the following statement:

```
cities[4] = new google.maps.LatLng(41.90, 12.50)   // the coordinates of Rome
```

the `cities` array will contain four elements, and you can verify this by requesting the length of the array with the `length` property:

```
alert(cities.length);
```

The elements at index values 0, 1, 2, and 4 have valid values. The element `cities[3]` has a peculiar value—it's *undefined*. The two alert statements that follow will print the contents of the first and third elements in the array:

```
alert(cities[0]);
alert(cities[3]);
```

and they will produce the following output:

```
(48.8742, 2.3470)
undefined
```

The value `undefined` is a special one that indicates that the variable (the array element) has not been initialized yet. All variables that have not been assigned a value are undefined.

After the execution of a statement that assigns a value to them, they have a proper value. To avoid undefined elements in an array, here's how you should add new elements to an array:

```
cities[cities.length] = new google.maps.LatLng(37.9778, 23.7278)
```

The length of an array is equal to the last index in the array plus one, so the position `cities.length` corresponds to the next available element in the array. Consider an array with three elements, which have the indices 0, 1, and 2. The length of the array is 3 and the index of the next available position in the array is also 3.

Or, you can simply call the `push()` method, which accepts as an argument a value and appends it to the array. To remove the last item in the array, use the `pop()` method, which removes the element at index `array.length - 1` and returns it. After the execution of the `pop()` method, the length of the array is decreased by 1.

The `reverse()` method reverses the order of the elements in the array. If you have an array sorted in ascending order, you can call the `reverse()` method to sort the array in descending order. The `reverse()` method reverses the element in-place: it rearranges the elements in the array.

The `indexOf()` method allows you to retrieve the index of a specific element in the array. If you need the index of the "Rome" value in the *cities* array, call the following method:

```
var idx = cities.indexOf("Rome");
```

You will use the `indexOf()` method when you want to remove a specific element from the array, or when you want to insert elements right after a specific element in the array. You can also use this method to find out if the array contains a specific element. If the `indexOf()` method returns –1, then the element you specified as an argument to the method does not belong to the array.

Sorting Arrays

Finally, the `sort()` method sorts the elements of the array. If the array contains simple values, such as strings or numbers, the `sort()` method sorts these values easily and returns the sorted array. It does so because it knows how to compare the basic data types (strings, numbers, and dates). If the array contains custom objects, however, the `sort()` method doesn't know how to sort the objects. To sort an array of custom objects, you must supply the name of a function that knows how to compare two instances of the custom object. All sorting algorithms work by comparing and swapping elements. The swapping part is straightforward, but the comparison operation is not trivial. How do you compare two `LatLng` objects, for example? In some applications, you might wish to sort locations from west to east, or north to south, in which case you would compare the `lat()` or `lng()` properties of the `LatLng` objects, respectively. If you wish to sort the locations according to their distance from the equator, you'd use the absolute value of their latitude in your comparisons. The first step is to determine how the custom objects should be compared in a way that makes sense to your application. Then, you must implement this comparison as a custom function and pass the name of this function as an argument to the `sort()` method.

The custom function should return zero if the two objects are equal, in which case no further action need be taken (the elements need not be swapped). If the first object should appear before the second one, then the custom function should return a negative value. Finally, if the second value should appear before the first one, the custom function should return a positive value. Here's a custom function that sorts LatLng objects based on their distance from the equator:

```
function pointCompare(p1, p2) {
    return (p1.lat() - p2.lat())
}
```

To use the sort() method with a custom comparer, pass the name of the function that compares two elements as an argument to the sort() method:

```
cities.sort(pointCompare);
```

You can also use an inline function to perform the comparison:

```
cities.sort(function(p1,p2){return p2.lat() - p1.lat()})
```

An inline function is like a regular function, but the entire function definition is passed as the argument to the sort() method. In the last example, the order of the variables p1 and p2 in the return statement is reversed, and this is how you sort arrays in descending order.

To iterate through the elements of an array, set up a for loop that goes through all elements of the array:

```
for (var i = 0; i < cities.length; i++) {
    // statements to process the current element: cities[i]
}
```

Another type of loop is the for...in loop, which has the following syntax:

```
for (var city in cities) {
    // statements to process element city
}
```

Note that the city variable doesn't represent the current element at each iteration; it's the index of the current element. Even if some of the array's elements are undefined, the code will skip the indices that correspond to these elements.

Slicing and Splicing Arrays

Two very useful methods of the array object are the slice() and splice() methods. The slice() method returns a segment of the array and accepts as arguments the starting and ending indices of the desired segment. The splice() method removes some elements from the array and inserts another array in their place. If you don't specify an array to be inserted, the splice() method simply removes the specified elements. This method returns a new array that contains part of the original array. The following statement returns an array that contains the second, third, and fourth elements of the `cities` array:

```
var cities1 = cities.slice(1, 3);
```

The selected subset of the array is stored in the `cities1` array.

The `splice()` method modifies an array by replacing a section of the original array with new elements. If you don't specify the replacement array, then the `splice()` method will simply remove the specified elements. The following is the syntax of the `splice()` method:

```
splice(start, count, newArray);
```

The method removes `count` elements starting at the index specified by the first argument and inserts in their place the elements of the `newArray` array. One of the forms of the `splice()` method that you will see in several sample applications in the rest of the book removes a single item from an array. To remove the element at position i in the array, call the `splice()` methods as follows:

```
array.splice(i, 1)
```

Let's look at a practical application scenario. The array `markers` stores all the markers you have placed on a map to identify points of interest. When the user clicks a marker to select it, this instance of the `Marker` object is stored in the variable `selectedMarker`. To remove the selected marker from the `markers` array, you must locate the `selectedMarker` object's index in the `markers` array and then call the `splice()` method with the appropriate arguments:

```
for (var i = 0; i < markers.length && markers[i] != selectedMarker; i++);
markers.splice(i, 1);
```

The first statement is a loop without a body! The second statement is not part of the `for` statement because the `for` statement ends with a semicolon. I mentioned at the beginning of this chapter that the semicolon isn't required, but this is a case where you must place a semicolon to indicate the end of the loop. Without it, JavaScript would think that the next statement is the body of the loop.

The loop keeps increasing the value of the counter variable i for as long as the `markers[i]` element is not the same as the `selectedMarker` object. When the `selectedMarker` is found, the loop breaks and the i variable maintains the value it had when the desired element was located in the array; its value is the index of the desired element in the array. The second statement in the code segment removes the *i*th element in the `markers` array by calling the `splice()` method.

NOTE If you're familiar with other high level languages (such as the .NET languages), you're probably wondering why the *i* variable maintains its value outside the loop in which it was declared. In JavaScript, the scope of variables is limited to a function and not a block of code. A variable declared in a `for` loop is visible inside the function that contains the declaration and not just the block that contains the declaration.

The following function demonstrates how to set up arrays in JavaScript and how to use the slice() and splice() methods. You can copy the following code as is in JSFIDDLE and use it as a starting point to experiment with arrays:

```
myFunction()
function myFunction() {
  var ancientCities = ["Troy", "Athens", "Rome", "Sparta", "Alexandria"];
  document.write("Array oldCities");
  document.write("<br/>");
  document.write(ancientCities);
  var rome = ancientCities.slice(2, 3);
  document.write("<br/>");
  document.write(rome);
  document.write("<br/>");
  var romeIndex = ancientCities.indexOf("Rome");
  document.write("<br/>");
  document.write(ancientCities[romeIndex]);
  document.write("<br/>");
  var modernCities = ["London", "Berlin", "Vienna"];
  var cities = [];
  cities.splice(0, 0, ancientCities);
  cities.splice(cities.length-1, 0, modernCities)
  document.write("Array cities");
  document.write("<br/>");
  document.write(cities);
  document.write("<br/>");
}
```

The script sets up an array with some ancient cities, the ancientCities array. It extracts one of them with the slice() method, which requires that you know the position of the desired element in the array. Then it extracts the same city, but this time it locates the element "Rome" in the array and then uses the value returned by the indexOf() method as an index to the array.

After that, a new array with the names of a few modern cities is declared, the modernCities array. The two arrays are then appended into the cities array with the splice() method. The cities array is initially empty and the code uses the expression cities.length-1 as the index of the first available element in the array. This is where each array is inserted with the splice() method.

You should keep in mind that the slice() method returns a segment of the array, but it doesn't remove this segment from the array. Unlike the slice() method, which does not alter the array, the splice() method does modify the array: It can remove elements, insert new elements, and replace existing ones with new values.

Summary

With the basics of HTML and JavaScript out of the way, you're now ready to explore some more advanced topics in coding with JavaScript. In the following chapter, you will find a few practical examples related to maps. You will learn about JavaScript's object manipulation features, and you'll see examples of how to handle some of the simpler objects of the Google Maps API. In Chapter 5, you'll explore the basic objects of the API in more detail and you will start developing practical map-enabled web applications.

4 Advanced JavaScript Topics

In this chapter, you continue your exploration of JavaScript with a few more advanced topics. While the code segments of the preceding chapter were rather generic to demonstrate basic features of the language, starting with this chapter you will see code examples specific to the Google Maps API. As with the previous chapter, the topics presented in this chapter are meant to assist you in programming the Google Maps API and not as a general introduction to JavaScript's features.

The basic topic of this chapter is the manipulation of multiple data values in arrays and collections. Arrays and collections are convenient mechanisms for storing data items, but the most convenient mechanism for storing data is to create custom objects that reflect the structure of the entities they represent. Custom objects allow you to store not only data, but their structure as well. Instead of using individual variables to store an airport's code, name, and location, you can use a custom object that has three properties (the code, name, and location properties) and assign the appropriate value to each property. All the information about a specific airport is stored in a single variable that contains multiple named values such as airport.code, airport.location, and so on.

Storing Data in Custom Objects

In addition to JavaScript's built-in objects, you can create your own custom objects. The map-related objects, such as the LatLng object or the Marker object, are implemented in the script you download from Google every time you include this script in your page. JavaScript knows nothing about LatLng objects, or the Map object for that matter, and this is why all map related objects are declared with the prefix google.maps.

You can create a new object on the fly by specifying its properties and their values as pairs embedded in a pair of curly brackets. The following statement creates a new object:

```
var obj = new Object()
```

and so does the following statement:

```
var obj = {}
```

If you attempt to display the value of the `obj` variable with this statement:

```
alert(obj);
```

you will see that its value is `[object Object]`. This is a string that JavaScript generates to describe an object. All variables provide a method called `toString()`, and every time you attempt to print a variable, JavaScript calls this function internally to convert an object to a string. The generic description of the preceding example says that `obj` is a variable of type `Object`. This is all the information JavaScript has about the object. If you attempt to print a `LatLng` object, you will get back a string with the location's coordinates like this:

```
(32.45, 109.10)
```

The `LatLng` object is identified by its coordinates, and the `toString()` method returns a meaningful string that identifies the object. Most objects do not lend themselves to a simple textual description, so their `toString()` method returns a generic string. The `Marker` object, for example, can't be uniquely identified by a simple string; this object has many properties, but not a single property, or combination of properties, that make it unique, so its `toString()` method returns a generic string to describe it.

Creating Objects On the Fly

Let's add some content to our custom object. Objects have properties, which are named values. The following statement creates an object that represents an airport (you'll use this definition in later chapters to generate a list of airports and place them on a map as markers).

```
var LAXAirport = {"Code": "LAX", "Name": "Los Angeles International Airport"}
```

The quotes around the property names are not mandatory, unless the names contain spaces. It's a very common practice, however, and it's followed in this book. The `toString()` method will return the usual `[object Object]` string, but your object has properties, which you can access using the dot notation:

```
alert(LAXAirport.Code);     // LAX
alert(LAXAirport.Name);     // Los Angeles International Airport
```

The values displayed are shown as comments next to each statement. You can also access the properties as elements of the `LAXAirport` array using the property names as index values:

```
LAXAirport['Code']
```

There's a catch here: The name of the property must be enclosed in a pair of quotes. If not, the JavaScript engine will not treat it as a literal; it will attempt to find a variable named `Code` and use its value to evaluate the expression. If no such value exists, then a run-time error will occur. Things will get really bad if a `Code` variable exists: JavaScript will use its value to access a property of the `LAXAirport` object!

The two notations are totally equivalent. The `LAXAirport` variable is not a common array, but it can be accessed as if it were an array, only instead on an index value you use a string to identify the desired element. You can also add new properties to the `LAXAirport` object using the same notation. The following statement adds a property of the `LatLng` type, which is the location of the airport:

```
LAXAirport['Location'] = new google.maps.LatLng(33.94250107, -118.4079971);
```

The `Location` property is itself another object. Any property of an object variable can be another object, or even an array of objects. The `Location` property is a nested object: It's an object contained within another object, the `LAXAirport` object, and you can nest properties in any depth.

If you think of an object as an array, then the property names are the keys of the values stored in the array. As a result, you can use the `for . . . in` loop to iterate through the properties of an object:

```
for (key in airport) {
    alert(key + '  >>>  ' + airport[key])
}
```

Here's a practical example of the `for . . . in` loop. Enter the following statements in a script and execute the script:

```
var LAXAirport = {
    "Code": "LAX",
    "Name": "Los Angeles International Airport"
}
LAXAirport['Location'] = new google.maps.LatLng(33.94250107, -118.4079971);
for (key in LAXAirport) {
    document.write(key + ' >>> ' + LAXAirport[key])
    document.write('<br/>')
}
```

The preceding statements will generate the following output (paste the preceding statements in the JavaScript pane of a new fiddle and run it):

```
Code >>> LAX
Name >>> Los Angeles International Airport
Location >>> (33.94250107, -118.40799709999999)
```

You may be wondering why the script declares an object with properties initially and then adds a new property (the `Location` property). There's no specific reason beyond demonstrating multiple methods of adding new properties to custom objects.

Extending Existing Objects

Creating custom objects and adding properties at will is straightforward. Does it mean that you can add custom members to existing objects such as a `LatLng` object? If you execute the following statements, you will see that it's quite possible (and easy):

```
var location = new google.maps.LatLng(32.90, -100.0)
location.dummy = "Extended property!"
alert(location.dummy);
```

The last statement will display the value of the dummy property! Note that if you attempt to read the value of the dummy property before it has been added to the location object, you will get back the value "undefined." This undefined value means that the property dummy hasn't been created yet. To find out whether an object supports a property before requesting its value, use the if statement to compare the property to undefined:

```
if (location.dummy != undefined) alert(location.dummy);
```

It's generally recommended that the strict comparison operator (!==) be used with undefined and null comparisons, but the != operator works fine in most situations.

It's not recommended to add new properties to existing objects, especially to objects that are implemented by a third-party script, such as the Google Maps API script. People reading your code will not understand it, and you may not always recognize that a specific property is not one of the object's built-in properties. Moreover, custom properties are added to specific variables, and not to all variables of the same type: You can't expect that all objects of the LatLng type have a property named dummy (only the one variable to which you added the custom property).

All objects in JavaScript support the objInfo property, which is a place to store custom information. If you want to extend the functionality of the LatLng object, create a new custom object with the additional information and assign it to the objInfo property of the original LatLng object.

Variables and Objects

Variables that store objects are called *object variables* and they behave differently than variables that represent basic data types. Let's create a string variable:

```
var str = "The Google Maps API"
```

Then create a new variable and assign to it the value of the str variable:

```
var newStr = str
```

So far, both variables store the same string. They actually store two copies of the same string. To verify this, modify each variable as follows:

```
str += " (version 2)"
newStr += " (version 3)"
```

and then display their values:

```
alert(str + '\n' + newStr)
```

The output will be:

```
The Google Maps API (version 2)
The Google Maps API (version 3)
```

Even though they contain the same value initially, each variable can be manipulated individually because they each contain a separate value. Let's do the same with two object variables. Execute the following statements:

```
var LAXAirport = {
    "Code": "LAX",
    "Name": "Los Angeles International Airport",
    "Location" : new google.maps.LatLng(33.94250107, -118.4079971)
}
var newLAX = LAXAirport;
newLAX.Name = "NEW Los Angeles Airport";
alert(LAXAirport.Name);
alert(newLAX.Name);
```

Both `alert()` statements will display the string "NEW Los Angeles Airport"! Objects are structures in memory and the corresponding variables do not contain the object data. Instead, they contain a pointer to the memory, where the structure with the object's data is stored. These variables are called *reference variables* because they hold a reference to their values, and not the actual values. The variables that hold simple values are called *value variables*. When you assign a value variable to another, the original variable's value is copied. When you assign a reference variable to another, then the reference (memory address) to the object is copied, not the object.

Objects and Methods

Typically, objects have properties, which are values, and methods, which are functions that perform specific tasks associated with the object. The `google.maps.Map` object, for example, exposes the `setCenter()` method. When you call this method, you change the map's center point, which is equivalent to scrolling the map from within your code. Objects in JavaScript are extremely flexible in that they can store anything, including functions. It's possible to add a method to an object by adding a function to it, just as you would add a property. The method has a name and a code block that implements it.

Let's revise the `LAXAirport` object by adding a simple function that returns the airport's full name (that is, its IATA code followed by its name). Let's call this method `getFullName()` and implement it with a single statement that returns the airport code followed by its name:

```
var LAXAirport = {
    "Code": "LAX",
    "Name": "Los Angeles International Airport",
    "Location" : new google.maps.LatLng(33.94250107, -118.4079971),
    "getFullName": function() {
        return(this.Code + ' - ' + this.Name)
    }
}
```

To call the `getFullName()` method of the `LAXAirport` variable, use a statement like the following:

```
alert(LAXAirport.getFullName())
```

and you will get back the string "LAX - Los Angeles International Airport." The getFullName() method is a good candidate for the object's toString() method, isn't it? You can replace the default implementation of the toString() method with a custom function by adding the toString() method to your object. Change the name of the getFullName function to toString in the definition of the LAXAirport object and you have a custom object that returns a meaningful representation of itself:

```
"toString": function() {
    return(this.Code + ' - ' + this.Name)
```

This is the definition of a custom object that stores airport data, including the airport's location, and it also provides a custom toString() method that returns a meaningful description of the object.

Adding a Custom Method

Let's add a method to create a marker at the location of the airport on the map. The Marker object has two basic properties as you recall from the previous chapter, the title and position properties. The marker's title property should be set to the same string returned by the custom object's toString() method. The position property of the same marker must be set to the custom object's Location property. Here's the definition of the createMarker() method:

```
"createMarker": function() {
    var M = new google.maps.Marker({
        position: this.Location,
        title: this.toString()
    });
    return(M);
}
```

The createMarker() method doesn't place a marker on the map; it returns a Marker object that represents the specific airport. To place the marker returned by the createMarker() method on the map, call the Marker object's setMap() method, passing as an argument a reference to the appropriate Map object:

```
var LAXMarker = LAXAirport.createMarker();
LAXMarker.setMap(map);
```

Assuming that the map variable represents the map on your page, the last statement will place the marker on the map. Alternatively, you can modify the createMarker() method so that it accepts a Map object as an argument and places the marker it creates on the map:

```
"createMarker": function (currentMap) {
    var M = new google.maps.Marker({
        position: this.Location,
        map: currentMap,
        title: this.toString()
    });
}
```

The revised function need not return a value, as it handles the insertion of the marker on its own. The `createMarker()` method, however, has a major drawback: It will place a new marker on the map, even if one exists already. You must somehow keep track of the marker that corresponds to each airport and not create a new marker, even if the application calls the `createMarker()` method multiple times on the same object. The `createMarker()` function must be modified as follows:

```
"createMarker": function(currentMap) {
    if (this.markerExists) return;
    this.markerExists = true;
    var M = new google.maps.Marker({
                position: this.Location,
                map: currentMap,
                title: this.toString()
            });
}
```

The `markerExists` property is set to `true` once the marker is created, and the comparison at the beginning of the function prevents the creation of a new marker for the specific variable if one exists already. If the current object, represented by the keyword `this`, has a property by the name `markerExists` already, then the function exists. It the object doesn't have a property by that name, the script creates it and sets it to `true`. When the `createMarker()` function is called again, it won't place another marker on the map.

Prototyping Custom Objects

So far, you have seen how to create individual objects in JavaScript. These objects are created on the fly and have no type: You can't create a new type and declare variables of this type. When you use the Google Maps script, you can create variables of the `LatLng` type, variables

"This" Keyword

Among JavaScript's keywords, `this` is a special one. The keyword `this` in JavaScript refers to the owner of a function and it's used frequently as a shorthand notation to the current object. When you create a new object with a function, `this` refers to the newly created object. It actually refers to the object you're about to create. When you use the keyword `this` in a method, it represents the owner of the method: the object to which the function is applied as a method. Finally, when you use the same keyword in an event listener, it refers to the object that fired the event. The keyword `this` is used in JavaScript very much like it's used in the English language: It denotes something that is close at hand. At various parts of the program, the same keyword refers to totally different entities, and it's not always obvious which object it represents. You can safely use it to refer to the custom objects you're creating in your code and the object you associate with a listener in the `addListener()` method. The topic of event listeners is discussed later in this chapter, and you will see shortly how the keyword `this` is used to identify the object that fired the event.

of the `Marker` type, and so on. How does one create custom types in JavaScript? Other OOP languages use classes. A class contains the definition of an object, its properties, and its methods, and you can create new variables based on this class. JavaScript doesn't recognize classes. You can still create custom types with JavaScript using prototypes. In this book, you're not going to build any prototypes, but a very short introduction to the topic is included for reasons of completeness.

Let's say you want to create a new custom type to represent cities, and let's assume that the type will be called "City."

Start by creating a function called `City`:

```
function City() {
}
```

In the body of the function, insert the new type's properties and methods. To do so, use the keyword `this`, which represents the object described by the function. Here's the definition of the `City()` function with a few properties:

```
function City() {
    this.name = undefined;
    this.population = undefined;
    this.location = undefined;
}
```

In the `City()` function, you don't care about the actual property values, and that's why they're all set to `undefined`. The function does not create a new object; it's simply the definition of an object. To create a new object of the `City` type, use the `new` keyword, and then assign values to its properties as shown here:

```
var LA = new City();
LA.name = 'Los Angeles';
LA.population = 1200000;
```

Now this object looks more like the objects of the Google Maps API you have seen so far: You can create a new object of the `City` type, not a generic object. The `City()` function is the object's constructor and it's executed every time you create a new object of the City type. You could initialize the properties to specific values rather than setting them to `undefined`. These values, however, would be the same for all new objects of the `City` type. Use this technique if you want to assign default values to some properties.

The constructor can also be called with arguments, which you can then assign to the object's properties. When you create a new variable of the `City` type, it's convenient to call the constructor passing the city's data as arguments. Developers using the `City` class should be able to pass the necessary parameters to the constructor of the new object, with a statement like this:

```
var LA = new City('Los Angeles', 12000000);
```

To enable the use of *parameterized* constructors, modify the constructor as follows:

```
function City(name, population, location) {
    this.name = name;
```

```
   this.population = population;
   this.location = location;
   this.toString = function() {
      return(this.name);
   };
}
```

Now you can use either notation to create new instances of the `City` custom type:

```
var NY = new City();
NY.name = "New York City'
NY.population = 8000000
NY.location = new google.maps.LatLng(40.7142, -74.0064);
```

or

```
var LA = new City('Los Angeles', 12000000,
                  new google.maps.LatLng(34.0522, -118.2428);
```

Custom Objects as Collections

It's evident from this chapter's examples that objects are multivalued variables. The same can be said for arrays, and there's a close relationship between arrays and objects in JavaScript. Arrays store multiple values, which are accessed by an index value. The index of the first element in the array is 0, the index of the second element is 1, and so on. The problem with this addressing scheme is that the indices are meaningless. Consider an array for storing state capitals. To access the capital of California, you need to know the index of the appropriate element. Wouldn't it be far more practical to access the capital of California as:

```
capitals["California"]
```

With this addressing scheme there's no need for indexing. Indeed, many languages support data structures known as associative arrays, hashtables, or dictionaries. These collections allow you to associate meaningful keys with their elements.

JavaScript doesn't support associative collections as a data structure. However, because an object's properties can be accessed by name, you can create objects and use the keys as property names and objects as values. Consider the `capitals` object defined with the following statement:

```
capitals = {}
capitals["California"] = "Sacramento"
capitals["New York"] = "Albany"
. . .
```

The `capitals` variable may be an object, but it looks and feels just like an associative array: an array whose elements can be accessed by a key value. You can view objects as associative arrays, if you wish, and use them in your code. The fact that JavaScript doesn't have a special structure for associative arrays is of no importance because objects can be used just like associative arrays.

The value assigned to a property of the `capitals` object (or equivalently to an element of the `capitals` associative array) need not be a single value. It can be another object with data about each state. Create an object with many properties, as in the following:

```
var CaliforniaData = {"Capital": "Sacramento",
                      "Population": 1293321,
                          . . .
}
```

and then append it to the `states` associative array using the state name as key:

```
var States = {};
States["California"] = CaliforniaData;
```

Some of the object's properties may be objects, or arrays of objects. The `majorCities` property could be an array with the state's largest cities:

```
States["California"].majorCities = ["Los Angeles", "San Francisco", "San Diego"];
```

If you want to store additional data about each city, use custom objects in the place of the city names:

```
States["California"].majorCities = [
          {"city": "Los Angeles", "population": 4000000,
           "Geolocation": new google.maps.LatLng()},
          {"city": "San Francisco", "population": 800000,
           "Geolocation": new google.maps.LatLng()}
]
```

The `majorCities` property is an array of custom objects! Do you want to store the major cities in a collection so you can access them by name? Almost trivial. Start by creating a collection with the cities, using city names as the keys:

```
var cities = {};
cities["Los Angeles"] =  {"population": 4000000,
                          "Geolocation": new   google.maps.LatLng(22,44)};
cities["San Francisco"] = {"population": 800000,
                          "Geolocation": new   google.maps.LatLng(11.2, 44.3)};
```

Then create the `states` collection and add the state of California and the major cities as a property:

```
var states={};
states["California"] = {
        "Code": "CA",
        "Population": 38000000,
        "majorCities": cities}
```

To see the advantages of using collections over regular arrays, take a look at the code for iterating through each state in the `states` array and through each city in the state.

There's only one state in the collection, but the same loop will work with as many states as it will find in the `states` collection.

```
for (var st in states) {
    resultsPane.innerHTML += "STATE: " + st + "<br/>";
    resultsPane.innerHTML += "   MAJOR CITIES: " + "<br/>";
    for (var ct in states[st].majorCities) {
        resultsPane.innerHTML += "    >> " + ct + "<br/>";
        resultsPane.innerHTML += "     
                                   Population:" +
                                  states[st].majorCities[ct].population + "<br/>";
    }
}
```

The preceding code segment, along with the declarations of the `states` variable shown earlier, generates the following output:

```
STATE: California
    MAJOR CITIES:
      >> Los Angeles
         Population:3820000
      >> San Francisco
         Population:812000
```

Figure 4-1 shows the code of the last example as a fiddle (it's the `CitiesAsObjects` `.html` sample page). Use this code as your starting point to add more properties to the individual objects and more states and cities in each state.

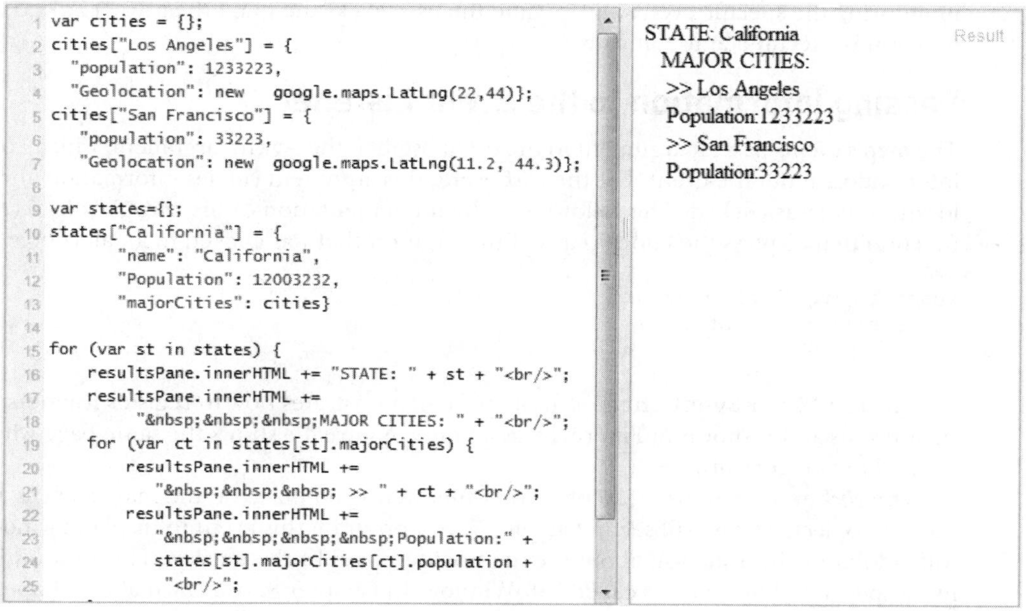

```
 1  var cities = {};
 2  cities["Los Angeles"] = {
 3      "population": 1233223,
 4      "Geolocation": new   google.maps.LatLng(22,44)};
 5  cities["San Francisco"] = {
 6      "population": 33223,
 7      "Geolocation": new   google.maps.LatLng(11.2, 44.3)};
 8
 9  var states={};
10  states["California"] = {
11          "name": "California",
12          "Population": 12003232,
13          "majorCities": cities}
14
15  for (var st in states) {
16      resultsPane.innerHTML += "STATE: " + st + "<br/>";
17      resultsPane.innerHTML +=
18          "   MAJOR CITIES: " + "<br/>";
19      for (var ct in states[st].majorCities) {
20          resultsPane.innerHTML +=
21              "    >> " + ct + "<br/>";
22          resultsPane.innerHTML +=
23              "    Population:" +
24              states[st].majorCities[ct].population +
25              "<br/>";
```

```
STATE: California                      Result
    MAJOR CITIES:
      >> Los Angeles
         Population:1233223
      >> San Francisco
         Population:33223
```

Figure 4-1   Using objects as collections in JavaScript

Event Listeners

JavaScript's programming model is based on events: When the user interacts with the page by clicking an element, typing a key, making a selection from a list, and so on, the element fires an event and the script reacts to it by executing a special function known as an *event listener*. Most elements provide attributes that allow you to associate an event listener with a specific event on that element. The button element, for example, provides the onclick attribute, to which you assign the name of the function that will handle the click event of the specific button; the text box element provides the textchanged attribute, to which you assign the name of the function that will handle the text as it's being edited (by converting it to uppercase, or by rejecting non-numeric keystrokes).

In the context of this book, you're interested in the events raised by the Map object. The Map object, which represents the map on your page, fires many of its own events as the user interacts with it, but you'll never handle all the events. You select the ones you're interested in and associate a listener to these events; all other events raised by the Map object will go unnoticed. Such events are the click and right-click of the mouse buttons, the dragging of the map, and more.

To associate a listener to an event, you must use the addListener() method passing as arguments the name of the object that fires the event, the name of the event, and the name of a function that will handle the event. The following statement associates the mapClicked() function with the click event of the map:

```
google.maps.events.addListener(map, "click", mapClicked);
```

This statement is said to "register" an event listener so that the JavaScript engine starts monitoring the specific events. Every time the user clicks the map, the mapClicked() function is executed automatically.

Passing Information to the Event Listener

The map's events pass an argument to the event listener, the event argument, which contains information about the event. For the *click* event, this argument carries information about the location that was clicked. The following is the implementation of the mapClicked() function that displays the coordinates of the location that was clicked in an alert box:

```
function mapClicked(event) {
    alert(event.latLng);
}
```

The MapClickEvent.html sample page demonstrates how to register listeners with their events and is shown in Figure 4-2 as a fiddle. Figure 4-3 shows the same page when opened in Google Chrome.

The *click* event may also take place on other items you place on the map, such as a Marker object. As you will see in Chapter 7, you program this event to display a window with additional information about the feature identified by the marker. This window looks like a speech bubble and it's called InfoWindow. In Chapter 8, you learn about shapes, such as lines, polygons, and circles, that you can place on the map. When the user clicks a shape, an event is raised and you can program this event to display additional information about

Figure 4-2   The `MapClickEvent.html` sample page implemented as a fiddle

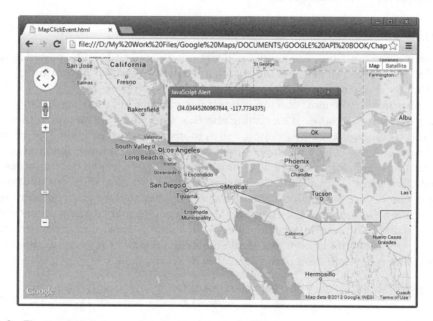

Figure 4-3   The `MapClickEvent.html` sample page in Chrome

the selected feature, or perform an action. A common design pattern is to add a marker when the map is clicked and to remove the marker when it's right-clicked.

All objects that fire the `click` event fire the `rightclick` event as well. The `rightclick` is extremely important, because this is how you can implement context menus on your maps, a topic that is discussed in detail in Chapter 5. Placing all the commands that apply to the item being clicked on a right-click menu will help you unclutter your interface, as you would normally have to create buttons for these operations. In addition, you would have to change the visibility of these buttons, as not all actions are applicable at all times.

Removing an Existing Listener

Event listeners usually remain in effect once registered, but this isn't mandatory. You can just as easily remove a listener from your application by calling the `removeListener()` method, which accepts an integer as an argument. This integer identifies the event handler and it's returned by the `addListener()` method. If you plan to remove a specific listener down the road, you must store the return value of the `addListener()` method to a script variable, and then pass this value to the `removeListener()` method.

Add a new event listener with a call to the `addListener()` method and save its return value:

```
var clickID = google.maps.addListener(map, "click",
processClickEvent(event));
alert("Event listener registered successfully. Its ID is :" + clickID)
```

and later in the code remove the listener with the following statement:

```
google.maps.removeListener(clickID);
```

Closures

Closures are functions that are defined without a name and can be passed as parameters to other functions. You first met these back in Chapter 3 as a way of providing a means of comparison during array sorting.

Closures are the most obscure concept in JavaScript. Yet there are situations when you will have to resort to closures, if everything else fails. I will not even attempt to present a definition of this technique; a simple example will demonstrate very clearly the type of problem that calls for closures. There are three sample projects in the support material of this chapter to demonstrate closures: the `No Closures.html` page, which demonstrates the problem, and `Closures 1.html` and `Closures 2.html`, with two different solutions to the problem. It's the same solution actually, just implemented with two different methods.

Here's the problem. Let's consider a code segment that creates markers and places them on the map. The coordinates and titles of the markers are stored in an array, the `Cities` array, and the script iterates this array and creates a marker for each array element. The following is the definition of the array that holds city data:

```
var Cities = [{'City': 'Santa Barbara',
            'location': new google.maps.LatLng(34.4, -119.7)},
```

```
{'City': 'San Diego',
 'location': new google.maps.LatLng(32.7, -117.2)},
{'City': 'Los Angeles',
 'location': new google.maps.LatLng(34.0, -118.2)}
]
```

The loop that iterates through this array and creates the Marker objects is shown in Listing 4-1. In addition to creating the markers, it also adds a listener for the click event. When each marker is clicked, the script displays a string with the selected city's name.

Listing 4-1
Creating multiple markers from within a loop

```
for (i=0; i <3; i++) {
    var marker = new google.maps.Marker({
                    title: Cities[i].City + "Marker " + i,
                    map: map, position: Cities[i].location});
    google.maps.event.addListener(marker, 'click', function()
                    {alert('You clicked on ' + Cities[i].City)});
}
```

The code is straightforward. Open the No closures.html page in your browser and hover the pointer over the three markers, located on three cities in California. The correct title will appear for each marker. Now click a marker. While you'd expect to see an alert box with the name of the city you clicked, nothing will happen. To find out what went wrong, double-click the status bar of Internet Explorer, or open the Developer tools of Google Chrome (open the Chrome menu and select the "Developer tools" command from the Tools submenu). If you're using Internet Explorer, you will see the error message shown in Figure 4-4.

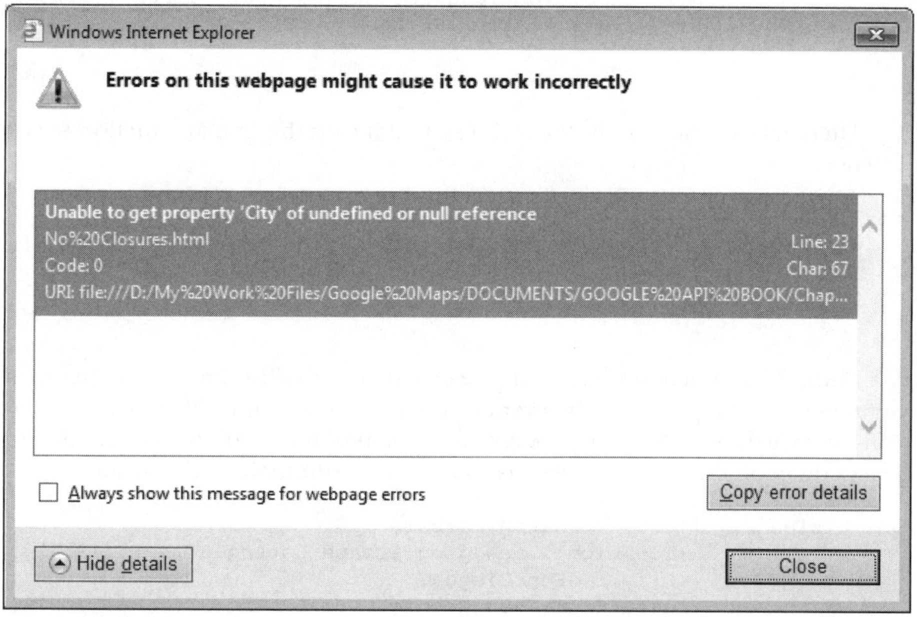

Figure 4-4   The message describing the error of the code shown in Listing 4-1

This error message is telling you that the expression `Cities[i]` is undefined and, as a result, the script can't access the `City` property of an undefined object. This is a hard-to-understand error message because the `Cities` array has been used to set up the markers, and the markers have been placed successfully on the map. The problem isn't with the `Cities` array, but with the specific element you're attempting to access. To understand what's happening, change the listener's code so that instead of the element `Cities[i]` `.City`, it displays the value of the variable `i`. This time you will see an alert box showing the value 3. This value corresponds to the fourth element of the array, but there's no such element in the array!

Here's what happens. The event listener contains a function definition, which is stored somewhere and executed when you click a marker. This is when the function reads the value of the variable `i`. When the listener is executed, the script has gone through the loop and the loop's counter variable has reached the value 3. This is how the loop ends (it keeps increasing its counter until it exceeds a maximum value). When the listener is executed, the value of `i` is 3 and the code fails to access the element `Cities[3]`.

You clearly need a mechanism that will execute some code in the loop, evaluate the variable `i`, and store it along with the definition of the function that implements the listener. This is where the closure comes in. The most important feature of a closure is that the inner function has access to variables of the outer function, even after the outer function has returned!

Write a function that accepts a `Marker` object and an index value as arguments, and associates the `Marker` object's `click` event with a listener.

```
var fnc = function(i, marker) {
        google.maps.event.addListener(marker, 'click', function() {
                alert('You clicked ' + Cities[i].City);
        });
}
```

Then, modify the loop in the script so that it calls the `fnc()` function to add the listener:

```
for (i=0; i <3; i++) {
    var marker = new google.maps.Marker({title: "Marker " + i,
            map: map, position: Cities[i].location});
    fnc(i, marker);
}
```

The `fnc()` function will actually be executed with different arguments each time. The arguments will be passed to the event listener, and the script will work as expected. For your convenience, Listing 4-2 shows the entire segment of the script that creates the three markers, places them on the map, and associates a listener with their `click` event.

Listing 4-2
Creating multiple markers from within a loop with closures

```
var Cities = [ {'City': 'Santa Barbara',
                'location': new google.maps.LatLng(34.4, -119.7)},
              {'City': 'San Diego',
                'location': new google.maps.LatLng(32.7, -117.2)},
              {'City': 'Los Angeles',
                'location': new google.maps.LatLng(34.0, -118.2)}
```

```
];
var fnc = function(i, marker) {
            google.maps.event.addListener(marker, 'click',
                function() {
                        alert('You clicked ' + Cities[i].City);
                });
}
for (i=0; i <3; i++) {
    var marker = new google.maps.Marker({title: "Marker " + i,
                        map: map, position: Cities[i].location});
        fnc(i, marker);
}
```

If you open the Closures 1.html page in your browser, you will see that it works as expected and each marker reacts to its own click event. Closures are defined as functions that capture the state of their environment: the values of the variables at the moment they're declared, and not the moment they're executed. By forcing some code to be executed while adding the markers, you effectively force the script to evaluate the values of the variables and pass to the listener the actual values, not the variable names.

Things can get even nicer with an inline function. The Closures 2.html page demonstrates a fancy technique of using closures, but this time without an external function. The fnc() function can be defined in-place, as shown in Listing 4-3:

Listing 4-3
Defining and
executing an
anonymous
function inline

```
for (i=0; i <3; i++) {
    var marker = new google.maps.Marker({title: "Marker " + i,
                        map: map, position: Cities[i].location});
    (function(index, selectedMarker) {
            google.maps.event.addListener(selectedMarker, 'click',
                        function() {alert('You clicked on ' + Cities[index].City)
                });
    }) (i, marker);
}
```

By embedding the function definition in a pair of parentheses, you're telling the JavaScript engine to execute it immediately. It's like calling another function, only the function being called is defined in-place. In the definition of the function, you specify the arguments, and as you can see, their names (arguments index and selectedMarker) need not match the names of the variables with the actual values (variables i and marker). At the end of the function, you pass the values as arguments and these values are the index of the current marker and the Marker object that represents the current marker.

If you're familiar with other object-oriented languages, you may find this approach elegant. If you're just learning JavaScript, just don't give up! When you see that several objects on your map have the same property values (while they shouldn't), it's time to use closures. And the most common scenario for closures is a code segment that adds event listeners for individual objects from within a loop. Define your own custom function, insert the same code you used in the script, and use this function in the statement that creates the event listener.

Am I suggesting that you need not try to master the concept of closures? Absolutely. There are tricks to avoid closures altogether, although there are situations in which you may not be able to do so. The source of the problem is that the code creates a `marker` variable and at each iteration stores a different `Marker` object to this variable. Once the marker has been placed on the map, the variable is no longer needed and can be reused. However, in the click event's listener of each marker, you must invoke a different alert box. The easy way out is to create an array and store your markers there. Each marker will be assigned its own listener for the `click` event and you're no longer required to handle the listeners of the markers in any special manner. The `Without Closures.html` page displays the same three markers without closures because it stores the individual `Marker` objects in an array. Here's the loop that places the markers on the map:

```
var markers = [];
for (i=0; i <3; i++) {
    var marker = new google.maps.Marker({title: Cities[i].City +
                            " (Marker # " + i +")", map: map,
                            position: Cities[i].location});
    marker.objInfo = 'You clicked on ' + Cities[i].City;
    markers.push(marker);
    google.maps.event.addListener(markers[markers.length-1],
                    'click', function() {alert(this.objInfo)});
}
```

The message to be displayed when a marker is clicked is stored in the `Marker` object's `objInfo` property and it's passed to the `alert()` function as an argument. The event listener is associated with an element of the markers array and there's no interference between the markers because they are stored in different elements of the array.

The drawback of this technique is that the array with the markers remains in memory while the page is open. If your map contains hundreds or thousands of markers, your script will take up a lot of resources. As you program more advanced applications, you will run into situations that call for closures and it won't always be possible to come up with an alternative technique. Closures aren't very common in programming with the Google Maps API, but remember to double-check any operations that take place in loops. All the objects you create in the loop may end up with the properties of the last object created in the loop, and this is a good indication to consider closures.

To use the sample code of this section with JSFIDDLE, do the following:

1. In the HTML pane, enter the following `<div>` element definition:

   ```
   <div id="map_canvas"></div>
   ```

2. In the CSS pane, enter the following style definition:

   ```
   #map_canvas {
       width:100%;
       height:300px;
       border: 2px solid darkgreen
   }
   ```

3. In the JavaScript pane, enter the definition of the `initialize()` and `addMarkers()` functions, as well as the statements to call the two functions. The `addMarkers()` function iterates through the `Cities` array and adds a marker to the map for each city.

```
var map;
initialize();
addMarkers();

function initialize() {
    var latlng = new google.maps.LatLng(34.0, -119.0);
    var settings = {zoom: 7, center: latlng,
        mapTypeId: google.maps.MapTypeId.ROADMAP
    };
    map = new google.maps.Map(
    document.getElementById("map_canvas"), settings);
}

function addMarkers() {
    var Cities = [{'City': 'Santa Barbara',
                   'location': new google.maps.LatLng(34.4, -119.7)},
                  {'City': 'San Diego',
                   'location': new google.maps.LatLng(32.7, -117.2)},
                  {'City': 'Los Angeles',
                   'location': new google.maps.LatLng(34.0, -118.2)}];
    var fnc = function (i, marker) {
        google.maps.event.addListener(marker, 'click',
        function () { alert('You clicked ' + Cities[i].City);});
    };
    for (i = 0; i < 3; i++) {
        var marker = new google.maps.Marker({
            title: "Marker " + i,
            map: map,  position: Cities[i].location
        });
        fnc(i, marker);
    }
}
```

You should also add a reference to the Google Maps API, as explained in the first section of this chapter.

Summary

In Chapters 3 and 4, you have seen all the features of JavaScript you'll be using in the sample applications of this book. You may have read about topics that you have never heard of before, or techniques that may appear unnecessarily complex. You will see many examples in the course of this book, and you will become quite familiar with JavaScript. The ability to write JavaScript code will help you design elaborate and highly interactive map-enabled applications.

You've learned how to create basic web pages with embedded maps and you have a basic understanding of JavaScript. Now that you're done with the prerequisites, and it's time to start exploring the Google Maps API in detail. In the following chapter, you learn about the basic components of the API and the objects you'll be using from now on to build applications based on the Google Maps API.

If you're interested in further exploring JavaScript, a good starting point is the JavaScript section of the w3schools site at http://www.w3schools.com/js/default.asp. Another excellent resource is John Pollocks' *JavaScript: A Beginner's Guide* from McGraw-Hill Education. If you need more information on building web pages with HTML and CSS, look into Powell's *HTML & CSS: The Complete Reference*, also from the same publisher.

CHAPTER 5

Google Maps API: The Building Blocks of Mapping Applications

In the examples of the first few chapters of this book, you learned how to embed maps on web pages, and in the process you saw some of the members of the `google.maps` library, which provides all the functionality for setting up and manipulating a map at the client through JavaScript. This library is part of the script you include in every page that contains a Google map, and it exposes its functionality through different objects. The `Map` object of the `google.maps` library represents the map itself. The maps you embed to your pages are instances of this object, and you manipulate the map through the `Map` object's methods. You can set the map's zoom level from within your script by calling the `setZoom()` method, which accepts the zoom level as an argument, or request the map's center point with the `getCenter()` method of the `Map` object.

To write custom applications on top of Google Maps and take advantage of Google's API, you must first understand the basic components of the `google.maps` library, and this is the topic of this chapter. The components you're going to explore in this chapter are the basic tools for manipulating maps; they will be used in every chapter of this book and every script you write from now on. While a reference chapter, this chapter also contains some interesting examples. Even if you're familiar with the Google Maps API, you should take a look at the last section of this chapter to see the implementation of a context menu for a Google map.

The Google Maps API at a Glance

The complete API is quite rich, and you will find a whole lot of information on how to make the most of it throughout this book. Let's start with an overview of the basic objects of the API, which represent the basic entities for coding mapping applications. These basic objects include the following:

- The `google.maps.Map` object, which represents the map itself.
- The `google.maps.LatLng` object, which represents locations on the map. This object is nothing more than a pair of decimal numbers: a point's latitude and longitude.

- The `google.maps.LatLngBounds` object, which represents the bounds of a rectangular area on the map, usually the bounds of the current viewport.

- The `google.maps.Marker` object, which represents the markers you use to visually identify features on the map.

- The `google.maps.InfoWindow` object, which is a window you use to display information about the selected marker.

- The `google.maps.event` object, which is an auxiliary object for handling all map-related events.

There are additional objects you can place on a map, which are also more complicated, such as lines and shapes. These objects are covered separately in Chapter 8. The `Marker` and `InfoWindow` objects are also covered separately in Chapter 7.

The `google.maps.Map` Object

This object represents the map and it's the most important object of the API. To display the map on the web page, you must create a new instance of this object and use its properties to customize the map's appearance. When you create a new instance of the `Map` object, you pass to the constructor the name of a container element where the map will be rendered. This container is a `<div>` element on which the map is displayed, and it usually takes up most of the available space on the page, but this isn't necessary. You can specify the size and position of the `<div>` tag on the page with HTML attributes, or apply a custom style to it. The map's `<div>` element may have a fixed size, or it can be dynamically resized with the browser's window. This element is passed as an argument to the constructor of the `Map` object, so it's imperative that it has a unique `id` attribute. The appearance of the element that hosts the map is controlled through HTML and has nothing to do with maps. If needed, you can create pages with multiple maps, which you can synchronize with some custom code. You will actually see this technique in action in the last section of this chapter.

The contents of the `<div>` element are generated by a server application running on a remote Google server, and you interact with the map through a script, `http://maps.googleapis.com/maps/api/js`, which is also downloaded from the remote Google server. This is a JavaScript file provided by Google and you can certainly read it; fortunately, you'll never have to read it. Understanding the script is not required (it's not even optional) for coding the mapping operations you wish to add to your application. The script is the client portion of Google Maps: It allows users to navigate the map, requests new tiles of the map from the remote server as needed, and renders them on the client application. When you zoom in, the script doesn't simply blow up the existing tiles; it requests new tiles, which contain additional information. All this takes place in the background and you don't need to write any code.

Map Initialization

The statement that creates the map calls the constructor of the `google.maps.Map` object passing two arguments: a reference to the `<div>` element and an auxiliary object that specifies the options of the map, as shown here:

```
var mapDiv = document.getElementById("map_canvas")
var map = new google.maps.Map(mapDiv, mapOptions);
```

`map_canvas` is the `id` of the `<div>` element that will hold the map, and it's part of the HTML page. Here's a typical declaration of a `<div>` element for displaying a map:

```
<div id="map_canvas"></div>
```

To control the position and size of the `<div>` element, you apply a style to it. The following is a typical CSS (Cascading Style Sheet) definition for the map's section:

```
<style type="text/css">
   #map_canvas {
      position: fixed; right: 0; top: 0;
      width: 100%; height: 100%;
      border:1px solid #0000FF; margin:0px;
   }
</style>
```

This style definition specifies that the `<div>` element to which it will be applied should take up all the available space on the page (100 percent of the page's width and height), have a blue border with a width of 1 pixel, and have no margins around the map.

The statement that initializes the `google.maps.Map` object must appear in a script that's executed as soon as the page is loaded. Typically, you create a script that contains the `initialize()` function with the initialization data and you call it when the page is loaded by setting the `onload` attribute in the page's `<body>` element to the name of this function:

```
<body onload="initialize()">
```

You can use any name for the function that initializes the map, but you will hardly ever find a page that doesn't use the `initialize()` name. The `onload` keyword is an attribute of the `<body>` element. It's also an event of the `window` object, which is activated as soon as the window is loaded. You can program the `window.onload` event to perform the initialization of the map with a statement like the following:

```
window.onload = function() {
   initialize()
}
```

This statement tells JavaScript to execute an anonymous function, which simply calls the `initialize()` function. You can also replace the call to the `initialize()` function with the actual contents of the `initialize()` function. The preceding statement must appear at the beginning of the `<script>` section.

The second argument of the google.maps.Map constructor, the mapOptions argument, is an array of key-value pairs that determine the map's overall appearance and its initial settings. You have seen how to use the mapOptions argument in Chapter 2, and in the following section, you'll find a detailed discussion of this object.

Map Options

The MapOptions object determines the appearance of the map and it has many properties, three of which are required: the center, zoom, and mapTypeId properties. The first two properties specify the map's initial center and zoom values. The MapTypeId property specifies the initial map type, and its value can be one of the members of the google .maps.MapTypeId enumeration, shown in Table 5-1.

The following statements create a MapOptions object with the most basic map attributes and then use it to set up a new map:

```
var mapOptions = {
        zoom: iniZoom, center: myLatlng,
        mapTypeId: google.maps.MapTypeId.ROADMAP,
    }
map = new google.maps.Map(
                document.getElementById("map_canvas"), mapOptions);
```

The MapOptions object exposes many more properties for customizing the map. Some of the properties allow you to manipulate the appearance of the various controls that appear in the default map: the Navigation control on the left; the Zoom control, which is normally part of the navigation control; and the MapType control, which allows users to change the map type.

Controlling the Map's Appearance

You can customize the appearance of the map by specifying which of the various controls will be displayed, and their style. The three controls are the Navigation control, the Scale control, and the MapType controls. These items are handled in a similar manner: There's a property you can set to a true/false value to specify whether the item will be shown on the map or not. You can further customize the appearance of these controls by setting their options.

All objects that can be customized accept an array of options in their constructor. They also provide a setOptions() method, which accepts the same argument: an array of option names and their settings. The setOptions() method can be called at any time to

MapType Name	Description
HYBRID	The map displays a semitransparent layer of major streets on top of satellite images.
ROADMAP	The map displays streets and administrative borders.
SATELLITE	The map displays satellite images.
TERRAIN	The map displays physical features such as terrain and vegetation.

Table 5-1 The Members of the google.maps.MapTypeId Enumeration

Zoom Style Name	Description
DEFAULT	The default control appearance. This control's look will vary according to map size and other factors. It may change in future versions of the API.
LARGE	A large control with the zoom slider in addition to +/– buttons.
SMALL	A small control with buttons to zoom in and out.
ANDROID	A small control at the bottom of the map, reminiscent of the Android interface.

Table 5-2   The zoomControl Styles

alter one or more options of the object to which it's applied. The following call to the setOptions() method changes the map's type to satellite view and its zoom level:

```
map.setOptions({
        mapTypeId: google.maps.MapTypeId.SATELLITE,
        zoom: 10});
```

Note that the property names and their new settings are passed to the method as an array of key-value pairs.

The Navigation Control   This is the control that normally appears in the left part of the map, and it contains the Pan control and the Zoom controls. To hide this control completely, set the navigationControl property to false (its default value is true). You can also manipulate the appearance of the Zoom control with the ZoomControlOptions object, which exposes only two properties: the position property, which determines the location of the control on the map, and the style property. The style property takes on the values as listed in the Table 5-2.

MapTypeControlStyle Options   The second control you can manipulate individually on the map is the MapType control, which determines the type of map you want to display. The property mapType control can be set to false to hide the entire control (if you don't want users to change the map type in a specific application). In addition, you can control the appearance of the control by setting the style property of the mapTypeControlOptions object to one of the values listed in Table 5-3.

Finally, you can move the map's controls to locations other than the default ones with the Position property, which can take one of the following values: BOTTOM_CENTER, BOTTOM_LEFT, BOTTOM_RIGHT, LEFT_BOTTOM, LEFT_CENTER, LEFT_TOP, RIGHT_BOTTOM, RIGHT_CENTER, RIGHT_TOP, TOP_CENTER, TOP_LEFT and TOP_RIGHT.

MapType Style Name	Description
DEFAULT	Uses the default map type control.
DROPDOWN_MENU	The options are listed in a drop-down menu to take up the least possible space on the map.
HORIZONTAL_BAR	The options appear as radio buttons on the map.

Table 5-3   The mapTypeControl Styles

The following example sets up a map by setting all the properties of the map controls. Paste the following definition in your script and experiment with all possible settings of the map's options.

```
var mapOptions = {
    zoom: 12,
    center: new google.maps.LatLng(40.0, -120.0),
    mapTypeId: google.maps.MapTypeId.ROADMAP,
    mapTypeControl: true,
    mapTypeControlOptions: {
        style: google.maps.MapTypeControlStyle.HORIZONTAL_BAR,
        position: google.maps.ControlPosition.BOTTOM_CENTER
    },
    panControl: true,
    panControlOptions: {
        position: google.maps.ControlPosition.TOP_RIGHT
    },
    zoomControl: true,
    zoomControlOptions: {
        style: google.maps.ZoomControlStyle.LARGE,
        position: google.maps.ControlPosition.LEFT_CENTER
    },
    scaleControl: true,
    scaleControlOptions: {
        position: google.maps.ControlPosition.TOP_LEFT
    },
    streetViewControl: true,
    streetViewControlOptions: {
        position: google.maps.ControlPosition.LEFT_TOP
    }
}
```

google.maps.LatLng

The LatLng object represents a point on the earth's surface; it consists of the point's latitude and longitude, in that order. The getCenter() method of the Map object returns a LatLng object with the coordinates of the center of the map. Whenever you need to pass a location to a function, you create a new LatLng object by specifying its latitude and longitude:

```
var pt = new google.maps.LatLng(38.409302, -103.326711);
```

To center the map around this point, call the Map object's setCenter() method passing the pt variable as an argument:

```
map.setCenter(pt);
```

The LatLng object exposes its two basic components, the point's latitude and longitude, as methods and their names are lat() and lng(). The following statements read the map's center coordinates and store them to two variables:

```
var center = map.getCenter();
var lat = center.lat();
var lon = center.lng();
```

google.maps.LatLngBounds

The LatLngBounds object represents the rectangle that encloses the current viewport. The bounds of the current viewport are specified by the coordinates of the upper-right and lower-left corners of the viewport. In terms of actual world coordinates, the upper-right corner is the north-east corner of the viewport, while the lower-left corner is the south-west corner of the viewport. The LatLngBounds object exposes the sw and ne properties, which are LatLng objects, and they represent the coordinates of the map's opposite corners. To find out the current viewport's minimum and maximum latitudes, you must call the map's getBounds() method and then extract the latitude values from the sw and ne properties, as shown here:

```
var bounds = map.getBounds();
var minLatitude = bounds.sw.lat();
var maxLatitude = bounds.ne.lat();
```

The LatLngBounds object exposes some very useful methods on its own, which can simplify your script, especially if you're coding a GIS application. The contains() method accepts as an argument a LatLng value (a geo-location) and returns true if the specified location lies within the bounds of the LatLngBounds object. The extend() method accepts as an argument a geo-location and extends the bounds of the current LatLngBounds object so that it will contain the specified geo-location. This method is especially useful when you place multiple markers on a map (say, the hotels in a city or neighborhood), and you want to make sure that all markers are shown. Instead of experimenting with the zoom level, you start by creating a new LatLngBounds object with the location of the first marker. Then, as you add markers to the map, you call the extend() method of the LatLngBounds object, passing the geo-location of the current marker as an argument. Finally, when you're done, you call the map's fitBounds() method, passing the LatLngBounds object you have created as argument, and the map will be panned and zoomed in or out as needed to display all markers. The new viewport will comfortably contain all the markers, as its actual size will be slightly larger than the absolute minimum rectangle that contains all markers.

The Fit Bounds Demo Page   The code in Listing 5-1 demonstrates the fitBounds() method, and comes from the Fit Bounds Demo.html web page. The script places a few markers at the locations of major airports in Germany. At the same time, it extends the bounds of a LatLngBounds object, the bounds variable, to include the location of the current marker.

Listing 5-1
Creating a
LatLngBounds
object based on
specific locations

```
var bounds = new google.maps.LatLngBounds();
var marker = new google.maps.Marker({
        position: new google.maps.LatLng(52.561111, 13.289444),
        map: map, title: 'Berlin-tegel / Otto Lilienthal'
    });
bounds.extend(marker.position);
```

These same statements must be repeated for each marker. After placing all markers on the map, the script calls the fitBounds() method to display the proper viewport:

```
map.fitBounds(bounds);
```

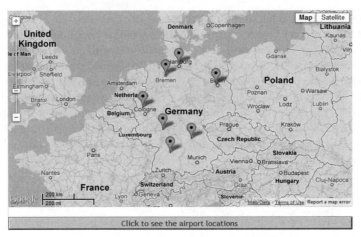

Click to see the airport locations

Figure 5-1 The Fit Bounds Demo.html web page demonstrates the fitBounds() method.

The Fit Bounds Demo.html web page is shown in Figure 5-1. The initial zoom level is 1, but after you click the button below the map and the airport markers are placed on the map, the zoom level is automatically set to 5 and the map's viewport is properly adjusted to display all markers. The Fit Bounds Demo.html page contains a very simple script, but you will find it useful when you need to display multiple markers (or other objects) on the viewport.

Map Methods

The Map object has many methods, including the getCenter() and getZoom() methods, which return the coordinates of the map's center point and the map's current zoom level, respectively. They retrieve the current zoom level, for example, you can call the Map object's getZoom() method as follows in a JavaScript script:

```
var zm = map.getZoom();
```

This method returns an integer in the range from 1 to 21. The getCenter() method, on the other hand, returns an object of the LatLng type, which is made up of two floating values: the geo-coordinates of the map's center point. If you include the following statement in a script:

```
alert('The map is centered at: ' + map.getCenter());
```

a popup window with a message like the following appears:

```
The map is centered at: (-134.21547360233408, 41.14455566406251)
```

The coordinates will be different, of course, depending on where the map is centered. Note that the parentheses were not inserted by the code; they're part of the getCenter() method's response when it's converted to a string.

All objects provide a toString() method, which is returned when you request the object's value as a string. The LatLng object's textual representation is a pair of comma-separated values embedded in parentheses. The toString() method was not called explicitly, but you requested the value of an object as text and JavaScript returned the object's textual description.

You can also retrieve the location's latitude and longitude values using the lat() and lng() methods of the LatLng object (the method toFixed() is a JavaScript method that rounds a floating point value to as many decimal digits as indicated by its argument):

```
var center = map.getCenter();
var lat = center.lat(); var lon = center.lng();
alert('The map is centered at latitude: ' +
      lat.toFixed(6) + ' longitude: ' + lon.toFixed(6));
```

Conversely, you can manipulate the map from within your script. To move to a different location, use the map object's setCenter() method, passing as an argument a LatLng object; to zoom in or out, use the map object's setZoom() method, passing as argument an integer value:

```
map.setCenter(new google.maps.LatLng(-134.25, 41.10));
map.setZoom(11);
```

Why should you ever control the map programmatically when it's so easy for the user to navigate to the desired location? You may have a page that displays cities, or monuments, or hotel names in an area, and want to center the map at the selected location and set the zoom to a value that makes sense for the item being selected. Your interface should allow users to select a monument or a hotel in a list and center the map on the selected feature every time the user makes a new selection. The fitBounds() method discussed in the preceding section does exactly the same.

The setCenter() method changes the map's location instantly. Another method, the panTo() method, also accepts a location as an argument and pans the map smoothly to its new location. A third related method, the panBy() method, accepts as arguments the horizontal and vertical displacements and scrolls the map smoothly to its new location. The Basic Map Events.html page, shown in Figure 5-2 later in this chapter, demonstrates the difference between the setCenter() and panTo() methods. Check either radio button below the buttons, and then click the destination buttons to change the viewport. With the setCenter() method, the map is relocated instantly; with the panTo() method, on the other hand, the map is panned smoothly to its new center. The operation lasts much less than a second, but the effect is quite noticeable. Of course, the panning is possible if the destination tiles are already in memory. If you move from one hemisphere to the other, the panTo() method is no different than the setCenter() method. The function jumpTo() in the page's script accepts the coordinates of the new location as arguments and calls the appropriate method depending on the status of the rbCenter radio button:

```
function jumpTo(lat, lng) {
    if (document.getElementById('rbCenter').checked) {
        map.setCenter(new google.maps.LatLng(lat, lng))
```

```
    }
    else {
        map.panTo(new google.maps.LatLng(lat, lng));
    }
}
```

The `Map` object is used routinely with all other objects of the Google Maps model object, such as markers, information windows, lines, and shapes. All of these objects expose the `setMap()` method, which accepts a single argument: the map to which the object will be attached. Assuming that the `marker` variable represents a marker, you can place the marker on the map by executing the following statement:

```
marker.setMap(map);
```

It's this statement that actually displays the marker on the page, and not the statement that creates the marker. To remove an object from the map, you call the same method, passing a null value:

```
marker.setMap(null);
```

The Marker and InfoWindow Objects

These two objects do not represent attributes of a map per se; they are the basic means for identifying locations, or points or interest (POI), on the map. The `Marker` object is used to mark a specific location on the map and it's usually rendered as a pin. Markers contain additional information about the location they identify, and this information can be displayed in a speech bubble icon, which is an `InfoWindow` object, when users click the marker. The `Marker` and `InfoWindow` objects are two of the most recognizable symbols in the computer world. They are very important in designing mapping applications and are described in detail in Chapter 7.

Working with Map Events

Google Maps are interactive by design: Users can zoom in and out, and they can drag the map around to bring any location into view. They can also switch views between roadmap view and satellite view. Users can interact with Google Maps and you don't need to write any code to enable the standard interaction techniques.

The most interesting mapping applications allow users to interact with maps in different and, in many cases, very imaginative and elaborate ways. To implement any type of interaction beyond the basic model, you must supply your own code. To be more specific, any custom interaction model must be implemented in JavaScript code. Need I present any examples? All hotel reservation sites display the hotels in the selected area on the map and they allow users to filter the results. You can select a hotel to see its details, including photos, in popup windows. Every major urban transportation company uses maps that allow users to select routes and stations to view details, banks have an interactive branch/ATM locator, and so on. The Web is full of interactive mapping sites, and this book shows you how to implement web applications with interactive maps.

Interactive mapping applications make extensive use of the Google Maps API, of course, and are based on *events*. An event is a notification passed from the map to your script, and your script should react to the event. Every time users click somewhere on the map, zoom in or out, and every time they drag the map, your application receives an event. Not all applications react to all events, but any model for interacting with the map on a web page is based on events. In the following section, you learn about the map events and how to write code to react to these events. The code is rather trivial, intended to help you understand the nature of the events and how they're handled at large. In the coming chapters, you will see practical examples for just about any event that the map can raise.

The Basic Map Events Application

To experiment with the basic map's events, use the `Basic Map Events.html` web page, shown in Figure 5-2. The application reacts to the most basic events. The various buttons at the bottom re-center the map at a different location. The text at the bottom (not shown in the figure) describes the map's events, and you can scroll the page to read it.

Drag Events

The following events are raised by the `Map` object when the map is dragged; they notify your application about the drag operations initiated by the user. User interaction with the map involves a lot of dragging and your application should be able to react to these events.

drag

This event is fired repeatedly while the user drags the map with the mouse. Because the `drag` event is fired continuously, it's wise to insert in this event's handler very simple and highly optimized code that's executed instantly. If the code in the `drag` event takes even a second to execute, it will cause the drag operation to become sluggish. For example, you can easily request the map's center point coordinates and display them on your page.

Figure 5-2   Monitoring the basic map events

This operation is carried out at the client and no trip to the server is required. If you want to translate the center point's coordinates to a physical address, which means an extra trip to the Google server, this will make your page less responsive. Use the `dragend` event instead for this operation.

On the Basic Map Events web page, you will find the following statements that handle the `drag` and `dragend` events. The script displays the string "dragging" in a `<div>` element on the page while you're dragging the map. In the `dragend` event, the script resets the same section on the page. First, add the listeners for the two events in the `initialize()` function:

```
google.maps.event.addListener(map, 'drag', function (event) {
        updateDragLabel('dragging')
});
google.maps.event.addListener(map, 'dragend', function (event) {
        updateDragLabel('')
});
```

The `updateDragLabel()` function is a trivial function that sets the contents of the `dragStatus` and `mouseStatus` elements on the page:

```
function updateDragLabel(eventName) {
    document.getElementById('mouseStatus').innerHTML = '';
    document.getElementById('dragStatus').innerHTML = eventName;
}
```

dragend
This event is fired when the user ends a dragging operation and it does not provide any argument. You've already seen an example of the `dragend` event in the preceding section.

dragstart
This event is fired when the user starts dragging the map with the mouse. If you want to provide a button to "undo" a drag operation, you can store the map's center location to a script variable in the `dragstart` event handler and use this variable to slide the map back to its initial location if needed. This event does not provide any arguments; yet you can retrieve the map's initial position in the `dragstart` event's handler, because it's fired before the map is moved.

mapTypeId_changed
This event is fired when the `mapTypeId` property changes. The `mapTypeId` property determines the type of map being displayed and it's fired when the user switches from a road map to a satellite/terrain view. Alternatively, you can omit the map type control from the map and change the map's type from within your script, either in response to a user action, or based on the map's current content. You can automatically switch to satellite view when the user zooms out beyond a threshold, and back to map view when the user zooms in below this threshold.

Mouse Events

The most common events in programming a Google map are the events generated with the mouse. The following subsections describe the mouse-related events.

click

This event is fired when the user clicks on the map: It's the most important of the events raised by the Map object. The click event reports the location of the pointer on the map the moment it is clicked through a LatLng object. Note that the click event isn't fired when the user starts a drag operation, so you can write code to take advantage of the click operation (to place a mark on the map, for example, or initiate a drawing operation), without interfering with the dragging operations.

To handle the map's click event, insert the following event listener into your script:

```
google.maps.event.addListener(map, 'click', mapClicked (event));
```

This statement appears usually in the initialize() function, right after the initialization of the map variable. The mapClicked() function, which will be invoked automatically every time the user clicks on the map, contains the code to handle the event. Note that the event automatically passes an argument to the listener of the click event, and this event exposes the coordinates of the mouse location. Here's a simple function that displays the coordinates of the location where the user clicked in a message box:

```
function mapClicked(location) {
    alert('mouse clicked at: ' + location.latLng)
}
```

The mapClicked() function is implemented with a single line of code, which is usually embed in the statement that adds the listener:

```
google.maps.event.addListener(map, 'click', function (event) {
    alert('mouse clicked at: ' + event.latLng)
});
```

The event argument conveys specific information about the event. For the click event, this information exposes a LatLng object as property; this property represents the point that was clicked. In the statement that adds the event listener, the name of the argument is always "event." In your function that handles the event, the name of the argument can be anything.

dblclick

This event is fired when the user double-clicks on the map. The dblclick event is not distinguished as a separate event from the click event, so when the user double-clicks on the map, a click event is fired, followed by a dblclick event. This behavior makes it impossible to program both the single-click and the double-click events in the same script. There are hardly any applications that make use of the double-click event. If you program the click event, the dblclick event will be raised, but never handled.

In effect, you have to choose between the two events and it's very unusual for an application to react to the double-click, but not to the single-click event. If you want to program the `dblclick` event, you must also disable its default function, which is to zoom in by one step. To disable the default function of the double-click, set the `disableDoubleClickZoom` option of the Map object to true. Like the `click` event, the `dblClick` event reports the location of the pointer on the map the moment it was double-clicked through a `LatLng` object.

mousemove

This event is fired continuously while the user moves the mouse over the map and you can use its listener to update the relevant elements of the interface. This event passes to the script the current location of the mouse.

mouseout

This event is fired when the user's mouse exits the map container and passes no additional information to its event listener.

mouseover

This event is fired when the mouse enters the map. It's fired only once and it's followed immediately by consecutive `mousemove` events. The three mouse events are fired in the following order:

- **mouseover** is fired once as soon as the pointer enters the map.
- **mousemove** is fired continuously while the user is moving the mouse over the map.
- **mouseout** is fired once as soon as the pointer leaves the map.

You can use the mouse events to update a label with the coordinates of the location under the mouse. This should take place in the `mousemove` event; you must clear the label on the `mouseout` event, as the pointer is no longer over the map.

rightclick

This event is fired when the user right-clicks the map. You can use this event to display a context menu at the current location on the map, a very convenient feature that's not used as much as one would expect in mapping applications. The menu displayed with the right mouse click is called a *context menu* because its items can change depending on the current operation. The `rightclick` event reports the location of the pointer on the map the moment it was clicked through a `LatLng` object. As you already know, right-clicking a map has no effect: The map doesn't have its own context menu. It's possible, though not trivial, to implement your own context menu by writing some JavaScript code that reacts to the `rightclick` event. You actually see how to add a context menu to a map later in this chapter.

Another common use of the `rightclick` event is to undo the effect of the click event in an application that annotates a map. Let's say you use the click event to insert a marker at the location where the mouse was clicked. You can intercept the `rightclick` event of the marker to remove an existing marker. Note that the markers are placed on the map from within the map's `click` event handler, but they are removed from within the marker's `rightclick` event handler.

State Events

There are few events that are fired based on certain user or internal actions, and they signal a change in the map's status. The `bounds_changed` event, for example, is fired when the map's viewport is changed, whether due to a change in the zoom level, or due to a user-initiated drag operation. These events report changes in the map's current status; you use them primarily as notifications to update the application's interface.

tilesloaded

The `tilesloaded` event is fired when the visible tiles that make up the current map have finished loading. This is a good place to execute any statements that add content on top of the map, or enable any buttons that update the map. The `onload` event is fired when the page with the map has been completely loaded. It will take a few seconds from the moment you request the map to the moment that the relevant map tiles actually arrive to the client computer. During that time, the map is a gray rectangle. The tiles arrive one at a time and the areas corresponding to tiles that have not arrived yet remain gray.

   If there are statements that should be executed after the map has been downloaded and rendered at the client, this event is your best choice. If your page has buttons that perform specific actions on the map, you should disable them initially and enable them from within the `tilesloaded` event's handler. A button that adds a new marker to the map shouldn't be enabled while the map is being loaded, for example.

zoom_changed

This event is fired when the map is zoomed in or out. The event doesn't report the current zoom level, so you must call the `getZoom()` method from within the event's listener to retrieve the current zoom level, if you need it in your code.

bounds_changed

This event is fired when the bounds of the visible part of the map change. It takes place when the map is scrolled, or when the map is zoomed in or out, and it reports no additional information. You must call the `getBounds()` and `getZoom()` methods to retrieve the new bounds and the new zoom level. Note that the event is fired after the completion of the operation that caused the event to fire. When the user drags the map, the `bounds_changed` event will be fired after the map has been dragged to a new location and the map's contents have been updated. The `zoom_changed` event is also followed by a `bounds_changed` event because a change in the zoom level also changes the bounds of the viewport.

center_changed

This event is fired when the map's center is changed and takes place when the map is dragged either with the mouse, or with the navigation control; when the map is zoomed, its center doesn't change. The `center_changed` event is hardly ever used in coding mapping applications; you use the `bounds_changed` event instead because the bounds of the map change when it's dragged as well as when the map is zoomed in or out.

idle

This is an important event, which is fired only once when the map becomes idle after a drag or zoom operation. Use this event's listener to insert the code that updates the interface based on the map's current viewport. Note that the event doesn't report any information about the map, so you must call the appropriate methods to retrieve the map's center point, its bounds, and its zoom level.

The `idle` event is fired only once after several operations that may affect the map's viewport, and it was designed specifically to facilitate the update of the interface with the current status. In the `Basic Map Events.html` page, the `idle` event is used to update the various `<div>` elements on the form. First, the script adds a listener for the event with the following statement:

```
google.maps.event.addListener(map, 'idle',
        function (event) updateLabels()
});
```

`updateLabels()` is a simple function that updates the interface by displaying the map's current center location and zoom level:

```
function updateLabels() {
   var center = map.getCenter();
   document.getElementById('centerLocation').innerHTML =
                 center.lat().toFixed(6) + ', ' +
                 center.lng().toFixed(6);
   document.getElementById('zoomLevel').innerHTML =
                       map.getZoom();
}
```

Note that the function calls the `getCenter()` and `getZoom()` methods because the `idle` event doesn't report any arguments back to the application. The preceding code segment could assign the return value of the `getCenter()` method directly to the `innerHTML` property, but the coordinate values are formatted with a small number of decimal digits.

A Customized Map

You've covered a lot of ground in this chapter: The topics discussed here will be of help in designing fully customized maps for your applications. Figure 5-3 shows a fairly customized map that looks very different from the default Google Map. The web page shown in Figure 5-3 is the `Customized Map.html` page, which is included in this chapter's support material. The first thing to notice about this page is that the usual controls on the map are missing. This was achieved by setting the `disableDefaultUI` property to `true`. To navigate, users can press the arrow buttons, while to zoom they can use the "+" and "−" keys. They can also pan the map around with the mouse and zoom in and out by double-clicking the two mouse buttons.

The entire map is embedded in a `<div>` element with a black background and rounded corners. Moreover, the map's section is another `<div>` element, slightly smaller than its

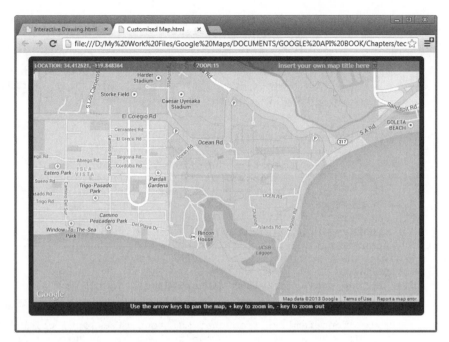

Figure 5-3   A map with a custom look

container. Some basic map attributes are displayed on a semitransparent pane at the top of the map. This pane is updated continuously with the map's basic attributes as the user interacts with the map. This pane is a combination of HTML (it's a `<div>` element with absolute position) and some code in the map's `idle` event that updates the contents of the `<div>` element. The HTML code that generated Figure 5-3 is shown in Listing 5-2.

Listing 5-2
Placing HTML
elements on top
of the map

```
<body onload="initialize()">
<center>
  <div style="
      border-radius:8px; padding:10px 10px;
      background:#303030;
      width:800px">
      <center>
    <div style="position:absolute;
          top:10; width:800px; height: 25px;
          background:#404040; color: #000000;
          opacity:0.60;z-index:999">
  <span
     style="font-family: Trebuchet MS; font-size: 8pt; " +
          "font-weight:bold; color:#000000;">
    <table width=100%>
        <tr>
          <td id="location",
            style="font-family: Trebuchet MS; " +
```

```
                              "font-size: 8pt; font-weight:bold; color:#ffff00",
                              width=320px, align=left >
                              LOCATION:
                          </td>
                          <td id="zoom", style="font-family: Trebuchet MS;" +
                              "font-size: 8pt; font-weight:bold; color:#ffff00",
                              width=80px, align="center">
                              ZOOM:
                          </td>
                          <td id="title",
                              style="font-family: Trebuchet MS; font-size: 10pt; " +
                                  "font-weight:bold; color:#00ffff",
                                  width=400px, align="center">
                                  insert your own map title here
                          </td>
                      </tr>
                  </table>
              </span>
          </div>
      </center>
      <div id="map_canvas" style=" width:800px; height:500px">
      </div>
      <div
          style="font-family: Trebuchet MS; font-size: 9pt; color:#ffffff">
              Use the arrow keys to pan the map, + key to zoom in,
                  - key to zoom out
      </div>
  </div>
</center>
</body>
```

This is straight HTML code; you will probably use a visual tool to design the interface, but these tools produce long listings with complicated style definitions and I wanted to avoid lengthy listings in the book's samples.

The contents of the semitransparent pane in the upper part of the map are updated from within the `idle` event's listener with the following statements:

```
google.maps.event.addListener(map, "idle", function() {
    var center = map.getCenter();
    var centerLabel = center.lat().toFixed(6) + ', ' +
                      center.lng().toFixed(6)
    document.getElementById("location").innerText =
                    "LOCATION: " + centerLabel;
    document.getElementById("zoom").innerText=
                    "ZOOM:" + map.getZoom()
});
```

Open the sample web page `Customized Map.html` to see how the various `<div>` elements are nested to produce the effect shown in Figure 5-3. The outer `<div>` element is the one with the rounded corners (property `border-radius`) and it contains a `<div>` element with the semitransparent header, followed by a `<div>` element with the map, and finally another `<div>` element with the instructions below the map. The header of the page is implemented as a table with named cells, the location and zoom cells, which are then assigned the appropriate values in the idle event's listener.

Adding a Context Menu to the Map

The second example of this chapter is a non-trivial, but extremely practical and useful, feature for any mapping application: the display of a context menu with commands that apply to the current status of the application and/or the current map location. The context menu appears when the user right-clicks an item on the user interface and it's a trademark of any Windows application. You can embed a whole lot of functionality in the context menu, which would otherwise require many buttons and/or hyperlinks on your page. If you're interested in embedding Google maps in a Windows application, then the context menu is a must.

The context menu you will implement in this section is shown in Figure 5-4; it contains three commands: one command to center the map at the clicked location, another command to display the coordinates of the point that was clicked, and a third nontrivial command to display the address of the clicked location. The procedure for requesting the address of any location is discussed in detail in Chapter 16, but I've added this command to make the menu a little more interesting.

To display a context menu, you need two items: a floating <div> element that contains the menu commands, and a listener for the map's rightclick event. This listener will display the <div> element with the context menu at the proper location on the map when the user requests it by clicking the right mouse button. Let's build a context menu by implementing the menu's div element and then the rightclick event listener.

The code presented in the following sections requires the jQuery component, so you must include a reference to a JavaScript file that adds jQuery functionality to your custom script. The sample applications of this book are limited to plain HTML to keep the complexity of JavaScript code to an absolute minimum. This section is an exception, because you can't display a context menu with straight HTML; you need some features

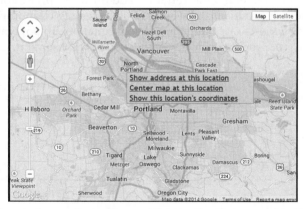

Figure 5-4   A typical context menu that appears at the location that was right-clicked on the map

available through jQuery. To access the functionality of jQuery, you must include the following statement at the beginning of the script:

```
<script type="text/javascript"
        src="http://code.jquery.com/jquery-1.4.2.min.js"></script>
```

Designing the Context Menu

The context menu is a `<div>` element that can be displayed on the current page at will; it may even contain a different set of commands depending on the current status of the application, or even the location that was clicked. If you found the last statement exaggerated, keep reading. The following statement creates the `<div>` element that will hold the menu's commands and assigns it to the script variable `contextMenuDiv`:

```
contextMenuDiv = document.createElement("div");
```

The next step is to apply a style to the `<div>` element that will host the menu:

```
contextMenuDiv.className  = 'contextmenu';
```

For that, you must create a style or, even better, customize the following style definition:

```
.contextMenu{
    visibility:hidden;
    background:#E0E0E0; border:1px solid #8888FF;
    z-index: 10; position: relative; width: 200px;
    font-family: "Trebuchet MS"; font-size: 9pt; font-weight: bold;
}
.contextItem{
    padding-left: 5px; height: 18px; cursor: default;
}
```

The first style is applied to the element that hosts the menu, while the second one is applied to each menu item. Last, you must add the appropriate commands to the menu. The commands are just hyperlinks. Instead of navigating to another page, however, they react to the `click` event by calling a different function. To populate this `<div>` element, set its `innerHTML` property to the appropriate HTML fragment, as shown in Listing 5-3.

Listing 5-3
Building the complete context menu of the Context Menu .html page

```
contextmenuDiv.innerHTML =
    "<a id='itemAddress' href='#' onclick='showAddress()'>" +
    "    <div class=contextItem>Show address at this " +
    "                           location<\/div><\/a>" +
    "<a id='itemZoom' href='#' onclick='recenterMap()'>" +
    "    <div class=contextItem>Center map at this location" +
    "    <\/div><\/a>" +
    "<a id='item3' href='#' onclick='showCoordinates()'>"
    "    <div class=contextItem>Show this location's " +
    "                           coordinates<\/div><\/a>
```

Each menu command is implemented as a hyperlink and its target is a local function. Because the definitions of the HTML elements are embedded in a string, you have to escape the slash character. Each menu item is embedded in its own `<div>` element and all these elements are formatted with a common style, the `contextItem` style. The first command displays the physical address at the location that was clicked by calling the `showAddress()` function; the second command centers the map at the location of the click with the `recenterMap()` function, and the last command displays the geo-coordinates of the same location with the `showCoordinates()` function. They're simple commands for demonstration purposes, except for the first one. You will see how you can request the physical address of a location on the map in Chapter 16.

All three functions need to know the geo-coordinates of the location that was clicked. This location is stored in a script variable, `rightClickLocation`, which is a `LatLng` object.

Displaying the Context Menu

The last step is the display of the context menu. To do so, you must first install a listener for the map's `rightclick` event:

```
google.maps.event.addListener(map, "rightclick",
            function(event){showContextMenu(event.latLng);});
```

The `showContextMenu()` function accepts as an argument the location that was clicked, creates the context menu by populating a new `<div>` element with the statement shown in Listing 5-3, and displays it on the map by setting its upper-left corner to the location that clicked. Note that you don't need to do anything in order to retrieve the coordinates of the location that was clicked. The listener's argument, `event`, is supplied automatically, and it exposes the coordinates of the location that was clicked through its `latLng` property. The code of the `showContextMenu()` function is shown in Listing 5-4. The ellipses in the listing stand for the statements that populate the `contextmenuDiv` variable, shown in Listing 5-3.

Listing 5-4
Displaying the
context menu

```
function showContextMenu(currentLocation  ) {
    $('.contextmenu').remove();
    contextmenuDiv = document.createElement("div");
    contextmenuDiv.className  = 'contextmenu';
    rightClickLocation=currentLocation;
    contextmenuDiv.innerHTML = ...
    $(map.getDiv()).append(contextmenuDiv);
    positionMenu(currentLocation);
    contextmenuDiv.style.visibility = "visible";
}
```

The function starts by hiding the context menu, should it be visible at the time; then it creates a new `<div>` element with the context menu's items. Finally, it displays the menu at the appropriate location by calling the positionMenu() function, which contains jQuery code to properly position the menu, as shown in Listing 5-5.

Listing 5-5
Calculating the
position of the
context menu on
the page

```
function positionMenu(currentLatLng){
    var mapWidth = $('#map_canvas').width();
    var mapHeight = $('#map_canvas').height();
    var menuWidth = $('.contextmenu').width();
    var menuHeight = $('.contextmenu').height();
    var clickedPosition = getPointerLocation(currentLatLng);
    var x = clickedPosition.x ;
    var y = clickedPosition.y ;
    if((mapWidth - x ) <menuWidth) x = x - menuWidth;
    if((mapHeight - y ) <menuHeight) y = y - menuHeight;
    $('.contextmenu').css('left',x  );
    $('.contextmenu').css('top',y );
};
```

Note that the positionMenu() function calls another function, the getPointerLocation() function, which converts the geo-coordinates of a location into screen coordinates (pixels) and places the context menu's upper-left corner at these screen coordinates. It also makes sure that there's enough space to display the menu and, if not, it places the menu's upper-right corner there so that the menu appears to the left of the location that was clicked. Similarly, if the user has clicked near the bottom of the screen, the menu is displayed above the clicked location, and not below as usual. To position the menu, the last two statements manipulate the left and top properties of the menu's style (these properties are introduced by jQuery and there's no equivalent HTML code).

If you're familiar with JQuery, you will have no problem following the code that displays the context menu. If not, here are the steps to include the maps' context menu in your web application:

1. Copy the following functions to your script:

   getPointerLocation(), positionMenu(),
   showContextMenu(), hideContextMenu()

   In the showContextMenu(), insert the appropriate statements to create the context menu.

2. Declare the .itemStyle and .contextMenudiv style definitions (and modify them accordingly).

3. Declare two variables at the script's level:

   var contextmenuDiv;
   var rightclickLocation;

4. Finally, add a listener for the map's rightclick event to call the showContextMenu() function.

The rightclickLocation variable is set to the location of the right-click from within the rightclick event listener and it's used by other functions in the script.

The implementation of the functions for centering the map and displaying the current coordinates is trivial:

```
function recenterMap() {
    hideContextMenu();
    map.setCenter(rightClickLocation);
}
function showCoordinates() {
    hideContextMenu();
    alert(rightClickLocation);
}
```

Note the call to the `HideContextMenu()` function, which removes the element with the context menu from the map by manipulating the `visibility` attribute of the `div` element that contains the entire menu:

```
contextmenuDiv.style.visibility = "hidden"
```

Open the `Context Menu.html` page and examine its script, which is well documented with comments that were not included in the listings. Try adding more options, apply different styles to the menu items and the menu itself, and implement commands that address your specific application requirements. If you're ambitious, design a menu with different commands, depending on the location that was clicked. You can retrieve the address of the current location and, if it's not a well-known address, you know that the user has clicked somewhere in the ocean or some other uninhabited place.

Context menus are not limited to the `Map` object. Practically every item you place on a map recognizes the `rightclick` event, which can lead to a custom context menu. In effect, you can add many different context menus: one for the map itself, another one for the lines on the map, another one for the shapes, and so on. You can even use different symbols to identify different features on the map, and each symbol could lead to a different context menu, specific to the feature represented by that symbol.

A More Elaborate Context Menu

The context menu shown in Figure 5-5 is very similar to the one you designed already, but it also contains a divider and an additional command, the "Show crosshair" command. This command is a toggle that shows/hides a crosshair at the center of the map. It also toggles the caption of the last command between the strings "Hide crosshair" and "Show crosshair" so that the user can hide the crosshair on the map by selecting the same command from the context menu The divider is just an `<hr/>` element. You can change the look of the menu as you wish, or as your HTML skills allow you.

The last command is added with an `if` statement because its caption may be "Show crosshair" or "Hide crosshair," depending on the current visibility of the crosshair. The code uses the `crosshair` script variable to keep track of the visibility of the crosshair. If this variable is `true`, the code sets the caption of the last command to "Hide crosshair";

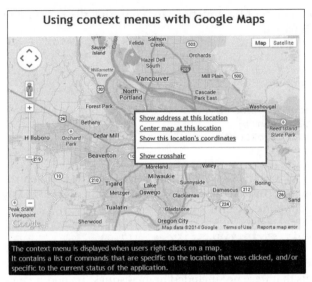

Figure 5-5   A more elaborate context menu with a divider and an additional command

otherwise, it sets it to "Show crosshair." Listing 5-6 shows the statements that generate the context menu.

Listing 5-6
The definition
of the enhanced
context menu

```
contextmenuDiv.innerHTML =
    "<a id='itemAddress' href='#' onclick='showAddress()'>" +
    "    <div class=context>Show address at this location<\/div><\/a>" +
    "<a id='itemZoom' href='#' onclick='recenterMap()'>" +
    "    <div class=context>Center map at this location<\/div><\/a>" +
    "<a id='item3' href='#' onclick='showCoordinates()'>" +
    "    <div class=context>Show this location's " +
    "        coordinates<\/div><\/a>" +
    "<hr/>"
if (crosshair == false)
    contextmenuDiv.innerHTML +=
        "<a id='item4' href='#' onclick='showCrosshair()'>" +
        "    <div class=context>Show crosshair<\/div><\/a>"
else
    contextmenuDiv.innerHTML +=
        "<a id='item4' href='#' onclick='showCrosshair()'>" +
        "    <div class=context>Hide crosshair<\/div><\/a>"
```

Note the use of the `crosshair` script variable: Depending on this variable's value, the script generates a command with a different name. This is the reason that you should generate the context menu on the fly, instead of creating a `<div>` element with the menu commands ahead of time and reusing it as needed. The implementation of the crosshair is a bit involved, and it's discussed in detail in Chapter 9. The code that draws the cursor is simple, provided you know how to draw lines, but it must be redrawn every time the map viewport changes. You can open the project and see the implementation of the `showCrosshair()` function, which draws two vertical lines at the middle of the map.

The Multiple Maps Application

The last application in this chapter, the `Multiple Maps.html` web page, demonstrates how to place three maps on the same page (see Figure 5-6). The three maps have different content, but they're synchronized. The small map at the lower-right corner shows an overview of a larger area, like a state or country. The main map is a basic roadmap of a very specific area (a university is shown in the figure), and the small map at the upper-right corner is a small detail in satellite view. The yellow semitransparent rectangle in the large map indicates the area of the satellite view.

As you expected, the page contains three distinct <div> elements and each one is assigned a different Google map in the page's `initialize()` function. Placing the three maps on three different <div> elements is straightforward: You simply initialize three different Map objects. Keeping the contents of the three maps synchronized is also simple. Each time any of the maps is dragged by the user, the other two maps are repositioned with the `setCenter()` or the `panTo()` method from within the appropriate event listener.

The script that drives the application is fairly straightforward: each time a map is dragged, the script repositions the other two maps. Along with the project in the chapter's support material, you will find the `MultipleMaps.pdf` file, which explains the code in detail.

Figure 5-6   This web page displays three Google maps with different settings. The three maps remain synchronized at all times.

Summary

This chapter contained mostly reference material. You explored the objects you'll be using from now on to make your mapping applications more functional and/or interactive. You will soon become proficient with these objects because you will see them in action in all of the examples in the following chapters.

Now that you know how to customize and manipulate the maps from within your script, as well as how to work with events to add interactivity to your mapping applications, it's time to learn how to embed a map in a Windows application and manipulate it from within a .NET application's code. In the following chapter, you design a .NET application for interacting with a Google map, intercept the map's events in your .NET application, and manipulate the map from within a Windows interface.

Windows Mapping: Embedding Maps in Desktop Applications

You have already developed map-enabled web pages and you know how to manipulate a map from within the page's script by programming the basic objects of the Google Maps API. In this chapter, you learn how to embed a Google map in a Windows application. The information in this chapter will help you design desktop applications that exploit all the functionality of Google Maps and at the same time take advantage of the rich user interface (UI) of Windows applications. The principles remain the same: You still manipulate the map through the script, only now you will develop a Windows interface and you'll be calling the script's functions from the Windows application's code.

This chapter is addressed to .NET developers. It doesn't require any specific programming knowledge, just an overall familiarity with Visual Basic and/or C#, and an installation of Visual Basic Express, Visual C# Express, or any of the licensed versions of Visual Studio. The Express versions of Visual Basic and C# are available for free. At the time of this writing, you can download either Visual Studio Express 2012 for Windows Desktop or the preview of Visual Studio 2013 Express for Windows Desktop. Just go to Microsoft's MSDN (msdn .microsoft.com) and follow the Visual Studio link. This chapter's sample project is a Visual Express 2010 project, which you can open with any higher version of Visual Studio. You will find both a Visual Basic and C# version of the application in this chapter's support material.

CAUTION   As with all web applications that make use of the Google Maps API, your desktop applications that rely on this API must be posted to a public facing URL. If you wish to use your application behind a firewall (and this is how most desktop mapping applications are used), you must purchase a business license from Google. For more information on licensing the Google Maps API, visit https://developers.google.com/maps/licensing.

You can still use the API to experiment with it, but the applications you develop with it can't be used in a corporate environment without a paid license. You may even sell your application, in which case the licensee must abide by the terms of the Google license.

Why a Desktop Application

Web applications have been on the rise for many years, but desktop applications remain the mainstream tools for our daily workload. Applications that require complex interfaces, or advanced calculations, are still implemented as desktop applications, not web applications. In particular, all major GIS and drawing applications are implemented as Windows applications that run on the desktop. Placing complex networks, such as the electricity network or the pipelines of a distribution network, on a map is not something you can do easily with a web application. It involves a lot of operations, fairly complex client-side programming, a server component, and many trips to the server.

Web applications are not yet as flexible and as elegant as Windows applications, especially when it comes to user interface issues. They can't provide multiple synchronized windows at once, and there are many simple operations that are quite cumbersome to implement in an application running in the browser. You can't access the local file system from within the browser and some browsers won't even allow you to access the Clipboard for security reasons. If your task involves more than just presenting data on a map, then you should consider the implementation of map-enabled applications as Windows applications that run on the user's desktop.

Embedding a simple map in a desktop application—as you will do in this chapter—will add great value to your desktop applications. Just a simple map with markers on selected points of interest will add points to your application, even if the map isn't truly integrated with the rest of the application. If you're manipulating business or scientific data with a spatial component, the ability to place your data on the map in your original application will come in handy sooner or later. Consider an application that presents aggregated sales figures per state or per country. In addition to the tabular report that contains names and values, you can present the individual data points as labels on a map. Reporting tools such as SQL Server's Reporting Services take into consideration the spatial components of one's data and present data on nice maps.

In this book, you learn how to go beyond nice pictures. You learn how to interact with the map from within the desktop application and eventually apply your programming skills to mapping applications. To get there, you need to understand the basics of embedding Google maps in Windows applications. This is the first chapter in this book that addresses the topic of embedding Google maps in desktop applications. You will find several interesting desktop applications that make use of Google maps in later chapters.

Using Google Maps with Desktop Applications

The Google Maps API was designed to be used exclusively with web applications. Google doesn't provide a mapping component that you can use to embed maps in a desktop application. However, it is quite possible to embed a web page on a Windows form and interact with the page's script from within a .NET application. If the web page you embed in a Windows form contains a map, then you can access the functionality of Google Maps from within your .NET Windows application. The basic components for harnessing the features of Google Maps from within your Windows application are: (1) a web page for displaying a map,

(2) a control to display the web page in your Windows application, and (3) some code to interact with the page's script from within the Windows application's code.

- **The web page**   You already have the web page that displays a Google map; it's the page you used for all sample applications in earlier chapters. This page contains the definition of a `div` element where the map will be displayed, and the `initialize()` function that requests a map from Google and displays it on the page. The web page should also contain a script with the functions you need to manipulate the map from within your application.

- **Embedding the map**   The means for embedding a web page into a form is the `WebBrowser` control; .NET developers are familiar with it. The `WebBrowser` control is nothing less than Internet Explorer packaged as a control: It encapsulates the functionality of Internet Explorer and allows you to embed web pages in desktop applications.

- **Controlling the script**   Beyond displaying a web page, the `WebBrowser` control exposes the script of the page to your application: You can write code in Visual Basic or C# to call the functions in the page's script, controlling in effect the map from a high-level language. The same control provides another unique feature: It allows the script to call methods in the Windows application's code, which is equivalent to firing events to the host application.

In this chapter, you're going to build a simple .NET mapping application with features that rival any similar web application: the WindowsMapping application, which is shown in Figure 6-1. The application's interface is a typical Windows application with a main window,

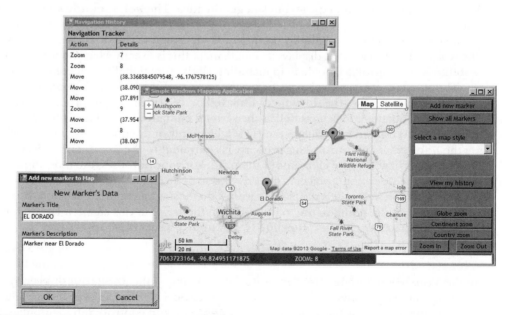

Figure 6-1   The WindowsMapping application is a simple desktop mapping application that combines the functionality of Google maps with a highly interactive UI.

where the map is displayed, and auxiliary windows that display data about the selected feature(s) on the map. Notice the multiple auxiliary windows that remain open at the same time and users can freely switch among them. This application is a simple one that introduces you to the topic of building map-enabled applications for the desktop. Later in this book, you will find more advanced mapping applications with true GIS features. In this chapter, you'll explore the architecture of a mapping application written in a .NET language.

The WebBrowser Control

The WebBrowser is a component that comes with Visual Studio and allows you to embed HTML documents on a Windows form. The control is a browser window without the menu bar and the status bar of a typical browser, just the area where web pages are rendered.

To display a web page on the WebBrowser control set the DocumentText property of the control to a string that contains valid HTML code. You can also call its Navigate2() method, passing the URL of a page as an argument. In this chapter, you use the DocumentText property because it allows you to build the HTML page on the fly in your code and display it instantly. The following Visual Basic statements display a trivial HTML document on the WebBrowser1 control:

```
Dim html = "<html><body>" &
           "<h1>Document Header</h1>" &
           "<span style='font-family: Verdana; font-size: 12pt'>" &
           "The document body goes here" &
           "</span>" &
           "</body></html>"
WebBrowser1.DocumentText = html
```

It's an extremely simple page, but you get the idea. The WebBrowser control enables you to not only display any web page in the context of a Windows application, but also to create the page you want to display on the fly. If you assign to the DocumentText property the typical HTML page that displays a Google map, this is exactly what you will get on the WebBrowser control: a Google map including all the functionality that comes with it.

The WebBrowser control exposes another very useful property, the Document property, which exposes the document displayed on the control. This property gives you access to the document itself, as well as the script it contains. You can use the Document property to access and manipulate the HTML elements of the document being displayed on the WebBrowser control. This property is equivalent to the document object you use in your script to access the elements of the page. For your purposes, the most important method of the Document object is the InvokeScript() method, which allows you to call a function in the web page's script from within the host application. Practically, this is the only method you're going to use to interact with the script in this chapter. Here's how you can call the map's setZoom() function from within a Visual Basic application:

```
WebBrowser1.Document.InvokeScript("setZoom", {3})
```

In this Visual Basic snippet, WebBrowser1 is the name of the WebBrowser control on the form and the script contains a function called setZoom(). You can even embed multiple maps on the same form (each one in its own WebBrowser control) and manipulate them independently. If you prefer C#, here's the equivalent method for calling the same function in the page's script:

```
var values = new object[] { 3 };
webBrowser1.Document.InvokeScript("setZoom", values);
```

The first argument to the `InvokeScript()` method is the name of the function you want to call. Note that the function is specified as a string so you must be careful to type it exactly as it appears in the script, including character casing. Unfortunately, any mistakes you make when using the `InvokeScript()` method will manifest themselves as run-time errors. The compiler has no way of knowing the names of the functions contained in the page's script, and it can't validate your code.

The second argument is an array of objects: You can place any values you want to pass to the function as arguments in this array and make sure that the order of the array's elements matches the order of the function's arguments. For the `setZoom()` function, you pass only an integer, which is the new zoom level. Even a single value must be placed into an array and this is what the curly brackets do: They create an array of objects and initialize it with the specified values.

The Windows Mapping Application

To demonstrate the process of building Windows mapping applications on top of Google Maps, you're going to build a simple application in Visual Studio and embed a Google map in its main form, which is shown in Figure 6-2. The map is displayed on a `WebBrowser` control, which covers most of the form.

Figure 6-2 shows two instances of the same application. As you can see, the user decides how much space will be assigned to the map and the remaining space will be taken by the application's interface (the pane with the buttons on the right). The divider between this pane and the map is draggable and users can change the relative widths of the two panes by dragging their divider. The map's pane on the left and the buttons on the right pane are resized by the user without any programming effort.

Note the status bar at the bottom of the form, where some trivial but useful data about the current map is displayed. The last item in the status bar is a text box, where users can type an address, and as soon as they press ENTER, the map will be centered on the requested address. This address could be as generic as a city name, or as specific as your home's address. It's not an award-winning interface, but it demonstrates some of the advantages of a typical Windows interface. You can use it as your starting point for building your own award-winning interface. Even this simple interface, however, is not as easy to achieve with HTML and JavaScript.

The Application's Architecture

The WindowsMapping application is a fairly simple one, but it combines two distinct layers: the web layer, which consists of HTML and JavaScript, and the .NET layer, which consists of Windows forms and .NET code. The application's user interface consists of the map, which is displayed on a `WebBrowser` control, and the Windows part, which contains everything else (buttons, labels, menus, any element that can be used to build the interface of a

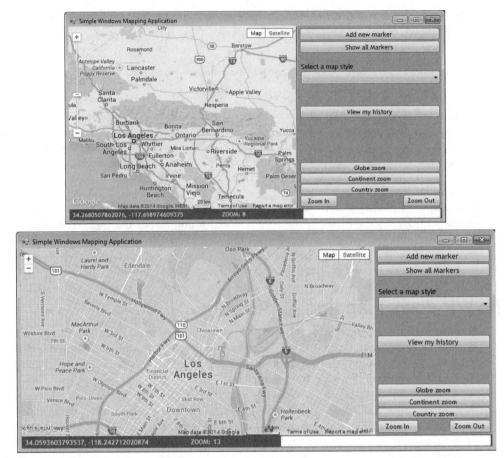

Figure 6-2 The main form of the Windows Mapping application

desktop application). Users can't tell what's going on behind the scenes. All they see is a rich interface that contains a Google map. Figure 6-3 outlines the structure of the application.

The user interacts both with Windows controls and the map. The events raised by the Windows controls are intercepted and handled by .NET code, which also manipulates the map through the script. The events raised by the map are intercepted by JavaScript and can be handled as they occur in JavaScript by the web page's script, or they can trigger an event in the .NET part of the application. Your task is to write two components in two totally different languages and make them talk to one another and operate in tandem so that users will perceive them as a single application.

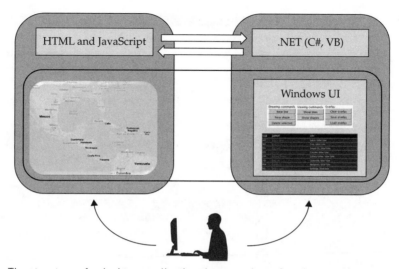

Figure 6-3   The structure of a desktop application that contains a Google map. Users see a unified interface, which is handled by two distinct components behind the scenes.

Designing the Application

Any Windows map-enabled application you will design with Visual Studio will be based on the `WebBrowser` control. The web page displayed on the control is a typical, very simple web page that displays a Google map, like the ones you have seen so far. The web page contains a trivial HTML section, just the definition of the `div` element that hosts the map, and the usual `initialize()` script.

Start Visual Studio and follow these steps to design the application:

1. Create a new project with Visual Basic Express 2012 or Visual Studio Express 2013. Name the new project **WindowsMapping**. The sample project you will find in this chapter's support material was written in Visual Basic Express 2010, and you'll be able to open it with Visual Studio 2012 Express as well. It goes without saying that the same projects can be opened with the licensed versions of Visual Studio.

2. Create a new folder in the solution, the Map Components folder. To do so, right-click the project's name and, from the context menu, select Add | New Folder. Name the new folder **Map Components**. In this folder, you will place the HTML file that contains the map.

3. Right-click the new folder's name and, from the context menu, select New Item. In the New Item dialog box that appears, select the Web Category item in the left pane and the HTML Page item in the right pane, as shown in Figure 6-4. Name the new page `MapPage.html`. If you're using Visual Basic Express, you won't be able to add an HTML page to the project. Add an XML file instead and rename to `MapPage.html`.

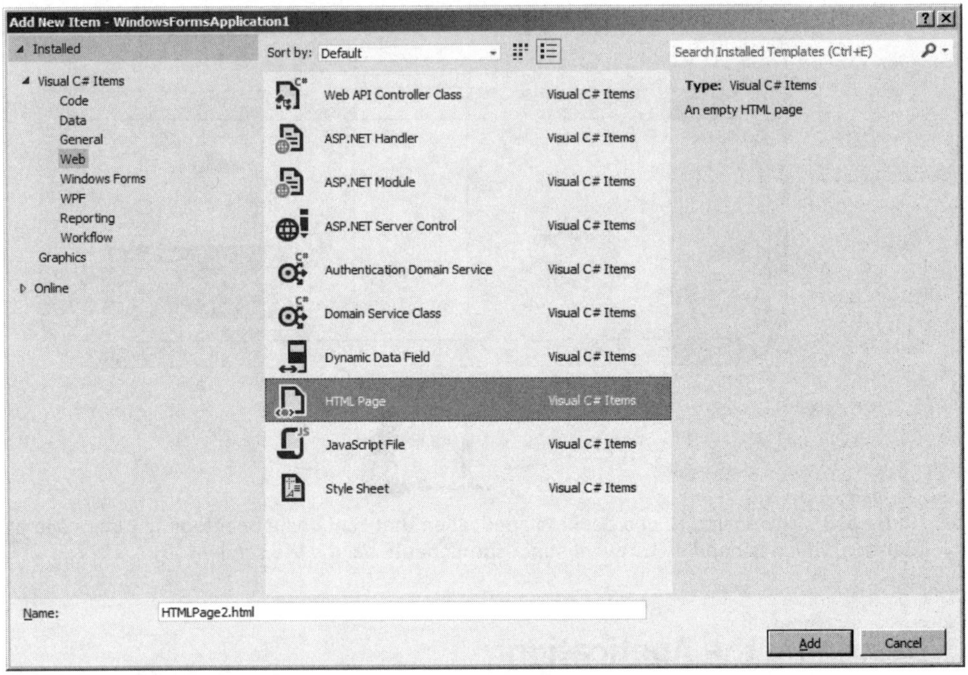

Figure 6-4 Adding an HTML page to a Visual Studio project

4. Then, paste the code of Listing 6-1 in the HTML file. The code shown is not new to you: It's the HTML page for displaying Google maps on web pages.

Listing 6-1
The basic web page for displaying a Google Map

```
<html>
  <head>
    <meta name="viewport" content="initial-scale=1.0, user-scalable=no"/>
    <meta http-equiv="content-type=" content="text/html; charset=UTF-8"/>
    <title>Google Maps Simple Page</title>
    <linkhref=http://code.google.com/apis/maps/documentation/
              javascript/examples/default.css
              rel="stylesheet" type="text/css" />
  <script type="text/javascript"
          src="http://maps.google.com/maps/api/js?
          sensor=false"></script>
  <script type="text/javascript">
    function initialize() {
      var iniLat = 0;variniLon = 0;
      var iniZoom = 1;
      var myLatlng = new google.maps.LatLng(iniLat, iniLon);
      var mapOptions = {
          zoom: iniZoom, center: myLatlng,
          mapTypeId: google.maps.MapTypeId.ROADMAP, panControl: false,
        zoomControl: true, scaleControl: true,
        streetViewControl: false, overviewMapControl: false
      }
```

```
        map = new google.maps.Map(
                    document.getElementById("map_canvas"), mapOptions);
      }
    </script>
  </head>
  <body bgcolor="#b0DDb0" onload="initialize();">
    <div >
      <div id="map_canvas" style="width:100%; height:100%"></div>
    </div>
  </body>
</html>
```

Preparing the Form to Accept the Map

Let's switch to the Visual Basic application and prepare it to recognize an external script and communicate with it. Double-click the form to open the Code window and you will see the event handler for the Form's Load event. Insert the following directive at the top of the file:

```
Imports System.Security.Permissions
```

In C#, you will use the using directive:

```
using System,Security.Permissions
```

The Permissions namespace is not included by default in a new project, but it's essential for communicating with the web page's script. Then, prefix the Form's declaration with the following declaration:

```
<PermissionSet(SecurityAction.Demand, Name:="FullTrust")>
<System.Runtime.InteropServices.ComVisibleAttribute(True)>
```

The WebBrowser control is a COM component and you must specifically instruct it to expose its public members (its properties and methods) to other COM components. You must also insert a statement in the Form's Load event handler to tell the WebBrowser control that your code needs to access the script contained by the page being displayed:

```
WebBrowser1.ObjectForScripting = Me
```

The last step is to load the HTML file you added to the project into the WebBrowser control. This must also take place in the form's Load event handler with the following statements:

```
Dim html = My.Computer.FileSystem.ReadAllText(
                "..\..\MapComponents\MapPage.html")
WebBrowser1.DocumentText = html
```

The first statement reads the contents of the MapPage.html file, and the following statement assigns the HTML document to the control's DocumentText property. Depending on the location of the HTML file, you may have to change the path of the file to be opened. You may also have to change the path if you deploy the project on a server at your company. If you are a .NET developer, you already know that you can create a resource with the contents of the HTML file and avoid the external component altogether.

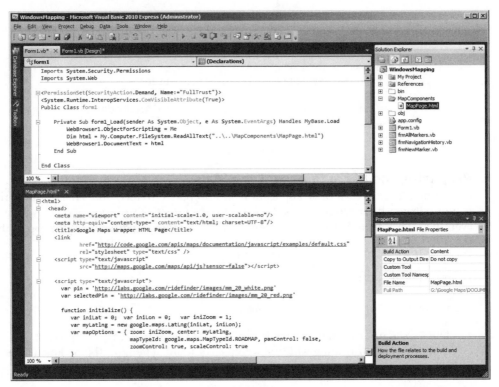

Figure 6-5   The initial steps in preparing a .NET application to access a web page with a Google map

Figure 6-5 shows what Visual Basic Express IDE should look like at this point. You're ready now to add some custom functionality to your application. To do so, you must implement functions in JavaScript and call them from within your .NET code.

Run the project by pressing F5. You already have a working Windows application that displays a map. You can even interact with the map using the built-in functionality provided by Google: You can zoom and drag the map, switch views, and so on.

Building the Windows Interface

The application's main form, shown earlier in Figure 6-1 and 6-2, contains a `SplitContainer` control with two panes: one with the map on the left and another one with the buttons to the right. Between the two panes is a thin vertical divider that users can slide on either side to make more room either for the map, or for the buttons. The `SplitContainer` control is not visible on the interface. It's a control that hosts other controls. You can only see the divider between the two panes of the control by hovering the mouse over it. The pointer will turn into a double arrow indicating the direction in which you can move the divider. Drag the divider and the controls on each pane will be resized automatically.

There's also a `Panel` control docked at the bottom of the form, where the map's center location and current zoom level are displayed. The contents of the controls on this Panel are updated as needed.

As you can see in Figure 6-1, the application's interface contains a number of buttons for performing various operations on the map. The Add New Marker button creates a new marker and adds it to the map. The user is first prompted with an auxiliary form for the marker's data and then the program instructs the script to create a new marker and place it on the map. The Show All Markers button displays yet another auxiliary form with all the markers on the map.

You can omit the navigation bar from the map and use the Zoom In and Zoom Out buttons for zooming. The other three zooming buttons set the zoom level to arbitrary values that roughly correspond to globe/continent/country zoom levels. The application uses the zoom levels 1, 3, and 6 for the zooming operations.

The ComboBox with the styles contains a few items, but no code behind it. You will see how to apply styles to your maps in Appendix C. The View My History button leads to an auxiliary form that contains the user's navigation history: the drag and zoom operations in the order that they were performed. You can add more actions to the history, such as the insertion of markers, and give users the option to undo certain actions, or review their edits.

The white box at the far-right edge of the status bar is a TextBox, where you can enter an address and press ENTER. As soon as you press ENTER, the map will be centered at the specified address. You will learn how to locate addresses on the map in Chapter 16, but this feature was included to make the application a little more functional.

Finally, the main form has its own context menu, which is shown in Figure 6-8 later in this chapter. It contains just two commands, one to center the map at the location that was clicked and another one to display the coordinates of the location that was clicked. This menu was included to demonstrate the process of initiating an action in the script (the right-click operation on the map is detected by the script with the appropriate event listener) and complete it at the .NET side of the application. The context menu was designed in Visual Studio, not in JavaScript.

The sample desktop application contains no features that can't be implemented with a web interface, but the Windows UI is rich, highly interactive, and very responsive, as it doesn't require any trips to the web server. It will make as many requests as it needs to Google's servers to update the map, but this can't be avoided.

Adding Custom Functions to the Script

You have successfully embedded a Google map in your Windows form and users of the application can interact with the map using the built-in navigational tools: They can zoom in and out, and drag the map around with the mouse. Now you must add custom functions to the script to implement all the operations you want to initiate from within your .NET application. No matter how you will use the application, here are a few functions that you will need in every mapping application. They're the functions for setting the map's center location and its zoom level. They're quite trivial, but you will see shortly much more useful functions that will be implemented along the same lines.

```
function setZoom(zoom) {
    map.setZoom(zoom);
}
function setCenter(latitude, longitude) {
    map.setCenter(new google.maps.LatLng(latitude, longitude))
}
```

The following Visual Basic statement in the host application sets the map's zoom level to 12:

```
WebBrowser1.Document.InvokeScript("setZoom", {12})
```

If you want to do the same in C#, use these equivalent statements:

```
var zoom = new object[1] { 12 };
WebBrowser1.Document.InvokeScript("setZoom", zoom);
```

The collection of custom functions you implement in JavaScript for the requirements of a specific application makes up a new API because you can build the interface for your mapping application by calling these functions and never having to "touch" the JavaScript code. Just as Google provides an API for its maps, you can build your own API for your custom mapping applications. You can actually pass the project to a group of developers who will call the script's functions with the InvokeScript() method and they'll never see the JavaScript code that implements them. You can do even better: You can design a class that sits between your .NET application and the page's script and hide in this class all the complexity of calling JavaScript functions in the script and passing arguments back and forth. The class will look like another .NET component to other developers and it will encapsulate the map's functionality in methods and custom objects. This technique is discussed in detail in Chapter 12. Before you get there, however, let's see how to pass data between the two sides of the application: the .NET application and the page's script.

Passing Arguments to JavaScript Functions

The script is the component that displays the map and handles the map's interaction with the user. The external application provides an advanced interface that allows users to initiate map-related commands, but it can't contact the map directly. The two components need to communicate with one another and exchange data. The exchange of data between any two components takes place through two basic mechanisms, which are the same whether you use components written in the same language, such as calling functions in JavaScript, or you use two totally different components, which are written in different languages and may not even reside on the same computer. The caller requests an operation by supplying a function name followed by a list of arguments. The function being called extracts the values of the arguments, processes them, and optionally returns a value to the calling component. Let's take a look at the operation of panning the map programmatically.

The host application provides a button or a command in a right-click menu that re-centers the map. To pan the map from within your application, you need to call a function in the script, which in turn will call the Map object's setCenter() method. Alternatively, you can use the panTo() method, which is smoother. Here's the script's function to center the map at another point:

```
function setCenter(latitude, longitude) {
    map.setCenter(new google.maps.LatLng(latitude, longitude))
}
```

You can call the script's `setCenter()` function from within your .NET code by using the `InvokeScript()` method, as explained already. The two arguments that determine the map's new center location can be passed either as strings, or as numeric values. JavaScript doesn't impose data types and it will convert the arguments to the appropriate data type. If you pass the two arguments to the `alert()` function, they will be treated as strings; if you pass them to the `setCenter()` method, they will be treated as numbers.

To center the map on Rome, you just pass two decimal values to the `setCenter()` function. The two values must be packaged as an array with the following notation:

```
{12.50, 41.90}
```

or

```
{"12.50", "41.90"}
```

The following Visual Basic statement calls the script's function:

```
WebBrowser1.Document.InvokeScript("setCenter", {12.50, 41.90})
```

and the following is the equivalent C# code:

```
var values = new object[] { 12.50, 41.90 };
webBrowser1.Document.InvokeScript("setCenter", values);
```

The arguments are always passed by value, which means that the function being called cannot alter their values. Even if the script function changes the value of one of its arguments, the changes are local to the function and will not affect the corresponding variable in the .NET part of the application.

Function Return Values

Functions usually return values, which are the result of a calculation. The `getCenter()` method is a typical example of a function returning a value. The string representation of the `LatLng` object returned by this method consists of two comma-separated values in a pair of parentheses. It's fine to pass this string to the host application and parse it there.

The Google Maps API Custom Objects

How about passing a `LatLng` object as argument? This is an option, but there's no equivalent object in any .NET language. You must either implement custom classes for the API objects you want to access in your .NET code, or use custom objects and late binding. The custom `LatLng` object must encapsulate all the functionality of the original `LatLng` object. And while it's easy to implement a `LatLng` object, you must do the same for other, less trivial objects. If you're designing an ambitious GIS system based on the Google Maps API, it is worth exploring this option. In this chapter, you're going to use strings to pass single values and custom objects to pass multiple arguments.

Some functions may pass multiple values as their result. To represent multiple data items, you can use a custom separator between them. Delimited data aren't the most flexible mechanism to pass multiple values; the separator may be part of a string argument and when this happens it will throw off your parser. A much more elegant approach is to package all the values you want to return to the calling application into a custom object and pass back this object.

Returning Custom Objects

Multiple values (of the same or different data type) should be coded as custom JSON objects, or even plain XML. Let's consider a marker, which has a position, a title, and a description (the description may be optional, but you must handle it when present). If the host application needs to retrieve all the properties of a `Marker` object, write a JavaScript function to package all the information in a custom object and return this object. Here's a possible implementation of the `getMarker(i)` function, which retrieves the data of a single marker on the map. The function's argument, `index`, is the index of the marker you wish to retrieve:

```
function getMarker(index) {
    return {"lat": markers[index].position.lat(),
            "lon": markers[index].position.lng(),
            "title": markers[index].title,
            "description": markers[index].objInfo}
}
```

The `getMarker()` function accepts as argument the index of a `Marker` object in the `markers` array, which stores all the markers on the map. The return value is a custom object created on the fly and this object provides the four properties of any marker: `lat` and `lon` are the coordinates of the marker's position on the map, `title` is the marker's title, and `description` is an extended description that will appear in an InfoWindow box when the marker is clicked. Because the `Marker` object doesn't have a description property, or any other property that can be used for this purpose, the extended description is stored in the marker's `objInfo` property.

On the .NET part of the application, you must extract the values of the custom object's properties and either use them as they are, or create a custom object in .NET. Here's how you could call the `getMarker()` function from within your Visual Basic application:

```
Dim obj = WebBrowser1.Document.InvokeScript("getMarker", {3})
```

This statement requests the properties of the fourth marker in the array. The `obj` variable is a COM object, and you can extract its individual properties by name:

```
Dim mLatitude = obj.lat
Dim mLongitude = obj.lon
Dim mTitle = obj.title
Dim mDescription = obj.description
```

The four variables are set to the properties of the custom object returned by the script and can be used in the code. They're also initialized to the appropriate types: The first two variables are of the Double type and the other two variables are strings. Each variable's type is determined by the type of the value you store in it.

To invoke the same script in C#, use the following statements:

```
varobj = WebBrowser1.Document.InvokeScript("getMarker", values)
varmLatitude = obj.lat
varmLongitude = obj.lon
varmTitle = obj.title
varmDescription = obj.description
```

You can also map the JSON objects to .NET objects with equally simple statements:

```
Dim marker = New With {
            .Location = New With {
                        .Latitude = obj.lat, .Longitude = obj.Longitude},
            .Title = obj.title, .Description = obj.description}
```

Notifying the Host Application with Method Calls

In the preceding section, you saw how to initiate an action in the script from within the .NET code, but not the opposite. An equally important aspect of the interaction model is the ability to notify the host application when certain events take place. The page's script detects all the events you're interested in, and may even react to some of them without passing any information to the host application. The motivation for developing a mapping desktop application, however, is to process as many events as possible in the host application.

To notify the host application about specific events, the script can call the `window` `.external` method, followed by the name of a method in the host application. Let's say you want to handle the map's `click` event in the .NET application. In the page that contains the `WebBrowser` control, create a public subroutine and name it `MapClicked`. The name can be any valid method name; the only requirement is that the method is prefixed with the `Public` keyword. Here's the declaration of a typical .NET method:

```
Public Sub MapClicked()
' .VB statements to handle the click event
End Sub
```

If you prefer C#, the equivalent declaration is

```
public void MapClicked() {
    // C# statements to handle the click event
}
```

To call the `MapClicked()` method from within your script every time the user clicks the map, switch to the HTML page and insert the following event listener in the script, after the map variable has been initialized:

```
google.maps.event.addListener(map, "click",
                function(event) {window.external.MapClicked});
```

With this event listener in place, every time the user clicks the map, the `MapClicked()` method of the host application will be invoked. You can think of the `MapClicked()` method as an event handler in your .NET application because this is exactly what it does: It handles an event. It's not the .NET runtime that detects the event and fires the method, but nevertheless the method is called in reaction to an event caused by a user action.

Calling Event Handlers with Arguments

What possible operations can you perform in the map's `click` event handler? You can update the interface, add a marker on the map—it's really your call. It turns out that for any operation you initiate from within the map's `click` event, you will need some additional information: the coordinates of the point that was clicked on the map. These coordinates must be passed to the method as arguments. To pass the latitude and longitude values of the point that was clicked, use the following signature for the external method:

```
Public Sub MapClicked(ByVallat As Double, ByVal Lon As Double)
' VB statements to handle the click event
End Sub
```

Then, change the event listener in the script as follows:

```
google.maps.event.addListener(map, "click",
            function(event) {
                  window.external.MapClicked(
                  event.latLng.lat(), event.latLng.lng()})
});
```

The function specified in the `addListener()` method includes two float values: the latitude and longitude of the point where the click event took place. These values will be interpreted as Double values by the .NET application's code.

You can also create a custom object that exposes multiple properties and pass this object as argument to the external method. The custom object can be created on the fly in JavaScript, its structure is not known to the .NET application. This means that the custom object's properties won't appear as members of the argument when you program the method that will handle the event in the host application. The following JavaScript statement passes a custom object with the point's coordinates.

```
google.maps.event.addListener(map, "click",
            function(event) {
                  window.external.MapClicked({
                        "latitude": event.latLng.lat(),
                        "longitude":event.latLng.lng()})
});
```

The external method must be declared with a single argument of the `Object` type. Here's the definition of the `MapClicked()` method, which matches the new argument and the statements that extract the two values from its argument:

```
Public Sub MapClicked(ByVal point As Object)
    Dim Lat = point.latitude
    Dim Lng = point.longitude
' .VB statements to handle the click event
End Sub
```

If you'd rather code your .NET application in C#, you should declare the argument with the dynamic keyword because C# doesn't support late binding by default. Here's the signature of the MapClicked() function in C#:

```
public void MapClicked(dynamic point){
  var lat = point.latitude;
  var lon = point.longitude;
}
```

The lat and lon variables have a type of Double in .NET, but note that their types haven't been specified explicitly. The compiler will infer their type from the values you assign to the variables, and the variables of the point argument are Double values.

The Interaction Model of the Two Components

This is all the information you need to control the map on a web page through a .NET application. Let's review the process, which is also outlined schematically in Figure 6-6.

- To embed a web page that displays the map in a .NET application, you assign the page's contents to a WebBrowser control's DocumentText property. To display a page with a Google map, you must assign to the DocumentText property the contents of the typical web page for displaying a Google map.

- Add functions to perform the basic mapping operations in the script. The number of functions and their complexity depend on the specific requirements of the application. The host application can't access the Google Maps API directly; instead, it must call the appropriate function in the page's script, which in turn will call the appropriate API methods.

- To initiate an action from your Windows UI, call the InvokeScript() method with a statement like the following (function_name is the function's name):

  ```
  WebBrowser1.Document.InvokeScript(function_name, {arguments})
  ```

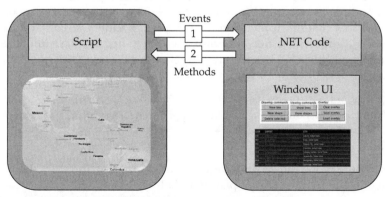

1. window.external.Method_Name (arguments)
2. WebBrowser1.Document.InvokeScript(script, {arguments})

Figure 6-6 The process of manipulating a Google Map from a .NET application through the map's script

- To react to user events on the map, such as a click or right-click action, call the relevant method in the host application from within your script with a statement like the following:

```
window.external.method_name(arguments)
```

where `method_name` is the method that will handle the event in the host application. Any arguments must be passed as value types in a pair of parentheses following the name of the method. Multiple arguments should be separated by commas, or passed as custom objects.

Initializing the Map

When the host application starts, it initializes the map through the `initialize()` function. The project's script initializes the map by centering it at point (0, 0) and setting its zoom level to 1. Any other settings would be just as valid, or just as meaningless. You should be able to initialize your map by setting its center and zoom level from within the external application's code; after all, your goal is to control the map from within the host application. Obviously, you can't rely on any values embedded in the script because you would have to edit the script every time. In a proper Windows application, you should store the map's initialization data to a configuration file and load it every time the program starts.

To set the map's initial position, simply call the `setCenter()` and `setZoom()` functions. These functions, however, must be called as soon as the map has finished loading all tiles. In the script, insert the following listener for the `idle` event. As you recall from the previous chapter, the `idle` event is fired every time the map completes an operation. When the map is initially loaded and all tiles have arrived at the client, the `idle` event is fired for the first time. You'll use this event to notify the host application that the map is ready. The host application can then enable the various controls on the interface so that users can start interacting with the map.

```
google.maps.event.addListenerOnce(map, 'idle',
                  function(){window.external.MapLoaded});
```

The listener is added with the `addListenerOnce()` method, which adds the event listener and removes it after it's executed once. The `MapLoaded()` method will be called once, and after that the application will no longer handle the `idle` event. Alternatively, you can associate another listener with the `idle` event after you have initialized the map.

In the application's `MapLoaded()` method, you can call the `setCenter()` and `setZoom()` functions to initialize the map:

```
Public Sub MapLoaded()
    WebBrowser1.Document.InvokeScript("setCenter", {iniLat, iniLon})
    WebBrowser1.Document.InvokeScript("setZoom", {iniZoom})
End Sub
```

The entire globe will be displayed for a brief moment and then the map will display a section of globe. The section displayed initially is determined by the values of the variables `iniLat`, `iniLon`, and `iniZoom`. Presumably, these variables are declared in the Windows application. You can persist their values at the end of a session, and the next time you start the application, initialize the map to the same location it was the last time the application was used.

Updating the Interface

Now you can focus on the host application's code, starting with the code that updates the host application's interface: Every time the user zooms in/out or drags the map around, the coordinates of the new center point and the new zoom level at the bottom of the form must be updated. These user actions are detected by the script, as long as it monitors the appropriate events.

You should first install two event listeners to detect changes in the map's status:

```
google.maps.event.addListener(map, "zoom_changed", function()
            {window.external.ZoomChanged(map.getZoom())});
google.maps.event.addListener(map, "bounds_changed", function()
            {window.external.BoundsChanged(map.getBounds())});
```

When a zoom_changed or a bounds_changed event takes place, the script calls two public methods in the host application, passing the appropriate values: The ZoomChanged() method accepts the new zoom level as an argument, while the BoundsChanged() method accepts the new bounds of the map. Note that the script uses the values returned by the corresponding API methods. JavaScript inserts the string representation of the zoom level, or the value of the current viewport's bounds. The latLngBounds object returned by the getBounds() object is a compound object, as you recall from the previous chapter, but it's represented with the following string (including the parentheses):

```
((36.31476273984809, -124.8402099609375),
 (37.722579674501546, -121.8299560546875))
```

The two methods in the host application are implemented as follows:

```
Public Sub ZoomChanged(ByVal zoom As String)
    lblZoom.Text = "ZOOM: " & zoom
End Sub

Public Sub BoundsChanged(ByVal bounds)
    Dim center = WebBrowser1.Document.InvokeScript("getCenter")
    lblCoordinates.Text = center
End Sub
```

The BoundsChanged() method accepts as an argument the new bounds, not the map's center point; this is why it has to call the getCenter() method to retrieve the map's center point coordinates. Figure 6-7 shows the JavaScript listeners for the bounds_ changed and rightclick events in the lower pane and the BoundsChanged and MapRClicked event handlers in Visual Basic in the upper pane.

Building Custom JSON Objects

As you recall from previous chapters, you can create a custom object on the fly in JavaScript. A very simple object could represent the map's center point with two floating type numbers.

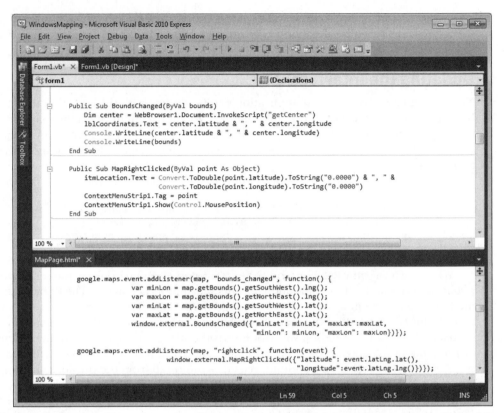

Figure 6-7 The definitions of two event listeners in the script and the corresponding methods of the host application

So, instead of passing the host application a string with the coordinates of the center point encoded as strings, here's an alternate implementation of the getCenter() method that returns a custom object with the latitude and longitude properties:

```
Function getCenter() {
    return {"latitude": map.getCenter().lat(),
            "longitude": map.getCenter().lng()}
}
```

The function uses simple object notation to create a custom object on the fly. The two properties of the custom object are set to floating values, which will be recognized by the .NET component of the application as Double values.

The Visual Basic code that reads the getCenter() function's return value can be rewritten more elegantly as follows:

```
Dim center = WebBrowser1.Document.InvokeScript("getCenter")
lblCoordinates.Text = center.latitude.ToString()& ", " &
                    center.longitude.ToString()
```

The properties `center.latitude` and `center.longitude` are Double values and can be used as they are in calculations.

Other objects of the Google Maps API are not as simple to implement as custom objects. The `LatLngBounds` object, for example, provides quite a few properties. It's up to you to determine the properties you need in your Windows application and create the appropriate custom object in your script. In most situations, you need the minimum and maximum latitude and longitude values of the bounding box, so here's a possible implementation of a custom object that represents the map's current bounds:

```
google.maps.event.addListener(map, "bounds_changed", function() {
        varminLon = map.getBounds().getSouthWest().lng();
        varmaxLon = map.getBounds().getNorthEast().lng();
        varminLat = map.getBounds().getSouthWest().lat();
        varmaxLat = map.getBounds().getNorthEast().lat();
        window.external.BoundsChanged({
            "minLat": minLat, "maxLat":maxLat,
            "minLon": minLon, "maxLon": maxLon
        })
});
```

The script extracts the coordinates of the bounding box and generates a new custom object with four simple properties. To use this object in the .NET code, write statements like the following:

```
lblCoordinates.Text = bounds.minLat.ToString& ", " &
                      bounds.maxLat.ToString&" to "&
                      bounds.minLon.ToString& ", " &
                      bounds.maxLon.ToString
```

To better exchange data between the host application and the web page's script, it's best to design custom objects, both in your script and in the host application's code. You'll return to this topic in Chapter 12, where you explore the topic of building a GIS application on top of Google Maps.

Adding the Context Menu

In the preceding chapter, you saw how to implement a context menu in your script. The context menu was designed as a `<div>` element in the script and it contained operations that could be easily coded in JavaScript. For a Windows application, you need something more elaborate. In the sample application, you pass the responsibility of displaying the context menu to the host application. Context menus are a standard feature in Windows applications; you can embed commands that can't be implemented in JavaScript but are trivial in .NET. Grabbing data from a local database, accessing the Clipboard, generating XML documents, and storing data to a local file are a few typical examples.

It's a bit early in the book to demonstrate any advanced features for the context menu, so the sample application's context menu contains a few simple commands, as shown in Figure 6-8. Later in this book, you will read about numerous operations that can be embedded as commands in a context menu. After you learn how to place shapes on the map, you can add commands to locate the nearest shape to the location that was clicked, remove the selected shape, and so on.

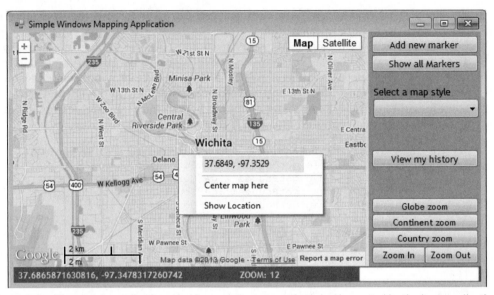

Figure 6-8   The sample application provides a context menu that's implemented by the host application.

The host application must be notified about the right-click operation, which is the action that causes the display of a context menu. It's very likely that you will need the coordinates of the point that was right-clicked on the map, so you'll pass this location as argument to the method that handles the right-click.

The first step is to design the context menu. Visual Studio allows you to create a context menu with visual tools. You can design nested menus and format each command differently. The WindowsMapping sample application provides a very simple context menu, which is shown in Figure 6-9. The same figure shows the Visual Studio menu editor for this menu.

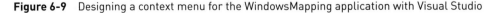

Figure 6-9   Designing a context menu for the WindowsMapping application with Visual Studio

Start by inserting a listener for the maps' `rightclick` event with the following statement in your script. This statement must appear right after the Map object's constructor in the `initialize()` function:

```
google.maps.event.addListener(map, "rightclick",
            function(event)
                    {window.external.MapRightClicked(
                            {"latitude": event.latLng.lat(),
                             "longitude":event.latLng.lng()})}
            )}
);
```

The page's script doesn't react to the right-click; it simply notifies the external application about the event passing the coordinates of the point that was clicked as arguments. The `MapRightClicked()` method in the .NET application displays the context menu that has already been created with visual tools at the location that was clicked. The context menu will appear on top of the map. The two components of the application are tightly integrated, and the user sees a desktop application with all the features of a typical Windows application plus all the functionality of Google Maps. Here is the implementation of the `MapRightClicked()` method:

```
Public Sub MapRightClicked(ByValpt As Object)
    itmLocation.Text =
        Convert.ToDouble(pt.latitude).ToString("0.0000") &
        ", " &
        Convert.ToDouble(pt.longitude).ToString("0.0000")
    ContextMenuStrip1.Tag = pt
    ContextMenuStrip1.Show(Control.MousePosition)
End Sub
```

The method stores the coordinates of the point that was clicked in the context menu's `Tag` property because this value may be required later in one of the menu's commands. Then it builds the string displayed on top of the context menu (see Figure 6-8) using the same coordinates.

The context menu is displayed by the last command, which uses the `Control` object to request the position of the mouse. The `Control` object is just a class in .NET and it provides the `MousePosition` property, which returns the screen coordinates of the point that was clicked, and this is exactly where the context menu will appear. The coordinates are expressed in pixels relative to the screen's upper-left corner, and you can pass the value of this property as is to the `Show()` method.

Note that you don't have to worry about positioning the context menu yourself; it will be positioned on the control automatically. The context menu's `Show()` method will determine the best location for the menu, depending on the free space on either side of it. To achieve this functionality in JavaScript, you had to write quite a few statements in the `positionMenu()` function of the `Context Menu.html` sample page of Chapter 5. The real advantage of implementing the context menu in the host application, however, is that you can include commands that couldn't be implemented in JavaScript, such as database lookups.

Coding the Context Menu's Commands

The context menu was designed with Visual Studio's visual tools; it contains just two commands: the Center Map Here and Show Location commands. The first command centers the map at the location that was clicked, while the second command displays the coordinates of the location that was right-clicked on the map. The top item in the menu is not a command; it's a box that displays the coordinates of the selected point rounded to four decimal digits. It was included as a demonstration of the custom functionality you can achieve with a Windows context menu. The top item is populated when the menu is displayed, as you saw earlier. The other two commands of the context menu are implemented with the following code:

```
Private Sub itmShowLocation_Click(sender As System.Object,
                  e As System.EventArgs)
                  Handles itmShowLocation.Click
   Dim coordinates = Convert.ToString(ContextMenuStrip1.Tag)
   MsgBox("The mouse was clicked at coordinates:" &
          vbCrLf& coordinates)
End Sub

Private Sub itmCenter_Click(sender As System.Object,
                  e As System.EventArgs) Handles itmCenter.Click
   Dim lat = ContextMenuStrip1.Tag.latitude
   Dim lon = ContextMenuStrip1.Tag.longitude
   WebBrowser1.Document.InvokeScript("setCenter", {lat, lon})
End Sub
```

The code reads the geo-location of the point that was clicked from the `Tag` property of the context menu and passes this location as an argument to the `setCenter()` function of the script. The `setCenter()` function in the script is a trivial function that accepts two coordinate values as arguments and calls the Map object's `setCenter()` method.

Tracking User Navigation

Another interesting feature you can add to a Windows mapping application is to track the user's navigational actions. The navigational actions include zoom and drag operations (whether performed with the mouse or with the help of the map's navigation control). These actions can be tracked just as easily in a script, but what you can't do from inside the web page is to display these actions in an auxiliary form, like the one shown in Figure 6-10. The navigational operations are added to the auxiliary window as they occur, even if the window isn't visible. To view the Navigation History window, users can click the View My History button on the main form. From this point on, the window remains open and new actions are added as they occur.

With a little extra coding effort, you can play back the user's history, or allow users to move to any of the previous map views, similar to a history option for Google Maps. You can also include entries for other actions, such as the insertion of a marker. If all user actions are logged, you can re-create the map by repeating all actions on a new map.

To implement this feature, you must first design the auxiliary form. The sample application's auxiliary form contains a `ListView` control with two columns: a title for each

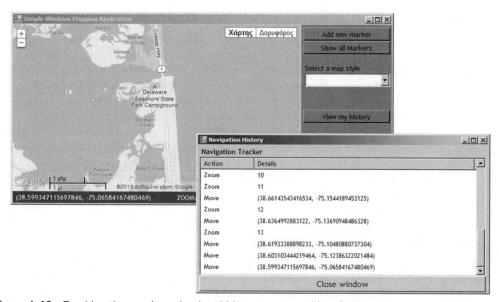

Figure 6-10   Tracking the user's navigational history on an auxiliary form

action, which is a Zoom or Move action, and the action's details. The details are the new zoom level for a Zoom action and a pair of coordinates for the Move action.

To add an item to the `ListView` control, the various parts of the application call the `Add2History()` method, passing as arguments two strings: the action's title and its details. Here's the `Add2History()` method that's called in several places in the application's code:

```
Private Sub Add2History(ByValactionName As String,
                        ByVal details As String)
    Dim li As New ListViewItem
    li.Text = actionName
    li.SubItems.Add(details)
    frmNavigationHistory.ListView1.Items.Add(li)
End Sub
```

This method is called by several of the application's methods. The `DragEnd()` and `ZoomChanged()` methods call `Add2History()` to append new terms to the list of navigational actions:

```
Public Sub ZoomChanged(ByVal zoom As String)
    lblZoom.Text = "ZOOM: " & zoom
    Add2History("Zoom", zoom)
End Sub

Public Sub DragEnded(ByVal ct As String)
    Add2History("Move", ct)
End Sub
```

Locating Addresses on the Map

In Chapter 16, you learn about the GeoCoding API, which allows you to look up addresses and convert physical addresses into geo-coordinates (and the opposite). Users of the WindowsMapping application can enter a location name in the text box at the right end of the status bar and center the map to the desired location by pressing ENTER. The .NET application's code includes an event handler for the text box's KeyPress event. Every time the user presses the ENTER, the host application makes a request to Google's GeoCoding service, passing as an argument the string in this box. If it's an address that Google can recognize, it returns the proper address of the specified location, including its geo-coordinates. These coordinates are then extracted from the web service's response and passed as arguments to the setCenter() function to reposition the map. In Chapter 16, you will see how to call the GeoCoding service from within a VB application and process the service's response.

Adding Markers to the Map

Another very common and easy-to-implement feature for mapping applications is the placement of markers on the map. You know how to place a new marker on the map using JavaScript, and you have seen the JavaScript code to do so (it's actually a single statement). A marker is identified by three data items: its coordinates, a title, and the map it belongs to. The following JavaScript function accepts as arguments the values of the marker's properties, creates a new marker, and places it on the map:

```
Function addMarker(lat, lon, title, description) {
   var marker = new google.maps.Marker({
                 map: map,
                 position:newgoogle.maps.LatLng(lat, lon),
                 title: title, objInfo: description
            });
   markers.push(marker);
   google.maps.event.addListener(marker, "click",
                 function() {openInfoWindow(this)});
}
```

The code behind the Add New Marker button displays an auxiliary form where users can enter the marker's title and description, and then calls the addMarker() function to create the new marker, passing the user-supplied values as arguments:

```
Private Sub bttnAddMarker_Click(sender As System.Object,
               e As System.EventArgs) Handles bttnAddMarker.Click
   If frmNewMarker.ShowDialog = Windows.Forms.DialogResult.OK Then
      Dim ctr = WebBrowser1.Document.InvokeScript("getCenter")
      Dim lat = ctr.latitude
      Dim lon = ctr.longitude
      WebBrowser1.Document.InvokeScript("addMarker", {
                    lat, lon, frmNewMarker.title,
                    frmNewMarker.description})
   End If
End Sub
```

The marker appears at the center of the map, and the VB code requests the center point's coordinates from the script with the `getCenter()` function. You could omit the first two arguments to the `addMarker()` function and let the JavaScript code place the marker on the center of the map. However, it's more flexible to pass the coordinates of the new marker as arguments to the `addMarker()` function, because you may wish to place a marker at a different location. You could also insert some code to make sure that no two markers are placed at the same location, or within a minimum distance from an existing marker.

The `addMarker()` function of the script stores all markers in an array, the `markers` array. To request the markers from within the host application, implement two functions: the `getMarkerCount()` function, which returns the total number of markers in the array, and the `getMarker()` function, which accepts as an argument the index of a marker in the array and returns the specified marker's data. The two functions are implemented with straightforward JavaScript code.

```javascript
function getMarkerCount() {
    return markers.length
}

function getMarker(index) {
    return {"lat": markers[index].position.lat(),
            "lon": markers[index].position.lng(),
            "title": markers[index].title,
            "description": markers[index].objInfo}
}
```

The `getMarker()` function returns a custom object with the marker's coordinates, its title, and its description. The code behind the Show All Markers button in the host application calls the `getMarker()` function for each marker and displays the marker data on the `frmAllMarkers` auxiliary form with the following statements:

```vb
Private Sub bttnShowMarkers_Click(sender As System.Object,
                    e As System.EventArgs) Handles bttnShowMarkers.Click
    Dim markerCount = Convert.ToInt16(
            WebBrowser1.Document.InvokeScript("getMarkerCount"))
    For i = 0 To markerCount - 1
        Dim obj = WebBrowser1.Document.InvokeScript("getMarker", {i})
'' statements to display marker data on auxiliary form
    Next
    frmAllMarkers.ShowDialog()
End Sub
```

The statements that display the actual data on the auxiliary form are not shown in the listing because they're simple Visual Basic statements that process the `obj` variable. The `obj` variable represents the current marker and it exposes the properties `lat`, `lon`, `title`, and `description`. The code extracts the individual properties and displays them on an auxiliary form, shown in Figure 6-11.

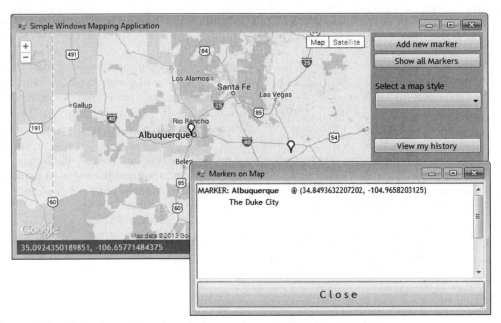

Figure 6-11   Displaying marker data on the map in an auxiliary Windows form

Summary

This has been a lengthy chapter, but it took you a step away from web pages with static maps toward an interactive desktop application that allows users to interact with maps, and a step closer to the implementation of a GIS system. You're going to get there gradually, as there are a few more topics to cover.

In the first five chapters of this book, you learned how to create web pages with mapping features, and in this chapter, you learned how to incorporate Google maps into desktop applications written in .NET. The map component of the interface, which is a `WebBrowser` control displaying a web page with an embedded map, carries with it all the functionality of a typical Google map, allowing you to create interesting desktop applications with mapping features. The sample application of this chapter was a simple one, but certainly not trivial, and you will see even more advanced mapping applications for the desktop in the following chapters.

CHAPTER 7

Markers: Identifying Locations on the Map

You have learned how to embed maps in your web pages, how to use the basic objects of the Google Maps API, and how to program the common map events to build interactive mapping applications. Now you're ready to create practical mapping applications by placing data on your maps. You'll start with point data, which are represented by markers; in the following chapter, you'll move to shapes.

A marker is an icon that identifies a location on the map. The default icon is a drop-shaped image pinned to a location, but you can assign custom icons to your markers. Google provides a few more images for markers, including colored pushpins, as well as symbols (airports, metro stations, hotels, and so on). There are many collections of images that can be used as symbols in Google Maps on the Web, some of them free while others available for purchase. If none of the existing symbols suits your needs, you can create your own marker images. This topic is demonstrated with examples in Google's documentation. The process of designing custom marker images is not discussed in this book because with so many symbols readily available, there shouldn't be many developers who really need to create their own symbols. If you're one of them, chances are that you're after some very unique and/or peculiar designs anyway.

Marking Locations on the Map

Markers are placed on a map to identify features and points of interest. They are icons with an arrow pointing to a specific location on the map, and have a title which is displayed in a tooltip box when users hover the mouse pointer over the marker's icon. The title is a short description of the feature, in most cases just a name, and the tooltip is not customizable.

Finally, a longer and frequently formatted description is displayed in a box that resembles a speech bubble when the user clicks the marker. The bubble is an `InfoWindow` object and it's customizable. You can control the width and the contents of the info window, but you can't change its pointer, nor make the Close button with the X mark disappear. As for the contents of the info window, it can host an HTML document with formatted text, hyperlinks, and images.

Figure 7-1 A few markers identifying airports in Germany, along with their info windows

Figure 7-1 shows two markers with custom icons that identify airports. Each marker leads to an info window with additional information about the selected airport. The textual description for each airport includes the airport's code and name, the city and the country name (feel free to include a whole lot of additional data about the locations you identify on the map). The code that displays all markers is identical, except for the HTML fragment with each airport's description. The figure was generated with the `Markers with InfoWindows.html` sample application.

Adding a New Marker

Placing a marker with the default look and functionality on a map is very easy. You create a `google.maps.Marker` object and you set the two required properties: the marker's location and the map on which the marker will be placed. Here's the statement that places a marker at the Space Needle monument in Seattle:

```
var spaceNeedle = new google.maps.Marker({
        position: new google.maps.LatLng(47.6205, -122.3493),
        map: map
});
```

The two mandatory arguments of the `Marker` object's constructor are its location and the map to which it belongs. If you place this statement in the page's `initialize()` function, the marker will be placed on the map as soon as the map is loaded. If you place the preceding statement in a button's `click` event, the marker will be placed at the same location when the button is clicked. If the user keeps clicking the same button, however, a new instance of the marker will be placed exactly on top of the previous one(s). Clearly, you need a mechanism to detect the presence of a marker and remove it from the map before adding a new instance of the same marker.

To remove a marker from the map, call its `setMap()` method with the null argument:

```
spaceNeedle.setMap(null)
```

Figure 7-2 The marker's title is displayed in a tooltip box when the user hovers the mouse over it.

The two required properties are essential, but the marker you designed so far is pretty useless because it conveys absolutely no information about the landmark it identifies, short of marking a location on the map. The most useful property of the `Marker` object is the `title` property, which is set to the text you want to appear in a tooltip box when the mouse is hovered over the marker. Modify the preceding marker by setting one more property, the `title` property:

```
var spaceNeedle = new google.maps.Marker({
       position: new google.maps.LatLng(47.6205, -122.3493),
       map: map,
       title: 'Space Needle, Seattle'
})
```

The title appears when the mouse is hovered over the marker, as shown in Figure 7-2.

By default, markers remain on the map exactly where you place them initially; users can't move them around with the mouse because markers indicate a fixed location on the map. However, there are occasions where you may wish to allow users to move markers around. To give users the option to reposition a marker on the map with the mouse, set the marker's `draggable` property to `true`.

Marker Animation

If your map contains a lot of markers, you may wish to provide some visual feedback to your users: for example, when a marker is placed on the map, or an existing marker is selected, you should somehow highlight the selected marker on the map. The best technique for highlighting a marker is to use the `animation` property to apply a visual effect to your markers. This property can be set either to `DROP` or to `BOUNCE`. The two keywords are members of the `google.maps.animation` class and you must use their fully qualified names in your code (i.e., `google.maps.animation.DROP` or `google.maps.animation.BOUNCE`).

The `DROP` setting causes the marker to drop from the top of the map and bounce for a few moments before reaching its final position. The `BOUNCE` effect makes the marker bounce until you stop the animation.

The `DROP` setting results in an effect that lasts for less than a second but is very noticeable. It's also easy to use; you specify the animation type in the marker's constructor:

```
var spaceNeedle = new google.maps.Marker({
       position: new google.maps.LatLng(47.6205, -122.3493),
       map: map,
```

```
      title: 'Exact location of Space Needle'
      animation: google.maps.animation.DROP
})
```

The BOUNCE effect is more complicated because you must provide a mechanism to end the animation. If you just set the `animation` property to BOUNCE in the constructor, you'll end up with an annoying marker that keeps bouncing. To make a marker bounce, you must call the `setAnimation()` method, passing the BOUNCE effect as argument and provide a function to end the animation after a number of milliseconds. Here's how you can animate a marker on the map that will stop bouncing after 1750 milliseconds:

```
marker.setAnimation(google.maps.Animation.BOUNCE);
setTimeout(function () {
    marker.setAnimation(null);
}, 1750);
```

The first statement starts the animation of the marker represented by the `marker` variable. As soon as the animation starts, the second statement calls the `setTimout()` method. The `setTimout()` function accepts two arguments: a function and a time interval. After the expiration of the time interval, the function specified by the first argument is executed.

The function in the sample code will wait for 1750 milliseconds and then it will stop the marker's animation by setting it to null. The value of 1750 milliseconds corresponds to three bounces. The `setAnimation()` function is discussed in detail in Chapter 18, where you will learn how to use this method to animate items on the map. You will find some examples of real animation techniques in this chapter. Here, we use the `setTimeout()` function to just end an animation effect initiated by the `setAnimation()` method of the Marker object.

In Chapter 14, you will develop an application that handles a large number of markers on the map, the `Map with Many Markers.html` page. This page contains the locations of nearly 9,000 airports around the world and displays only the ones that fit in the current viewport. Below the map, there's a table of the airports in the current viewport; users can click an airport name to view it on the map. The selected airport's marker bounces for a second or so when its link in the table is clicked. You can open the project and view the implementation of the `HighlightMarker()` function, which uses the technique just described.

Qualifying Markers with InfoWindows

Another Google trademark is the balloon that appears when you click a marker. This balloon is an `InfoWindow` object, and it displays additional information about the selected marker. The `InfoWindow` may contain plain text or an HTML fragment with formatted text.

The `InfoWindow` object exposes many properties, the most important being the `content` property. This property is mandatory and all others are optional. Here's a typical constructor of an `InfoWindow` variable (which would appear on clicking a marker over New York):

```
var infowindow = new google.maps.InfoWindow({
                content:'The Big Apple'
});
```

This statement creates an `InfoWindow` object, sets its contents, but doesn't place it on the map. To display the info window, you must call the `InfoWindow` object's `open()` method, passing two arguments: the map on which it will appear and the marker to which it applies. When displayed, the arrow of the info window will point at the marker specified in the `open()` method. To display the preceding info window, you must call the `open()` method as follows:

```
infowindow.open(map, NYMarker)
```

where `NYMarker` is a `Marker` object that has already been placed on the map.

Obviously, the `open()` method must be called in the marker's `click` event listener. The following statements create a marker located in Manhattan and associate an `InfoWindow` object with it:

```
var NYMarker = new google.maps.Marker({
        position: new google.maps.LatLng(40.7257, -74.0047),
        map: map,
        title: 'Manhattan'
})
var infowindow = new google.maps.InfoWindow({
                content:'Welcome to the Big Apple!'
});
google.maps.event.addListener(NYMarker, 'click', function() {
    infowindow.open(map, NYMarker);
});
```

You're probably thinking that you shouldn't have to specify the name of the marker twice in the `addListener()` method. The first instance of the `NYMarker` keyword is an argument to the `addListener` method, and the second instance is an argument to the `InfoWindow` object's `open()` method. It's actually possible to click one marker and display the info window of another marker! Just make sure this doesn't happen in your application.

The problem with info windows is their size, which can't be controlled through properties. To change the size of an info window, you can set its contents to a `<div>` element and apply a style to this element. The info window will be sized accordingly, while at the same time you can display a small HTML fragment on the info window.

TIP   Info windows are a convenient mechanism to provide additional information about the selected feature, but it's by no means your only option. You can place a `<div>` element on your page and update its contents from within the marker's `click` event listener. This element can be anywhere on the page outside the map's `<div>` element, but it can also be a floating element over the map. This technique is demonstrated with an example in the last section of the chapter.

Customizing the Marker's Icon

Markers provide the `icon` property, which allows you to specify your own icon for the marker This property can be set to the URL of an alternate icon or to a new `Icon` object. There are many custom icons you can use with Google Maps on the Web and some of them are provided by Google. The best aspect of Google's icons is that you can use them directly from Google's servers. Most third-party markers must be copied to your web server before they're used. The reason for this is that not too many people want to service so many requests. It goes without saying that you must also pay attention to the icon designer's license terms. Not all icons are free!

There's a collection of differently colored pins at Google, and you'll find them at https://sites.google.com/site/gmapicons/home/. The URL of the small red pushpin icon is http://labs.google.com/ridefinder/images/mm_20_red.png.

You can use any image, with the appropriate size, with your markers. In addition, you can use SVG (Scalable Vector Graphics) files. SVG is a language for generating vector graphics, which you can scale at will; SVG icons are ideal for placing custom symbols on your maps. An advantage of SVG graphics is that you can embed the definition of a vector shape in your script, and not necessarily reference an external file. Later in this book, you will find examples of SVG files; Appendix A is an introduction to the SVG format.

To use a different icon with a marker, you must first locate the image that will identify the marker and then use it with the marker's `icon` property. The following is the URL of an airplane icon, which is used by the sample page `Markers with Custom InfoWindows.html`, to indicate the locations of a few airports in Germany: http://google-maps-icons.googlecode.com/files/airport.png.

A popular site with icons is the Map Icons Collections by Nicolas Mollet, located at http://mapicons.nicolasmollet.com. You can download any of these icons and use them in your pages, or edit them if you wish. They're free as long as you include a credit to the Maps Icons Collection site. If you decide to use any icons from this or any other collection, be sure to read the licensing terms at that time.

Placing Multiple Markers on the Map

Mapping applications involve more than a single marker. The `Markers with Custom InfoWindows.html` web page, shown in Figure 7-3, demonstrates the most straightforward technique for placing multiple markers on the map. Each marker, which represents an airport in Germany, is represented by a `Marker` object with a custom icon, and it has its own associated `InfoWindow` object. As you can see in Figure 7-3, you can open all info windows at once; the application leaves it to the user to close the info windows they don't need on the map. It takes some extra programming effort to close any open info window before opening another one; you will adjust the application's code to display a single info window at any time.

Each marker and its associated info window are generated with separate statements in the script. You really need to write the statements to display the first marker and its infowindow;

Figure 7-3   Markers and their associated info windows

then, you can copy and paste the statements in the script. In Chapter 10, you will see how to iterate through an array of custom objects and create a marker for each item in the array. In this chapter, will find an example that generates the markers from a dataset, which is a JavaScript array of custom objects embedded in the script. This section's sample application uses straightforward JavaScript statements to generate the map annotations.

The following statement creates a new `Marker` object that represents the marker of the Aachen airport. The marker's `position` and `title` properties are set in the `Marker` object's constructor. It also sets the `map` property so that the marker is displayed immediately on the map.

```
var marker1 = new google.maps.Marker({
        icon: 'http://google-maps-icons.googlecode.com/files/airport.png',
        position: new google.maps.LatLng(50.823056, 6.186111),
        title: 'AAH  -  Aachen/Merzbruck', map: map});
```

You must now attach an `InfoWindow` object to the marker so that users can click the marker and view additional information about the selected landmark. If you don't care about the appearance of the text in the info window, you can display plain text. Plain text is too rough even for a sample application like this, so you should use HTML code to format your text. It's common to embed the text into a `<span>` or `<div>` element, as in the following statement:

```
var info1 = new google.maps.InfoWindow({
        content:     '<span style="font-family: Trebuchet MS; /
                    font-size:10pt; color: maroon"> /
                    <b>AAH</b>     /
                    Aachen/Merzbruck<br/>Aachen, Germany'});
```

After creating the two objects, another statement connects the marker's `click` event with a JavaScript function that opens the info window:

```
google.maps.event.addListener(marker1, 'click',
                  function() {info1.open(map, marker1)});
```

The code contains several copies of identical statements that create the corresponding objects for a few more airports. When the application is opened, all markers are displayed. Every time you click a marker, its info window pops up and displays some data about each airport.

The problem with this approach is that the open info window isn't closed when the user clicks another marker, as you can see in Figure 7-3. To handle info windows better, the script introduces a global variable, `currentWindow`, which points to the current info window. This variable must be declared at the script level, outside the function(s) that use it. The function that's executed when the user clicks a marker must be modified a little, as shown here:

```
google.maps.event.addListener(marker1, 'click',
                  function() {
                      if (currentWindow != null) currentWindow.close();
                      info1.open(map, marker1);
                      currentWindow=info1;});
```

This time the function closes the current info window, if one is open, then opens the selected marker's info window, and finally sets the `currentWindow` variable to point to the info window that was just displayed. The next time the user clicks a marker, the `InfoWindow` object pointed to by the `currentWindow` variable will be closed before the new marker's info window is opened.

The RichMarker Control

Along with markers, info windows are the most recognizable items on Google Maps. They're practically branding symbols for Google Maps, and every web page based on Google Maps uses them. Info windows have two major drawbacks, both related to their size. To begin with, they're bulky (even though the info window's size was one of the most prominent changes in the recent visual refresh of Google Maps). Not only that, but in many cases the map is scrolled when users click a marker to accommodate the display of the selected info window. Moreover, you can't totally control their size. The `InfoWindow` object has a minimum size of 200 pixels, which makes info windows inappropriate for displaying a short description, or for use with a small font size. Another problem with the `InfoWindow` object is that you can't make the Close button disappear; there's no option to remove the X icon from an info window.

Fortunately, there's an alternative to the `InfoWindow` object: the `RichMarker` object. The `RichMarker` object is rendered on the map as a rectangle that can display HTML fragments and has no arrow by default. You can create an arrow as a bitmap, but rich markers work best for placing labels on the map. The labels describe a rather large area of the map, as shown in Figure 7-4, rather than very specific locations. The application used to place the annotations on the map of Figure 7-4 is discussed in the next section.

Figure 7-4   The annotation labels on this map are RichMarker objects.

The `RichMarker` object's basic properties are its contents and its location on the map. The contents are assigned to the `content` property, and the exact location is determined by the `position` property, which is a `LatLng` object. The RichMarker's `anchor` property determines the edge of the rich marker that will be placed at the location specified by the `position` property. The valid settings for the `anchor` property have self-explanatory names as follows:

```
TOP_LEFT, TOP, TOP_RIGHT, LEFT, MIDDLE,
RIGHT, BOTTOM_LEFT, BOTTOM, BOTTOM_RIGHT
```

The `RichMarker` object is implemented by the script in the following file, which you must reference in your script with the following `<script>` directive (it must appear on a single line in your code):

```
<script type="text/javascript" src="http://google-maps-utility-library-
v3.googlecode.com/svn/trunk/richmarker/src/richmarker.js"></script>
```

To place a rich marker on the map, create a `<div>` element that holds the label's content. The following statement assigns an HTML fragment to the `div1` variable. The text is a short description of an airport, but the `div1` variable holds a lot of HTML code:

```
var div1 =  '<div style="padding: 4px; border:2px solid maroon; ' +
            'font-family: Trebuchet MS; font-size:10pt; background-color: ' +
            'white; color:blue">' +
            '<b>AAH</b>Aachen/Merzbruck<br/>' +
                'Aachen, Germany</div>'
```

Then, create a new instance of the `RichMarker` object and set the label's `content` property to the variable with the label's content and its `position` property to the `position` property of an existing marker:

```
var info1 = new RichMarker({
            position: marker1.position, anchor: RichMarkerPosition.LEFT,
            content:  div1 });
```

To display the rich marker when the `marker1` marker is clicked, set the `RichMarker` object's `map` property from within the marker's `click` event handler:

```
google.maps.event.addListener(marker1, 'click', function() {
        if (currentWindow != null) currentWindow.setMap(null);
        info1.setMap(map);
        currentWindow=info1;
    });
```

The `currentLabel` variable represents the `RichMarker` object that's currently active. This instance must be closed before you open a new one, just as you did with the `InfoWindow` objects earlier in the chapter.

The `RichMarker` object has no arrow and it's used as a label to annotate maps. However, it can be used in the place of an info window to display additional information about the selected marker. The sample application `RichMarker Demo.html`, shown in Figure 7-5, is identical to the `Markers with InfoWindows.html` application, but instead of info windows it uses rich markers to display the same information. The application displays only one rich marker at a time, not multiple ones, as shown in Figure 7-5. The advantage of using the `RichMarker` object is that the additional information is displayed exactly next to the marker. It has no Close button and you can control its appearance from within your script.

Another idea you may find interesting in designing custom labels is to make the `<div>` element transparent by omitting the `background-color` style attribute. The end result is to print the text right on the map. You must use a bold typeface and a color that stands out so the users will notice your custom labels. Clearly, this technique shouldn't be used in areas of a map that are crowded with feature names. Even better, apply a custom style to the entire map, which will make your custom labels stand out.

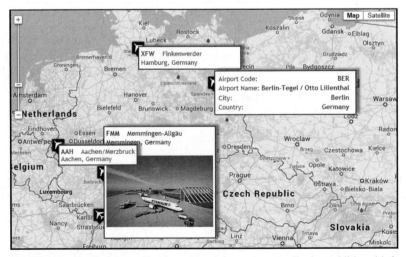

Figure 7-5 The RichMarker Demo application uses rich markers to display additional information about the selected marker.

Annotating a Map with RichMarkers

In this section, you're going to build an interactive web page for annotating maps with rich markers. The `RichMarkers.html` application, shown in Figure 7-6, allows users to place rich markers on the map and set their contents through an interactive interface. This is the application used to generate the page shown in Figure 7-4. The buttons at the top of the page allow you to place a new caption on the map, edit or remove an existing caption, and finally create a new static web page that contains the map and the annotations, but not the editing buttons. The contents of the new web page that displays the same map and the annotations are shown in a `<div>` element at the bottom of the page. Just copy the code and paste it into a new HTML file. The process of converting annotated maps to stand-alone web pages is known as *map generation*, and it's a standard feature of any GIS application. In later chapters, you will see more examples of scripts that generate map-enabled web pages. The auto-generated maps can be hosted to a web server so that other users can view, but not edit, them.

New labels are generated when the user clicks the Add New Marker button. This button opens a new window on top of the map with the caption's data, and users can edit the width of the label, its font size, the background color, and the caption itself. These attributes were selected to demonstrate the process, but you can easily add the text color, border width, and other attributes that affect the appearance of the caption. When the user clicks the Add New Label button, the function shown in Listing 7-1 creates a new `RichMarker` object with a default appearance and places it on the map.

Listing 7-1
Adding a new
RichMarker
object with
custom content

```
function addRichMarker() {
    var div = document.createElement('DIV');
    div.innerHTML='This is a marker';
    div.style.width='120px';
```

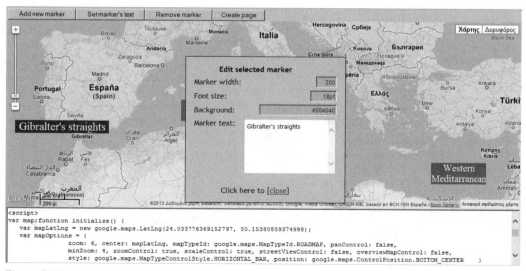

Figure 7-6   Annotating a map with RichMarker controls

```
        div.style.fontSize='12pt';
        div.style.background='#004040';
        div.style.color = '#ffffff';
        div.style.textAlign = 'center';
        var newMarker = new RichMarker(
                            map: map, position: map.getCenter(),
                            draggable: true, flat: false,
                            anchor: RichMarkerPosition.MIDDLE,
                            content: div, objInfo: 'This is a RichMarker'
        });
        markers.push(newMarker);
        google.maps.event.addListener(newMarker, "click", function()
                        {selectedMarker=this;});
}
```

The function generates a `<div>` element in code and applies a style to it. The code sets the label's initial appearance and places the new label at the center of the map. The user is allowed to change the attributes of the style on a pop-up window, and the new settings are applied to the `<div>` element's style, changing the appearance of the label on the map.

The pop-up window that appears modally on the map and allows users to customize the contents of the selected rich marker is implemented as a `<div>` element, whose visibility is turned on and off depending on the application's status. The `<div>` element that acts as a pop-up window is implemented with straight HTML code, which is shown in Listing 7-2.

Listing 7-2
A `<div>` element that's used as a pop-up window in an HTML application

```
<div id="overlay">
    <div style=
        "background-color: #d0d0d0; font-size:12pt; font-family: 'Trebuchet MS'">
        <b>Edit selected marker</b>
        <table width=100%>
            <tr><td>Marker width:</td>
                <td align='right'>
                    <input type="text" id="markerWidth" class="textbox" size="5"/>
                </td>
            </tr>
            <tr><td>Font size:</td>
                <td align='right'>
                    <input type="text" id="fontSize" class="textbox" size="7"/>
                </td>
            </tr>
            <tr>
                <td>Background:</td>
                <td align="right">
                    <input type="text" id="bgColor" class="textbox" size="25"/>
                </td>
            </tr>
            <tr>
                <td valign="top">Marker text:</td>
                <td>
                    <textarea id="caption" class="text"
                            cols="25" rows="4">enter your text here</textarea>
                </td>
            </tr>
        </table>
    </div>
</div>
```

The `overlay()` function, shown in Listing 7-3, populates the pop-up window with the selected label's attributes and then displays it on top of the map. If the pop-up window is already visible, the script reads the user-supplied data from the various elements on the pop-up window and applies them to the currently selected label.

```
function overlay() {
    if (selectedMarker == null) return;
    popup = document.getElementById("overlay");
    var div = selectedMarker.content;
    if (popup.style.visibility == "visible") {
        div.innerHTML = document.getElementById("caption").value;
        div.style.width = document.getElementById("markerWidth").value + 'px';
        div.style.fontSize = document.getElementById("fontSize").value;
        div.style.backgroundColor = document.getElementById("bgColor").value;
        div.style.color = '#ffffff';
        selectedMarker.objInfo=document.getElementById("caption").value;
    }
    else {
        document.getElementById("caption").value = selectedMarker.objInfo;
        document.getElementById("markerWidth").value = selectedMarker.width;
        document.getElementById("fontSize").value = div.style.fontSize;
        document.getElementById("bgColor").value = div.style.backgroundColor;
    }
    popup.style.visibility = (popup.style.visibility == "visible") ?
                            "hidden" : "visible";
}
```

The `overlay()` function implements the pop-up window for editing the current marker by examining the visibility of the `<div>` element. If the element is visible, it changes the settings of the `RichMarker` object on the map. If not, it reads the settings of the same object and populates the pop-up window with the object's properties. The role of this function is to transfer the data that controls the appearance of the selected label into the pop-up window and the values supplied by the user on this window back to the selected label and change its appearance.

Generating the Static Map

After you have placed a number of labels on the map and you have finalized their positions and appearance, you can create a static web page of the map overlaid with the labels. The static page does not provide any buttons for editing the labels, and it does not allow users to drag the labels around, of course. To generate the static page, click the Create Page button. The code will generate a new page, complete with HTML and JavaScript, and will insert the code for the page in the `TextArea` control below the map, as you can see in Figure 7-6. You can copy the text, paste it into a new text file, and save it with the .html extension to create a stand-alone web page with the same content. The `Autogenerated_Map.html` page in this chapter's support material was generated by the `RichMarkers.html` sample page.

The code behind the Create Page button is quite lengthy, but rather trivial: It gradually builds a very long string with the page's script, followed by some trivial HTML code. The only interesting part of the code in the context of handling the labels is the loop that goes through the labels on the map and generates their declarations:

```
var strScript = '';
for (i=0; i<markers.length; i++) {
    var strMarker = '';
```

```
    var mkWidth = markers[i].content.style.width;
    var mkBgColor = markers[i].content.style.backgroundColor;
    var mkFontSize = markers[i].content.style.fontSize;
    var mkCaption = markers[i].content.innerHTML;
    var div = document.createElement('DIV');
    strMarker += ' var div = document.createElement("DIV");' + '\n';
    strMarker += '    div.innerHTML="' + mkCaption + '"; div.style.width="' +
            mkWidth + '"; div.style.background="' + mkBgColor +
            '"; div.style.color = "#ffffff"; div.style.fontSize="' +
            mkFontSize + '";div.style.textAlign = "center";' + '\n';
    strMarker += ' var marker' + i + ' = new RichMarker({map: map, ' +
            ' position: new google.maps.LatLng' +
            markers[i].position + ', \n draggable: false, '
    strMarker +=
            'content: div, flat: false, anchor:' +
            'RichMarkerPosition.MIDDLE});\n';
    strScript += strMarker + '\n';
}
```

You can look up the generateMap() function in the RichMarkers project to see how it generates the static page with the annotated map. Of course, the page need not be static. You can embed code to generate listeners for the labels' click events and display additional data about the selected labels. You can make the page as interactive as you wish—just don't give users the tools to keep customizing the map. You can store the auto-generated pages into a folder of your web server with meaningful filenames and let the users discover the pages they're interested in.

An Alternate Approach to InfoWindows

Info windows and rich marker lablels are not your only options for displaying additional data for the selected marker (or any feature on the map). You can display the relevant data on a section of the page that hosts the map. Or, you can display the additional data on a floating data window like the one shown in Figure 7-7. Users can drag this window out of the way when they explore the data on the map, or they can minimize and restore it as needed. The data window should be updated every time the user selects another marker on the map.

The data window shown in Figure 7-7 is a <div> element and it's not as elegant in appearance. The sample application shown in Figure 7-7 uses a tabular layout for the data, but any HTML code you can apply to this window goes. There are also jQuery components that you can use in your HTML pages to achieve this functionality, including shaded boxes with rounded corners, but this book isn't about third-party components or HTML design. Moreover, the <div> element that implements the floating window was designed manually, to avoid long listings with embedded styles. Actually, the page uses a jQuery component to make the window draggable, but this component is fairly easy to use in your script (it's also optional).

The sample page with the draggable window of Figure 7-7 is the Map with data window.html application, included in this chapter's support material. The data window is implemented with the following <div> element:

```
<div id='window'>
    <div id='top'><table width=100%><tr><td align="left">
```

```
          Floating window title</td><td align="right">
          <a href='#' onclick='minimizeDataWindow()'>
          Minimize   </a></td></tr></table></div>
   <div id='main'><div>
</div>
```

The floating data window is implemented with two `<div>` elements, one that contains the window title and the Minimize/Restore links, and another one that contains the contents of the window. Both elements are nested under another `<div>` element, which is made draggable. The container element, the one with the ID `window`, is made draggable with the following statement, which must appear at the script level, to be executed as soon as the page is loaded:

```
$(function() {
     $( "#window" ).draggable({containment: "parent", zIndex:999});
});
```

This statement applies a jQuery method to the container `<div>` element, so you must also embed the following jQuery scripts to your page:

```
<script src="http://code.jquery.com/jquery-1.9.1.js"></script>
<script src="http://code.jquery.com/ui/1.10.3/jquery-ui.js"></script>
```

These few lines turn any element on the page into a draggable element. As each marker is selected, you must embed its data to the contents of the main section in the floating window. To display a marker's data window, attach the following listener to the marker's `click` event:

```
google.maps.event.addListener(marker, 'click', function() {showInfo(this)});
```

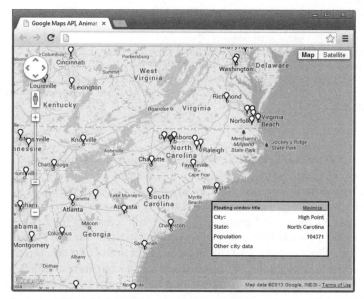

Figure 7-7 Displaying additional information about the selected markers on floating windows on top of the map. Note that the auxiliary window can also be minimized.

The showInfo() function, shown in Listing 7-3, populates the custom floating window with data regarding the selected city:

```
function showInfoWindow(m) {
     document.getElementById("main").innerHTML="<html><body>" +
               "<table width='100%'>" + "<tr>" +
               "<tr><td>City:</td><td align='right'>" + m.objInfo.City +
               "<td/></tr>" + "<tr><td>State:</td><td align='right'>"+
               m.objInfo.State + "</td></td>" +
               "<tr><td>Population</td><td align='right'>" +
               m.objInfo.Population + " </td></tr>" +
               "<tr><td>Other city data</td></tr>" +
               "</table>" +
               "</body></html>"
     if (currentMarker != null) {currentMarker.setOptions({icon: whitepin})}
          currentMarker=m;
          m.setOptions({icon: redpin});
}
```

The code shown here stores a custom object with the city data to the marker's objInfo property. In addition to setting the main section of the floating window, this function also highlights the selected marker by assigning the icon of a red pin to the marker. The selected marker is stored in the currentMarker script variable so that it can be reset to a white pin when another marker is selected. This highlighting technique will not work if you're using differently colored pins to indicate another property, such as the city's population.

The top section of the window contains a title and a hyperlink, which is initially set to Minimize and minimizes the window by hiding its main section when clicked. The window is reduced to a narrow bar and the title of the link becomes Restore. Clicking the link again makes the entire window visible and resets the caption of the link to Minimize again. The following is the minimizeDataWindow() function:

```
function minimizeDataWindow() {
    document.getElementById('main').style.height = '0px';
    document.getElementById('main').style.overflow = 'hidden';
    document.getElementById('window').style.height = '18px';
    document.getElementById('window').style.overflow = 'hidden';
    document.getElementById('top').innerHTML = '<a href="#"
                    onclick="maximizeDataWindow()">Restore </a>';
}
```

There's also a maximizeDataWindow() function with similar statements, which set the properties of the window to their original values.

As mentioned already, the floating window is implemented with straight HTML code. If you think this technique can enhance your application's interface, you will probably go for a much more elegant third-party component with a distinct look. The floating window isn't limited to displaying HTML fragments; you can actually embed a small form and interact with the user. For example, you can include checkboxes and react to their onchange event. Use this technique to allow your application's users to filter the markers on the map based on certain attributes. Such attributes could be the population of a city, the category of an airport (international, military, and so on), or any other classification scheme appropriate for your application. Another interesting idea would be to maintain a list of the features and make its items react to the mousemove event so that as users move the mouse over the list, a different feature is selected on the map.

GIS applications that display a lot of items on the map use this technique to display only the items in specific categories and even subcategories. You can also display items that were built under the same contract, or in the context of the same project, and so on and so forth. The ability to easily filter items on floating windows that can be moved out of the way, or minimized, and restored as needed, is a great aid to users viewing maps with a large number of complex annotations. It goes without saying that you can have multiple auxiliary panes, each one displaying different data.

Summary

You're done with typical mapping applications! You know how to embed Google maps in your web applications, as well as how to embed a Google map in a Windows application. You know how to manipulate the map through the page's script with the help of the Google Maps API, how to identify features on the map with markers and how to annotate maps with text.

Starting with the next chapter, you will learn advanced and very useful topics, such as how to draw shapes on a map, store these shapes in files and reuse them, and later in the book how to animate the various items on the map. In the following chapter, you learn about some new objects, such as the Polyline and Polygon objects, which can be used to annotate maps with shapes. Later in this book, you will see how to draw lines and polygons on the map interactively using the same objects.

8

Feature Annotation: Drawing Shapes on Maps

So far in the book, you have learned how to create map-driven web applications by embedding Google maps in your web pages. You also know how to place markers to identify points of interest on the map and how to write JavaScript functions to react to the basic map events. In this chapter, you learn about a more advanced, and very practical, feature of Google Maps: how to draw basic shapes on top of a map. Using shapes, you can mark features on the map, such as roads, borders of all types (besides administrative borders, which are displayed by default), even networks of lines that represent subway tracks, bus routes, gas pipes, electricity cables, any type of network. In some cases, it even makes sense to maintain the borders of states or countries as polygons. You can use these outlines to calculate the area of a state, or find out the state or county that was clicked, and so on. The borders shown on the map part of the image and you can't select countries or states on Google Maps.

The Google Maps API provides four objects that represent shapes: the `Polyline`, `Polygon`, `Rectangle`, and `Circle` objects. Routes are represented by polylines, while property and administrative outlines are represented by polygons.

> **NOTE** The word "shapes" refers to closed geometric entities, which are represented on Google Maps as polygons. Strictly speaking, a shape is a polygon. In the context of this book, I use the word "shape" to refer to polylines, rectangles, polygons, and circles. And sometimes I use the term "line" to refer to polylines. Also, the terms "polyline," "polygon," and "circle" in the text refer to the usual geometric entities, while the terms "Polyline," "Polygon," and "Circle" are the names of the objects that represent the corresponding entities on the map.

Polylines

A polyline is a collection of connected line segments, defined by a series of locations. The locations form the polyline's path, which is an array of `LatLng` objects. These locations are the line's breakpoints and are known as *vertices*. Figure 8-1 shows a polyline that corresponds to one of the lines of the Los Angeles metro system, the Golden Line. The figure was

The Golden Line of the LA Metro System

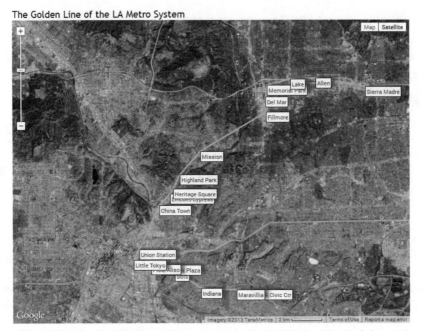

Figure 8-1 The polyline on the map is based on a path formed by the locations of the stations of the Golden Line of the Los Angeles Metro System.

generated by the LA Golden Metro Line.html page, included with this chapter's material. The stations are marked with RichLabel controls, as you recall from the preceding chapter.

The polyline that represents the metro track is defined by the locations of the stations along the metro line and the tracks between stations are straight line segments. This is an oversimplification, of course, because rail tracks don't change direction abruptly. If you can specify more points along the line's path, you'll be able to display a smoother line on the map that follows more closely the path of the metro line and has the appearance of a smooth curve. Even so, when users zoom deeply, they will be able to see the breaks in the line.

When you trace a map feature such as a freeway, a river, or a rail track with too many points, the resulting polyline can approximate any shape, including smooth curves. Figure 8-2 (see page 166) shows the outline of Italy. The shape is actually a polygon (a closed polyline), but it's still defined by a path. Italy's outline is made up of 639 vertices and up to a reasonable zoom factor it approximates the country's borders nicely.

The data was generated with a Windows application, the Map Tracing application, which is discussed in Chapter 9. The Map Tracing application allows users to trace any map feature interactively and keeps track of the locations specified by the user on the map.

Polyline Construction

To place a polyline on the map, you must create a `Polyline` object and place it on the map by calling its `setMap()` method. The constructor of the `Polyline` object expects an array of `LatLng` objects that define the polyline's path. This array must be passed to the constructor with the `path` attribute. Here's a short segment of the definition of the metro line's path:

```
var GoldenPath = [
    new google.maps.LatLng(34.03339791, -118.15446943);
    new google.maps.LatLng(34.03336123, -118.1612058);
    ...
    ];
```

The first two coordinates correspond to the Atlantic and East LA Civic Center stations of the Golden Line; open the sample page to see the entire track. The following statement creates a very basic `Polyline` object, which will be rendered on the map with the default color and default width:

```
var GoldenLine = new google.maps.Polyline({
                path: GoldenPath});
```

The `path` attribute is the only mandatory attribute of the `Polyline` object. To specify any of the optional attributes, add more items to the array following the constructor. The other two basic attributes of the `Polyline`'s constructor are the line's width, which is specified in pixels, and its color. Because the polyline has a color, it can also have an opacity value.

```
var GoldenLine = new google.maps.Polyline({
                path: GoldenPath,
                strokeColor: "orange", strokeWeight: 2,
                strokeOpacity: 0.25
});
```

To actually place the `GoldenLine` object on the map, you must call its `setMap()` method, passing the name of a `Map` object as an argument:

```
GoldenLine.setMap(map);
```

You can change any of the properties of the line in your code by calling the `Polyline` object's `setOptions()` method, which accepts as an argument an array of key-value pairs: The keys are property names and the values are the property values. The following statement changes the color and width of the line on the map:

```
GoldenLine.setOptions({strokeColor: "#a0a0a0", strokeWeight: "3"});
```

You can also change the path of a polyline with the `setPath()` method, which accepts as an argument another path.

Polygons

Polygons are very similar to polylines: In effect, polygons are closed polylines. They're also specified with an array of locations (or vertices) with the `path` attribute, and they have a `strokeColor` and a `strokeWeight` attribute. In addition, you can specify the polygon's `fillColor` attribute. Note that polygons are always closed and you don't have to repeat the initial point to close the shape because the end point will be connected to the initial point automatically. In effect, you can use the path of a polyline to create a polygon with the exact same shape.

You can change any attribute of a polygon at will by calling the `setOptions()` method and passing as argument an array with the attributes you want to change and their new values, similar to the array passed to its constructor.

To prepare a nontrivial shape, the outline of Italy was traced with the Map Tracing application, which is discussed in detail in Chapter 9. The path of the outline consists of 639 `LatLng` objects, and the polygon of Figure 8-2 was based on this path. The polygon encloses the continental part of Italy. As you probably know, Italy encompasses two large islands, as well as many smaller ones. Additional shapes can be defined with additional paths, as you will see in the section "Polygon Islands" later in this chapter. The polygon looks quite reasonable at a moderate zoom level. As you increase the zoom level, the differences between the actual borders on the map and the polygon's shape become noticeable.

Polygons with Holes

A polygon may contain a hole, like the one shown in Figure 8-3. To define the shape shown in the figure, you need two polygons: one for the outer shape and another one for the hole.

Figure 8-2 A polygon encompassing Italy

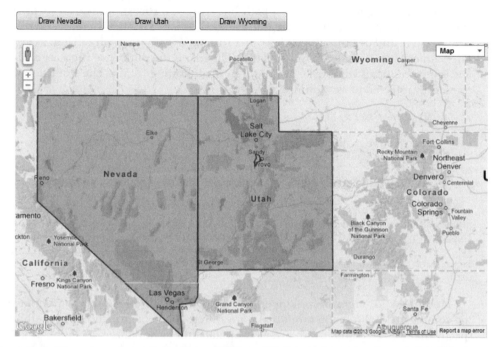

Figure 8-3   The outer polygon is the state of Utah and Utah Lake is rendered as a hole within the state's polygon.

Indeed, the path of a polygon with holes is an array of paths. In JavaScript terms, this is an array of arrays. The first path in the array is the path of the outer polygon and the remaining paths correspond to holes, as long as these paths are fully contained within the outer polygon. Figure 8-3 shows the state of Utah with a hole that corresponds to Utah Lake. If the shape of the lake is hard to see on the printed page, please open the `Polygons.hml` page.

The `Polygon` object provides two methods for specifying its shape: `setPath()` and `setPaths()`. The difference between the two methods is that `setPaths()` allows you to specify multiple paths for the polygon. The first shape is the basic polygon and the remaining ones represent holes in the outer shape. The state of Utah with a hole that corresponds to Utah Lake was generated with the `drawPolygon()` function, which accepts as an argument the path of the shape to draw:

```
function drawPolygon(state) {
    var poly = new google.maps.Polygon({
    strokeWeight: 2, strokeOpacity: 1,
    fillColor: '#AA00BB',    strokeColor: '#3030FF'
    });
    poly.setPaths(state);
    poly.setMap(map);
}
```

The `state` argument is either a path (an array of vertices) or an array or paths, each path being an array of vertices. The statements shown in Listing 8-1 create the path for the state of Utah, and call the `drawPolygon()` function with the path of Utah as argument. The path of Utah is made up of two paths. The first is the outline of the state and the other one is the outline of Utah Lake, as shown in the following listing. The resulting shape is commonly referred to as "donut-shaped."

Listing 8-1
Constructing a
"donut"-shaped
path

```
var utah = new Array();
utah = [
        new google.maps.LatLng(42.0083149369298, -111.039287109375),
        new google.maps.LatLng(41.9838201251284, -114.0385546875),
                    . . .
        new google.maps.LatLng(41.0045986236626, -111.02830078125)
          ];
var lake = new Array();
lake.push(new google.maps.LatLng(40.3589241562642,-111.898967285156));
lake.push(new google.maps.LatLng(40.3557814813435,-111.849528808594));
. . .
lake.push(new google.maps.LatLng(40.2458126855149,-111.852275390625));
utah = [utah, lake];
```

Most of the locations were skipped in the preceding listing, as the number of vertices or the complexity of the shape won't make any difference. Note the different methods used to specify the two arrays: the `utah` array is populated in its initializer, while the `lake` array was populated by pushing one element at a time. Open the file `Polygons.html`, which draws the outlines of three states on the map. One of the states is Utah, which includes a polygon that delimits Utah Lake. The other two polygons correspond to Nevada and Wyoming, whose borders are made up of large straight lines.

Polygon Islands

Figure 8-4, on the other hand, shows the outline of Los Angeles County, which is made up of three polygons: one for the continental part of the county and two more for the islands outside Los Angeles. Because the two islands are totally outside the polygon that corresponds to Los Angeles County, they're rendered on the map as regular polygons.

If you open the `Islands Polygons.html` file, you will see that the script creates a single `Polygon` object with a path that contains three arrays. Listing 8-2 shows just the basic statements of the script.

Listing 8-2
Creating a path
with "islands"

```
var SanClemente=[ ... ];
var SantaCatalina = [ ... ];
var LA = [ ... ];
var LosAngelesPath = [LA, SanClemente, SantaCatalina];
 var poly = new google.maps.Polygon({
            strokeWeight: 2, strokeOpacity: 1,
            fillColor: 'yellow', strokeColor: '#202020'});
            poly.setPaths(LosAngelesPath);
            poly.setMap(map);
}
```

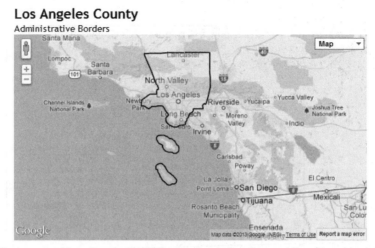

Los Angeles County

Figure 8-4   The county of Los Angeles includes the Santa Catalina and San Clemente islands, in addition to the continental part of the country.

The ellipses indicate missing definitions of `LatLng` objects. The three individual paths are combined into an array of paths, the `LosAngelesPath` variable, which is then passed to the `Polygon` object's `setPaths()` method. Note that you must use the `setPaths()` method, even if you're passing a single array as an argument, because the argument is an array of arrays.

Displaying a Crosshair on the Map

Another interesting use of the line drawing feature of the API is the implementation of a crosshair at the center of the map. Typical mapping applications allow users to precisely locate the desired features on the map. You can program the map's `click` event and expect that users will identify a location with the mouse and click on it. This approach is neither precise nor user friendly. A better approach is to display a crosshair cursor at the center of the map, like the one shown in Figure 8-5, and allow users to scroll the map until they bring the location they're interested in exactly under the crosshair.

The crosshair is a pair of vertical lines that meet at the center of the map. To draw them, you need to know the horizontal and vertical extents of the map's viewport and then draw two lines through the middle of each axis and extend from the minimum to the maximum latitude or longitude. The drawing of the lines takes a few statements, but it's straightforward; you will use the map's `getBounds()` method to retrieve the horizontal and vertical extents of the current viewport.

However, you must redraw the two lines every time the user drags the map around, as well as when the user zooms out. The code that draws the two lines of the crosshair on the map must be executed from within the map's `bounds_changed` event. Otherwise, the crosshair will scroll with the map because it was drawn at a specific location on the map. Moreover, users may not wish to keep the crosshair visible at all times, so you must give

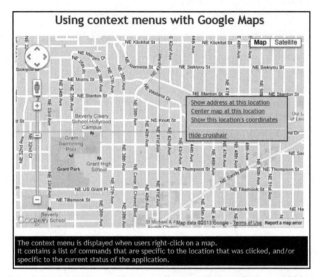

Figure 8-5 The Context Menu.html web page allows users to show and hide a crosshair cursor on the map.

them the option to show or hide the crosshair. In Chapter 5, you saw how to add to the context menu a command that shows/hides the crosshair. Now that you know how to draw lines on the map, let's look at the statements that actually draw the crosshair of the Context Menu.html sample page of Chapter 5.

First, you must declare three variables: two variables that represent the two lines and the crosshair variable that indicates the visibility of the crosshair. Set the crosshair variable to true or false to control whether the crosshair will be displayed initially.

```
var centerHLine;
var centerVLine;
var crosshair=false;
```

The drawCrosshair() function does all the work. It extracts the coordinates of the minimum and maximum latitude and longitude values, calculates the coordinates of the endpoints of the two lines, and then draws them on top of the map. The code of the drawCrosshair() function is shown in Listing 8-3, which is a bit condensed to fit on the printed page.

Listing 8-3
Drawing the two lines that form a crosshair cursor at the map's center

```
function drawCrosshair() {
    if (crosshair == true)      {
        if (centerHLine != null)     centerHLine.setMap(null);
        if (centerVLine != null)     centerVLine.setMap(null);
        var bounds=map.getBounds();
```

```
        var sw = bounds.getSouthWest();
        var ne = bounds.getNorthEast();
        var minLat = sw.lat();   var maxLat = ne.lat();
        var minLon = sw.lng();   var maxLon = ne.lng();
        var mapCenter = map.getCenter();
        var ctrLat = mapCenter.lat();  var ctrLon = mapCenter.lng();
        var centerCoordinatesV =
            [new google.maps.LatLng(minLat, ctrLon),
             new google.maps.LatLng(maxLat, ctrLon) ];
        var centerCoordinatesH =
            [new google.maps.LatLng(ctrLat, minLon),
             new google.maps.LatLng(ctrLat, maxLon) ];
        centerVLine = new google.maps.Polyline({
            path: centerCoordinatesV,
            strokeColor: "#FF0000", strokeOpacity: 1.0, strokeWeight: 0.5
        });
        centerHLine = new google.maps.Polyline({
            path: centerCoordinatesH,
            strokeColor: "#FF0000", strokeOpacity: 1.0, strokeWeight: 0.5
        });
        centerVLine.setMap(map);
        centerHLine.setMap(map);
    }
  else {
      if (centerHLine != null)  centerHLine.setMap(null);
      if (centerVLine != null)  centerVLine.setMap(null);
    }
}
```

The variables centerHLine and centerVLine are two Polyline objects that represent the two lines that make up the crosshair. The horizontal line's latitude is the latitude of the map's center point, and it extends from the minimum to the maximum visible longitude. Similarly, the vertical line's longitude is the longitude of the center point, and it extends from minimum to the maximum visible latitude. The script relies on the crosshair variable, declared at the script's level, which indicates whether the crosshair cursor is visible at the time. If the cursor is not currently visible, the script draws two perpendicular lines that meet at the center of the map. If the crosshair is visible, then the script removes the cursor from the map by setting the map attribute of the centerHLine and centerVLine variables to null.

Rectangles

Rectangles are, in effect, polygons with four vertices, but they're defined without a path. Instead, they're based on a LatLngBounds object, which describes both the location and size of the rectangle. Other than that, they have the same properties as polygons. In fact, you can create rectangular polygons and ignore the Rectangle object. Use the StrokeColor and FillColor to specify their appearance, the StrokeOpacity and FillOpacity properties to set the rectangle's opacity, and the StrokeWeight to set the width of the rectangle's outline.

To create a new `Rectangle` object, use a constructor like the following:

```
var rectangle = new google.maps.Rectangle({
    strokeColor: 'red',   strokeOpacity: 1,    strokeWeight: 2,
    fillColor: 'orange',  fillOpacity: 0.40,
    map: map,
    bounds: new google.maps.LatLngBounds(
        new google.maps.LatLng(33.671068, -116.25128),
        new google.maps.LatLng(33.685282, -116.233942))
    });
```

Only the *bounds* property is mandatory; all other properties are optional. The `LatLngBounds` object's constructor accepts two arguments, which are the coordinates of the lower-right (south-west) and upper-left (north-east) corners of the rectangle. While polylines and polygons are used extensively in mapping applications, there aren't many features that can be approximated by rectangles and circles. These two shapes are too perfect for the shapes you usually mark on the map.

Circles

Circles are defined by a center point and a radius. The center is a `LatLng` object as usual (a location on the map), and the radius is specified always in meters. Here's the constructor of the `Circle` object:

```
var location = (40.6898, -74.0453);
var circle=
    new google.maps.Circle({ strokeColor: '#FF0000',
            strokeOpacity: 1, strokeWeight: 2,
            fillColor: '#FF0000', fillOpacity: 0.3,
            center: location, radius: 1000});
```

The circle is located at the center of Liberty Island in New York and its radius is 1 kilometer. You can set the circle's center and radius from within your code at any time by calling the `setOptions()` method as usual, or the `setCenter()` and `setRadius()` methods, passing the appropriate value as argument. As far as events go, you can detect the usual mouse on the circle as well as the `center_changed` and `radius_changed` events, which aren't very common in coding mapping applications. You can fill the circle with a solid color to create a disk with the `strokeColor` and `strokeOpacity` properties.

Unlike polygons, you can't place holes in circles or use circular holes in polygons. However, you can create a polygon that approximates a circle with a function that generates points along the circle's circumference and then uses these points as a path. If you generate 100 or 200 points along the circumference, the polygon will be a good approximation of the corresponding circle. This approximation isn't recommended because the more points you add to your polygon to better approximate the circle, the slower your script will get. On the other hand, it's the only way to create circles with holes, or circular holes, in another polygon.

Listing 8-4 show the `drawGeodesicCircle()` function, which approximates a circle by creating a polygon with 500 vertices, all on the circumference of the underlying circle.

The function performs simple trigonometric calculations. Okay, they aren't simple because the circle is drawn on a sphere, but it's not much different from calculating points along the circumference of a circle on a flat surface. Most readers who need this function will simply paste it in their script, so I won't get into advanced trigonometric topics here.

Listing 8-4
Approximating
a circle with a
polygon

```
var R = 6371000; // the earth's radius in meters
function drawGeodesicCircle(center, radius) {
    var d2r = Math.PI / 180; var r2d = 1 / d2r;
    var count = 1000;  // generate 1,000 points to approximate circle
    var Rlat = radius/R * r2d;
    var Rlng = Rlat / Math.cos(center.lat() * d2r);
    var points = new Array();
    for (i=0; i < count; i++) {
        var theta = Math.PI * (i / (count/2));
        var lat1 = center.lat() * d2r;
        var lng1 = center.lng() * d2r;
        var x = Math.asin(Math.sin(lat1) * Math.cos(radius/R) +
                Math.cos(lat1) * Math.sin(radius/R) * Math.cos(theta));
        var y = lng1 + Math.atan2(Math.sin(theta) *
                Math.sin(radius/R) * Math.cos(lat1),
                Math.cos(radius/R) - Math.sin(lat1) * Math.sin(x));
        points.push(new google.maps.LatLng(x * r2d, y * r2d));
    }
    return points;
}
```

The `drawGeodesicCircle()` function accepts two arguments, the circle's center and its radius, and returns an array of `LatLng` objects, the `points` array, which you can use to draw a polygon that approximates the equivalent circle. You may have noticed that the name of the function is `drawGeodesicCircle()` and not `drawCircle()`. A geodesic circle is a perfect circle on the sphere, not on the flat map. At smaller scales, the two circles are identical because small sections of the earth's surface are practically flat. At large scales, when the circle's radius exceeds 1,000 kilometers, for example, the perfect circle on the sphere is not nearly as perfect when projected onto the flat map. The topic of geodesics, along with the distortion introduced by projecting large earth features on a flat map, is discussed in detail in Chapter 10. In the same chapter, you will find more interesting examples of circles drawn on a Google map.

Fixed-Size Circles

There's no option to specify the `Circle` object's radius in pixels; this will cause you problems if you're trying to use a circle as a marker on the map. Because the circle's radius is defined in meters, its actual size will follow the zoom level. If you zoom out far enough, the circle will practically disappear, and if you zoom too deeply, the circle may fill the entire map.

What if you want to display a circle that retains its size at all zoom levels? The solution is to specify the radius not in absolute units, but as a percentage of the map's width. Moreover, you must redraw the circle with its new radius every time the user changes the zoom level. In Figure 8-6, you see a web page created to demonstrate animation techniques for Chapter 20. When the user clicks somewhere on the map, a "vanishing" circle is displayed for a few

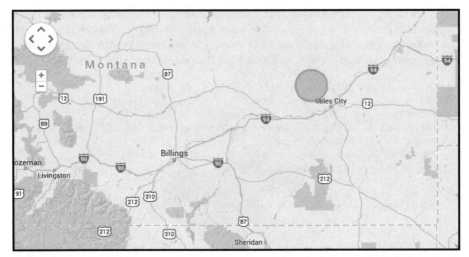

Figure 8-6 The `Highlight Points.html` page uses animated circles to highlight locations on the map.

moments at the location of the click. The circle's opacity goes from 1 to 0 in a second or so, and the circle disappears. This simple animation effect, however, is a very effective way of highlighting the point that was clicked.

You will see the complete code of this technique in Chapter 21, but let me show here quickly the code that calculates the radius of the circle. When the user clicks on the map, the following statement calculates the horizontal extent of the map in degrees:

```
latExtend = Math.abs(map.getBounds().getNorthEast().lat() -
                     map.getBounds().getSouthWest().lat());
```

To convert this value to meters, you multiply it by 111,320 because each degree corresponds to 113.32 kilometers on the surface of the earth (near the equator, of course). Then, you can set the circle's radius to 2 percent or 5 percent of the viewport's width. The following statement sets the radius to 2 percent of the map's viewport:

```
var radius = latExtend * 111320 / 50;
```

The actual size of the circle will be different at different latitude values; this technique draws a consistently small disc that may not have the exact same size at all locations, but it changes size as you zoom in or out so that it appears to have a more or less constant size at any zoom level.

Another approach to drawing circles the same size at all zoom levels it to use icons instead of circles. In the section "Placing Symbols Along Polylines" later in this chapter, you will see how to use the built-in symbol of a filled circle to identify a feature on the map.

Storing Paths in MVCArrays

The `path` property of the polylines and polygons is an array of geo-locations; you can manipulate the shape's outline by manipulating the elements of the path. However, changing an element's value won't have an immediate effect on the shape that has been rendered on the map. You must create a new object based on the revised path and place it on the map, in place of the previous version of the same shape.

Google provides a special object, the `MVCArray`, which can be bound to another entity. As you recall from Chapter 4, MVC stands for *Model-View-Controller*. It's a design pattern that allows the same data to be presented in different manners. As soon as the data is updated, the view of the data is also updated. The `MVCArray` object can be bound to a path or other object and update the object it's linked to. If you use a `MVCArray` to store the shape's path and then assign this object to the shape's `path` property, the `path` property will remain bound to the `MVCArray`. This means that every time you change an element in the `MVCArray`, or add a new vertex to the path, the shape will be updated automatically. `MVCArrays` are extremely useful in programming with the Google Maps API because they allow you to focus in your code, and not the plumb work required to keep the map up-to-date. If you stored the vertices of a path to a regular array and then assigned this array to the `path` property of a polygon, the polygon would assume the shape of the path the moment of the assignment. After that, you could change the array without affecting the shape; you would have to reassign the array to the *path* property to change the polygon's shape.

Figure 8-7 shows a Google map with a polyline on it. The vertices of the polyline are identified by markers and you can edit the shape by moving the markers around with the mouse. Figure 8-7 was created by the `Editable PolyLine.html` application; the script that drives the functionality of this page is discussed in the following section.

The core of the script is an `MVCArray` object with the path's vertices. This array is used as the shape's path so that when a vertex is moved and the code updates the selected vertex's location, the shape changes instantly.

An Editable Polyline

Specifying a polyline and placing it on the map is straightforward, and you can create complex overlays on top of the map using the `Polyline` and `Polygon` objects. What if you want to create a new shape by tracing a feature on the map, such as a train track, a delivery route, a network of cables, and so on? Wouldn't it be useful to be able to edit the polyline right on the map? Indeed, this is one of the most basic features of a GIS system, and you're going to build an application for tracing maps in Chapter 9. In this chapter, you will find all the information you need for designing editable polylines and polygons. The `Editable PolyLine.html` page shown in Figure 8-7 demonstrates a technique for editing a polyline interactively. Each vertex of the polyline is identified by a marker and users can edit the polyline by dragging the markers with the mouse. This isn't exactly an editable polyline because this technique doesn't allow users to delete vertices or insert new ones, but it's the first step in designing truly editable polylines.

The polyline shown in the figure represents a metro line, and its vertices are the stations along the line (which happens to be the Golden line of the Los Angeles Metro). The data is

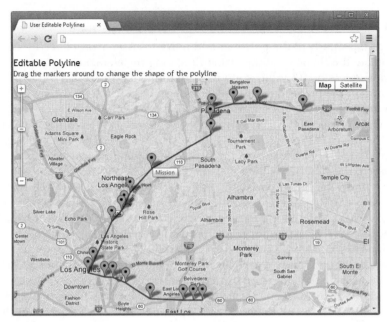

Figure 8-7 Editing a line on the map by dragging the markers on its vertices with the mouse

stored in two arrays in the script: the first array, GoldenLine, contains the coordinates of the metro stations, which are also the polyline's vertices, and the other one, the stations array, contains the names of the stations. Here are the constructors of the two arrays:

```
var GoldenLine = [
    new google.maps.LatLng(34.03339791, -118.15446943),
    new google.maps.LatLng(34.03336123, -118.1612058),
    new google.maps.LatLng(34.03331678, -118.16813663),
    ...
    ];
var stations = [
    "Atlantic", "East LA Civic Ctr", ... , "Sierra Madre"];
```

The script starts by creating a variable for storing the polyline's vertices, the linePath variable. The linePath variable holds the coordinates that define the polyline based on the GoldenLine array. However, the script generates an MVCArray object based on the GoldenLine array. It does so by passing the GoldenLine array as an argument to the constructor of an MVCArray object. The linePath array is then used to specify the polyline's path in the Polyline object's constructor. The following two statements place on the map a polyline that represents the Golden line of the Los Angeles Metro:

```
var linePath = new google.maps.MVCArray(GoldenLine);
var line = new google.maps.Polyline({
                map: map, path: linePath, strokeColor: "#006400"});
```

The script iterates the `GoldenLine` array and generates a marker for each station. The statement that generates the markers is straightforward; just note that the *draggable* property is set to `true` so that the users of the application can edit the polyline by dragging around the markers that correspond to the polyline's vertices:

```
for (i=0; i < GoldenLine.length; i++) {
    var marker = new google.maps.Marker({
                    position:  GoldenLine[i], title: stations[i],
                    map: map, draggable:true});
    marker.setMap(map);
    markers.push(marker);
}
```

Note that each new marker is added to the `markers` array so that the script can access the markers later. If you don't store the individual markers to an array, you won't be able to manipulate them after they have been placed on the map.

So far, you have displayed a polyline on the map and placed a marker at each vertex. The markers are draggable, but they can't be used yet to edit the shape of the polyline. For this to happen, you must change the location of the corresponding vertex in the path as the user moves the marker. This action must clearly take place in each marker's `drag` event listener. In the listener's code, you must find out the index of the marker being dragged in the `markers` array and use this index to access the corresponding vertex in the path to change its coordinates. Here's the statement that adds the appropriate listener to each marker's `drag` event:

```
google.maps.event.addListener(marker, "drag", function (event) {
    for (var i = 0; i < markers.length; i++) {
        if (markers[i] == this) {path.setAt(i, this.getPosition()) }
    }
});
```

The loop iterates through the `markers` array and compares each marker to the marker that fired the event (identified by the keyword `this`). When the marker being dragged is located, the code changes the value of the corresponding item in the `path` array and sets it to the marker's current location, which is given by the expression `this.getPosition()`. The code is short and simple, but thanks to the ability of the elements of the `MVCArray` object to remain bound to the polyline's vertices, the polyline's shape is changed as soon as you change the location of any vertex. Listing 8-5 shows the complete script of the `Editable PolyLine.html` page (the ellipses in the two array initializers stand for additional elements omitted from the listing).

Listing 8-5
Displaying a polyline with markers at its vertices on the map

```
<script>
    var GoldenLine = [
            new google.maps.LatLng(34.03339791, -118.15446943),
            new google.maps.LatLng(34.03336123, -118.1612058),
            ...
            new google.maps.LatLng(34.14774151, -118.081205)
    ];
    var stations = [
```

```
                  "Atlantic", "East LA Civic Ctr", ..., "Sierra Madre"
  ];
  var markers = [];
  var map;
  function initialize() {
     var iniLat = 34.10;
     var iniLon = -118.15;
     var iniZoom = 12;
     var myLatlng = new google.maps.LatLng(iniLat, iniLon);
     var mapOptions = {
           zoom: iniZoom, center: myLatlng,
           mapTypeId: google.maps.MapTypeId.ROADMAP, panControl: false,
           zoomControl: true, scaleControl: true,
           overviewMapControl: false, streetViewControl: false,
           style: google.maps.MapTypeControlStyle.HORIZONTAL_BAR,
           position: google.maps.ControlPosition.BOTTOM_CENTER
     }
     map = new google.maps.Map(document.getElementById("map_canvas"),
                             mapOptions);
     var linePath = new google.maps.MVCArray(GoldenLine);
     var line = new google.maps.Polyline(
                       {map: map, path: linePath, strokeColor: "#006400"});
       for (i=0; i < GoldenLine.length; i++) {
         var marker = new google.maps.Marker({
                 position:  GoldenLine[i], title: stations[i],
                 map: map, draggable:true});
         marker.setMap(map);
         markers.push(marker);
         google.maps.event.addListener(marker, "drag", function (event) {
             for (var i = 0; i < markers.length; i++) {
                       if (markers[i] == this) {
                           path.setAt(i, this.getPosition()) }
             }
         });
       }
  }
}
</script>
```

Open the Editable Polyline.html page and test-drive it. You have a truly interactive map that allows you to position markers very precisely with the mouse. To create an editable polygon, you need only change the definition of the Polyline object to a Polygon object. The polygon you specify with the same path will remain closed at all times as you edit its path, without any additional code.

As soon as an element of the path array changes, the polygon is redrawn on the map and its new shape is dictated by the current locations of its path's vertices. The short application you created in this section is the beginning of an interactive map drawing application. This is the topic of the next chapter, where you will implement an application that allows users to edit shapes interactively on top of the map.

Placing Symbols Along Polylines

An interesting feature added to version 3.0 of the Google Maps API is the capability to place symbols along polylines, as shown in Figure 8-8. The highway was drawn with the `Highway 5.html` page, included in this chapter's support material.

The symbols may be placed at fixed positions, or they can be repeated along the polyline, and they usually indicate direction. If you make the underlying polyline invisible and place the symbols close to one another, then the symbols are no longer "decorations"; they become the line. This is how you can create dotted and dashed lines on top of a map.

Consider the following path definition:

```
var US5 = [
   new google.maps.LatLng(32.7595620256501, -117.204208374023),
   new google.maps.LatLng( 32.7657692211219, -117.205581665039),
   new google.maps.LatLng( 32.7711099498904, -117.207126617432),
   ...
]
```

These are the first few vertices of a path that correspond to a large segment of the US 5 Highway from San Diego to Portland. It's a plain polyline that was traced manually with the Map Traces application, which will be discussed in the following chapter.

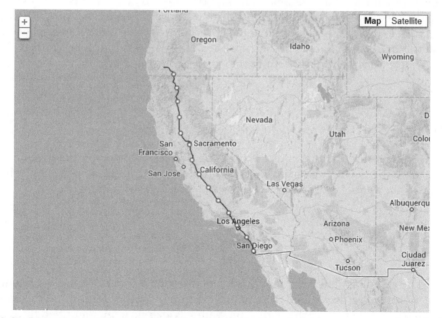

Figure 8-8   Repeating a symbol along a polyline path. The line shown here corresponds to the US 5 highway in California.

Let's add a few marks along the highway. First, you must create a new symbol with a statement like the following:

```
dotSymbol = { path: google.maps.SymbolPath.CIRCLE, offset: "0%",
              scale: 3, strokeColor: "red", strokeWeight: 2,
              fillColor: "white", fillOpacity:1
            };
```

The symbol is defined as an array of property values. The symbol's shape, specified with the path property, is one of the predefined symbols that come with the API, and it's a circle. The predefined symbols are members of the google.maps.SymbolPath enumeration, which includes the following: CIRCLE, BACKWARD_CLOSED_ARROW, FORWARD_CLOSED_ ARROW, BACKWARD_OPEN_ARROW, and FORWARD_OPEN_ARROW. In addition to the API's predefined symbols, you can create your own symbols using the SVG (Scalable Vector Graphics) notation, which is discussed briefly in Chapter 20 and Appendix A. The symbol created with the preceding statements is a white circle with a medium-width red outline. The scale attribute is very important: It's the scaling factor of the symbol in pixels. The default size of the symbol (when scale is 1) is the same as the polyline's stroke width. Because their sizes are specified in pixels, symbols are not affected by the zoom level: They have the same size at all zoom levels.

To place instances of the selected symbol along the path of the polyline, you must set the Polyline object's icons property. This property is an array of symbols, and it usually contains a single item. In addition to the symbol, you must also specify one of the offset or repeat properties. The offset property is the distance from the beginning of the line, where the symbol will appear; it can be expressed either in pixels or as a percentage. This property's default value is "100%" (it's a string). The repeat property is used when you want to repeat the symbol along the line's path; its value is the distance between successive symbols on the line and it can be expressed either in pixels or a percentage. The following is a typical icons property definition:

```
icons: [{
    icon: dotSymbol,
    offset: "0%"
}]
```

If you use this definition in a Polyline object's constructor, the specified symbol will appear at the beginning of the line. A more interesting example is the following, which repeats the symbol every 25 pixels along the path, as shown in Figure 8-8.

```
icons: [{
    icon: lineSymbol,
    offset: "0%", repeat: "25px"
}]
```

The complete statement that produced the path shown in Figure 8-8 follows. The array US5 holds the vertices of the path, and the icons property determines the symbol and how it will be repeated along the path. The symbol is a circle icon, identified by the dotSymbol variable created earlier, and it's repeated every 25 pixels. All these settings are combined in the constructor of the US5Route object, which is a `Polyline` object.

```
var US5Route = new google.maps.Polyline({
                path: US5, map: map,
                strokeOpacity: 0.75, strokeWeight: 1.5,
                strokeColor: "blue",
                icons: [{
                    icon: dotSymbol,
                    offset: '0%', repeat: '25px'
                }],
                map: map
});
```

The most important aspect of symbols is that they can be animated. In Chapter 20, you will see applications that animate a symbol along a line to simulate an object, such as a train or airplane, traveling between any two locations.

Another interesting application of symbols is to create dashed and dotted lines. To create dashed lines, you must use the SVG notation, which is discussed in detail in Appendix A. In the same appendix, you will find examples of different line types. There's also a short demo page by Google that demonstrates various types of dotted lines. The page animates the symbols too, but you can ignore the animation for the time being. Just copy the SVG definitions of the various line shapes and re-use them in your code. The URL of this page is http://gmaps-samples-v3.googlecode.com/svn/trunk/symbols/polyline-symbols.html.

The definition of the chevron symbol on this page, for example, is as follows:

```
icons: [{
  icon: {
    path: "M -1,1 0,0 1,1",
    strokeOpacity: 1,
    strokeWeight: 1.5,
    scale: 6
  },
      repeat: "20px"
}]
```

The highway was traced with over 1,000 vertices, and you can see that it doesn't quite follow the freeway's path when you zoom in too closely. Figure 8-9 shows two details of the same highway. Note that the symbols do not get closer or further apart as you zoom in and out because the icon's `repeat` attribute is specified in pixels, not as a percentage. The distance between consecutive symbols in Figure 8-9 is the same, even though the second map of Figure 8-9 covers a tiny segment of the highway.

Handling Large Paths

In this chapter's examples, all the coordinates required to generate paths were embedded in the corresponding scripts. This is convenient for sample applications, but it's not very practical for real-world applications. The main drawback with this approach is the size of

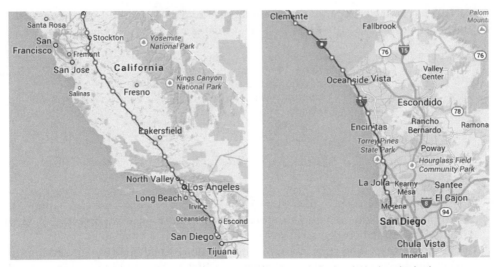

Figure 8-9   When the symbols are placed apart by a number of pixels, their density is the same regardless of the zoom factor.

the script. There are two techniques for transferring the definitions of large paths to the client, both of which are discussed later in this book. Here's an overview of these two techniques.

The first technique uses compressed paths. Google provides the tools necessary to encode long paths as text in a compressed format. This format isn't readable; it looks like this:

```
sl`qEx`ozU}Br@y@tDoD`BDwMkEqAgMWHgDrJyXjD
```

Just a segment of an encoded path is shown here. It's a binary value encoded as text using the Base64 format, but you need not understand anything about Base64 encoded values. You can encode your paths into similar strings, transmit the strings to the client, and then decode the path in your script to generate the original path. The topic of encoding and decoding paths is discussed in Chapter 10 and in the file "The Encoding Library.pdf" included in this chapter's support material. The advantage of embedding the data into the script, using either encoded format or the plain-text format, is that after the page has been loaded, the data is instantly available to the script and no more trips to the server are required.

The second approach is to request the necessary paths on demand from the web server where your application is hosted. The script contains just code (and a few data items to initialize the map, perhaps) and is short. The data that defines the shapes on the map is fetched as needed from the server. On the server, you may store the data in files, or write a web service that retrieves the requested data from a database (or a local XML file, or even another remote web service) and returns it to the client script in any format you see fit. XML is a format for data exchange discussed in Chapter 10, along with an XML variation specific to geographic data known as KML (Keyhole Markup Language). XML is the universal standard for data exchange between systems today, and it's also easy to understand.

You can also push the data to the client in JSON format (the format used to describe custom objects in JavaScript, as you recall from Chapter 4). The web service may also accept arguments that determine specific datasets. For example, you can write a web service that returns the path of a metro line and expects the number or the name of the metro line as an argument. The advantage of requesting data through a web service is that the client application gets up-to-date data every time it calls the web service, and it retrieves just the data needed at the time. The topic of accessing remote web services from within a script is discussed in detail in Chapter 15.

Summary

In this chapter, you learned how to place simple drawings on a map. The shapes you read about in this chapter are all the shapes supported by Google Maps, and they're the same shapes you would use with most GIS systems.

The three geometric entities you can place on a map are lines, polygons, and circles. Lines are one-dimensional objects and have a length. Polygons are two dimensional objects and have a perimeter (which is basically their length) and area. In Chapter 10, you will learn how to calculate these attributes. It should be mentioned here that these shapes are "plastered" on a sphere and the calculation of length and area are not trivial. Fortunately, the geometry library of the API provides methods for these calculations. The geometry library of the Google Maps API is covered in detail in Chapter 10, where you will also learn how to compress paths by encoding their vertices. The geometry library also exposes methods for calculating polyline lengths and polygon areas.

You also saw the basics of editing simple shapes interactively on top of the map. The following chapter elaborates on this technique, and then you can proceed to build a highly interactive GIS application.

Interactive Drawing: The Basics of Drawing on Google Maps

In preceding chapters, you learned how to place markers to identify points of interest on the map, and how to draw shapes (lines and polygons) on the map. The process of creating a geometric shape and placing it on the map is straightforward, as long as you know the coordinates of its vertices. For example, you can easily place a colored polygon that fits your property, as long as you know the coordinates of your property's vertices. This map, however, is static. The only way to change the shape on the map is to edit the page's script and provide the new, corrected, coordinates.

In this chapter, you learn how to design applications that enable users to truly interact with the map and design shapes right on the map. You will build a web application that allows users to annotate maps dynamically by drawing lines and polygons on the map with the mouse, using the map's features as guidelines. The ability to interact with Google Maps requires quite a bit of code, but after mastering the basic techniques, you will be able to build highly interactive mapping applications with rich GIS features. You will also learn how to exploit this functionality from within your Windows applications and how to control the drawing process from within a Windows application's interface.

NOTE This chapter contains some "serious" JavaScript. The good news is that the scripts you're going to develop in this chapter are self-contained: You can embed a file with the script in any page, or include it in your client script with the `<script>` directive, and the "shape drawing" functionality will become instantly available to your application. I will try to explain every bit of JavaScript code presented in this chapter, mostly for the benefit of readers who are not familiar with JavaScript, or readers who wish to understand JavaScript well enough to write mapping applications.

Who Needs to Draw on a Map?

Do you really need applications for drawing on a map? The need for specialized and/or customized tools for interacting with maps increases by the day. As maps become mainstream technology and data acquire spatial characteristics, the need for all types of mapping applications is on the rise. Spatial data types are supported by most modern databases; Google is making available all kinds of spatial data through Fusion tables; even traditional tools such as PowerPoint and Visio now provide tools for adding a spatial dimension to business data.

There's a world of difference between placing items on the map from within your script and enabling your users to draw on the map. Both types of applications are useful, but one of them is static, while the other one is dynamic. If you need to place a large pipe network or the outline of a new apartment complex on the map, then you will get the required coordinates from the engineering or architectural plans. AutoCAD, for example, can export lines and shapes in many different geocoding formats, including KML. If you can obtain the coordinates of the various shapes you want to view on the map, then you don't need anything more than a bunch of statements that place lines and shapes on the map. You will create a static, or a semidynamic web page, to present the shapes to the users.

But what if the coordinates are not available? If this is case, you must zoom into a roadmap or aerial view of the map and pinpoint the coordinates of a location. You already know how to request the coordinates of any point on the globe by clicking at its location. In many situations, we use Google services to locate features on a map, rather than look at features based on their coordinates. Sure, if you have access to the blueprints of a subway structure, you can create lines for the various routes and place them on the map, even though the actual tunnels are under the earth's surface. If you don't have access to precise geo-coordinates, however, your best bet is to use Google Maps to request the geo-coordinates directly from the map's features by requesting the mouse coordinates, as you saw in the Basic Map Events sample application of Chapter 5. The interactive drawing features you're going to read about in this chapter will help you build applications that enable users to literally design on the map: to create a line or shape by clicking one feature after the other in an aerial or map view. These features could be the corners of a property, the stops along a route, points along a railroad track, trails, and so on. Other applications include placing on the map paths generated by a GPS device, the design of geo-fences manually on the map, and endless others.

Beyond a basic web application for drawing on maps, in this chapter you're also going to see a Windows application for tracing natural or man-made features. The Map Traces Windows application, which is discussed in the last section of this chapter, was used to trace the lines of the Paris Metro system and some highways. These datasets are used in sample applications in later chapters. The most advanced application contained in this book is a GIS application based on Google Maps. This application, which is discussed in detail in Chapter 12, relies on the techniques introduced here.

Why Windows Applications

Most major GIS systems are implemented as Windows applications that run on the desktop. Placing complex networks on a map is not something you can do with a web application. It involves a lot of operations and many trips to the server. Web applications are not yet as flexible and as elegant as Windows applications. Web applications can't provide multiple synchronized windows; they cannot even access the local clipboard or the target computer's file system to store the spatial data in a local file. Generating custom printouts from within a web application is another thorny issue. A lot of work is being done to bring the ease of the desktop to the Web but we aren't there yet. While it's easier to create a sassy interface with rich graphics for the Web, a highly interactive web interface with custom components requires a lot of JavaScript code.

Once you have placed your network on a map, you can create web applications to present various views of the map to viewers. But you will need the richness of a typical Windows interface to lay out your data on the map, validate your data, and create custom views for your users.

Web applications are great for reaching a potentially huge audience but certain types of applications are best implemented as desktop applications, especially if they're going to be used within the confines of a corporate environment. Luckily, it's possible to embed maps in a Windows application and manipulate the map from within a rich Windows interface using a .NET language. The main sample application of this chapter is implemented both as a web and as a Windows application, and you will decide the type of application that suits your specific requirements best.

A Simple Web Application for Drawing on Maps

In this chapter, you will build the the Interactive Drawing application, which is shown in Figure 9-1. It's a web application that allows users to draw lines and shapes on top of Google Maps with the mouse. The figure shows a polygon delimiting the island of Madagascar; the polygon was drawn with the mouse on top of a Google map. The markers you see in the figure identify the vertices of the polygon, and you can adjust the polygon's exact shape by moving the markers with the mouse.

The script of the `Interactive Drawing.html` web page contains all the logic for interactive drawing and the code that implements it. Figure 9-2 is the Windows version of the same application, which is based on the script of the web application. Users can draw on the map using the very same techniques, only this time the commands are initiated from within a Windows application's interface. Depending on your HTML skills, you can implement a much better looking interface for the web application, but it will never be as rich as the Windows interface.

Before you start writing code for either application, you need to design a model for the user's interface: How will the user initiate the various actions and how will the application react to the mouse events. Then you can write code to implement the interaction model. The interaction model will be implemented mostly in JavaScript because the API can't be accessed directly from within a .NET language.

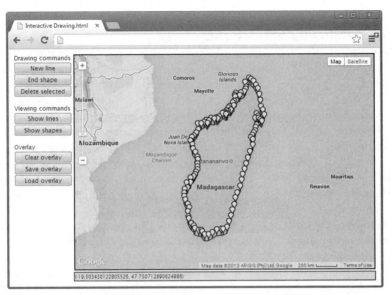

Figure 9-1   A web application for drawing shapes on maps interactively

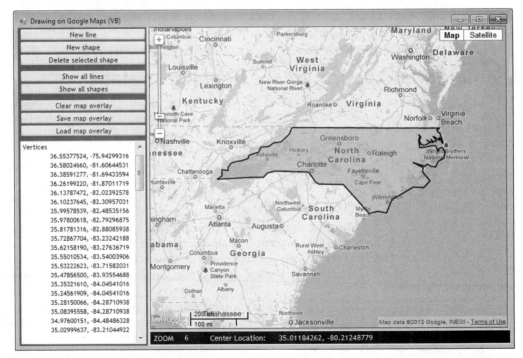

Figure 9-2   The Windows version of the web application shown in Figure 9-1 with a different polygon

Outlining the Interaction Model

Let's start by laying out a model for the user's interaction with the map, beginning with the most basic operation, which is the drawing of a path. Because both polylines and polygons are based on a path, all you really need is a mechanism to draw and edit the underlying path. To draw a path with the mouse, you need to provide an intuitive interface for the following operations:

- Insertion of new vertices
- Relocation of existing vertices
- Deletion of existing vertices

The following is the (proposed) process of drawing a new path with point-and-click operations:

1. The user signifies his intention to draw a shape by clicking a button or a link on the page, such as the buttons in the left pane of the page shown in Figure 9-1. The application sets up a `Polyline` or `Polygon` object that will be shaped as the user adds new vertices to it.

2. From this point on, and every time the user clicks somewhere on the map, a new vertex is appended to the path and a line segment that connects this vertex to the last one (if one exists) is drawn automatically. The shape consists of vertices, which are identified with markers on the map. Consecutive markers are connected by line segments that are drawn as each vertex is added to the path.

3. The markers on the shape's vertices remain visible until the user ends the editing operation. These markers allow users to edit the shape while they're drawing it: Users can move any of the existing vertices around by dragging the corresponding marker with the mouse. The path is reshaped as the user drags each marker.

4. The user can also insert new vertices to the current path by clicking any of the existing markers. A new vertex is inserted in the existing path halfway between the current vertex and the previous one, and the new vertex is identified with its own marker so that users can reposition the new vertex as desired.

5. The user can remove a vertex from the polygon by right-clicking it. As with the other editing operations, the path on the map is updated instantly.

6. To end the path, the user must click another button, or link, on the page (or the same button, if it's used as a toggle). Upon ending the editing operation, the markers that identify the path's vertices are removed and the shape is finalized on the map.

Figure 9-3 demonstrates the process of drawing a polygon with the mouse. Every time you click the map, a new vertex is added to the polygon. The numbers next to each marker were placed to show the order of the clicks on the map. Upon ending the drawing, the shape remains on the map, but the markers are removed.

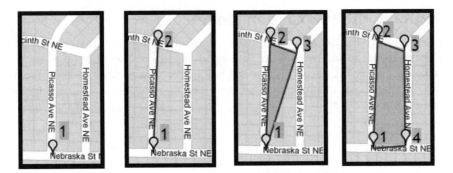

Figure 9-3 Drawing a new polygon with the mouse on top of Google Maps

The proposed technique works nicely even for shapes with many vertices. The application becomes sluggish if you attempt to edit a shape with over 1,000 vertices, but for reasonable sized shapes there are no delays. Very large shapes, however, can't be created or edited manually. They're generated by an application, or loaded from a resource. In Chapter 11, you will see an example of loading a KML file with over 500 polygons and a total of over 100,000 vertices on Google Maps.

Obviously, the user can't start another shape while editing one. Moreover, the usual map operations, like dragging the map and zooming in/out, should remain functional. All the user interaction with the map must take place in the `click` event of the map (for inserting new vertices) and the `drag`, `click`, and `rightclick` events of the markers that identify the vertices (for moving a vertex, inserting a new vertex, and deleting an existing vertex respectively).

Google's Editable Shapes and the Drawing Manager

The `Polyline` and `Polygon` objects provide the `editable` property, which you can set to `true` to create editable polylines and polygons. The problem with the editable shapes is that they implement their own interaction model, which you can't customize to suit your needs. Google also provides the Drawing Library, which contains a graphical interface for drawing shapes on the map. It displays its own icon menus and, somehow, helps users draw on the map. You can look it up in the documentation, but it requires quite a bit of programming, while at the same time you're limited by its interface.

If you're going to interact heavily with Google Maps, I recommend that you implement your own interface. Besides, the custom script you will develop to suit your exact requirements will be readily available to external applications, so you can embed the map in a Windows application. In this chapter, I am laying the foundation for building an ambitious GIS application, not merely providing a simple mechanism for placing a few shapes on the map.

A Simple Starting Point

If you're learning JavaScript to develop map-enabled applications and you're not comfortable with the structure of long scripts and events, you should start with the `Basic Drawing` `.html` application, presented in this section. This application is a web page, very similar to the Basic Map page used in preceding chapters to display a map on a web page. The only drawing feature added to the basic map is the drawing of polygons. It's the simplest possible application for demonstrating the fundamentals of drawing on the map. If you're comfortable with JavaScript, or you find the application really trivial, just skip it and explore the full application discussed in the section "The Interactive Drawing Application." Figure 9-4 shows the web page you're going to build. The page contains a Google map, as usual, and three buttons: the New Shape button, which starts/ends the process of drawing a new shape; the Delete Shape button, which deletes the selected shape; and the Show Shapes button, which displays the basic data for each shape on the map in an alert box. The image was captured while drawing the outline of the Île de la Cité island in Paris, and the first button's caption has changed from New Shape to End Shape. For the time being, ignore the Delete Shape and Show Shapes buttons.

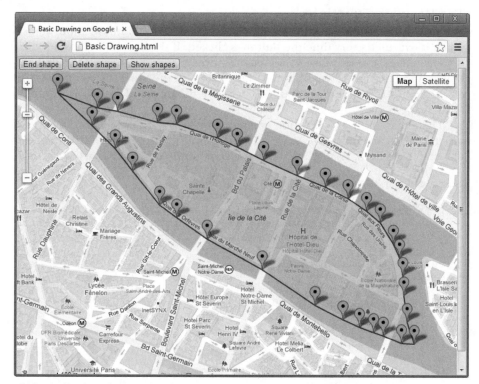

Figure 9-4   A simple web page that demonstrates the most basic drawing features

To create the `Basic Drawing.html` page, make a copy of the `Basic Map.html` application of Chapter 2 and place the three buttons at the top of the page, as shown in Figure 9-4. Here's the `<body>` section of the new page:

```
<body bgcolor="#b0DDb0" onload="initialize();">
  <input type="button" id="bttnShape" value="New shape"
         onclick="if (this.value == 'New shape') {
                     this.value='End shape'; startShape(randomID())}
                   else {
                     this.value='New shape'; endShape()}"
  />
  <input type="button" id="bttnDelete" value="Delete shape"
         onclick="removeSelectedShape()"/>
  <input type="button" id="bttnShow" value="Show shapes"
         onclick="showShapes()"/>
  <div>
    <div id="map_canvas"></div>
  </div>
</body>
```

The Drawing Functions

The `onclick` attribute of the New Shape button is set to an inline anonymous function, which is executed every time the button is clicked. If the button is clicked while its caption is "New shape," the script calls the `startShape()` function to start the drawing of the new shape. If the caption of the button is "End shape" at the time, the script calls the `endShape()` function to commit the shape on the map and resets the button's caption to "New shape."

The `startShape()` function creates a new `Polygon` object, the `poly` variable, and sets its path to an empty `MVCArray`. The polygon is then placed on the map with the `setMap()` method. Listing 9-1 shows the code of the `startShape()` function.

Listing 9-1
Starting the
drawing of a new
shape on the map

```
function startShape(shapeGuid) {
    if (drawingShape == true ) {
        alert('You are already drawing a shape. Please end ' +
              'the current operation before starting a new shape');
        return;
    }
    currentShapeGuid=shapeGuid;
    drawingShape = true;
    poly = new google.maps.Polygon({
                strokeWeight: 2, strokeColor: 'maroon',
                fillColor: selectedColor
            });
    poly.setMap(map);
    poly.setPath(new google.maps.MVCArray([path]));
    map.setOptions({ draggableCursor: 'crosshair' });
}
```

Each shape is identified by an ID value; you will see shortly how this ID is generated. You may prefer to prompt the user for the shape's ID or name; just make sure it's a unique name.

The function starts by making sure that the user isn't drawing a shape already by examining the `drawingShape` variable. If this variable, which is declared outside the function, is `true`, the function exits and doesn't initiate a new shape while the user is already drawing one. Otherwise, it sets the variable `currentShapeGuid` to the value passed as an argument, which is the ID of the current shape. It also sets the `drawingShape` variable to `true` to indicate that the user is drawing a new shape.

Then the code creates a new `Polygon` object, the `poly` variable. The polygon's path is set to a dark red color, the width of the outline is set to 2 pixels, and the fill color is set to the global variable `selectedColor`. These settings are applied to the polygon while it's being drawn so that it will stand out from the other polygons on the map. The `poly` variable is declared at the script level and is used later in the `endShape()` function, which ends the drawing of the path and commits the shape.

The path of the shape is stored in the `path` array, which is another global variable. The `path` variable is used to store a collection of points, which in turn set the shape's path. The path is initially empty, but it will be populated gradually as the user creates new vertices by clicking on the map.

Adding New Vertices to the Path

Next, you must provide the code to add new points to the shape's path. This action takes place from within the map's `click` event handler so that every time the user clicks on the map, a new vertex is appended to the current path. You must define a listener for the map's `click` event, the `addPoint()` function, and associate it with the event using the following statement:

```
google.maps.event.addListener(map, 'click', addPoint)
```

The `addPoint()` function must append a new point to the shape's path every time the user clicks on the map and is shown in Listing 9-2.

Listing 9-2
Appending a
new point to the
current path,
when the map is
clicked

```
function addPoint(event) {
    if (drawingShape == true ) {
        path.insertAt(path.length, event.latLng);
        var shapeMarker = new google.maps.Marker({
                            position: event.latLng,
                            map: map, draggable: true
                        });
        shapeMarkers.push(shapeMarker);
    }
}
```

The `addPoint()` function reacts to the `click` event only if the `drawingShape` variable is `true`. Otherwise, the event is ignored. The script starts by adding a new point to the `path` array. Because the `path` variable is an `MVCArray`, and not a simple array, the code uses the `setAt()` method to append a new location to the path and not the `push()` method. As the `path` array is modified, the shape is updated automatically. Then it creates a new marker to identify the new point, the `shapeMarker` object. Each vertex is identified with a marker to help users edit the shape by dragging its vertices around with the mouse. Note that the `Marker` object's `draggable` attribute is set to `true`. The marker is then added to the `shapeMarkers` array, this time with a call to the `push()` method.

Note that the listener for the click event accepts the coordinates of the point that was clicked through the event argument, which is passed to the listener by default; you don't even have to specify the argument in the addListener() method that calls the addPoint() function.

Repositioning Vertices

You must keep a reference to all markers on the map because you want to be able to access them at any time. The markers are draggable, but the shape won't be affected when a marker is dragged to a new location. You must provide the code to change the corresponding entry in the path array. This action must take place from within another event listener, the listener for the dragend event of the marker. Add a listener to the dragend event of the shapeMarker variable with the following statement, which must appear before the statement that adds the shapeMarker variable to the shapeMarkers array:

```
google.maps.event.addListener(shapeMarker, 'dragend',
    function (event) {
        var idx = null;
        for (var j = 0; j <shapeMarkers.length; j++) {
            if (shapeMarkers[j] == this)   idx = j;
        }
        if (idx != null) path.setAt(idx, this.getPosition());
    }
);
```

The listener for the dragend event is defined as an inline function, which iterates through all markers in the shapeMarkers array and locates the current marker. It does so by comparing each element of the array with the marker that was dragged (represented by the keyword this). The index of the marker that was dragged is stored in the idx variable and the last statement sets the matching element of the path array to the marker's new location. As soon as this statement is executed, the path is updated and the shape is adjusted on the map automatically. In short, when the user drags one of the markers that define the shape on the map, the marker's dragend event listener changes the coordinates of the corresponding vertex of the path variable, which causes the shape to change immediately.

Ending the Drawing of a Path

Finally, you must program the End Shape button by providing the endShape() function. The endShape() function ends the editing process and commits the shape on the map. To commit the shape on the map, the script changes its fill color and its border width to indicate that the shape is no longer being edited. In addition, the endShape() function must reset the drawingShape variable to false and the button's caption to "New Shape" so that the user can initiate the drawing of a new shape by clicking the same button again. Listing 9-3 shows the function that ends the drawing of a shape.

Listing 9-3
The endShape()
function
terminates the
drawing of a
shape on the
map.

```
function endShape() {
    if (drawingShape == false) {
        alert('You are not editing a shape at the moment!');
        return
    }
    if (poly.getPath() != undefined &&poly.getPath().length >2) {
        poly.setOptions({strokeColor: 'black',
```

```
                        fillColor: unselectedColor});
        var localGuid=currentShapeGuid;
        shapes[currentShapeGuid]=poly;
    else {
        poly.setMap(null);
        poly = null;
        currentShapeGuid = null;
    }
    drawingShape = false;
    clearShapeMarkers();
    path = new google.maps.MVCArray;
    map.setOptions({ draggableCursor: 'null' });
}
```

The endShape() function ends the drawing of the current shape: It changes the stroke and fill colors of the shape, adds the poly variable to the shapes collection, and removes the markers that identify the shape's vertices on the map by calling the clearShapeMarkers() function. It also resets the variables drawingShape and currentShapeGuid before exiting. Note that the script makes sure that the new shape has more than two vertices; if not, it's not a closed shape (polygon). It's either a single point, or a line with two points, and it's rejected. In this case, the function just removes the shape from the map and sets the poly variable to null.

The Missing Features

Two very basic operations were not implemented in this simple drawing application: the insertion of new vertices in the path, and the deletion of existing vertices. In the map's click event, you handle the addition of new vertices at the end of the path, but not the insertion of new vertices at arbitrary positions of the path.

You must also provide a mechanism for users to edit and delete the selected shape. To edit a shape, you must bring back the markers on the vertices and program some of their events, such as the dragend and rightclick events, to enable users to edit the shape through its markers, just as you did for new vertices. Deleting an existing shape is simpler: You must remove it from the map and also from the corresponding array. These features are implemented in the Interactive Drawing.html application, already shown in Figure 9-1, which is discussed next.

The Interactive Drawing Application

The Interactive Drawing application is similar to the Basic Drawing application, and it includes the missing features mentioned in the last paragraph. It's also based on a more elegant interface, which you can easily extend with custom features.

The Interactive Drawing application allows you to draw both lines and polygons on the map. Let's start with the script variables for storing the shape data. The lines and shapes collections store the Polyline and Polygon objects placed on the map, and they're declared with the following statements:

```
var lines = {};
var shapes = {};
```

The shape being drawn is stored in one of the two variables: *line* or *poly*. This shape's path is updated as the user draws on the map, and when the operation completes, the variable is appended to the `lines` or `shapes` collection. The `currentShapeGuid` variable stores the ID of the currently selected variable. This variable is set to the ID of the shape selected on the map by clicking it with the mouse. Finally, the toggle variables `drawingLine`/`editingLine` and `drawingShape`/`editingShape` indicate the current operation. The following is the definition of the button that initiates the drawing of a new shape on the map:

```
<input id="bttnLine" type="button" value="New line"  class="button"
        onclick="if (this.value == 'New line') {
                this.value='End line'; startLine(GenerateGuid())}
            else {
                this.value='New line'; endLine()}"/>
```

The `onclick` event handler starts a new line, or ends the current editing operation by calling one of the `startLine()` and `endLine()` functions, respectively. The `startLine()` function creates a new `Polyline` object and sets its path to an empty `MVCArray` object, the `path` variable. Then the `addPoint()` function takes over: Every time the user clicks on the map, the `addPoint()` handles the event by appending a new point to the path variable, as with the Basic Drawing application.

Handling Vertices

You saw how to append new vertices to a path in the preceding sections. The `addPoint()` function takes care of this operation. Inserting new vertices between existing ones and deleting existing vertices are two more important tasks, which are carried out not in any of the map's event listeners, but in the `click` and `rightclick` event listeners of the markers.

Inserting New Vertices

When the marker that identifies the new vertex is created, its `click` event is associated with a handler that inserts a new vertex to the path. The new vertex is inserted halfway between the marker that was clicked and the following one. Here's the definition of this event handler:

```
google.maps.event.addListener(shapeMarker, 'click', function () {
        insertPoint(shapeMarker);
});
```

The `insertPoint()` function is fairly lengthy. It creates a new marker that will be placed at the location of the new vertex. The script finds out the index of the new vertex in the `path` array and inserts a new vertex at this index. Finally, it adds the usual event handlers for the `click` and `rightclick` events of the new marker. The new marker bounces for a second when placed on the map so that users notice it immediately. Once a new vertex becomes part of the shape's path, users can edit it just like any other vertex. Listing 9-4 shows the insertPoint() function.

Listing 9-4
The implementation of the insertPoint() function

```
function insertPoint(thisMarker) {
    var image = new google.maps.MarkerImage(smallYellowPin,
                        new google.maps.Size(20, 20),
                        new google.maps.Point(0, 0),
                        new google.maps.Point(5, 20))
    var insMarker = new google.maps.Marker({
        position: thisMarker.getPosition(),
        map: map,
        draggable: true,
        icon: image,
        animation: google.maps.Animation.DROP
    });
    var idx = -1;
    for (i = 0; i < shapeMarkers.length; i++) {
        if (shapeMarkers[i] == thisMarker) { idx = i; }
    }
    var pt1 = idx;
    var pt2 = idx - 1;
    if (pt2 == -1) {
        idx = 1; pt2 = 1; pt1 = 0
    }
    var positionLat = (shapeMarkers[pt1].getPosition().lat() +
                        shapeMarkers[pt2].getPosition().lat()) / 2
    var positionLng = (shapeMarkers[pt1].getPosition().lng() +
                        shapeMarkers[pt2].getPosition().lng()) / 2
    var newMarkerPosition =
                    new google.maps.LatLng(positionLat, positionLng);
    path.insertAt(idx, newMarkerPosition);
    insMarker.position = newMarkerPosition;
    shapeMarkers.splice(idx, 0, insMarker);
    google.maps.event.addListener(insMarker, 'rightclick', function () {
        insMarker.setMap(null);
        for (var i = 0; i < shapeMarkers.length &&
                        shapeMarkers[i] != insMarker; i++);
        shapeMarkers.splice(i, 1);
        path.removeAt(i);
    });
    // Attach an event handler to the new marker's click event.
    google.maps.event.addListener(insMarker, 'click', function () {
        insertPoint(insMarker);
    });
    // Attach an event handler to the new marker's dragend event.
    google.maps.event.addListener(insMarker, 'dragend', function () {
                var idx;
                for (var i = 0; i < shapeMarkers.length; i++) {
                    if (shapeMarkers[i] == this) idx = i;
                }
                path.setAt(idx, this.getPosition());
    });
}  // end of insertPoint() function
```

This is the lengthiest function of the application, but it's worth understanding how it works. The code calculates the midpoint between the marker that was clicked and the preceding one. The coordinates of the new point are stored in the positionLat and positionLng variables, which are then used as the location of the marker that identifies the new vertex. These two variables are the coordinates of the point to be inserted, which lies halfway between the two consecutive vertices.

For each new vertex inserted into the path, the script inserts a new element in the path array and a new marker in the shapeMarkers array. The path variable is an MVCArray object, and it provides the insertAt() method, which inserts a new item at the specified index. As soon as the new vertex is inserted, the path on the map is updated automatically. The shapeMarkers variable is a plain array and doesn't support this method. To insert an item in an array, you must call the splice() method, passing as an argument the index of the element to be inserted and the element to be inserted. Contrast the statement that inserts a new element in an MVCArray object:

```
path.insertAt(idx, newMarkerPosition);
```

with the statement that inserts a new element in a regular array:

```
shapeMarkers.splice(idx, 0, insMarker)
```

The first argument of the splice() method is the index where the array will be split, the second argument is the number of elements to be removed, and the last argument is the object(s) to be inserted in the array. The script always inserts a single element into the shapeMarkers array; to insert multiple elements, you must pass an array as the last argument. As with the new vertices that are appended to the path, the script adds the handlers for the click, rightclick, and dragend events of the newly created vertex.

Deleting Existing Vertices

Let's get another trivial editing operation out of the way, that of deleting a marker from the shape while editing it. The removal of the vertex will take place from within the marker's rightclick event: When the user right-clicks a marker, the corresponding vertex is removed from the shape, along with the matching marker. First, you must add a listener for the rightclick event to the shape. The event listener's code is shown in Listing 9-4.

The listener is implemented with an inline function that goes through all elements in the shapeMarkers arrays until it finds the element insMarker. When this happens, it uses the value of the i variable, which is the index of the marker that was clicked in the collection and removes the element at that index. The path variable is an MVCArray and you must use the removeAt() method to remove an element.

The code for creating new polygons and placing them on the map is practically identical. Just like lines, polygons are based on paths and instead of creating a Polyline object based on the path created by the user on the map, the script creates a Polygon object.

Handling Shapes

Once the shape is on the map, you need to provide a mechanism to select it. Users need to be able to select a shape in order to edit or delete it, or request additional attributes of the shape. You will see in the following chapter how to request the length of a line and the area of a polygon. You may also associate additional data with each shape, such as a description, operational characteristics, history and maintenance data, anything that suits your application. To enable these operations, you must provide a mechanism for selecting a shape with the mouse, and this will obviously take place in the shape's click event, which you haven't associated with a listener yet.

Handling the Shape's Events

Every time a new shape is created, its click event is associated with an event handler that allows users to select the shape by clicking on it. To select a shape, the script calls the selectShape() function, which changes the background color of a polygon, or the color and width of a line. The selectShape() function must first unselect the previously selected shape (reset its outline and fill colors) and then select another one. To unselect the currently selected shape, it calls the unselectShapes() method, which resets the colors of all shapes, regardless of whether they're selected or not. Alternatively, you can keep track of the currently selected shape and reset the colors of this shape only. Listing 9-5 shows the implementation of the selectShape() and unselectShapes() functions.

Listing 9-5
The select
Shape() and
unselect
Shapes()
functions

```
function selectShape(Guid) {
    unselectShapes();
    shapes[Guid].setOptions({fillColor: selectedColor});
    alert('The ID of the shape you selected is: ' + Guid);
    currentShapeGuid = Guid;
}

function unselectShapes() {
    for (key in shapes)
    shapes[key].setOptions({fillColor: unselectedColor});
}
```

When the user clicks a shape on the map, the script detects the action through the shape's click event and displays a simple message with the selected shape's ID. You can use this ID to access a database through a web service and request additional data about the selected item. The data may reside in a database and your application can access it at will, or you may store additional information in custom objects, which you can then assign to each shape, through the objInfo attribute.

Run the application and check out how it interacts with the user. You can easily create any shape (line or polygon) by adding points to the shape's path. The more vertices you add, the better you will approximate the shape's outline. Note that sometimes you'll want to place a vertex at a point that's in the shape's interior. Clicking into the shaded area that represents the shape doesn't create a new vertex because the click event is intercepted by the shape, not the map. In this case, you must create a new vertex outside the shape and then drag it into position with the mouse.

Deleting Shapes

To remove an existing shape from the map, add a new button to the form, the Delete Shape button, and associate its `onclick` event with a script that removes the selected shape. The following HTML code adds the Delete Selected button:

```
<input type="button" id="bttnDelete" value="Delete selected"
       class="button" onclick="removeSelectedShape()"/>
```

The `removeSelectedShape()` function removes the selected shape from the map, as well as from the `shapes` collection. Listing 9-6 shows the implementation of `removeSelectedShape()` function:

Listing 9-6
The remove
SelectShape()
function

```
function removeSelectedShape() {
    if (drawingLine || editingLine || drawingShape || editingShape)
        alert('Please end the current edit operation first, then
                delete the selected item');
        return;
    }
    if (lines[currentShapeGuid]) {
        lines[currentShapeGuid].setMap(null);
        delete lines[currentShapeGuid];
    }
    if (shapes[currentShapeGuid]) {
        shapes[currentShapeGuid].setMap(null);
        delete shapes[currentShapeGuid];
    }
    currentShapeGuid = null;
}
```

The `removeSelectedShape()` function removes the currently selected shape, be it a polyline or a polygon. The ID of the currently selected shape is stored at all times in the `currentShapeGuid` variable. When no shape is selected on the map, this variable is set to null. The expression `lines[currentShapeGuid]` returns true if the `lines` collection contains the element with the specified key.

The selected shape is identified by the `currentShapeGuid` variable, and the code uses this variable as the key to the `shapes` collection to (a) remove the shape from the map by settings its map attribute to null and (b) remove it from the collection as well. If you remove the shape from the collection but not from the map, you will have a shape on the map that you will no longer be able to access from within your code. Finally, the code sets the `currentShapeGuid` to null to indicate that no shape is selected on the map.

Customizing the Vertex Icons

If the proposed interaction model isn't quite what you need, you still have the option to adjust it. If you find the markers too bulky, for example, use a smaller or a custom icon. You can even use small draggable discs to represent the vertices, as in the shape shown in Figure 9-5.

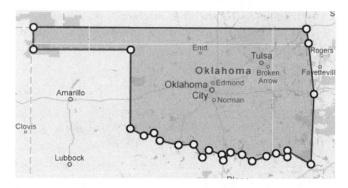

Figure 9-5 Using filled circles as marker symbols in the drawing application

The icon used to identify the vertices in Figure 9-5 is not a `Circle` object; it's one of the built-in symbols, as discussed in Chapter 8. Changing the marker's icon, as you'll recall from that chapter, is really simple. Define the icon with a statement like the following:

```
Var vertexIcon = {
     path: google.maps.SymbolPath.CIRCLE, offset: "0%",
     scale: 5, strokeColor: 'black', strokeWeight: 2,
     strokeOpacity: 1, fillColor: 'yellow', fillOpacity:1 };
```

and then assign the `vertexIcon` variable to the `icon` attribute of the Marker object. Simply replace the statement that creates the marker in the `addPoint()` function with the following:

```
shapeMarker = new google.maps.Marker({
               position: event.latLng, icon: icon, map: map,
               draggable: true
               });
```

The new statement is identical to the old one, with the exception of the `icon` attribute. The vertices are identified by markers as before, only this time the marker has a custom shape. Note that the colors of the icons are customizable. If you really need some unique icons for your application, you can use SVG graphics. SVG graphics are used in Chapter 19 and they're discussed in more detail in Appendix A.

You're in control of the script that manipulates the shapes on the map and you can easily adjust it to suit your specific requirements. For example, you can create an initial path with dozens of vertices between the two endpoints, equally spaced apart, which you can move in place using the underlying map's features as guides.

Retrieving Shape Data

Another useful operation of the `Interactive Drawing.html` web page is the ability to retrieve information about the shapes on the map and display it to the user in a pop-up dialog. To view a summary of all shapes on the map, click the Show Shapes button. For each shape, the script displays its ID and the number of vertices that make up its path. The data retrieval takes place in the ShowShapes() function of the script, which is shown in Listing 9-7.

Listing 9-7
Displaying shape
data

```
function showShapes() {
    var contentString = '';
    for (key in shapes) {
        contentString += 'ID: ' + key + '\n';
        contentString += '        Number of vertices: ' +
        shapes[key].getPath().length + '\n';
    }
    if (contentString == '') {
        alert('No shapes were found on the map!');
        return;
    }
    else
        alert(contentString);
}
```

The code iterates through the items in the shapes collection. Each item in this collection is a Polygon object, and the script uses the current item in each iteration to retrieve information about a different shape. You can easily add the coordinates of the shape's vertices, or other data. You can print the coordinates of all vertices on an element in your page and export them to any other application in the target computer with a copy and paste operation. In the next chapter, you're going to learn how to calculate the lengths of lines and areas of shapes, and you'll be able to display even more useful data about the shapes on the map.

The loop uses the expression key in shapes to iterate through the collection's keys, and then accesses the current element in the shapes collection with the expression shapes[key]. Each element of the shapes collection is a Polygon object so you can call its getPath() method to retrieve its path. The strokeColor property will return the shape's outline color, the fillColor property will return the shape's fill color, and so on.

A Pseudo-GUID Generator

As I mentioned, each shape is identified by a GUID value. JavaScript doesn't provide a function to generate GUIDs. The script contains the GenerateGuid() function, which generates random hexadecimal values. These values are not true GUIDs and are not globally unique. In your application, you will probably use meaningful names for the entities you place on the map.

A Windows Map Drawing Application

The Interactive Drawing application you just created is a web page. It allows you to draw shapes on the map interactively, and it has an interface that's both functional and intuitive. How about a Windows application with the same drawing features based on the same script? This is quite possible, almost trivial if you have read Chapter 6, which describes how to embed a web page in a Windows interface and use the web application's script from within the Windows application's code. To make this section a little easier to read, let's refer to the Windows application as the host application and the web page as the embedded application (because this is exactly what it's all about).

This section's sample project is the Simple Drawing project. It's a .NET drawing application implemented as a solution with two projects: one in Visual Basic and one in C#. If you're not familiar with either language, but you wish to see this application in action, you can find the application's executable in this chapter's support material.

NOTE   If you're not familiar with Visual Studio, you can still use the application by double-clicking the .exe file in the EXECUTABLE folder. You may be prompted to install the .NET Framework 4.0, if it's not already installed on your system. The .NET Framework will be installed automatically, after you give your permission in the appropriate prompt. The executable was included to help readers who have not used Visual Studio yet to get the feel of a desktop application with embedded Google maps.

Let's look at the approach from a designer's perspective: The Windows application must take advantage of the script you have already developed for the web application. Once the web application is embedded into a .NET project, its functionality should become available to the host application as if it were another .NET component. Imagine that someone has packaged all the functionality you need in order to control the map from within a .NET application in a reusable class. This is exactly what you're going to do in the following sections.

Interacting with the Script from a .NET Application

To interact with the script of the embedded application from within your .NET application's code, you need to:

1. Call functions in the embedded application's script
2. Allow the script to call methods in your application

By calling script functions, you can initiate certain actions, similar to invoking the same functions in a button `onclick` event listener. As the user interacts with the map, some of the user's actions will be handled by the script, but certain actions must be reported to the host application. The script can call public methods in the host application and these method calls are basically event notifications.

If you had designed your own class to control a Google map, you would have exposed the `startLine()` method to initiate the drawing of a line, and you would call this method with an expression like the following:

```
google.startLine(Guid)
```

Instead, you must call the `startLine()` function with the following statement:

```
WebBrowser1.Document.InvokeScript("startLine", {Guid})
```

Not much of a problem, is it? In Chapter 12, you're going to package the functionality of the script in a custom class, but let's take it one step at a time. In this section, you'll be manipulating the embedded application's script directly from within your .NET code.

The .NET Code

You're ready to look at the code of the Simple Drawing Windows application that provides the same functionality as the Interactive Drawing web application. The interface looks pretty much the same, but it's designed differently. The Windows interface consists of Windows controls, such as buttons, labels, and the like. The map is displayed on a `WebBrowser` control, which is the container for a web page and its script.

Loading the Map

When the form is loaded, the following code is executed to load the map into the `WebBrowser` control:

```
lblOperation.Text = ""
WebBrowser1.ObjectForScripting = Me
WebBrowser1.ScriptErrorsSuppressed = False
Dim html = My.Computer.FileSystem.ReadAllText(
            "..\..\Map Components\MapPage.html")
WebBrowser1.DocumentText = html
```

The `MapPage.html` file contains both the HTML code for the page to be displayed in the `WebBrowser` control as well as the script of the application, and it's stored in the Map Components folder under the project's folder, as discussed in Chapter 6.

The code behind the various buttons is straightforward. The buttons invoke the same script functions as with the web version of the application, only they use the `InvokeScript()` method of the `WebBrowser` control to access the script.

When the user clicks the New Shape button, for example, the following statements are executed to initiate the line drawing process with the `startShape()` function of the script. If the application is in the process of drawing a line, it calls the `endShape()` function. The following Listing 9-8 is the code behind the button:

Listing 9-8
Initiating the drawing of a shape from within a Visual Basic application

```
Private Sub bttnNewShape_Click(sender As Object, e As EventArgs)
                Handles bttnNewShape.Click
    If bttnNewShape.Text = "New shape" Then
        WebBrowser1.Document.InvokeScript("startShape",
                    System.Guid.NewGuid.ToString})
        bttnNewShape.Text = "End shape"
        bttnNewLine.Enabled = False
        bttnDeleteSelected.Enabled = False
    Else
        WebBrowser1.Document.InvokeScript("endShape")
        bttnNewShape.Text = "New shape"
        bttnNewLine.Enabled = True
```

```
            bttnDeleteSelected.Enabled = True
        End If
End Sub
```

Most of the statements actually modify properties of the controls on the form to reflect the current state of the application. You should focus on the statements that invoke the appropriate function in the script. The code behind the New Line button is equivalent to the code of the New Shape button: Instead of calling the `startShape()` function, it calls the `startLine()` function to initiate the drawing of a line.

The script used in the Simple Drawing project is practically identical to the script you used for the Interactive Drawing web application, except that the new script "fires" events by calling methods in the host application. The host application's code is also very short and almost trivial. All the action takes place in the script and the external application does two things: It initiates certain actions when the user clicks the buttons in the left pane, and it handles the events it receives from the script in the embedded application.

Handling the Map's Events

A typical map event is the `drag` event. When the user drags the map, the script receives the `drag` event. Instead of handling it on its own, the script passes this event to the external application with the following event listener:

```
google.maps.event.addListener(map, 'drag',
                function () { window.external.MapDragged() });
```

The host application contains a public subroutine called `MapDragged` (with the exact same spelling), which is invoked by the script to handle the `drag` event. The event handler in the .NET application does what most scripts would have done: It updates its own interface with an event handler like the following:

```
Public Sub MapDragged()
    Dim cPoint = Convert.ToString(
            WebBrowser1.Document.InvokeScript("getCenter"))
    lblCoordinates.Text = Xml.XmlConvert.ToDouble(
                cPoint.Split("|")(0)).ToString("0.00000000") & ", " &
            Xml.XmlConvert.ToDouble(
                cPoint.Split("|")(1)).ToString("0.00000000")
End Sub
```

The `MapDragged()` method doesn't accept any arguments, so it must call the `getCenter()` function in the script to retrieve the coordinates of the map's center location and display its latitude and longitude on a `Label` control. This control is placed right below the `WebBrowser` control with the map and functions as a status bar. The code extracts the individual coordinates and formats them with eight decimal digits. In Chapter 6, you saw how to exchange data with the script using custom objects. I haven't used custom objects in this application, because I wanted to demonstrate how to use the same script developed for the web version of Simple Drawing application as the foundation of the equivalent Windows application.

You can open the Simple Drawing solution in Visual Studio and examine its code. The solution contains two identical projects, one in Visual Basic and one in C#. Both projects share the same web page to embed a Google map into the WebBrowser control on their main form and the same script. Choose your favorite language and add more features to the application. The project contains a relatively small number of statements to invoke functions in the script. Other than that, it's the script that does all the work and interacts with the user.

The Map Tracing Application

In this section, you explore a different approach to an application for annotating a map with drawings. This time you will build another .NET application, which handles the interaction with the user. It is a highly interactive application that would be considerably more difficult to implement in JavaScript as part of a web page. The application's interface is a typical Windows interface with rich controls and auxiliary forms. As you will see, this application uses simpler JavaScript functions at the cost of additional .NET code. If you're a JavaScript developer, you may not like the idea of relinquishing control to the external application, but it's an alternative you should consider for applications that require lots of customization. If you're a .NET developer, you'll probably love the idea of keeping the JavaScript code to a minimum and implementing the more advanced features in a high level language—whenever this is possible, of course.

The Map Traces application is written in a full-blown object-oriented language, takes advantage of the .NET Framework, and is much easier to maintain, not to mention that you can add new features to the application without touching the script. In the folder with this chapter's support material, you will find both a VB and C# version of the application.

The Map Traces application, shown in Figure 9-6, allows users to create paths by tracing features on the map. The traces you generate with the Map Traces application are paths: They're collections of vertices and each vertex has a name and a geo-coordinate. The name is optional and can be added/edited at any time; the geo-coordinates, however, are mandatory. Figure 9-6 shows the Map Traces application while it's used to trace the stations of the Paris metro system.

How to Use the Application

To create a new trace, click the New Line button. From this point on, every time you click on the map, a new point is appended to the current path. A location item is also added to the list on the right side of the form. This item is a named location, made up of the feature's name and its coordinates. The name of the new feature is initially blank, but you can edit it in-place: Just click the item's name and the program will allow you to edit the Name cell. When done, just click outside the name's area. This functionality comes out of the box with the ListView control of Visual Studio.

To insert a new location anywhere in the path, just select a point in the list and then click on the map. The new location will be inserted after the selected location in the list. You can also delete any vertex by selecting it in the list, or on the map, and pressing the DELETE key.

A key concept in this application is the selected line. This is the line whose name is selected in the ComboBox control and its vertices appear in the grid below. Every time you select another line in the ComboBox control, the corresponding `Polyline` object on the map is selected and all editing operations explained in this section apply to the selected line.

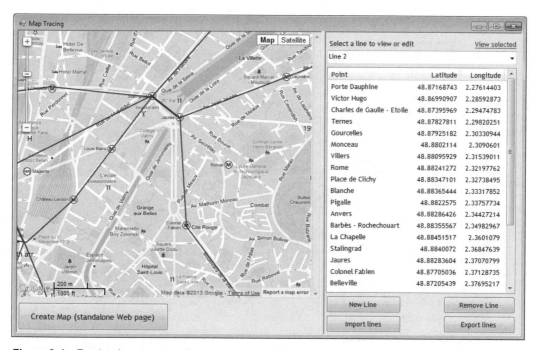

Figure 9-6   Tracing features on a Google map with a Windows application

Before you can edit a vertex, you must first locate it. If the vertices have names, you can just click the desired vertex in the list of the right pane with the mouse. A marker will appear on the map at the location of the selected vertex. The marker will bounce for a few moments so that the user can spot it immediately. You can also select a vertex on the map with the mouse. The selection technique used in this application is based on the map's `rightclick` event. Every time you right-click somewhere on the map, the program locates the nearest vertex in the selected line and places a marker at its location to identify it. A vertex of another line may be closer to the mouse location, but the application forces you to work with the selected one. This is the new line you're creating, or the line you're editing. You can, of course, change the selection logic, if you wish. You could locate the nearest vertex and then select the line it belongs to from within your code.

If you know the exact coordinates of a feature but you can't locate it on the map (it could be an underground feature not marked on the map), you can still add its location to the path using the coordinates. Just add a new point to the path, and then double-click this point in the grid and enter its coordinates in an auxiliary window. Figure 9-7 shows the auxiliary window where you can edit any vertex's data. To open this window, just double-click a vertex entry in the list. As soon as you close the auxiliary form, the path will be updated.

If you have a list of geo-coordinates, you can easily add modify the .NET application to enable users to paste a long list of coordinates in the grid and then process them sequentially. The advantage of map-enabled Windows applications is that you can implement user interaction techniques that are very difficult (or impossible) to code in JavaScript. The Map Traces application is a typical mapping application that should be implemented as a

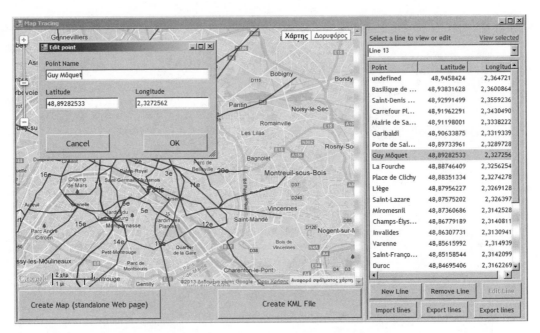

Figure 9-7   Editing the name and location of a vertex on an auxiliary form

desktop application. It takes advantage of the rich features of the Windows interface, it makes use of multiple forms, and it can save its data to a local file without the need of a server side component. Keep in mind that an application like Map Traces is not meant to be used by end users; you create the routes and then make them available to end users as stand-alone pages, or special data files that can be laid over the map. A special format for describing spatial data is the KML format, which is discussed in detail in Chapter 11. A detailed presentation of the application's code can be found in the Map Traces.pdf documents, included in this chapter's support material.

Summary

This has been a lengthy chapter, but we dealt here with a non-trivial topic. If you're interested in developing mapping applications with GIS features on top of Google Maps, by now you have all the information you need in order to design applications that enable users to interact with Google Maps.

It's relatively straightforward to draw shapes on a Google map, and the action takes place in the map's `click` event and in the `click` event of the objects that represent the shape's path, thanks to the `MVCArray` object. By setting a shape's path to an `MVCArray`, you reduce the problem of drawing polylines and polygons into manipulating the locations of a `MVCArray` with the mouse on the map.

In Chapter 12, you'll build a complete GIS application based on Google's maps and you will see two versions of a GIS application: the Web and the Windows versions.

10 Geodesic Calculations: The Geometry Library

The shapes you explored in Chapter 8 are made up of line segments that appear straight on the map. On the sphere, however, there are no straight lines; even if you could hold your hand steady and draw a "straight" line on a sphere, it would be an arc. Conversely, if you draw a straight line on a map and then wrap the paper around a sphere, the straight line will no longer be straight; it will end up as a curve on the sphere. The curved lines on the sphere are called *geodesic*. To make a long story very short, the shortest distance between any two points on the surface of a sphere lies on a geodesic circle. Google Maps treats the earth as a perfect sphere, and you need to understand the difference between the straight lines you draw on the map and the curved lines on the sphere.

A Quick Overview of the Mercator Projection

As you recall from Chapter 1, the Mercator projection introduces a substantial distortion to the sizes of the various features of the earth, such as islands and lakes. The distortion becomes more pronounced as you move away from the equator. There are several examples in this chapter that will help you "see" this distortion and understand why it can't be avoided. For the benefit of readers that skip the introductory chapters, let me repeat the best explanation of the Mercator distortion I've read so far (a very illuminating description proposed by mathematician Edward Wright in the seventeenth century). Imagine that the earth is a balloon and the features you're interested in are drawn on the surface of the balloon. Place this balloon into a hollow cylinder so that the balloon simply touches the inside of the cylinder. The points of the balloon that touch the cylinder form a circle that divides the balloon in two halves. This circle is the equator by convention. Because the balloon is a perfect sphere, any circle that divides it into two hemispheres is an equator and there's an infinity of equators you can draw on a sphere.

Now imagine that the balloon expands inside the cylinder and the features drawn on the balloon's surface are imprinted on the inside surface of the cylinder. As the balloon is inflated, more and more of its surface touches the cylinder's surface. No matter how much the balloon is expanded, however, the two poles will never touch the cylinder. This explains why you'll never see the two poles on a conventional map. Go to the Google Maps site, or open one of the mapping applications you have explored in receding chapters, and zoom out all the way. You will see part of the two arctic circles, all in white, but never the two poles.

When you unfold the cylinder, the imprint left on its inside surface is the map. The features near the equator touch the surface early in the process, before the balloon is substantially inflated. The further away you move from the equator, the more you have to expand the balloon in order to touch the cylinder. The balloon's expansion, however, causes the features to expand, which explains why the Mercator projection distorts sizes. This process preserves the local shapes and angles of the various features, at the expense of features at higher latitudes being expanded by different amounts. The meridians, which all meet at the poles, will become parallel lines, and the parallels, which wrap the earth at various latitudes, remain parallel on the flat map. And this is another reason why you'll never see the poles on a Mercator projection: The meridians run parallel to each other and they never merge (they should merge at the two poles, of course). While consecutive meridians maintain their distance around the earth, consecutive parallels are closer to one another near the equator than they are near the poles (see Figure 10-4 a little later in this chapter).

Any measurements you carry out on the map should include the distortion introduced by the projection. If you're working in small scales, you can trust the map and the current scale. Calculations that involve global features, such as the area of an island or the distance between remote cities, must be carried out on the sphere (the balloon) and not on the map, and this is the topic of this chapter. The geometry of the shapes on the sphere is known as *geodesy* and the shapes on the sphere are called *geodesic*. This chapter will help you understand geodesic shapes and the tools for calculating lengths and areas of geodesic shapes.

Understanding the Map's Scale

To verify the inaccuracy of measuring distances on the map, follow this experiment. View on Google Maps two locations, one way up north and the other near the equator. Two good candidates are Rovaniemi, Finland and the Lake Bosomtwe in Ghana, as shown in Figure 10-1. Make sure you view both places at the same zoom level, as was done to produce the two maps of Figure 10-1.

What's wrong with Figure 10-1? The two maps have the same size at the same zoom level. Did you notice how different their scales are? A segment that corresponds to one mile near the equator corresponds to more than two miles in northern Norway. That can't be correct, of course; it's a distortion introduced by the Mercator projection. When you view Rovaniemi on the map, the relative distances are correct and the distances you measure on the map are also correct, as long as you use the scale at Rovaniemi's latitude to convert inches to miles. The same is true everywhere in local scale. But as you move from Lake Bosomtwe to Rovaniemi, the scale itself changes! Even the map's scale isn't constant and it varies with latitude. The parts of the balloon near the equator touch the cylinder faster (with a lesser expansion) than the parts far away from the equator (which happens with further expansion of the balloon).

Santa Claus' Village, Rovaniemi, Finland

Lake Bosomtwe, Ghana

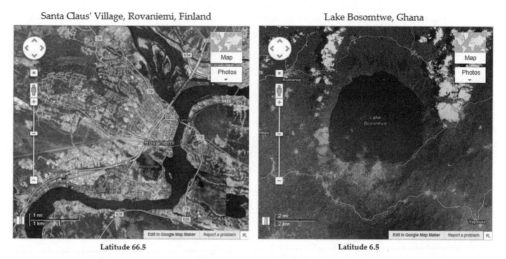

Latitude 66.5

Latitude 6.5

Figure 10-1 Two parts of the earth displayed at the same zoom level aren't immediately comparable because their scales are different.

Geodesic Lines and Shapes

The `Polyline` and `Polygon` objects have a property called `geodesic`, which is false by default. If you set it to `true`, the lines (and polygons) will be rendered on the map as geodesic shapes. Figure 10-2 shows two lines with common endpoints. The figure was generated by the `Long Geodesic Lines.html` application (the symbols of the airplanes at the start of the lines are discussed in Chapter 20). One of them has its `geodesic` property set to `true` and is rendered on the map as a curve, while the other one that appears straight has its `geodesic` property set to `false`. What's hard to understand by looking at the figure is that the geodesic path is shorter than the other one; in fact, the shortest path between the two points is the geodesic path.

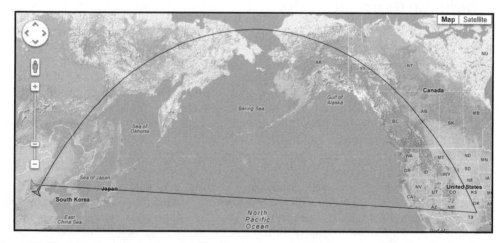

Figure 10-2 A geodesic line on the map is the shortest path between the two points on the globe.

The endpoints of the two lines are the coordinates of the Beijing and the Dallas/Fort Worth airports. Start by declaring the two endpoints as LatLng objects:

```
var DallasAirport = new google.maps.LatLng(32.89680099, -97.03800201);
var BeijingAirport = new google.maps.LatLng(39.78279877, 116.3880005);
```

Then, create a path between the two endpoints as an array of LatLng objects:

```
var path = [DallasAirport, BeijingAirport]
```

and finally, create two Polyline objects with the same path, but different settings for the geodesic property:

```
var straightRoute = new google.maps.Polyline({
        path: path, map: map,
        geodesic: false,
        strokeOpacity: 1, strokeWeight: 1,
    });
var geodesicRoute = new google.maps.Polyline({
        path: path, map: map,
        geodesic: true,
        strokeOpacity: 1, strokeWeight: 1,
    });
```

The two lines will be rendered quite differently on the map. An airplane flying from Dallas to Beijing should follow the geodesic line to make a shorter trip. (The route will be different, but only because of the air space regulations over China; what you see in the figure is indeed the shortest path between the two cities.) If the two endpoints were close together, however, you wouldn't be able to see much difference in the two paths. Modify the Long Geodesic Lines application to draw the two lines, only this time from Dallas to Austin, or from Austin to San Antonio. Over small areas of the map, the earth is practically flat and you won't notice much difference between geodesic and non-geodesic paths. The difference becomes obvious when the lines cover a substantial part of the globe.

Defining Geodesic Paths

As mentioned already, geodesic paths represent the shortest distance between two points on the globe, and they're calculated automatically by the API when the geodesic property is set to true. But how are they defined? All paths on the sphere are created as intersections of the sphere and a plane, and this intersection is always a circle. Depending on the orientation of the plane, you can create an infinite number of paths on the sphere with the same endpoints. One of these circles will split the sphere in two hemispheres, and this circle is called a *greater circle*. All other circles are called *minor circles*. Any plane that splits the earth into two hemispheres also goes through the earth's center, and this is the basic definition of the greater circle between two points: It's the intersection of the earth with a plane that touches the two points and goes through the center of the earth. The shorter arc of this circle is the geodesic route between the two locations.

This is an accurate mathematical definition and, fortunately, you don't need to understand how to draw geodesic paths on the globe. The API will do it for you, as long as you set the geodesic property to true. In addition to the Polyline object, the geodesic property applies to Polygon and Circle objects.

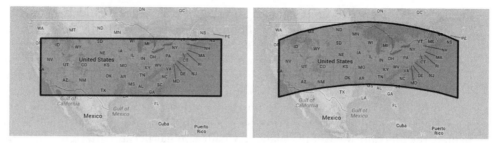

Figure 10-3   This "band-aid" shape is a rectangle wrapped around the earth.

Let's do the same with polygons. This time, you will create a `Polygon` object that spans a large area on the globe, like the ones shown in Figure 10-3. Both rectangles shown in Figure 10-3 are `Polygon` objects with their `geodesic` property set to `false` and `true`, respectively. The two shapes were created by the `The Global Bandaid.html` web page. Edit the page and change the setting of the `geodesic` property to see how it affects the way the rectangle is rendered on the globe. You can also experiment with the size of the rectangle to verify that as the rectangle is reduced in size, the distortion is reduced. The distortion depends on the location of the polygon as well; drag it around with the mouse to see how its shape changes.

Start by defining the rectangle that spans most of the United States with the following path:

```
var points = [
     new google.maps.LatLng(45.0, -60.0),
     new google.maps.LatLng(45.0, -120.0),
     new google.maps.LatLng(30.0, -120.0),
     new google.maps.LatLng(30.0, -60.0)
];
```

and then create a polygon based on this path:

```
var polygon = new google.maps.Polygon({
                 path: points,
                 map: map, geodesic: true
              });
```

This is the default polygon defined by its path and no other options, except for the `geodesic` property. The geodesic rectangle looks like a huge Band-Aid applied on the earth, doesn't it? (It wouldn't save the planet, but at least you know what it would look like.) That's pretty much what the sphere geometry does to lines and rectangles: It distorts them by converting straight lines into arcs. The source of the distortion is the Mercator projection of a spherical object onto a flat surface, which is the map. The distortion, however, becomes negligible as the area you're examining on the map becomes smaller and smaller. If the "Band-Aid" is small, the size of your neighborhood, for example, then it will remain a perfect rectangle even when applied on the globe. At small scales, the projected view of the earth is totally accurate, regardless of whether you're near the equator or not. Of course, you must take into consideration the current scale to read the map correctly.

There are other types of projections beyond the Mercator projection, yet none without some distortion. The Mercator projection is the oldest one and there are many people who consider it outdated, but for the purposes of Google Maps, it's quite adequate. For most people, the Mercator view of the planet is totally familiar because they grew up with it and all the maps they have seen in classrooms are based on this projection. Additionally, no one really cares if Greenland appears to be larger than Australia, when in reality it's less than one-third of Australia. Many people have criticized Google for its decision to go with the Mercator projection, but the phenomenal acceptance of Google Maps indicates that the engineers at Google made the right choice.

Changing Properties On the Fly

To add a twist to the preceding application, and also to demonstrate the use of the `setOptions()` method, you can program two mouse events of the `Polygon` object. When the mouse is dragged into the shape (`mouseover` event), set the polygon's `geodesic` property to `true`, and when the mouse is dragged out of the shape (`mouseout` event), set the same property to `false`. To implement this functionality, you only need to add the following event listeners:

```
google.maps.event.addListener(polygon, 'mouseover',
            function() {polygon.setOptions({geodesic: true})});
google.maps.event.addListener(polygon, 'mouseout',
            function() {polygon.setOptions({geodesic: false})});
```

The event listeners change the setting of the `geodesic` attribute when the mouse enters or leaves the polygon, respectively, and every time this happens, the polygon changes shape. To see the effects of the Mercator projection, you can make the polygon draggable and move it around with the mouse. Set the `polygon` object's `draggable` property to `true` and comment out the two statements that add the event listeners.

A Different View of Geodesics

Readers with an interest in math might further research the topic of geodesics. The mathematical definition of a geodesic shape is quite interesting. According to Wolfram MathWorld, *a geodesic is a length minimizing curve.* On the plane, it's a straight line. On a sphere, it's a greater circle. Geodesics describe the motion of small objects on the surface of the earth under the influence of gravity alone: objects that have no power of their own and those that at a constant speed.

The path taken by an object traveling at a constant speed under the influence of gravity alone is known as a *minimum energy path.* A minimum energy path is the path that a particle would follow when no forces are acting on it, just its initial speed.

Any other path would require additional energy. All minimum energy paths are parts of greater circles. Inevitably, all greater paths split the earth into two hemispheres. All meridians are greater circles because they lie on planes that go through the center of the earth and they split the earth into two hemispheres. Parallels are not greater circles; the only parallel that's also a greater circle is the equator.

How does minimum energy affect the trajectories of paths? A fundamental law in physics, one that applies to the entire universe, is the principle of minimum energy. Objects move, or assume shapes, that require the absolute minimum energy. Imagine you stretch a rubber band between any two points on the surface of a sphere. The rubber band will assume minimum length; any other shape would violate the principle of minimum energy. Just as you can't expect to stretch a rubber band on the plane and assume a shape other than a straight line, you can't expect to stretch a rubber band on the sphere and assume a shape that does not lie on a greater circle (which is the minimum energy path). The rubber band would further minimize its length by following a totally straight path under the crust of the earth, but this is not an option because it has to lie on the surface of the earth. Given this limitation, the minimum length path between any two points on the sphere is an arc of a greater circle.

If you have a globe at home and try to repeat this experiment, keep in mind that the friction between the rubber band and the globe is the primary force that will determine the path. A soft stretchable spring will work much better.

The Meridians and Parallels Project   One of the short projects of this chapter is the `Meridians and Parallels.html` project, which is shown in Figure 10-4. The meridians are drawn as gray lines and the parallels in black.

The page's script draws lines every 10 degrees. The meridians extend in latitude from 90 to –90 degrees and are drawn every 10 degrees of longitude with the following loop:

```
for (i=0; i<= 360; i += 10) {
    var path = [new google.maps.LatLng(90, i), new google.maps.LatLng(-90, i)];
    var meridian = new google.maps.Polyline({
                    path: path, geodesic: false,
                    strokeOpacity: 0.85, strokeWeight: 1,
                    strokeColor: "white"
                });
    meridian.setMap(map);
}
```

You can change the setting of the `geodesic` property from `false` to `true`; the script's output won't be affected because meridians are great circles by definition.

The parallels are drawn with another loop, and they extend from –180 degrees to 180 degrees (a full circle). Here's the loop that draws the parallels (each parallel in the northern hemisphere is represented by the `parallelN` variable and each parallel in the

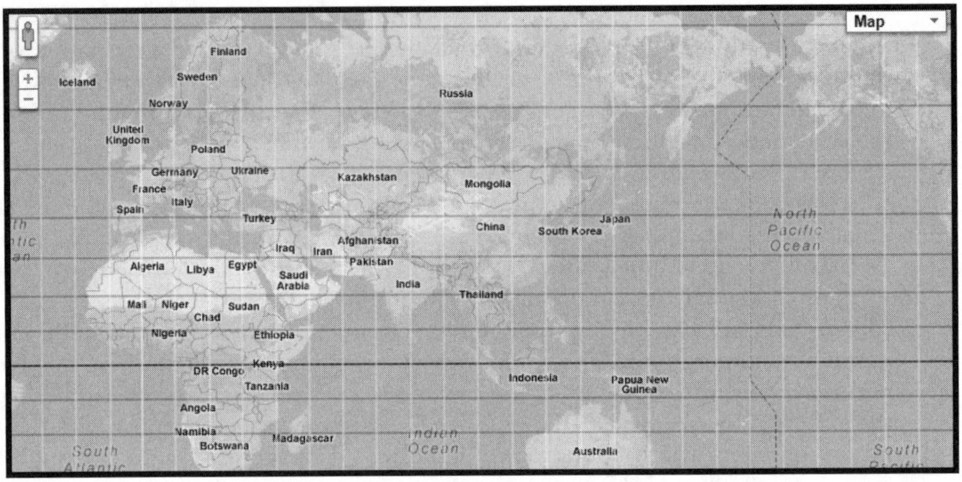

Figure 10-4 A segment of the earth covered with meridians and parallels

southern hemisphere is represented by the `parallelS` variable in the corresponding loop):

```
for (i = 0; i < 90; i += 10) {
    var pathN = [new google.maps.LatLng(i, 0),
                 new google.maps.LatLng(i, 180),
                 new google.maps.LatLng(i, 180),
                 new google.maps.LatLng(i, 359.9999)];
    var parallelN = new google.maps.Polyline({
        path: pathN,  geodesic: false,
        strokeOpacity: 0.5,  strokeWeight: 1,  strokeColor: "black"
    });
    parallelN.setMap(map);
    var pathS = [new google.maps.LatLng(-i, 0),
                 new google.maps.LatLng(-i, 180),
                 new google.maps.LatLng(-i, 180),
                 new google.maps.LatLng(-i, 359.9999)];
     var parallelS = new google.maps.Polyline({
        path: pathS,  geodesic: false,
        strokeOpacity: 0.5,  strokeWeight: 1,  strokeColor: "black"
    });
    parallelS.setMap(map);
}
```

The parallels are defined with four pairs of coordinates, not just two. The reason for of this is that a line going from 0 degrees to 360 degrees is just a point. Here, you don't want to draw the shortest line between two points, but the part that goes around the globe. The script does so by forcing the parallel to go through the prime meridian. The `geodesic` property of the lines that represent parallels is set to `false`. If you change it to `true`, then all parallels will be drawn as meridians! It shouldn't surprise you because parallels are not great circles, and you're requesting that they be drawn as great circles. A great circle that connects two points at opposite sides of the globe must go through the poles!

Geodesic Circles

Just like polygons, circles can also be geodesic. Geodesic circles are heavily distorted near the poles and appear much larger than circles with the same radius near the equator. All the circles you see in Figure 10-5 have the same radius, but they're drawn at different parallels. As a result, their sizes vary drastically and they demonstrate the type of distortion introduced by the Mercator projection.

The pattern generated by the circles of Figure 10-5 is known as the Tissot's Indicatrix and it's a mathematical contrivance that demonstrates the effects of Mercator projections. The circles on the map of the preceding figure have the same radius and are drawn at parallels of 0, +/−15, +/−30, +/−45, +/−60, and +/−75 degrees. At each parallel, the circle is repeated every 30 degrees, so you get 12 circles along the map. Listing 10-1 shows the code used to generate the circles; it's repetitive, but it demonstrates the effects of Mercator projections very clearly. Only the code that renders the circles on the map is shown here, not the listing of the entire page. Open the `Circles on Sphere.html` application to examine the code and experiment with it.

Listing 10-1
Drawing the circles that form the Tissot's Indicatrix

```
for (loc=180; loc > -180; loc=loc-25.0) {
    var location = new google.maps.LatLng(30.0, loc);
    var circleOptions = {
        strokeColor: "#FF0000", strokeOpacity: 1, strokeWeight: 2,
        fillColor: "#FF0000", fillOpacity: 0.3,
        map: map,
        center: location, radius: 250000
    };
```

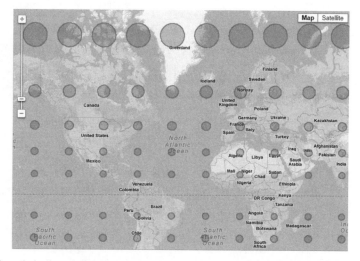

Figure 10-5   Tissot's Indicatrix is a pattern of equal radii circles repeated at varying latitude/longitude values.

```
// nothern hemisphere
   circleOptions.center = new google.maps.LatLng(15, loc);
   var C0n=new google.maps.Circle(circleOptions);
   circleOptions.center = new google.maps.LatLng(30, loc);
   var C1n=new google.maps.Circle(circleOptions);
   ...
   circleOptions.center = new google.maps.LatLng(75, loc);
   var C4n=new google.maps.Circle(circleOptions);
// southern hemisphere
   circleOptions.center = new google.maps.LatLng(-15, loc);
   var C0n=new google.maps.Circle(circleOptions);
   circleOptions.center = new google.maps.LatLng(-30, loc);
   var C1s=new google.maps.Circle(circleOptions);
   ...
   circleOptions.center = new google.maps.LatLng(-75, loc);
   var C4s=new google.maps.Circle(circleOptions);
   }
```

The script's code creates five circles for each hemisphere: c0n, c1n, … c4n for the Northern Hemisphere, and c0s, c1s, … c4s for the Southern Hemisphere. Instead of repeating the same statements with different numeric values, you can write a nested loop that draws a circle at the appropriate parallel.

Large Geodesic Circles

The circles that make up the Tissot's Indicatrix may be of different sizes depending on their latitude, but they're perfectly circular. Shouldn't they be deformed like their polygon counterparts? Circles are distorted too, but this effect is visible only if they're large enough. Figure 10-6 shows a circle with a radius of 3,500 kilometers. As this circle moves away from the equator, it looks more and more like an ellipse.

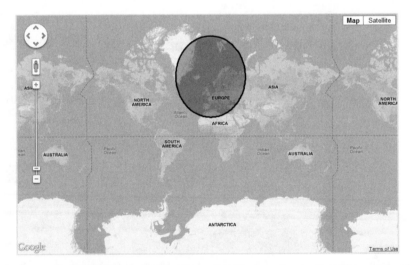

Figure 10-6 Large circles lose their aspect ratio as they're moved away from the equator, as demonstrated by the Draggable Circle application

The sample application `Draggable Circle.html` draws a large draggable circle on the map. Open the application in your browser and move the circle around with the mouse to see the effects of the Mercator projection. An even better demonstration is a site by Google, the Mercator Puzzle site, which is shown in Figure 10-7. The Mercator Puzzle is a fun application, but a very illuminating one. It allows users to drag country shapes around with the mouse and drop them at their proper locations. Once in the correct spot, the polygon of a country is locked in place.

You can find the Mercator Puzzle site at http://gmaps-samples.googlecode.com/svn/ trunk/poly/puzzledrag.html.

Locate Australia's outline (it's the large shape shown over Greenland and parts of Europe in Figure 10-7) and move it around with the mouse. If you move it over Europe, you will see that Australia appears to be larger than Europe! Move it a little closer to the Arctic Circle and it will appear enormous. To get a feel of the distortion, Australia is 7,700,000 square kilometers, and Europe is 10,100,000 square kilometers. This shows you that any shapes near the equator are approximately equal to their actual size when "flattened" on a map. Shapes far from the equator appear much larger when projected onto the same flat map.

For an even more dramatic illustration of the Mercator distortion, move the polygon of Greenland close to Australia and you will see how much smaller it is. Yet when seen at its place on the map, Greenland appears to be almost the size of Africa.

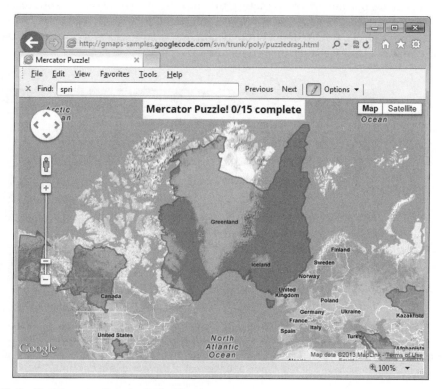

Figure 10-7   The Mercator Puzzle site by Google

What does it really mean to slide a country's or a continent's outline on the map? The Mercator projection distorts sizes, not directions. The shape of Australia remains the same, but it gets larger the closer it's moved to the poles. Moving a continent to a different location is equivalent to "placing" a continent with the exact same size and shape somewhere else on the globe. What you see on the map is the projection of this imaginary shape. If Australia is moving gradually toward Antarctica without changing its size, it will remain as large as it is today, but on the map it will look much larger (in several million years, of course). The Mercator Puzzle is a simple tool for teaching geography, but it's much more valuable as a visualization tool for the effects of the Mercator projection.

Another way to look at geodesic shapes is that you can't measure distances on a Google map. Geometric calculations should yield the same results regardless of where the shapes are located on earth, and this isn't the case for Mercator projections. Google provides the `geometry` library, which exposes functions for calculating lengths and areas on the sphere given the vertices of a shape. These functions are quite accurate because they're not affected by the Mercator distortions, yet they yield the correct result no matter where a specific feature is located. The geometry library is discussed in the second half of this chapter.

Viewing the Daylight Zone on Google Maps   Let's return for a moment to the large geodesic circle. In Figure 10-8, you see a circle (the dark area on the globe) with radius equal to one quarter of the earth's equator. The diameter of this circle is exactly one-half of the earth's perimeter. Try to picture the imprint of a circle on the sphere. As the radius grows, the circle will eventually cover one-half of the sphere. On the map, however, the circle isn't quite a circle, is it? When a circle becomes too large, and its center gets far away from the equator, the circle is seriously deformed.

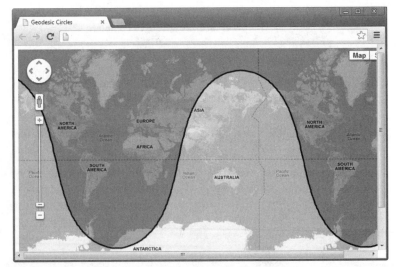

Figure 10-8   The dark shape on the map is a circle that covers exactly one-half of the planet. The areas under this circle are in night time and the rest of the world is in day time.

Open the Draggable Circle.html page and set the radius of the circle to this value:

```
var R = Math.PI * 6371000 / 2;
```

The radius is equal to the length of an arc that lies on the equator and covers one-quarter of the equator. A circle drawn with this radius covers exactly one-half of the globe. As the center moves away from the equator, the circle assumes an odd, but very familiar shape. The smoothly curved shape you see in Figure 10-8 is very similar to the daylight zone, isn't it? Indeed, at any given time the sun's light covers one-half of the planet and you can approximate the daylight zone very well by drawing a geodesic circle that covers one-half of the planet. What you actually see is the nighttime zone because you can't cast light on Google Maps; you can only make part of the globe darker. The daylight zone is what's left of the globe outside the shadow.

Keep in mind that the sun never gets directly over parts of the world whose latitude exceeds 23.5 degrees north (in the summer) or 23.5 degrees south (in the winter). If you wish, you can draw the parallels at 23.5 and –23.5 degrees as two lines and place a marker at the center of the circle.The center of the circle is the location on the globe directly under the sun (high noon).

The Geometry Library

The google.maps.geometry library provides a few invaluable methods for performing global geometric calculations. The functions of the geometry library take into consideration the shape of the earth and produce very accurate results. While they perform complex geodesic calculations, they expose their functionality through a few simple methods that accept locations as arguments. These methods encapsulate all the complexity of performing trigonometric calculations on the sphere.

The geometry library's main component is called spherical and it contains the methods for calculating lengths and areas. The other two components of this library are the Poly component, which provides just two methods for computations involving polylines and polygons, and the Encoding library, which provides the utilities for encoding and decoding paths. The most useful methods are the ones in the spherical component, which are explained in the following section.

To access the functionality of the geometry library, you must include a script from Google in your page with the following directive:

```
<script type="text/javascript"
src="http://maps.google.com/maps/api/js?
    libraries=geometry&sensor=false"></script>
```

You're still loading the basic script for Google Maps, but also request that the geometry library be included. With this directive in place, you can call the functions of the geometry library in your script by prefixing the function names with the complete name of the library. To call the computeLength() function, for example, use the following expression (and provide the appropriate arguments, of course):

```
google.maps.geometry.spherical.computeLength(...)
```

The `geometry.spherical` Methods

The most important component of the geometry library is the `spherical` component, which provides methods for computing lengths and distances. The methods of the `geometry.spherical` component are discussed in the following sections.

computeDistanceBetween(origin, destination)

The `computeDistanceBetween()` method returns the distance between the two points specified as arguments. The calculations are geodesic: They're performed on the sphere. They take into consideration the shape of the earth and the method returns the length of the shortest possible path between the two points (the geodesic distance). To calculate the length of the shortest flight path between Dallas and Beijing airports, use the following statements:

```
var P1 = new google.maps.LatLng(32.89680099, -97.03800201);
var P2 = new google.maps.LatLng(39.78279877, 116.3880005);
alert('The distance from Dallas, TX to Beijing, China is: ' +
    google.maps.geometry.spherical.computeDistanceBetween(P1, P2))
```

The geodesic distance between the two cities is 11,244 kilometers. This is the length of the shortest flying route between Dallas and Kentucky. The `computeDistanceBetween()` method calculates the geodesic length between the two points because this is the shortest path between them.

computeLength(path)

This method is similar to the `computeDistanceBetween()` method, but it calculates the length of a path with multiple vertices. If you want to measure the perimeter of an island, for example, trace it with as many points as possible and then pass the array of the geo-locations that define the outline of the island to the `computeLength()` method to retrieve the path's length. The outline of Iceland in the `Iceland.html` application is made up of 156 polygons (Iceland has a number of small islands around it) and a total of 7,590 vertices. When the `computeLength()` function is called for each of the polygons that make up then outline of Iceland, the total value is 6,260 kilometers. An alert box with the information is displayed every time you load or refresh the page. To better approximate complex shapes such as islands, you need to use as many points as possible to define their paths. The `Iceland.html` example is a simple page with a long list of polygons that correspond to the islands that make up Iceland. The polygons are drawn on the map as a draggable shape.

computeArea(path)

The `computeArea()` method is similar to the `computeLength()` method, but instead of the perimeter, it calculates the area under the shape defined by the `path` argument. If you return to the `Iceland.html` example, the total area covered by the polygons that make up the island is calculated with the statements shown in Listing 10-2, which also calculate the island's perimeter.

Listing 10-2
Computing the
perimeter and
area of a polygon
with multiple
paths

```
var area = 0;
var perimeter = 0;
var points = 0;
for (i=0; i<polygon.getPaths().length;i++) {
    perimeter += google.maps.geometry.spherical.computeLength(
                       polygon.getPaths().getAt(i));
    area+= google.maps.geometry.spherical.computeArea(
                       polygon.getPaths().getAt(i));
    points += polygon.getPaths().getAt(i).length;
}
```

NOTE Note that both the `computeLength()` and `computeArea()` methods accept a single array as their argument; you can't call these methods passing an array of arrays, such as an array of paths. The calculations are performed on a single path at a time, which explains the use of a loop that iterates through the individual paths that make up the total path of the polygon. The individual paths represent the islands around Iceland, which are added to the total length and total area of the shape that represents Iceland.

`interpolate(origin, destination, fraction)`

This method returns the geo-coordinates of a point (as a `LatLng` object), which lies the given fraction of the way between the specified origin and destination. The interpolate function works on geodesic paths defined by their two endpoints; you can't interpolate a path based on a polyline (or an array of `LatLng` objects).

The methods of the `geometry.spherical` library perform geodesic calculations, because this is the only way to calculate distances and areas on the sphere. Even if you wish to know the length of a "straight" line from Los Angeles to London, the `computeLength()` method will return the length of the geodesic line. The "straight" line simply isn't the shortest path connecting the two cities! The straight line is actually called the *rhumb* line and it's a line of constant bearing: It crosses all meridians at the same angle. Rhumb lines were used for centuries in sailing, but are of little interest in modern cartography. I'll come back to rhumb lines in the final chapter of this book, where you learn how to animate the flight of an airplane over a geodesic and a rhumb path. Later in this chapter, you will see a custom function that calculates the length of the rhumb line between any two points on the surface of a sphere.

The `geometry.poly` Functions

The `Poly` library is much simpler as it provides just two methods: the `containsLocation()` and `isLocationOnEdge()` methods. They both return a `true`/`false` value that indicates whether a point is contained within a polygon and whether a point lies on a polyline or polygon's edges.

`containsLocation(point, polygon)`

This method returns `true` if the `point` argument (a `LatLng` object) is within the bounds of the `polygon` argument, which represents a `Polygon` object.

`isLocationOnEdge(point, shape, tolerance)`

This method computes whether the `point` argument lies on or near a polyline, or the edge of a polygon, with a specified tolerance. It returns `true` when the distance between the point and the nearest point on the edge of the shape is less than the specified tolerance. The `tolerance` argument is specified in degrees, and it's the angle between the two lines that connect the center of the earth and the two points. The default tolerance is very small: 0.000000009, or 10^{-9} degrees. As a reminder, an angle of 1 degree corresponds to approximately 110 kilometers on the surface of the earth, which explains the very small default value.

Exercising the Geometry Library

Let's look at a couple of examples of the methods of the `Geometry` library. The first example uses the `computeDistanceBetween()` method to calculate distances of airports from a specific location and select the airports within a specific number of kilometers from a location. The sample application is called `Nearest Airports Client Side.html` and is shown in Figure 10-9. The data for this application was downloaded from www.openflights.org, which provides airport-related data free of charge (they do accept donations, however, if you find their site useful).

The range specified by the user around the map's center is marked with a semitransparent circle, and its radius is set to one of the values in the drop-down list at the top of the form. The circle isn't draggable; instead, it's drawn at the middle of the map and

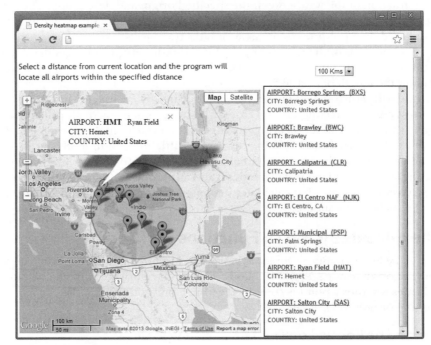

Figure 10-9   Locating airports within a given range from the map's center location

you should drag the map to center it at the desired location. As you drag the map, the script queries the data and displays the airports within the specified range from the map's center location.

The application is based on the geo-locations of approximately 9,000 airports around the world. Every time the map is dragged, the script calculates the distance between the center of the circle and each airport. If the distance is smaller than the selected value, the airport is displayed on the map as a marker. The following statement associates a custom function with the map's `dragend` event:

```
google.maps.event.addListener(map, 'dragend',
                              function() {showNearestAirports()});
```

Listing 10-3 shows `showNearestAirports()`, the function that calculates the distance of each one of 9,000 or so airports to the map's center location and selects the ones in the specified range.

Listing 10-3
The
showNearest
Airports()
function

```
function showNearestAirports() {
    var R;
    var idx = document.mapForm.radius.selectedIndex;
    R = parseInt(document.mapForm.radius.options[idx].value);
    var center = map.getCenter();
    var markerCount = 0;
    for (i=0; i < airports.length; i++) {
        var airportLocation = new google.maps.LatLng(
                airports[i].Location.Latitude, airports[i].Location.Longitude);
        var dist = google.maps.geometry.spherical.computeDistanceBetween(
                center, airportLocation)
        if (dist <= R * 1000) {
            var airportMarker = new google.maps.Marker({position:  airportLocation,
                            title: 'AIRPORT: ' + airports[i].Name + ' in ' +
                            airports[i].City + ', ' + airports[i].Country});
                airportMarker.setMap(map);
                airportMarkers.push(airportMarker);
                markerCount++;
        }
    }
}
```

The script iterates through all airports, calculates the distance of every airport from the map's center point (represented by the `center` variable), and then compares this distance to the specified range. If smaller, the script selects the current airport by adding it to the `airportMarkers` array. The actual script in the sample application contains many more statements that generate the contents of the right pane. The list of airports is a long `<div>` element constructed one item at a time as the script goes through the list of the selected airports. The code that generates the HTML content is not shown in the listing, because it's not related to the topic discussed here. If you're interested in generating a sidebar with additional data related to the items on the map, you can open the sample project and examine the code. Another interesting aspect of the sample application is that the name of each airport in the list is a hyperlink, and you can select an airport on the map by clicking the corresponding entry in the list. When an airport name is clicked in the list, the corresponding airport's info window is displayed on the map.

Rhumb Lines

A straight line on the map isn't totally useless, however. For centuries sailors have used such lines to navigate and there's a name for them: They're called *rhumb* lines. There was a time when the main navigation aids were the compass and the stars. Back then, rhumb lines were used to maintain a course at sea. Rhumb lines are also known as paths of *constant bearing*.

What exactly is a line of "constant bearing?" As you recall from Chapter 1, and the "Meridians and Parallels Project" earlier in this chapter, the meridians are all parallel lines. If another straight line crosses a meridian at a given angle, then it will cross all other meridians at the same angle! In other words, the rhumb line is a line with a constant direction, or constant bearing. The advantage of rhumb lines is that they're easy to navigate and were used by sailors for centuries. To some extent, they're actually being used for sailing even today.

An interesting aspect of rhumb lines is that if you draw a rhumb line on the globe, making sure it crosses every meridian at the same angle, you'll end up with a curve spiraling toward one of the poles, as shown in Figure 10-10 (courtesy of Wikipedia). Because of its constant inclination, rhumb lines are also known as loxodromes. Interestingly, if you were to drive on a loxodrome, you wouldn't need to turn the driving wheel. To drive along a geodesic path, you would have to turn the wheel. You would also have to turn it more sharply as you approached the poles.

Figure 10-10   A line of constant bearing spirals toward the poles. (Image courtesy of Wikipedia.)

Calculating the Length of a Rhumb Line

Rhumb lines are the paths that an airplane will never take, but a sailor might (no high tech instruments are required for navigating along a rhumb line). Eventually, you may need to know the length of a rhumb line. At the very least, you may be interested in knowing the relation between a rhumb line and the equivalent geodesic line. The calculateRhumbDistance() function, shown in Listing 10-4, accepts two geo-locations as arguments and returns the length of a straight line that connects the two points on the flat (projected) map.

Listing 10-4
Calculating the length of a rhumb line

```
function calculateRhumbDistance(pt1, pt2) {
      var R = 6371000;
      var d2r = Math.PI/180;
      var lat1=pt1.lat()*d2r; var lat2=pt2.lat()*d2r;
      var lng1=pt1.lng()*d2r; var lng2=pt2.lng()*d2r;
      dLat= (lat2-lat1); dLon= (lng2-lng1);
      var dPhi = Math.log(Math.tan(Math.PI / 4 + lat2 / 2) /
              Math.tan(Math.PI/4+ lat1 / 2));
      var q = (isFinite(dLat/dPhi)) ? dLat/dPhi : Math.cos(lat1);
      dPhi = 0;
      if (Math.abs(dLon) > Math.PI) {
          dLon = dLon>0 ? -(2*Math.PI-dLon) : (2*Math.PI+dLon);
      }
      var d = Math.sqrt(dLat*dLat + q * q * dLon * dLon) * R;
      return d;
}
```

The length of the rhumb line from Dallas to Beijing is 13,134 kilometers, or 16 percent longer than the equivalent geodesic path, which was calculated by the computeDistanceBetween() function of the geometry library of the Google API and was found to be 11,244 kilometers. Of course, this is an extreme example of a path that spans nearly one-half of the planet.

Flight Paths   Another demonstration of geodesic lines is shown in Figure 10-11. This map shows the flight paths from several airports in the United States (and the world) into Louisville, Kentucky. Once you have the coordinates of the airports you need, you can easily create geodesic lines between them. An interesting aspect of this application is that it displays airport data right on the map, when the mouse is hovered over an airport. In Chapter 19, you learn how to animate planes along these paths.

The page's script contains two lists with a few dozen airports each: one for U.S. airports and another for world airports. The script draws a polyline between the international airport in Kentucky and all other U.S. airports, or all the other international airports. The Polyline objects that represent the flight paths are geodesic lines and are rendered as curves on the map. When the mouse is hovered over an airport (the small red circle), the airport's icon changes to a large yellow circle and its name appears near the top of the map, as shown in Figure 10-11 for the Duluth International Airport.

Figure 10-11   Flight paths over the United States

Encoded Paths

The second component of the `geometry` library is the `encoding` component, which
provides two methods for encoding and decoding paths. As you already know, paths are
specified as arrays of `LatLng` objects and their textual representation is quite verbose.
Embedding such arrays in scripts bloats the file(s) that must be downloaded at the client.
Using the `geometry.encoding` library, you can compress this array, transmit the
compressed form of the array to the client, and decode it in your script. Encoded paths are
substantially shorter than the equivalent arrays of `LatLng` objects that describe the shape's
path. The `geometry.encoding` library isn't among the most commonly used libraries, so
it's not discussed in detail in this chapter. If you're interested in working with encoded
paths, please read the tutorial "The Encoding Library," included as a PDF file in this
chapter's support material.

Summary

This chapter should have helped you understand the difference between drawing on the flat map and drawing on the globe. All shapes drawn on the surface of the earth are called geodesic and take into consideration the curvature of the surface on which they're drawn. A non-geodesic shape, on the other hand, is a shape on the flattened map. When geodesic shapes are projected onto the flat map, they're distorted: Lines become curves. Measuring a large distance on a map, like the distance from Los Angeles to London, makes no sense. You need special functions to calculate the large distances on the globe and these functions are, fortunately, readily available in Google's `geometry` library. On the other hand, measuring small distances on the map, such as the perimeter of your backyard, or your jogging route, is quite accurate. The non-geodesic polygon that outlines your property, or Disneyland's parking lot, is practically the same as the equivalent geodesic polygon. When dealing with global features, however, you must take geodesy into account and be aware of the distortions introduced by the Mercator projection.

11 The KML Data Format: Persisting Spatial Data

Being able to place markers and shapes on a map is very exciting and opens a world of capabilities, but it wouldn't be of much use without the ability to save the shapes and reload them in a later session. For all types of data, there exist standards for describing it so they can be shared among systems and users, and geographical data are no exception. Among the many standards for spatial data, Google has adopted the KML standard, which is the topic of this chapter.

KML stands for Keyhole Markup Language, and it's an XML schema for representing items on a map. KML was actually adopted by Google for Google Earth and can become very complex. When used with Google Earth, it can describe even the movement of the camera, should you wish to create flyovers. Google Maps supports a subset of the KML language, and this subset supports all the features I've discussed so far: markers, polylines, and shapes. You can also use extended attributes to describe just about anything on the map. In this chapter, you learn the basic elements of the KML language, how to create KML documents on your own, and how to display KML documents on the map.

XML 101

KML is pure XML with tags specific to geographical data. If you're familiar with XML, you can skip this section and read about KML. This section contains a very short introduction to XML, which is the most widely accepted protocol for storing structured data of any type, and it's used in all computing fields.

So, what's XML? XML is a way to describe data in unambiguous ways. XML was created to address a very basic need, that of exchanging data between applications and systems. It's also a pure text protocol. Yes, you can embed binary information in an XML file, but it must first be encoded as a sequence of letters and digits. Because of this, XML is firewall-friendly: It can be safely transmitted from one computer to another over HTTP and overcomes the problem of moving binary data between computers (a basic requirement for data exchange in our connected world).

XML Uses Named Delimiters

XML uses delimiters to identify each data item. Unlike other delimited formats, however, XML allows you to define the names of these delimiters. The only requirement is that delimiters be placed in a pair of angle brackets and appear in pairs before and after the data item they delimit.

Let's say you want to store data about states in a format that can be easily moved between computers. Standard file types may come to mind, such as comma or tab-delimited files, structured data files with headers, and so on. Here's one possible method of coding the state of California in XML:

```
<State>
  <Name>California</Name>
  <Code>CA</Code>
  <Capital>Sacramento</Capital>
  <Population>36000000</Population>
  <Temperature>81</Temperature>
</State>
```

Every data item is placed between a pair of named tags. A tag is a name embedded in angle brackets, such as `<Name>`, `<Capital>`, or `<Code>`. The segment of the XML document that these tags delimit is called an *element*. XML contains delimited data, but the delimiters are not some special characters; they're strings that describe their contents. Moreover, the actual tag names are irrelevant: You get to choose the names that best describe your data. HTML uses identical syntax, only the tags are predefined and they describe how the content will be rendered in the browser. The `Temperature` element is enclosed by two tags with the same name in angle brackets, the `<Temperature>` and `</Temperature>` tags. The only difference between the two is that the closing tag's name is prefixed by backslash. The name of the closing tag must match exactly the corresponding opening tag as XML is case sensitive. In between the opening and closing tag there's usually a value, which is the element's value. The value of the `Temperature` element is 81 (degrees Fahrenheit, presumably).

You'll rarely create an XML document to store a single entity. In practice, you'll store a collection of `State` elements. To do so, you can embed any number of `<State>` tags under another tag, say the `<States>` tag. The following code segment outlines the structure of a XML document with three states. (I've omitted the details to focus on the outline of the collection in XML format.)

```
<States>
  <State>...</State>
  <State>...</State>
  <State>...</State>
</States>
```

XML elements can be nested to reveal the structure of the data they contain. This is the most prominent characteristic of XML, but more on this later.

Element contents are simple values such as strings, dates, and numbers. However, elements are not limited to simple values (or primitive data types); they may contain other elements. You can think of elements as objects. Just as objects can have properties that are objects themselves, elements may enclose other elements. The `<Coordinates>`

tag may contain two nested tags, the `<Latitude>` and `<Longitude>` tags, which are decimal numeric values. XML elements may contain other elements to any depth; the deepest nested elements, however, are simple values: strings, numbers, and dates.

Nesting XML Elements

XML owes its flexibility to the fact that elements can be nested to any depth: You can insert elements within elements to specify the structure of the entity you're describing. Take a look at the following XML segment that represents the country of France:

```
<Country>
  <Name>France</Name>
  <Capital>
    <Name>Paris</Name>
    <Population>2300000</Population>
  </Capital>
  <Language>French</Language>
  <Currency>Euro</Currency>
  <Population>65000000</Population>
  <Temperature>
    <High>59.9</High>
    <Low>47.3</Low>
  </Temperature>
</Country>
```

Under the root element `County` are six distinct elements: the `Name`, `Language`, `Currency`, and `Population` elements that represent single values, and the `Capital` and `Temperature` elements that contain nested elements. The `Capital` element contains two subelements: the name and population of the country's capital. The `Temperature` element is also a compound one because it contains the `High` and `Low` subelements.

You have probably noticed in the preceding example that the `<Population>` tag is used to denote the population of the country, as well as the population of the capital. These are two distinct `Population` elements because they belong to different parent elements. What makes an element unique is not its name, but its path in the document. It's the same as storing multiple files with the same name in different folders on your hard drive.

Here's another fairly simple example of an XML document with nested elements. The `CityData` element stores data about cities and includes geographical data.

```
<CityData>
  <Name>Los Angeles</Name>
  <Temperature>81</Temperature>
  <Coordinates>
    <Latitude>34.09</Latitude>
    <Longitude>-121.92</Longitude>
  </Coordinates>
  <State>
    <StateCode>CA</StateCode>
    <StateName>California</StateName>
  </State>
</CityData>
```

Qualifying Elements with Attributes

In addition to nested elements, each element may contain *attributes*, which are named values contained in the tag. The temperature in the preceding example is expressed in degrees Fahrenheit, as is obvious from its value. To be on the safe side, you should include this piece of information as well. If you were recording evaporation temperatures, or the temperature of the upper layers in the atmosphere, their units would no longer be "obvious." Yet this isn't essential information that deserves its own tag; it's more of a clarification that qualifies the value of the `<Temperature>` tag. It's possible to include a qualifier in the tag itself, as shown here:

```
<Temperature degrees="Fahrenheit">
```

`degrees` is an attribute of the `<Temperature>` tag, and you may include any number of attributes in a tag. Its name is a string that doesn't contain spaces and its value is always a string and as such it must be enclosed in double quotes. Attributes qualify in some way the tag to which they belong, but the element's primary value is the one between the two tags. An attribute's value may be an arbitrary value, or a member of a collection of values. In the example, the `degrees` attribute could have one of the values `Celsius` and `Fahrenheit`. However, an attribute has to be a primitive data type: You can't nest attributes.

You have your choice of specifying some data as attributes and others as elements. There are no hard rules as to what should be coded as attributes and what should be coded as elements. You may run into XML documents with a few elements and many attributes, or many elements and no attributes at all. In most XML documents, attributes are used to qualify the elements to which they belong.

The Three XML Rules

That's all there is to know about XML! It's made up of elements, which may contain other nested elements and attributes. Elements are delimited by tags, and tag names are arbitrary. You make up the tag names so that they reflect the entity they contain; once you've determined the element names, however, you must use them consistently. There are only a few rules you need to know in order to build valid XML documents:

- Tags are case-sensitive, may not contain spaces, and they always appear in pairs: the opening and closing tag. When you work with XML, you must pay attention to casing as `<Name>` and `<name>` are two totally different tags.
- All attribute values must be enclosed in double quotes—even integer values.
- It goes without saying that the tags must be properly nested; otherwise, the document wouldn't have a structure. You must always close the innermost element first, then its immediate parent, and so on.

Now that you have a basic understanding of the nature and structure of XML, let's switch out attention to KML and see the specific tags for describing geographical data. KML is pure XML with a specific schema.

XML Schemas

The basic characteristic of XML is that, in addition to the data, it also describes the structure of the data. This structure is called *schema* and there are ways to specify the schema of an XML document. The schema specification is another XML file and it's called XML Schema Definition (XSD). XSD files contain the names of the tags and the data type of their values. I'm not going to discuss how to build schema files here, but the idea is that XSD files allow you to create XML documents that conform to a structure. XML editors can take into consideration the schema and won't let you insert your own tags or tags out of place. In effect, the schema both serves and protects you. A dedicated KML editor, for example, is nothing more than an XML editor that complies with the KML schema. As you type your KML document, the editor suggests the possible elements at the current location and will not accept elements or attributes that do not conform to the schema definition. Let's sidetrack for a moment to see the XSD schema for the `<Cities>` tag (an element that may contain one or more `<City>` tags). The following schema tag specifies that the `City` element is a string, and it may occur multiple times under the same parent element:

```
<xsd:element name="City" type="xsd:string" maxOccurs="unbounded"/>
```

Just as you use XML to describe your data, you can use XML to describe the structure of XML documents for storing specific data. Schemas are published by industry consortiums and all commonly used schemas can be found on the Web. You're welcome to view the complete schema for KML documents; it's fairly intimidating, so focus on the basic information presented in this chapter to become familiar with its basic features first.

Understanding KML

KML is an XML-based protocol for describing geographic data on top of a map. The data include points (which are usually rendered as markers), lines, and polygons. The KML protocol is a very rich protocol because it was designed to be used with Google Earth. You can use it to describe buildings (with a third coordinate that corresponds to their height), set your view point, and even create a fly-by animation. These features are available in Google Earth only, so in this chapter you're going to learn about a subset of the KML, which is adequate for describing annotations on a flat map. All modern GIS applications support KML and many related applications provide tools to import/export their native data in KML format. AutoCAD is a typical example and the ArcInfo suite is another.

The Structure of a KML Document

The top element in a KML document is the `Document` element. As odd as it may appear, the `<Document>` tag is optional. The items that appear in the document are *placemarks*.

A placemark is a feature on the map; it can be a location (a point), a line, or a shape. As far as KML goes, everything you place on a map is a placemark. Google Earth supports additional types of placemarks, but for Google Maps these are the three types of placemarks.

A placemark is identified by the `<Placemark>` tag, and it may contain multiple items. If you create a placemark that corresponds to a university, or a county, you may include both a location and a shape that outlines the item. At a high level, viewers are interested in the location of an item and a short description. As they zoom in, they may wish to see more details about the item, in which case the outline may become visible.

Whatever item you place in a placemark represents a map feature and is described with its geo-coordinates, so let's start our discussion of KML by examining how geospatial data are represented in KML.

Defining Points

The most basic element in KML is the `coordinates` element, which represents a single point, or a series of points that define a path. This element's value is a comma-separated list of values: longitude, latitude, and altitude values. A location's coordinates are separated by a comma without spaces. Here's a `coordinates` element that corresponds to the location of Rome on the earth's surface:

```
<coordinates>12.50,41.90,0</coordinates>
```

The first value is the longitude, the second value is the latitude, and the last one is the altitude. The altitude value is optional and it's used only in KML files intended for Google Earth. In the context of Google Maps, you can omit the last value, or set it to zero. The coordinates can be expressed with many decimal digits, but there's no point in expressing a city's coordinates with too much accuracy. To specify the coordinates of St. Peter's Basilica in Rome, you would use more decimal digits:

```
<coordinates>12.456389,41.902222</coordinates>
```

TIP Note that there are no spaces between the values and that the geo-coordinates of a point are specified with the longitude first. This is the reverse order in which you specify coordinates with the Google Maps API (the `LatLng` object, for example). It would be much safer if the KML protocol included elements such as `<Longitude>` and `<Latitude>`, but its designers decided to reduce the total file size at the cost of a potential ambiguity.

The `coordinates` element of the preceding example specifies a single point on the globe. A point can be the location of a monument, a house, anything that can be represented with a marker. To represent a point item, use the `<Point>` tag with a nested `<coordinates>` tag:

```
<Point>
  <coordinates>12.456389,41.902222</coordinates>
</Point>
```

Defining Paths and Polygons

You can also represent items with multiple coordinates in KML. These items are specified as a path, which can be a route, a country outline, and so on. To represent multiple point items, you use the `coordinates` element with multiple coordinates, such as the following:

```
<coordinates>
  32.201402,47.940021,0 34.983212,47.339283,0 33.489371,45.355493,0
</coordinates>
```

This element specifies a path with three points. Note that the coordinates of successive points are separated by a space; the comma delimits the individual components of each point's coordinates. The delimiter between point coordinates need not be a space character; you can use any white space in its place. Here's an equally valid (yet much easier to visualize and read) way of specifying the same path as in the preceding example:

```
<coordinates>
  32.201402,47.940021,0
  34.983212,47.339283,0
  33.489371,45.355493,0
</coordinates>
```

To insert the definition of a path in a KML file, use the `LineString` element:

```
<LineString>
  <coordinates>
    32.201402,47.940021,0 34.983212,47.339283,0 33.489371,45.355493,0
  </coordinates>
</LineString>
```

The `LineString` element is used to insert a path in the KML document. To insert a polygon (which is a closed path), use the `LinearRing` element instead. The `LinearRing` element contains a series of geo-coordinates, just like the `LineString` element, but it closes the path automatically, even if the last coordinate doesn't coincide with the first one.

Closed polygons must also be enclosed in another element, the `outerBoundaryIs` element. To insert a simple polygon in the document, you should use the following compound element:

```
<outerBoundaryIs ...>
  <LinearRing>
    <coordinates>
      32.201402,47.940021,0 34.983212,47.339283,0
      33.489371,45.355493,0 32.201402,47.940021,0
      ...
    </coordinates>
  </LinearRing>
</outerBoundaryIs>
```

The name of the outer element is quite odd, but there's a good reason for it. A polygon may contain a hole, which is defined as another polygon with the `innerBoundaryIs` element. This way, the KML protocol differentiates between the outer polygon and the inner polygon (or polygons) that describe one or more holes in the outer polygon.

TIP When you draw polygons with the Google Maps API, you don't have to specify the outer polygon and the inner polygons that correspond to holes. Every polygon that's contained in another polygon is a hole of the containing polygon. This is not the case with KML

Everything Is a Placemark

All items you specify in the KML file are placemarks and are represented by `<Placemark>` tags. This element has a name and a description and, at the very least, either a `<Point>` or a `<LineString>` (or `<LinearRing>`) tag. The entire KML file is a sequence of `Placemark` elements, as in the following:

```
<Placemark>
  <Point>
    <coordinates>32.201402,47.940021,0</coordinates>
  </Point>
</Placemark>
<Placemark>
  <LineString>
    <coordinates>
      32.201402,47.940021,0 34.983212,47.339283,0 33.489371,45.355493,0
    </coordinates>
  </LineString>
</Placemark>
```

The preceding example contains two placemarks, one of them a marker and the other one a path. When rendered on the map, they will have the default appearance.

Besides a geographical entity, the `Point` element may contain a name and a description element. Both elements must appear under the `<Placemark>` tag, as shown here:

```
<Placemark>
  <name>St. Peter's Basilica<\name>
  <description>
    St. Peter's Basilica (Latin: Basilica Sancti Petri;
    Italian: Basilica di San Pietro in Vaticano) is a Late
      Renaissance church located within Vatican City.
  </description>
  <Point>
    <coordinates>12.456389,41.902222</coordinates>
  </Point>
</Placemark>
```

The description may contain HTML, too. To include HTML in the `description` element, you must either escape the special symbols (in other words, replace the < symbol with the text < and similar escape codes for all symbols that have special meaning in HTML), or use a CDATA tag within the `<description>` tag. Then, you can embed any HTML code in the CDATA tag, as shown here:

```
<Placemark>
<name>St. Peter's Basilica</name>
  <description>
```

```
        <![CDATA[
        <b>St. Peter's Basilica</b>
        (Latin: <u>Basilica Sancti Petri</u>;
        Italian: <u>Basilica di San Pietro in Vaticano</u>)
                  is a Late Renaissance church located within
        <i>Vatican City</i>.
      </description>
      <Point>
        <coordinates>38.595626,-114.996729</coordinates>
      </Point>
</Placemark>
```

When this item is opened either in Google Maps or in Google Earth, the specific point will be identified by a marker. The item's name will become the marker's title and the item's description will appear in the marker's info window.

Finally, all <Placemark> tags are nested under a <Document>tag:

```
<Document>
  <Placemark>
  ...
  </Placemark>
  <Placemark>
  ...
  </Placemark>
</Document>
```

In short, a KML document contains one or more <Placemark> tags (usually many such tags), which represent features on the map. The features supported on a Google map can be points, lines, and polygons, and they're identified by one of the <Point>, <LineString> or <LinearRing> tags. These tags contain a nested <coordinates> tag, which contains as many points as necessary. Finally, they can have two descriptive subelements, the name and description elements.

Viewing KML Files on Google Maps

The few elements presented so far are adequate for describing the shapes you can place on a map in a KML document. Let's look at a KML document with the outline of a state and the locations of a few major cities. Figure 11-1 shows the KML file displayed in the Google Maps site.

Opening a KML file on top of a map requires that the file reside in a public server because the file won't be processed at the client. Google will read the file, create the document with the map and the necessary overlays, and then send it to the client. To verify this, take a look at the source code of the file displayed—if you dare. There's no link to the file and you won't find a single city name in the page's HTML file. If you have your own web server, you can copy the sample KML files to this server. If not, you can still follow this section's examples using the KML files that were uploaded to a Google site for your convenience.

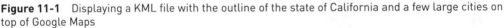

Figure 11-1 Displaying a KML file with the outline of the state of California and a few large cities on top of Google Maps

Create a URL for the Google Maps site followed by the q parameter and the URL of the KML document you want to view: http://maps.google.com?q=*KML_URL*. In this URL, *KML_URL* is the URL of a KML document posted on a public server. Enter this URL in your browser address box and press ENTER. The KML document shown in Figure 11-1 can be located at https://sites.google.com/site/samplekmlfiles/, which is a Google Site set up for this book's examples. The file is shared and you can access it without a password.

On this site, you will find the California.kml file, which is also included in this chapter's material. To insert a reference to this file in your page, right-click the Download link under the file name and from the context menu, select the Copy Shortcut command. The complete URL of the file is https://sites.google.com/site/samplekmlfiles/home/California.kml?attredirects=0&d=1.

If the KML file is a valid one, it will be rendered on top of the map, as shown in Figure 11-1. In addition to the shapes and markers on the map, the same items will appear in the left pane of the page. The names of the items are hyperlinks: When clicked, they cause an info window to appear at the corresponding feature. You can also show or hide items by checking or clearing the box in front of an item's name in the list.

The data for the outline of California was created manually with the Map Tracing application of Chapter 9. The entire state is approximated with a couple hundred points only. As for the city coordinates, they were also generated with the Map Tracing application but saved as individual points rather than as a path's vertices. Listing 11-1 is a segment of the `California.kml` file (most of the cities were omitted, as well as most of the vertices of the state's polygon). The definitions of the styles were omitted from the listing for the sake of brevity; please open the file with an XML editor to view it in its entirety.

Listing 11-1
A KML document
with California's
outline and a few
major cities

```
<?xml version="1.0" encoding="utf-8"?>
<Document>

  <Placemark>
    <name>California</name>
    <styleUrl>#CaliforniaStyle</styleUrl>
    <Polygon>
      <outerBoundaryIs>
        <LinearRing>
          <coordinates>
              -114.63332,34.87057,0.0  -114.63305,34.86997,0.0
              -114.56953,34.79181,0.0  -114.48236,34.71453,0.0
               -114.44166,34.64288,0.0  -114.38169,34.47903,0.0
              ...   more points
          </coordinates>
        </LinearRing>
      </outerBoundaryIs>
    </Polygon>
  </Placemark>
  <Placemark>
    <name>Santa Barbara</name>
    <Point>
      <coordinates>-119.70153809,34.42050488</coordinates>
    </Point>
  </Placemark>
  <Placemark>
    <name>Long Beach</name>
    <Point>
      <coordinates>-118.19641113,33.77001515</coordinates>
    </Point>
  </Placemark>
  ...  moreplacemarks
</Document>
```

To demonstrate the use of the CDATA section, the KML document contains the following description for the town of Santa Barbara:

```
<description>
  <![CDATA[
  <span style="font-size: 9pt; font-family:verdana;  color:'green' ">
    <table>
        <tr><td>Country</td><td align='right'>United States</td></tr>
        <tr><td>State</td><td align='right'>California</td></tr>
        <tr><td>Region</td>
          <td align='right'>
                Southern California</td></tr>
```

```
       <tr><td>Incorporated</td><td align='right'>
                  February 18, 1850</td></tr>
       <tr><td>County seat</td>
           <td align='right'>Santa Barbara </td></tr>
       <tr><td>Area</td><td align='right'>
              9,813.7 km2 (3,789.08 sq mi)</td></tr>
       <tr><td>Population</td><td align='right'>423,895 </td></tr>
       <tr><td>Time zone</td><td align='right'>
              Pacific Standard Time (UTC-8)</td></tr>
       <tr><td>Area code(s)</td><td align='right'>805</td></tr>
       <tr><td>Website</td>
           <td align='right'>www.countyofsb.org</td></tr>
     </table>
  </span>
  ]]>
</description>
```

The [CDATA] section contains straight HTML code that formats the city data as a table. When the California.kml document is viewed on Google Maps, the info window for Santa Barbara looks like the one shown in Figure 11-2. It's worth noting on the same figure that the text of the CDATA section is shown in the left pane, under the corresponding marker's name. This is the default mechanism for displaying KML files on top of Google Maps, and there's nothing you can do about it. You will see shortly how to place KML documents on top of your own map.

The icons for the cities were specified in the California.kml file with the Icon attribute of the style element that applies to cities.

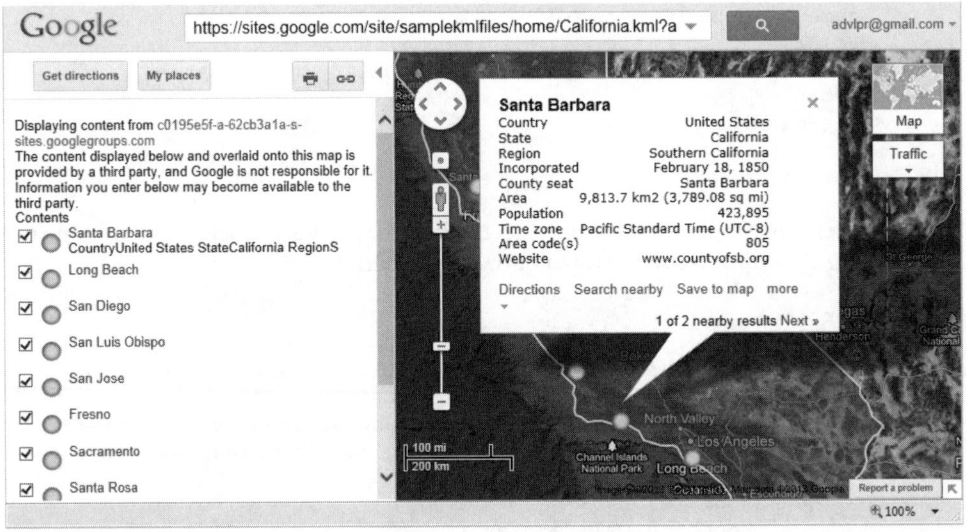

Figure 11-2   Displaying additional data about locations in HTML format

Tools for Preparing KML Files

As mentioned earlier, the shapes described in the KML file will be rendered on the map only if the file contains valid KML code. If not, no specific warnings will be generated; instead, you will see a message to the effect that the file you've loaded is not a valid KML file. So, before you use your KML files, make sure that they're valid. In most cases, KML files are generated by applications that process large sets of data, which most likely come from databases. There are also dedicated KML editors, which you may wish to use to become familiar with KML, but there's not much point in editing large sets of coordinates manually.

An Online KML Editor

You can edit a KML file and view it on a map at http://display-kml.appspot.com/, shown in Figure 11-3. You can't use this online editor for large KML files, but it's a good starting point. Practical KML files can grow very large, but you will probably use a tool or your own program to produce such files.

KML Validators

Another useful operation on KML documents is to check that they contain valid KML code. Displaying a KML document correctly on the map doesn't mean that every bit of the document is correct; browsers are very forgiving and chances are that your new KML file may contain some invalid data, which may result in a few markers not being shown on the map, or some other hard-to-notice mistake. There are KML validation tools that you can download and install at your computer. You can also use KML editors, which are nothing more than XML editors that validate against the KML schema as you type.

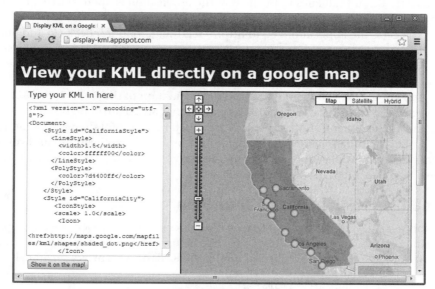

Figure 11-3   Connect to this site to edit and preview small KML files.

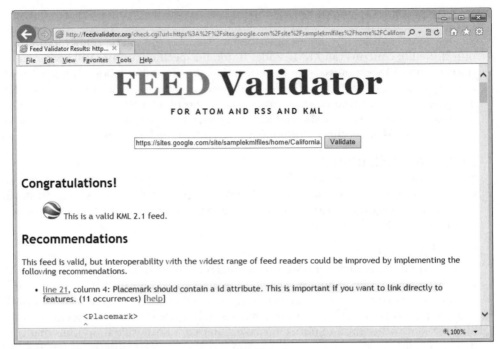

Figure 11-4 The FEED Validator site for validating KML documents

An online KML validator is shown in Figure 11-4. This site allows you to enter the URL of a KML file and validates it. By the way, the application is open source and you can download and use it locally.

To access the application, go to http://feedvalidator.org/check.cgi and enter the URL of the document you wish to validate. The document must reside in a public server, as explained in the earlier section "Viewing KML Files on Google Maps"; if you don't have your own web server, use a public one as you did in the preceding section.

In Figure 11-4, you see the results of the validation of the `California.kml` file. The document is valid, but the validator suggested that an `id` attribute be added to the `Placemark` elements. KML validators are much more useful than KML editors because KML files are usually generated automatically by custom applications, and you need only verify that your application generates a properly structured KML document. You'll never have to create a KML document manually.

Adding a KML Layer to Your Map

In this section, you're going to overlay a KML document on top of a Google map. Start by creating a simple page that displays a Google map, initialize the map as usual, and then insert the following statements to read and render the KML document as a separate layer:

```
var kmlUrl = 'https://Your_KML_File.kml';
var kmlOptions = {map: map};
var kmlLayer = new google.maps.KmlLayer(kmlUrl, kmlOptions);
```

The last statement creates a `KmlLayer` object, which is a layer that contains the shapes described in the KML document and is rendered on top of the specified map. The `KmlLayer` object's constructor accepts two arguments—the URL of the KML file and the layer's options. The `map` option is the only mandatory one, but there are a few more options, such as `suppressInfoWindows` and `preserveViewport`, which tell the browser whether it should (or should not) display an info windows upon the selection of an item in the KML layer, and whether to scroll the viewport in order to fit the info window, if needed. The default value for both options is false. Unfortunately, the `preserveViewport` is a property of the `KmlLayer` object and not of the `InfoWindow` object; you can't prevent the scrolling of the map when any other info window is opened.

The KML Demo Application

The annotation layer's data is stored in a KML file at a web server and downloaded by the script as needed. The KML layer is rendered on the map automatically with no user action or any special programming effort. The statement that creates the new `KmlLayer` specifies the location of the KML file and tells Google Maps to render the items contained in the file. To see how to open a KML file and create an overlay with the file's data on top of the map in your own web page, open the `KML Demo.html` application, shown in Figure 11-5.

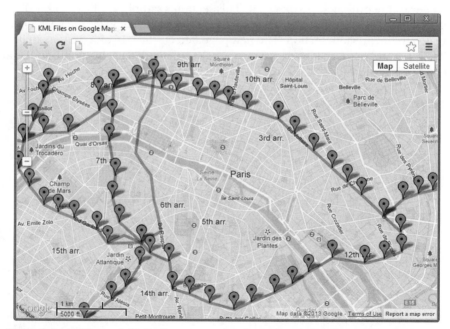

Figure 11-5 Selected lines of the Paris metro and their stations specified as placemarks in a KML file and viewed as a map overlay

It's a simple web page with a script that displays a map in the usual `<div>` element and then creates a new layer with the KML data using the following two statements:

```
var metroLayer = new google.maps.KmlLayer(
          'https://sites.google.com/site/mykmltestsite/' +
          'kml-samples/Paris%20Metro%20Folders.kml?attredirects=0&d=1');
metroLayer.setMap(map);
```

These two statements appear at the end of the page's `initialize()` function. The first statement creates a `KmlLayer` object with the data of the file specified with the argument of the constructor of the `KmlLayer` object, and the second statement places the new layer on top of the map. It's that simple (as long as the specified file resides at a public server).

The `KML Demo.kml` file contains the path of a few lines of the Paris metro along with their stations and the path of line 12 without any stations. The overlaid data looks fine on the map, but the page is totally static. You can't select any item on the map with the mouse to view its details, not even a marker. It's possible to detect the selection of an item on the KML layer and react to this action, but only through custom code, as you will see in the following section.

Handling KML Events

In this section, you're going to revise the `KML Demo.html` page by adding an event listener to the overlay's `click` event. This section's sample application is called `KML Demo with Events.html`, and it's based on the simple page that loads the KML document you created in the previous section. The new page detects the `click` event on an item of the KML layer and reacts to it by displaying the selected item's data, including an ID value, as shown in Figure 11-6.

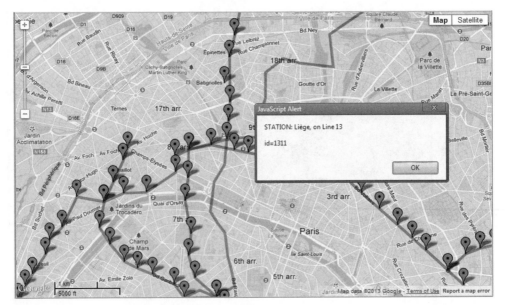

Figure 11-6 Capturing events on the KmlLayer object

The `KmlLayer` object fires a few events of its own, regardless of the item that was clicked. To customize the interaction of the user with the layer's items to some extent, you must (a) disable the default reaction of the layer to the click event and (b) provide a custom function to handle the event. To disable the default interaction, set the `suppressInfoWindows` attribute to `true` in the `KmlLayer` object's constructor, as shown here:

```
new google.maps.KmlLayer(KML_File_URL, {suppressInfoWindows: true});
```

Then, add a listener for the `click` event in the layer that contains the items you're interested in, with a statement like the following:

```
google.maps.event.addListener(metroLayer, 'click',
    function (KmlEvent) {
        // function's statements
    }
}
```

The `KmlLayer`'s Events

The `KmlLayer` object recognizes three events in all: the `status_changed` event, which is fired when the layer has finished loading, the `click` event, and the `defaultviewport_changed` event. The most commonly used event is the `click` event, which is fired when any of the layer's features is clicked; it passes to the script the `KmlEvent` argument, which provides information about the feature that was clicked. The `KmlEvent` argument exposes the `KmlFeatureData` object, which represents the item that was clicked. The `KmlFeatureData` property of the `KmlEvent` argument contains information about the selected KML item; you can access this information from within your script through the properties which are listed in Table 11-1.

In practice, the most useful property is the `id` property, which uniquely identifies a feature in the layer. This feature most likely is stored in a database with the same id so that you use the id stored in the KML document to request additional data from the database.

Property	Description
description	A string with the feature's description, as specified in the KML document.
id	The ID of the selected feature. The ID is specified with the `id` attribute of the `Placemark` element. If the `Placemark` element has no `id` attribute, a unique ID for the selected feature will be generated on the fly. The next time you retrieve the `id` property in the same session, its value won't change, of course.
name	The feature name. It's the value of the placemark's `name` element.
infoWindowHtml	The HTML document you wish to display in an info window when the user clicks the feature.

Table 11-1 The properties of the KmlEvent argument

Handling the KmlLayer's Click Event

To use the `featureData` property in a client script, you must first add a listener to the `click` event of the KML layer as follows:

```
google.maps.event.addListener(metroLayer, 'click',
function (kmlEvent) {
    // code to handle the event
});
```

The `click` event is fired when any item on the layer is clicked; you can't attach an event listener to specific objects in the KML layer. You can extract the `id` of the selected item in your script and call a function to process the selected item. The sample application displays the `id` along with the feature's name in an alert box to keep the code simple (see Figure 11-6). In Chapter 15, you learn how to call web services from within your script and display the service's response on the same web page that contains the script. The following is the event listener of the KML Demo application:

```
google.maps.event.addListener(metroLayer, 'click',
    function (kmlEvent) {
        var name = '';
        if (kmlEvent.featureData.name != null)
          name = kmlEvent.featureData.name;
        var description = '';
        if (kmlEvent.featureData.description != null)
          description = kmlEvent.featureData.description;
        alert(name + '\n' + description + '\nid=' +
            kmlEvent.featureData.id );
});
```

CAUTION Please note the following odd behavior of the `id` attribute: If the KML is posted on a production server, the script will retrieve its value as explained here. If you use a drive like Google Drive for your test, the script will read a random `id`, which is a long hexadecimal number.

The KmlEvent Argument You must also call the `preventDefault()` method of the `kmlEvent` argument to cancel the event's default action from within the event listener:

```
kmlEvent.preventDefault( )
```

The following `Placemark` element represents a metro line and is rendered on the map with a `Polyline` object. Note that the element has the following subelements: a name, a description, and a series of coordinates that correspond to the polyline's vertices.

```
<Placemark>
  <name>Line 13</name>
  <description>
    <![CDATA[
      <font color="green" size="4">Saint-Denise-Univesite<br/>
                Châtillon - Montrouge</font>
      <br/><br/><font color="black" size="3">13.18 Kms / 9.43 miles
```

```
      </font>
  ]]>
</description>
<LineString>
  <coordinates>
      2.364721300000042,48.9458424,0
      2.3600864400000319,48.93831628,0
      2.3559236500000225,48.92991499,0
      2.3430490499999905,48.91962291,0
      ...
      2.3016786599999932,48.81073548,0
  </coordinates>
</LineString>
</Placemark>
```

Figure 11-7 shows the custom info window that's displayed when the user clicks the `Polyline` object that represents the metro line 13. To make the application more useful, you can display additional information, such as the number of passengers on the selected line, or the number of passengers boarding at the selected station every day, the arrival time of the next train at the station, and any other type of information you can retrieve from a database. Note that the placemarks are organized in a tree structure in the left pane of the

Figure 11-7   When you select an item in the KML list in the left pane, the custom info window is displayed automatically on the map.

page. This organization is possible because KML supports the `Folder` element. The concept of organizing placemarks in folders is discussed in the following section.

The data used in the examples is embedded in the KML document, but you can modify the application and make it interact with a remote database. If all geography items (stations and lines) are stored in a database and they have a unique ID, you can pass this ID to the client through the initial KML file. The client application can then request additional information about each item from the database by passing the ID to a web service.

Organizing Placemarks in Folders

A very useful KML tag is the `<Folder>` tag, which allows you to organize the various items in groups and even nest groups within others. If you open a KML file that contains groups in Google Maps, you will see this structure in the left pane, as shown in Figure 11-7. The folders and their contents are displayed in a tree structure and you can display/hide an entire folder by checking or clearing the box in front of the folder's name.

The `Folder` element may contain practically any KML element. The `name` and `description` elements under the `Folder` element are equivalent to the same two subelements of the `Placemark` element; they specify the folder's name and a description either in plain text or HTML format.

Let's create a KML with folders to store the lines of the Paris metro. Each metro line will be represented by its own folder, which will be named after the specific line it contains. Under each line's folder, you'll store the line's path, which is a single item. The line's stations will be stored in their own folder, the `Stations` folder, nested under the line's folder. Listing 11-2 shows the outline of the suggested KML file:

Listing 11-2
A KML fragment with `<Placemark>` tags organized in folders

```
<Folder>
  <name>Line 13</name>
  <Placemark>
    <name>Track</name>
    <description> . . . </description>
    <LineString>
      <coordinates>
        2.364721300000042,48.9458424,0
        2.3600864400000319,48.93831628,0
        . . .
        2.3016786599999932,48.81073548,0
      </coordinates>
    </LineString>
  </Placemark>
  <Folder>
    <name>Stations</name>
    <Placemark>
      <name>Saint-Denise-Univesite</name>
      <Point>
        <coordinates
          2.364721300000042,48.9458424,0
        </coordinates>
      </Point>
    </Placemark>
```

```
<Placemark>
. . .   Placemarkdata  . . .
</Placemark>
. . .morePlacemarks
</Folder>
</Folder>
```

A sample file, Paris Metro Folders.kml, with a few metro lines is included in this chapter's material. You can open this file in Google Maps as explained already to view its structure and render its elements on the map. The same file can also be accessed at https://sites.google.com/site/samplekmlfiles site. KML folders can be nested to any level and will come in very handy when you work with large datasets. Of course, the data must lend itself to a hierarchical representation to organize it efficiently within folders.

Generating KML Files

Before ending this chapter, let's discuss briefly the topic of generating KML documents with a Windows application. As mentioned at the beginning of this chapter, it's possible to generate KML files in JavaScript, but you can't store them at the client—not without resorting to a server component and not without the hassles of moving very large data sets to the server. Your best bet is to generate KML documents with dedicated applications at the server, or to export data in this format from SQL Server (see Chapter 13 for a detailed discussion of SQL Server's spatial features).

The Map Tracing application of Chapter 9 converts the lines traced by the user and their vertices into a KML document. The function that generates the KML document is surprisingly simple (see Listing 11-3).

Listing 11-3
Generating KML for a collection of paths in Visual Basic

```
Private Function export2KML() As XDocument
    Dim kmlDoc = New XDocument
                    kmlDoc.Add(New XElement("Document"))
    For Each itm In ComboBox1.Items
        Dim guid = itm.ToString
        Dim obj = Convert.ToString(
                    WebBrowser1.Document.InvokeScript("getLine", {guid}))
        Dim line = obj.Split(vbLf)
        Dim lineName = line(0).Split("|")(0)
        Dim coordinates = ""
        For i = 1 To line.Count - 2
            Dim ptName = Convert.ToString(line(i).Split("|")(0))
            Dim ptLat = System.Xml.XmlConvert.ToDouble(line(i).Split("|")(1))
            Dim ptLon = System.Xml.XmlConvert.ToDouble(line(i).Split("|")(2))
            Dim ptCoordinates = ptLon.ToString & "," & ptLat.ToString & ",0"
            coordinates &= ptCoordinates & vbCrLf
            kmlDoc.Element("Document").Add(
                    New XElement("Placemark",
                        New XElement("name", ptName),
                        New XElement("Point",
                            New XElement("coordinates", ptCoordinates))))
        Next
        kmlDoc.Element("Document").Add(New XElement("Placemark",
                New XElement("name", lineName),
```

```
                        New XElement("LineString",
                            New XElement("coordinates", coordinates))))
        Next
    Return kmlDoc
End Function
```

The code iterates through all the lines drawn on the map and requests each line's data from the script by calling the `getLine()` function. This function returns a string with the data, and then the VB code extracts each line's vertices. First, it splits the long string into separate lines (one line per vertex), and then splits it again at the pipe symbols to extract the vertex data: the vertex's name, its latitude, and its longitude.

The `getLine()` function returns a string like the following for each metro line (only the first few stations are shown here):

```
Line 8
Balard|48.8359952|2.27803229999995
Lourmel|48.83856566|2.282023429999981
Boucicaut |48.8410795|2.287774089999971
Félix Faure |48.84271768|2.2916364600000634
Commerce|48.84477943|2.293825149999975
```

The first line contains the line's name. The following lines correspond to the line's stations and each of them contains the name of the station followed by a vertical line (the pipe symbol), the station's latitude followed by the same separator, and finally, the station's longitude.

The program iterates through all lines and at each iteration it calls the `getLine()` method to retrieve the line's data. Then it builds the KML document, one line at a time. For each station, the code adds a new `<Placemark>` tag with two nested tags: the `<name>` and `<Point>` tags. The `<Point>` tag has a nested tag, `<coordinates>`, where the vertex coordinates are placed. All these actions are carried out with a single statement:

```
kmlDoc.Element("Document").Add(
                    New XElement("Placemark",
                        New XElement("name", ptName),
                        New XElement("Point",
                            New XElement("coordinates", ptCoordinates))))
```

This statement adds to the `<Document>` tag the data passed as argument, which is a new element, the `Placemark` element. This element's value, in turn, is an array of two elements: the name and `Point` elements. Finally, the `Point` element's value is a `coordinates` element that contains the actual coordinates of the station. This statement produces an element like the following:

```
<Placemark>
  <name>Saint-Denise-Univesite</name>
  <Point>
    <coordinates>
      2.364721300000042,48.9458424,0
    </coordinates>
  </Point>
</Placemark>
```

To generate the preceding KML segment, the `Add` method was called with the following arguments:

```
kmlDoc.Element("Document").Add(
New XElement("Placemark",
        New XElement("name", "Saint-Denise-Univesite"),
        New XElement("Point",
            New XElement("coordinates",
                    .364721300000042,48.9458424,0)))))
```

Even if you're not familiar with Visual Basic's XML features, you can understand what's going on by examining the statement that generates the placemark for a station and the output generated by that statement. While generating the `<Placemark>` tags for each station, the code also builds the `coordinates` variable's value by appending the coordinates of each vertex:

```
Dim ptCoordinates = ptLon.ToString& "," & ptLat.ToString& ",0"
coordinates &= ptCoordinates&vbCrLf
```

After going through all the stations of the line, the code generates another `Placemark` element that corresponds to the line. It's very similar to the stations' `Placemark` elements, but it contains a `<LineString>` tag with the coordinates of the line's vertices:

```
kmlDoc.Element("Document").Add(
                    New XElement("Placemark",
                        New XElement("name", lineName),
                    New XElement("LineString",
                        New XElement("coordinates", coordinates))))
```

Generating KML documents in a high-level language with built-in support for XML, such as Visual Basic or C#, is very easy. You can use statements like the ones shown here to build very long KML documents and save them to local files or submit them to a client application through web services, as you will see in Chapter 15.

Summary

In the last several chapters, you learned how to place lines and shapes on the map, how to allow users to draw on maps interactively, and how to store the geographical data in KML format. KML is not your only option; you could have used your own XML schema to persist the data, or you could have used the JSON format, which is equivalent to XML. No matter what format you use, you can persist the data laid over the map and reuse them later. After placing all the data on the map, you can even generate static pages that include all the data and post them on a web server, where users can select the map they're interested in and view it.

In short, you have all the information you need in order to build a complete GIS application, which is the topic of the next chapter. In the following chapter, you put together information from previous chapters to build a Windows application for performing basic GIS operations on Google Maps.

CHAPTER

12

Adding GIS Features to Mapping Applications

Now that you know how to annotate a map with lines and shapes and you have seen the basics of interactive drawing on a Google map, you're ready to develop a custom map-enabled application with GIS (Geographical Information Systems) features. GIS are some of the most complicated software packages, and they incorporate an endless list of features. According to Wikipedia, a geographic information system is a system designed to capture, store, manipulate, analyze, manage, and present all types of geographical data. Systems that support all these features are very, very costly. They also come in modules because most companies are interested in specific sets of features, not all of them. The modules themselves are expensive, but they also require backend support, large databases, conversion programs, and a whole lot of parameterization.

In this chapter, you'll only scratch the surface of applications that incorporate GIS features; the applications you will build in this chapter could be considered simply as drawing applications on top of a map. You have seen all the pieces of building a map-enabled application with GIS features. You know how to mark the features of interest on the map with markers and shapes, how to display data about the selected features in data windows, and how to annotate the map with labels. Now you're ready to build custom applications that incorporate the features you're interested in. For example, you can combine mapping components with reporting tools to produce reports with spatial data. Practical data have an inherent spatial component, even if this component is an address or a larger area on the map, and you can add value to any application by incorporating GIS features to it.

The Simple GIS Application

The application you build in this chapter is called Simple GIS, and there are two versions of it: the `Simple GIS.html` web page (shown in Figure 12-1) and the Simple GIS desktop application (shown in Figure 12-2) developed with Visual Studio (you will find a VB and a C# version of the desktop application in the chapter's support material). Both applications

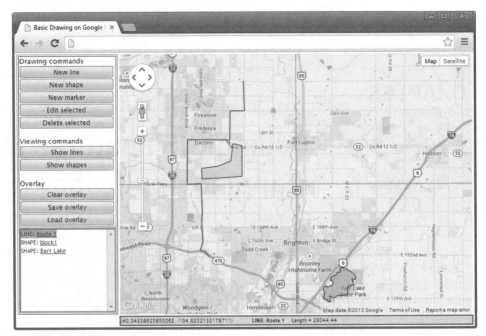

Figure 12-1 The Simple GIS web page allows users to draw shapes on the map.

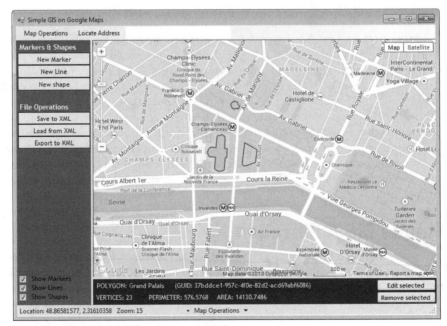

Figure 12-2 The Simple GIS application is a .NET application with the same functionality as the Simple GIS web page, but unlike its web counterpart, it deploys a rich Windows interface

use similar interfaces, and they're both based on the same script (well, not exactly the same—there are a few minor differences). The script that's used with the desktop application, for example, fires events in the external application with the `document.external` statement, which has no place in the context of a stand-alone web application. There are a few more minor differences, but the two scripts are very similar and you'll be able to leverage your understanding of the Google Maps API to both Windows and web applications.

This chapter doesn't introduce any new topics. Instead, it combines many of the topics covered in preceding chapters to demonstrate how they work together and how you can apply the knowledge you have acquired so far to build a practical application. The code is well documented and the best way to understand it is to dive in, explore it, and add new features. I discuss the most important parts of the code in this chapter, but skip the trivial operations. The sample applications of this chapter are quite lengthy, because they include a number of practical features and can become your starting point for specialized applications that address your specific requirements.

The Basic Features of the Application

Both applications allow users to annotate the map with markers, lines, and polygons. Users can literally draw on the map with the mouse and all entities they place on the map are editable. They can select an item by clicking on it and then edit it, or remove it from the map. Because it's difficult to locate a shape on a map with many items, an alternate selection technique was implemented. Users can locate an item by clicking its name in a list that contains all the items placed on the map—as long as the items have meaningful names, of course. The web version of the application displays the names of these items in a list displayed in the lower left pane, below the command buttons. Users can click the hyperlink with the shape's name in the list to select the item on the map.

The Windows version of the application uses a different selection mechanism. One of the map's context menu commands is the Show Items command, which displays an auxiliary window with the names of the items drawn on the map, and users can select one by clicking the appropriate entry on this form. The auxiliary form, along with the application's context menu, is shown in Figure 12-3. The selected item is drawn with a different fill color and the map's viewport changes so that the selected shape fits comfortably in it.

The desktop application's interface is a bit more elaborate, as the items on the auxiliary window are placed in a tree structure and users can expand/collapse individual branches of the tree. When the item is selected on the map, the list is updated to highlight the selected item. Likewise, when an item is clicked in the list, the corresponding item on the map is selected.

Drawing the Crosshair Cursor

To help users identify locations accurately, the application displays a crosshair cursor at the middle of the map. Users can drag the map until the location of interest is right in the middle of the map. The web page draws the crosshair cursor at all times. The desktop version of

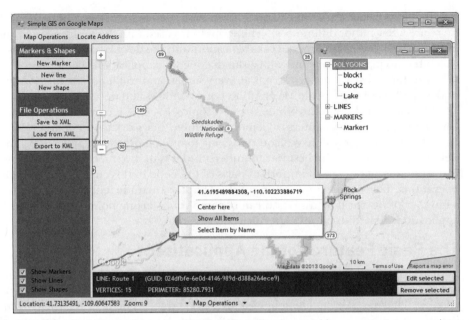

Figure 12-3 The desktop version of the Simple GIS application provides a context menu and one of the menu's commands leads to an auxiliary window with all the items on the map.

the application allows users to turn the crosshair on and off either with a menu command (Maps Operations | Show Crosshair) or with the same command in the status bar, as shown in Figure 12-2. The drawing of the crosshair cursor takes place in the script for both applications and it involves a few script variables and a function. The script variables are as follows:

```
// crosshair cursor support variables
var crossHair = true;
var centerHLine;
var centerVLine;
```

The first variable determines whether the crosshair cursor will be drawn or not. The other two variables represent the two perpendicular lines that form the cursor. The function that draws the crosshair cursor in the middle of the map is the drawCrosshair() function, shown in Listing 12-1.

Listing 12-1
The draw
Crosshair()
function

```
function drawCrosshair() {
    if (crossHair == true) {
        if (centerHLine != null) centerHLine.setMap(null);
        if (centerVLine != null) centerVLine.setMap(null);
        var bounds = map.getBounds();
        var sw = bounds.getSouthWest(); var ne = bounds.getNorthEast();
        var minLat = sw.lat(); var maxLat = ne.lat();
        var minLon = sw.lng(); var maxLon = ne.lng();
```

```
        var mapCenter = map.getCenter();
        var ctrLat = mapCenter.lat(); var ctrLon = mapCenter.lng();
        var centerCoordinatesV = [new google.maps.LatLng(minLat, ctrLon),
                            new google.maps.LatLng(maxLat, ctrLon)];
        var centerCoordinatesH = [new google.maps.LatLng(ctrLat, minLon),
                            new google.maps.LatLng(ctrLat, maxLon)];
        centerVLine = new google.maps.Polyline({
            path: centerCoordinatesV,
            strokeColor: "#FF0000", strokeOpacity: 1.0,
            strokeWeight: 0.75
        });
        centerHLine = new google.maps.Polyline({
            path: centerCoordinatesH,
            strokeColor: "#FF0000", strokeOpacity: 1.0,
            strokeWeight: 0.75
        });
        centerVLine.setMap(map); centerHLine.setMap(map);
    }
    else {
        if (centerHLine != null) centerHLine.setMap(null);
        if (centerVLine != null)  centerVLine.setMap(null);
    }
}
```

The code that displays the two perpendicular lines on the map is shown here for your convenience, since it has been discussed in earlier chapters. The drawCrosshair() function is associated with the map's bounds_changed event; every time the user drags the map, the cursor is redrawn. In the web version of the application, the crossHair variable is always true, and in the desktop version of the application, the same variable is controlled by the host application through the two functions:

```
function activateCrosshair() {
    crossHair = true;
}
function deactivateCrosshair() {
    crossHair = false;
}
```

Drawing a Path on the Map

The drawing of both lines and shapes is handled in the same manner: Both entities are based on a path, which is a collection of LatLng objects. The collection is an MVCArray object declared at the script level. Every time the user starts drawing a new line or a new polygon, the path variable is initialized to an empty MVCArray object with the following statement:

```
var path = new google.maps.MVCArray;
```

The process of drawing a new shape was described in detail in Chapter 9 and is repeated here briefly.

When users click on the map, a new vertex is added to the path. For this action, you must program the map's click event and react to it only if the user is actually drawing a new shape. To edit an existing vertex, users can simply drag the marker that identifies the vertex with the mouse. For this action, you must program the marker's drag event. Users can also insert new vertices and remove existing ones. The insertion of a new vertex takes place from within the click event of the markers that identify the vertices. When a marker is clicked, a new vertex is inserted halfway between the one that was clicked and the preceding one. The removal of a vertex is similar and it takes place from within the rightclick event of the marker that identifies the vertex. Let's see the code that implements these operations.

Start by adding a listener to the map's click event:

```
google.maps.event.addListener(map, 'click', addPoint);
```

The addPoint() function handles the map's click event and performs more actions than simply adding new vertices to the current path. For example, it clears the current selection if the user isn't editing a shape at the time. To distinguish between the operations, the script makes use of the variables drawingShape/editingShape and drawingLine/editingLine. Listing 12-2 shows the addPoint() function.

Listing 12-2
The
addPoint()
function

```
function addPoint(event) {
    if (editingShape == true) endShape();
    if (editingLine == true) endLine();
    var pinImage = new google.maps.MarkerImage(
            smallPin,
            new google.maps.Size(20, 20), new google.maps.Point(0, 0),
            new google.maps.Point(5, 20));
    if (drawingLine == true || drawingShape == true) {
        path.insertAt(path.length, event.latLng);
        var shapeMarker = new google.maps.Marker({
            position: event.latLng,
            map: map,  draggable: true,  icon: pinImage
        });
        google.maps.event.addListener(shapeMarker, 'rightclick',
            function () {
                shapeMarker.setMap(null);
                for (var i = 0; i < shapeMarkers.length &&
                                shapeMarkers[i] != shapeMarker; i++);
                shapeMarkers.splice(i, 1);
                path.removeAt(i);
            });
        google.maps.event.addListener(shapeMarker, 'click',
            function () {
                insertPoint(shapeMarker);
            });
        google.maps.event.addListener(shapeMarker, 'dragend',
            function (event) {
                for (var i = 0; i < shapeMarkers.length; i++) {
                    if (shapeMarkers[i] == shapeMarker)
                        path.setAt(i, shapeMarker.getPosition());
                }
            });
        shapeMarkers.push(shapeMarker);
        return;
```

```
  }  // ends if clause
  // user has clicked the map while not editing a shape.
  // Unselect the currently selected shape
  unselectPolyline();
  unselectPolygon();
  clearSelectedLink();
  selectedGUID = null;
  showSelectionDetails();
}
```

At the beginning, the code examines the current operation. If the user has clicked the map while editing a line or a shape, the function ends the current edit operation and terminates. There's no return statement, but the following `if` statements exclude any other action after ending an edit operation.

If the user is in the process of creating a new path, the script adds the coordinates of the location that was clicked to the `path` collection, which is an `MVCArray` object and it holds the path of the current line or shape. As soon as the new vertex is added to the `path` collection, the corresponding line or shape on the map is updated. Then it creates a new marker, the `shapeMarker` object, places it on the map and adds it to the `shapeMarkers` array. Note the statements that associate the `click`, `rightclick`, and `dragend` events of the newly created marker with the appropriate listeners. Two of these listeners are implemented with simple inline functions. The `rightclick` listener finds the marker that was clicked and removes it from the markers array, and its coordinates from the `path` array. The `dragend` event listener also finds out the marker that was clicked in the same array and updates its `position` property. You can also use the `drag` event for this action, in which case the shape will be updated as the user drags the marker. For very long paths, the `drag` event is not the best choice because it may take more than a few moments to locate the selected vertex.

The marker's `click` event is associated with the `insertPoint()` function, which is substantially more complex. This function finds out the index of the marker that was clicked, which is the same as the index of the corresponding vertex in the path, and then calculates the coordinates of the point that lies halfway between the marker that was clicked and the preceding one. This point lies on the line segment that connects the two points: This is where the new vertex, along with its marker, will be placed. Each marker added to the path with the `insertPoint()` function is also associated with three listeners for the `click`, `rightclick`, and `dragend` events. Listing 12-3 shows the implementation of the `insertPoint()` function of the script.

Listing 12-3
The
insertPoint()
function

```
function insertPoint(thisMarker) {
    var pinImage = new google.maps.MarkerImage(smallPin,
                         new google.maps.Size(20, 20),
                         new google.maps.Point(0, 0),
                         new google.maps.Point(5, 20))
    var insMarker = new google.maps.Marker({
        position: thisMarker.getPosition(),
        map: map, draggable: true, icon: pinImage,
        animation: google.maps.Animation.DROP
    });
    var idx = -1;
    for (i = 0; i < shapeMarkers.length; i++) {
```

```
        if (shapeMarkers[i].title == thisMarker.title) { idx = i; }
    }
    var pt1 = idx;  var pt2 = idx - 1;
    if (pt2 == -1) pt2 = shapeMarkers.length - 1;
    var positionLat = (shapeMarkers[pt1].getPosition().lat() +
                        shapeMarkers[pt2].getPosition().lat()) / 2
    var positionLng = (shapeMarkers[pt1].getPosition().lng() +
                        shapeMarkers[pt2].getPosition().lng()) / 2
    var newMarkerPosition =
            new google.maps.LatLng(positionLat, positionLng);
    path.insertAt(idx, newMarkerPosition);
    insMarker.position = newMarkerPosition;
    shapeMarkers.splice(idx, 0, insMarker);
    // iterate the shapeMarkers array and
    // rename all the vertices that make up the shape
    for (i = 0; i < shapeMarkers.length; i++) {
        shapeMarkers[i].setTitle("vertex: " + (i + 1));
    }
    google.maps.event.addListener(insMarker, 'rightclick', function () {
            insMarker.setMap(null);
            for (var i = 0; i < shapeMarkers.length &&
                                shapeMarkers[i] != insMarker; i++);
            shapeMarkers.splice(i, 1);
            path.removeAt(i);
            for (i = 0; i < shapeMarkers.length; i++) {
                shapeMarkers[i].setTitle("vertex: " + (i + 1));
            }
    });
    google.maps.event.addListener(insMarker, 'click', function () {
            insertPoint(insMarker);
    });
    google.maps.event.addListener(insMarker, 'dragend', function () {
            var idx;
            for (var i = 0; i < shapeMarkers.length; i++) {
                if (shapeMarkers[i].title == this.title) idx = i;
            }
            path.setAt(idx, this.getPosition());
    });
}
```

Editing Paths

Users can also edit existing shapes. To edit a shape, users must first select it with the mouse and then click the Edit Selected button. When this button is clicked, the editSelected() function is executed. This function makes sure that no other edit operation is currently in progress. If so, it displays a message in an alert box and returns. Next, it locates the selected shape from the value of the selectedGUID variable. This variable holds the ID of the selected shape and is also the key to the corresponding associative array with the markers that identify the shape's vertices. Depending on the type of the selected item, the function calls one of the editPolyline(), editPolygon(), or editMarker() functions, passing as an argument the selected item's GUID. Listing 12-4 shows the editSelectedShape() function:

```
function editSelectedShape() {
    if (drawingShape || editingShape || drawingLine || editingLine) {
        alert('You can't edit the selected item at this time.');
        return;
    }
    if (!(selectedGUID == null || selectedGUID == undefined)) {
        if (polygons[selectedGUID]) {
            if (editPolygon(selectedGUID)) {
                return true;
            }
            else
                return false;
        }
        if (lines[selectedGUID]) {
            if (editPolyline(selectedGUID))      return true;
            else return false;
        }
        if (markers[selectedGUID]) {
            if (editMarker(selectedGUID))      return true;
            else return false;
        }
    }
}
```

If the GUID is an existing key in the polygons array, the function calls the editPolygon() function, which initiates the edit operation for the selected polygon. To prepare the polygon for editing, the editPolygon() function, shown in Listing 12-5, creates an array of markers, one for each vertex of the polygon's path. Then, it associates a listener with their click, rightclick, and drag events. They're the same event listeners used by the insertPoint() function because the vertices are manipulated in the same manner. Users can edit the polygon's path when they create it, as well as when they edit it. The actual code for the three event listeners is not shown in the listing as it's exactly the same as in Listing 12-3 (you will find placeholders in Listing 12-5 where the code of the event listeners should appear).

```
function editPolygon(GUID) {
    if (editingShape || editingLine || drawingShape || drawingLine)
        return false;
    selectPolygon(GUID);
    editingShape = true;
    shapeMarkers = [];
    poly = polygons[GUID];
    currentPolygonGUID = GUID;
    path = new google.maps.MVCArray;
    var vertices = polygons[GUID].getPath();
    for (var i = 0; i < vertices.length; i++) {
        var xy = vertices.getAt(i);     // the current vertex's coordinates
        var image = new google.maps.MarkerImage(smallPin,
```

```
                               new google.maps.Size(20, 20),
                               new google.maps.Point(0, 0),
                               new google.maps.Point(5, 20))
        path.insertAt(path.length, xy);
        var shapeMarker = new google.maps.Marker({
            position: xy,
            map: map,
            draggable: true,
            title: "vertex: " + (i + 1),
            icon: image
        });
        shapeMarkers.push(shapeMarker);
        google.maps.event.addListener(shapeMarker, 'dragend',
                    function (event) {
                        // the dragend event's listener
                    });
        google.maps.event.addListener(shapeMarker, 'click',
                    function (event) {
                        insertPoint(this);
                    });
        google.maps.event.addListener(shapeMarker, 'rightclick',
                                    function () {
                        // the rightclick event's listener
        });
    } // end for
    poly.setPath(new google.maps.MVCArray([path]));
    poly.setMap(map);
    return true;
} // end function
```

This function starts by selecting the polygon to be edited, just in case, and then creates a new path with the vertices of the polygon being edited. For each vertex, it creates a marker and places it on the map. These markers identify the vertices of the path, which are draggable so that users can reposition them to modify the shape's path. Moreover, two listeners for their `click` and `rightclick` events are added.

These two actions correspond to the insertion of a new vertex and the removal of an existing vertex, similar to the listeners you added to the new markers while the shape was being drawn. In effect, this function re-generates the path that describes the shape, places markers at the shape's vertices, and attaches the same events as the function that draws a new shape. Its job is to leave the shape in the same state as it was before the last edit operation was completed.

Handling the Markers

The part of the application that handles the markers is also simple. The marker data is displayed on a `<div>` element, the `MarkerData` element, which contains the various input boxes arranged on a table. The `MarkerData` element is usually hidden and it's displayed when the user chooses to add a new marker, or edit an existing one. When the New Marker button is clicked, the script calls the `newMarker()` function, which clears the fields on the dialog box, as shown in Figure 12-4, and makes the `MarkerData` element visible.

After supplying the appropriate values on the dialog box's fields, users can click OK to invoke the `addMarker()` function, which creates a new `Marker` object based on the

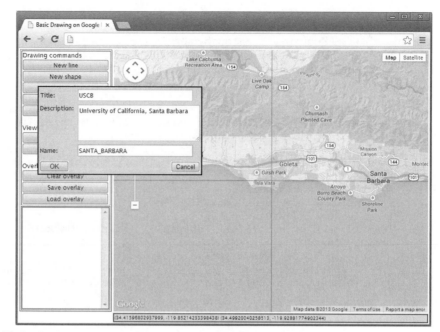

Figure 12-4   Editing a marker's data in a modal dialog box

supplied values and places it on the map. The `addMarker()` function handles both the insertion of a new marker as well as the update of an existing marker after an edit operation.

The implementation of the `addMarker()` function is rather lengthy, so let's run through its operations quickly. Listing 12-6 shows the code that implements the function.

Listing 12-6
The `addMarker()` function adds a new marker on the map, or updates the attributes of an existing one after an edit operation.

```
function addMarker() {
    // if no marker selected, create a new one
    if (currentMarkerGUID == null) currentMarkerGUID = GenerateGuid();
    // extract user-supplied values from the dialog
    var title = document.getElementById("txtMarkerTitle").value;
    var description =
            document.getElementById("txtMarkerDescription").value;
    var name = document.getElementById("txtMarkerName").value;
    if (!markers[currentMarkerGUID]) {
        var markerPos = map.getCenter();
        var marker = new google.maps.Marker({
                    position: markerPos, title: title, draggable: true
        });
        marker.objInfo = {'Name': name, 'Description': description};
        marker.setMap(map);
        markers[currentMarkerGUID] = marker;
        var localGUID = currentMarkerGUID;
        // add event listener for the click event of the new marker
        google.maps.event.addListener(markers[localGUID], 'click',
                function () {
                    var markerContent = "<div style='width: 260px;'><h2>" +
```

```
                    this.title + "</h2>" + this.objInfo.Description+
                "<br/>" + this.position + "</div>";
            selectedGUID = localGUID; showSelectionDetails();
            infowindow.close(); infowindow.setContent(markerContent);
            infowindow.open(map, markers[localGUID]);
        })

        // add event listener for the dragend event of the new marker
        google.maps.event.addListener(markers[currentMarkerGUID],
                    'dragend', function (event) {
                            this.position=event.latLng;})
        document.getElementById("MarkerData").style.visibility =
                                            "hidden";
        // create a new hyperlink for the list <div> element.
        var itemDiv = document.createElement('a');
        itemDiv.style.fontSize = "8pt";
        itemDiv.setAttribute('id', 'shapeDIV' + currentMarkerGUID);
        itemDiv.innerHTML  =  'MARKER: ' +
                '<a href="javascript:selectShape(\'' +
                currentMarkerGUID + '\')">' +  name + '</a>' + '<br/>';
        document.getElementById("list").appendChild(itemDiv);
    }
    else {
        markers[currentMarkerGUID].title =
                    document.getElementById("txtMarkerTitle").value;
        markers[currentMarkerGUID].objInfo = {
            Name : document.getElementById("txtMarkerName").value,
            Description :
                document.getElementById("txtMarkerDescription").value};
        var element =
                document.getElementById("shapeDIV" + currentMarkerGUID);
        element = element.getElementsByTagName("A")[0];
        element.innerHTML=document.getElementById("txtMarkerName").value;
        document.getElementById("MarkerData").style.visibility = "hidden";
    }
}
```

The script starts by creating a new marker with the user-supplied data (the marker's title and description, which should appear on an `InfoWindow` object when the user clicks the marker). The data are read from the `MarkerData` element's fields and the new marker is represented by the `marker` variable. This variable is then stored in the `markers` collection and also placed on the map. Then, the script creates the hyperlink that corresponds to the new marker and adds it to the list of items in the lower-left pane. The process, which is the same for all items, is described in the following section. Finally, the script adds three listeners for the following events of the newly created marker:

- **click event** This listener displays the marker's description in an info window.
- **dragend event** The markers are draggable and users can relocate them at will. When a marker is dragged to a new location, the `dragend` event's listener updates the position of the marker in the `markers` array.

The last few statements print the selected marker's name in the status bar.

Updating the List of Shapes

Another interesting aspect of the application is the insertion of the hyperlink that identifies
the current shape in the lower-left pane. This pane maintains a list of all items currently on
the map. Each item is identified by its type and its name. The item's type is identified by
one of the strings "Marker," "Line," and "Shape." The item's name is formatted as a hyperlink,
and you can click this hyperlink to select and bring into view the corresponding item on the
map. Whether the user selects an item by clicking it on the map or by clicking its matching
hyperlink in the pane with the item names, the script calls one of the selectPolygon(),
selectPolyline(), or selectMarker() functions. All three functions are similar:
They unselect the currently selected shape to ensure that there will never be two selected
items on the map; then, they redraw the selected items in a different color so that they
stand out; and finally, they call another function to display the attributes of the selected
items in the status bar below the map.

Let's start with the statements that create the <a> element with the selected item's
hyperlink and add it to the list:

```
var itemDiv = document.createElement('a');
itemDiv.style.fontSize = "8pt";
itemDiv.setAttribute('id', 'shapeDIV' + currentMarkerGUID);
itemDiv.innerHTML  =  'MARKER: ' +
        '<a href="javascript:selectShape(\'' +
        currentMarkerGUID + '\')">' +  name + '</a>' + '<br/>';
document.getElementById("list").appendChild(itemDiv);
```

The itemDiv variable represents an <a> element and it's created on the fly. This
element has a unique name that contains the selected item's GUID. The hyperlink's
destination is the selectShape() function. Finally, the element is added to the list
element of the page.

The polygonSelected() and lineSelected() functions call the
showSelectionDetails() function to display the attributes of the selected item in the
status bar. The same function is also called when the user unselects any item on the map,
and also when they remove an item. When the showSelectionDetails() function is
called with a null argument, it simply clears the section of the status bar where the item
details are shown. Otherwise, it prints the selected item's name and its basic properties: a
line's length, a shape's perimeter and area, and a marker's title.

The showSelectionDetails() function handles each item differently because lines
don't have areas and markers have a name and a title only. The description of the selected
item is printed in the application's status bar (a stripe below the map). The implementation
of the function is rather trivial, and you can look it up in the sample HTML file.

The Desktop Version of Simple GIS

Now let's switch our attention to the desktop version of the application, which is a .NET
application. To simplify the coding of the application, a class was introduced to handle the
communication between the host application and the HTML page's script. This is the
GMap.vb file in the project and it assumes that the main form of the application, which is
called frmGIS, contains the WebBrowser1 control. The GMap class provides methods that
call the script's functions and raises events every time the script calls an external function in

the class. The class isolates the HTML/Javascript components of the application from the main application, which calls methods in the GMap class.

To initiate the drawing of a new line, the GMap class provides the StartPolygon() method, which accepts as an argument the polygon's GUID and name and calls the startShape() function of the script. The following are the relevant statements of the StartPolygon() method:

```
Public Sub StartPolygon(ByVal _polygonName As String,
                        ByVal _newPolygonID As String)
   _newPolygonID = System.Guid.NewGuid.ToString
   _editingPolygon = True
   frmGIS.WebBrowser1.Document.InvokeScript("startShape",
        {_newPolygonID, PolygonName})
End Sub
```

To end the drawing of the current polygon, the EndPolygon() function must be called:

```
Public Sub EndPolygon()
    _newPolygonID = Nothing
    frmGIS.WebBrowser1.Document.InvokeScript("endShape")
    _editingPolygon = False
End Sub
```

By embedding all the code that controls the script in a class and exposing its functionality through methods, you can greatly simplify the host application's code. The code behind the New Line button, for example, is as follows:

Listing 12-7
The .NET code
to initiate the
drawing of
a line

```
Private Sub bttnLine_Click(sender As Object, e As EventArgs)
                  Handles bttnLine.Click


    If bttnLine.Text.ToUpper = "New line".ToUpper Then
        If GMap1.IsInDrawMode Then
            MsgBox("Please edit the current edit operation first")
            Exit Sub
        End If
        bttnLine.Text = "End line"
        Dim pName As String =
            InputBox("Please enter an optional name for the new line",
                    "New line name", "New line")
        If pName.Trim.Length = 0 Then
            bttnLine.Text = "New line"
            Exit Sub
        End If
        Try
            GMap1.StartLine(pName)
        Catch ex As Exception
            MsgBox("Operation failed. A shape by the same name (" &
                    pName & ") exists already" & vbCrLf & ex.Message)
            bttnLine.Text = "New line"
            Exit Sub
        End Try
    Else
        bttnLine.Text = "New line"
```

```
        GMap1.EndLine()
    End If
End Sub
```

Quite a bit of code, but it doesn't contact the script directly; instead, it calls methods of another .NET component, the `GMap` class. Apart from the statement that calls the `StartLine()` method, the event handler contains mostly error checking code.

The Basic Data Structures

Before exploring the Windows application's code, let's review the structure of the custom objects that are used to represent the various items placed on the map. These objects are based on the following classes, which are declared in the `GMap.vb` module of the application, shown in Listing 12-8.

Listing 12-8
The structure of the application's basic objects

```
Public Class GeoPoint
    Public Property Latitude As Double
    Public Property Longitude As Double
End Class

Public Class Polygon
    Public Property PolygonID As String
    Public Property Name As String
    Public Property LineColor As Color
    Public Property LineWidth As Integer
    Public Property Area As Double
    Public Property Perimeter As Double
    Public Property Vertices As New List(Of GeoPoint)
End Class

Public Class Polyline
    Public Property PolylineID As String
    Public Property Name As String
    Public Property LineColor As Color
    Public Property LineWidth As Integer
    Public Property Perimeter As Double
    Public Property Vertices As New List(Of GeoPoint)
End Class

Public Class Marker
    Public Property MarkerID As String
    Public Property Title As String
    Public Property Name As String
    Public Property Description As String
    Public Property Position As GeoPoint
End Class
```

The `GeoPoint` class represents a location, and it's used by all other classes. The marker's `Position` property, for example, is a `GeoPoint` type. The paths of lines and shapes are lists of `GeoPoint` types.

The Application's Context Menu

The desktop application uses a context menu for the map. It's a very simple menu with just a few commands. The most interesting one is the Show All Items command, which iterates through the elements of each array of items (lines, polygons, and markers) and displays their basic data on a TreeView control.

This control was selected to allow users to expand and collapse items at will as they're trying to locate the desired item, as shown in Figure 12-3. Listing 12-9 shows how the TreeView control is populated with the polygons already on the map.

Listing 12-9
Adding polygon data to a tree structure

```
Private Sub menuItemCommand2_Click(sender As Object,
                        e As EventArgs) Handles nenuItemCommand2.Click
    Dim allPolys = GMap1.GetAllPolygons
    frmItemsTree.tvItems.Nodes.Clear()
    Dim ndPolys = frmItemsTree.tvItems.Nodes.Add("POLYGONS")
    For Each marker In allPolys
        Dim Nd = ndPolys.Nodes.Add(marker.Name)
        Nd.Tag = marker
    Next
End Sub
```

The code shown here shows only how to populate the sub-tree with the polygons. The code for the other two sub-trees is very similar. Note that the object's name is used as a caption, and the actual object is stored in the node's Tag property. When an item is selected on the tree with the mouse, the statements of Listing 12-10 are executed:

Listing 12-10
Selecting an item on the map when its name is clicked in the tree

```
Private Sub tvItems_NodeMouseClick(
            sender As Object, e As TreeNodeMouseClickEventArgs)
            Handles tvItems.NodeMouseClick
    If e.Node.Level = 0 Then Exit Sub
    Dim guid As String = ""
    Dim type As String = e.Node.Parent.Text
    If type = "LINES" Then
        guid = CType(e.Node.Tag, Polyline).PolylineID
        GMap1.SelectLine(guid)
    End If
    If type = "POLYGONS" Then
        guid = CType(e.Node.Tag, Polygon).PolygonID
        GMap1.SelectPolygon(guid)
    End If
    If type = "MARKERS" Then
        guid = CType(e.Node.Tag, Marker).MarkerID
        GMap1.SelectMarker(guid)
    End If
End Sub
```

When the user selects a different item on this auxiliary window, the code calls one of the SelectLine(), SelectPolygon(), or SelectMarker() methods of the GMap1 object to highlight the selected item on the map. The auxiliary window is updated the moment it's requested. If a new shape is added to the map while this window is open, the contents of the tree structure on the auxiliary window won't be updated. If you want to incorporate this selection technique in your applications, you should provide the code to update the contents of the tree structure as new shapes are added or existing shapes are deleted so that it's always up to date. A simpler, but less elegant, approach would be to provide a Refresh button on the auxiliary form so that users can update it at will.

The highlighting of the selected items on the map is based on the following script variables, which you can set to the desired values:

```
var selectedFillColor = '#773377';
var selectedStrokeColor = "#008000";
var unselectedFillColor = '#00EEEE';
var unselectedStrokeColor = "#000000";
var selectedPenWidth = 2;
var unselectedPenWidth = 1;
```

You can also provide methods to set the values of these variables from within the host application and make them parameters of the application. To make the application more useful, you can create layers and assign each shape to a layer. The layer isn't represented on the map with a special entity; just create an additional property for each item you place on the map, say the `layer` property, and assign an integer value to it. By separating the items on the map in virtual layers, you can manipulate these items in groups: You can show/hide an entire layer at once, change the basic attributes of all items on the same layer, and so on. Simply write a loop that iterates all items and examines their `layer` setting. If they belong to a specific layer, you can change their stroke or fill color, or show/hide them. You just need a user-friendly mechanism to associate items with layers as well as to move items from one layer to another. This type of functionality can be implemented easily in a desktop application with point-and-click or even drag-drop operations. Doing the same on a web interface requires a considerable amount of code.

Requesting the Map Items

The various shapes you place on the map aren't stored in the host application, although it would be very simple to maintain a collection of objects in a .NET application. The shapes are stored in arrays maintained by the script, because there are functions in the script that iterate through these arrays to locate items. Because the script is responsible for manipulating the map's objects, it makes perfect sense to maintain these objects in the script. What doesn't make any sense is to maintain two identical lists, one in the page's script and another one in the host application. If your code is perfect, the two arrays will be always synchronized. This approach, however, means more code to write and test and more potential error sources. Data should be stored at a single location; otherwise, you may end up with two different versions of the same data, and then you're in for some serious debugging.

The host application, therefore, needs a mechanism to request data from the script. The `GMap` class provides the `GetAllPoygons()`, `GetAllLines()`, and `GetAllMarkers()` methods, which return a list populated with objects of the appropriate type. All three functions are nearly identical, and here's how they request the various shapes from the script.

First, they call a function to retrieve the IDs of the shapes. The `getPolylineIDs()` function of the script, for example, returns the GUIDs of all lines that have been drawn on the map. Then, they iterate through the appropriate collection using the GUIDs as keys and call another function in the script, `getPolylineData()`, passing as an argument the GUID of the current line. The `getPolylineData()` function returns a custom object describing the requested `Polyline` object. Listing 12-11 shows the code of the `getPolylineData()` function.

Listing 12-11
The get
Polyline
Data() function
returns a custom
object with the
selected line's
attributes.

```
function getPolylineData(guid) {
    var linePath = lines[guid].getPath();
    var lineLength =
      google.maps.geometry.spherical.computeLength(lines[guid].getPath());
    var linePath = polylines[guid].getPath();
    var path = "";
    for (i = 0; i < linePath.length; i++) {
        path += linePath.getAt(i).lat() + ',' +
                linePath.getAt(i).lng() + '\n';
    }
    var L = { "Name": polylines[guid].objInfo,
              "Length": lineLength,
              "Path": path.substring(1, path.length - 1) };
    return L;
}
```

The object returned by the `getPolygonData()` function has three properties: the name of the polygon (`Name` property), the length of the polygon (`Length` property), and a long string with the coordinates of the path's vertices `Path` property). The `Path` property has the same structure as the `<coordinates>` element of KML: Each point's latitude and longitude values are separated by a comma and consecutive points are separated by a space. The `GetAllPolygons()` and `GetAllPolylines()` methods of the `GMap` class parse this string and create a series of `Point` objects, one for each vertex. Listing 12-12 shows the implementation of the `GetAllPolygons()` method of the `GMap` class, which returns a list of Polygon objects.

Listing 12-12
The GetAll
Polygons()
method of
the GMap class

```
Public Function GetAllPolygons() As List(Of Polygon)
    Dim allKeys = Convert.ToString(
            frmGIS.WebBrowser1.Document.InvokeScript("getPolygonIDs"))
    Dim keys = allKeys.Trim.Split(vbLf)
    Dim polygons As New List(Of Polygon)
    For p = 0 To keys.Length - 1
        If keys(p) <> "" Then
            Dim key = keys(p).Split("|")(0).Trim
            Dim name = keys(p).Split("|")(1).Trim
            Dim Plgn = frmGIS.WebBrowser1.Document.InvokeScript(
                         "getPolygonData", {key})
            Dim PG As New Polygon
                PG.Name = name
                PG.PolygonID = key
                PG.Area = Plgn.Area
                PG.Perimeter = Plgn.Length
                Dim vertices = Plgn.Path.split(" ")
                For i = 0 To vertices.length - 1
```

```
              PG.Vertices.Add(New GeoPoint With {
                  .Latitude = Double.Parse(vertices(i).
                                     Split(",")(0), clt),
                  .Longitude = Double.Parse(vertices(i).
                                     Split(",")(1), clt)})
          Next
          polygons.Add(PG)
        End If
    Next
    Return polygons
End Function
```

Saving the Map Annotations

A major aspect of both applications is the persistence of the shapes you place on the map. While with the desktop version of the application you can use any format and store the data to a local file, things are not as simple with the web version of the application. To put it simply, there's no way for a web application to store data to a local file. Even with HTML5, which provides the `FileSystem` object and enables the client application to access files on the local file system, you can only use files in the Download folder. To save the map's data to a file with the web version of the application, you need to use a server component. This component could be a web application running on your server, or a web service that can accept and service requests from the client. Web services are discussed in Chapter 15, and they are a very good option for an application like this. However, you still need a mechanism to enable users to select the desired set of annotations—the equivalent of a file—and limit users to the annotation files they have created in earlier sessions. Developing such an interface with a web application is quite a task. To keep the example manageable, this book doesn't cover server side applications.

Handling the Data in the Web Application

The sample application generates JSON arrays of custom objects for each entity type and displays the array definition in the browser, in the place of the map, as shown in Figure 12-5. This window is just a `<div>` element that covers the same area as the map. The application makes the map invisible and the `<div>` element with the data visible. Users can return to the map by clicking the Close hyperlink at the top.

When the Save Overlay button is clicked, the application calls the `saveOverlay()` function, which generates the array definitions and prints them. Listing 12-13 shows the implementation of the function.

Listing 12-13
The JSON descriptions of map's annotations

```
function saveOverlay() {
    document.getElementById("notepad").style.height="100%";
    document.getElementById("map_canvas").style.height = "0px";
    var divHTML="<a href=# onclick='javascript:closeWindow()'>" +
                "<b>Close window</b></a>";
    divHTML += '<br/><br/>';
    // show all lines
    if (lines != undefined) {
        var strLines = "var Polylines = [";
        for (key in lines) {
```

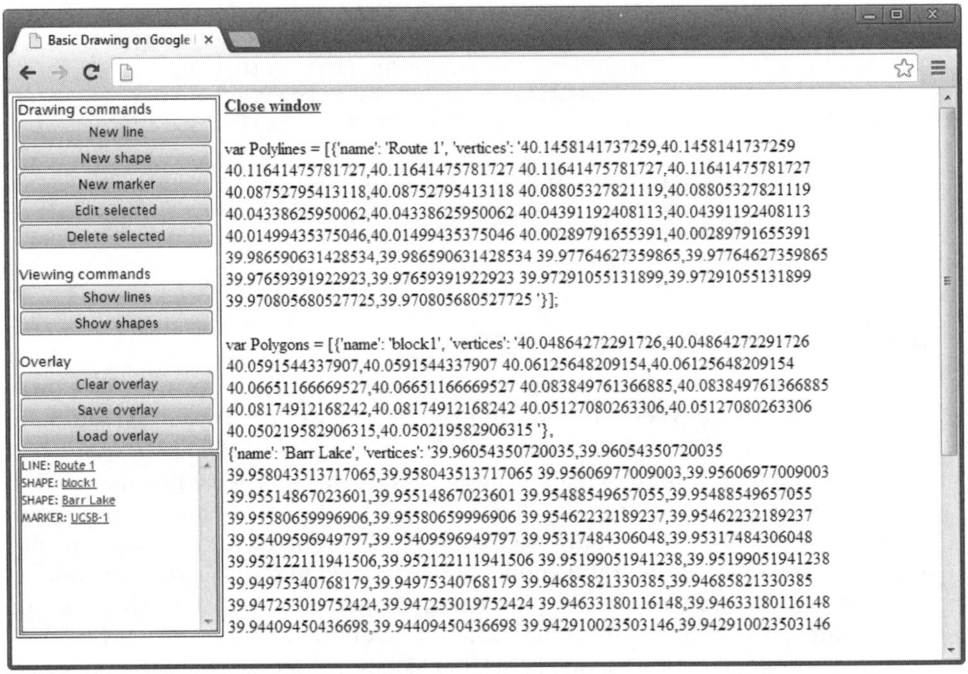

Figure 12-5 Displaying the definition of the arrays with the descriptions of the various items placed on the map

```
        strLines += "{'name': '" + lines[key].objInfo + "'";
        var vertices="";
        for (idx= 0; idx < lines[key].getPath().length; idx++) {
            vertices += lines[key].getPath().getAt(idx).lat() + "," +
                        lines[key].getPath().getAt(idx).lat() + " ";
        }
        strLines += ", 'vertices': '" + vertices + "'},<br/>";
    }
    divHTML += strLines.substring(0, strLines.length-6);
    divHTML += "];" + "<br/><br/>";
}
    divHTML += strShapes.substring(0, strShapes.length-6);
    divHTML += "]";
}
document.getElementById("notepad").innerHTML = divHTML;
}
```

The listing shows only the code that generates the definition of the array with the lines. The arrays with the shapes and markers are generated with similar statements, which were omitted from the listing for brevity. The last statement in the listing assigns the divHTML variable, which holds the text to be printed on the notepad element of the page.

Saving the Annotation Data in the Desktop Application

Persisting the data in the .NET version of the application is much simpler, not to mention that you have many options, including the storing of the shape descriptions to a local file. You can create a KML file with the shapes on the map, a custom XML document to describe the same shapes, arrays of custom objects, and you can even submit the data to a database. The sample application creates a KML document to describe the same data and saves the document to a local file. The KML file contains three `<Folder>` elements, which in turn contain the items of each type (lines, polygons, and markers) as `<Placemark>` tags. The structure of a KML file generated by the application is shown in Listing 12-14. The KML document in the listing contains the descriptions of two lines and one polygon.

Listing 12-14
The structure of the KML document with the map's annotations

```
<kml xmlns="http://www.opengis.net/kml/2.2">
    <Document>
        <Folder>
            <name>Lines</name>
            <Placemark>
                <name>Route1</name>
                <LineString>
                    <coordinates>
                        -105.125427246094,9.98238166771568 ...
                    </coordinates>
                </LineString>
            </Placemark>
            <Placemark>
                <name>Route2</name>
                <LineString>
                    <coordinates>
                        -105.100708007813,9.8918262417256 ...
                    </coordinates>
                </LineString>
            </Placemark>
            <name>Polygons</name>
            <Placemark>
                <name>Block1</name>
                <OuterBoundaryIs>
                    <Linestring>
                        <coordinates>
                            -105.110321044922,9.84175880481816 ...
                        </coordinates>
                    </Linestring>
                </OuterBoundaryIs>
            </Placemark>
        </Folder>
    </Document>
</kml>
```

The code that generates the KML document is straightforward Visual Basic/C# code and will not be presented here. You can open the project and examine it. You will also find some additional information on generating XML documents in Chapter 15. The code that reads the KML document is equivalent, and you can examine it on your own. You can also overlay the KML files generated by the application on a map, as explained in Chapter 11.

Summary

In this chapter, you developed a map-enabled application with GIS features, both as a web page and as a .NET program. Either version of the Simple GIS application can be used as your starting point for a highly customized application. You will provide the code for features that are unique to your application and address very specific requirements.

In the following chapter, you're going to learn how to store spatial data to a database. KML files and arrays of custom JSON objects are fine for small scale applications, but if you have a large collection of items to place on the map, you need to be able to use a database. You should be able to store your data to the database and then select only the items you need. The topic of querying databases based on spatial criteria, such as the distance of a location from another or the intersection of a highway (line) and a county (polygon), is an extremely interesting topic.

13 — SQL Spatial: Backend Databases for Spatial Data

We're at a point now to discuss the storage of large volumes of spatial data in databases. What good is it to annotate maps with markers and shapes if you can't store these features into a central database and reuse it as needed? While KML will serve you well for isolated features and small-scale applications, as you accumulate more and more data the need for central storage will become pressing. The question of storing large sets of data isn't unique to spatial data; it's a universal problem and it's addressed with databases.

Database Management Systems (DBMS) are special systems designed for storing large volumes of data. You can also use very large files to store data, but databases are very complex objects that abstract the complexity of manipulating individual data items and provide mechanisms to quickly locate the items you're interested in. Traditionally, DBMSs were designed to handle typical business and scientific data types, such as text, numbers, and dates. Modern databases, such as SQL Server and Oracle, can also handle spatial data.

Do You Really Need Spatial Databases?

You can store the numeric values that represent longitude/latitude pairs as numeric values in any database table, can't you? That's true, but when it comes to querying the data, you'd have to write some serious code to efficiently locate the items you're interested in. Such items could be all hotels within a 5-mile radius from your current location, or the cities that fall into a polygon that represents a county. Thanks to Google, you don't have to write any code to perform distance calculations in your scripts. If your data resides in a database, however, you should be able to perform similar queries with ease. And this is exactly why a new data type is needed. All major DBMSs include support for spatial queries, which enables you to quickly retrieve data based on geographical features. You will find many examples of querying data with a spatial component in this chapter, but let's start by examining how spatial data are stored in databases and how spatial data are described.

Using Tables with Spatial Features

While all major DBMSs (such as SQL Server, Oracle, MySql, and so on) support spatial data, this chapter deals with SQL Server's spatial features. I selected SQL Server because there's a free version, SQL Server 2012 Express, which fully supports spatial features. As for the methods you use to query spatial data, they're part of the OGC (Open GeoSpatial Consortium) standard and are supported by both Oracle and MySql. The topic of handling spatial data is huge, and this chapter is only an introduction to the spatial features supported by SQL. In this chapter, you learn about the methods you'll use to retrieve spatial data from a SQL server in the context of developing map-enabled applications with the Google Maps API.

All major databases provide a language for manipulating the data, and all languages are based on the SQL standard (Structured Query Language). The examples in this chapter are written in T-SQL (Transactional SQL), which is the language of SQL Server. T-SQL is based on SQL and it contains its own extensions to standard SQL. Oracle's SQL is called PL/SQL (Procedural Language/SQL); it supports the core of SQL and enhances it with its own extensions. All queries in this chapter are standard SQL queries and use the OGC geography extensions.

To start your exploration of spatial data, you can open the `Samples.sql` file, which comes with this book's support material in SQL Server's Management Studio, and execute it. It will create a new database, the GEO database, and will add five tables:

- **USCities**   Contains city names along with populations and geo-locations.
- **USStates**   Contains just state names and is used in conjunction with the USCities table.
- **World Airports**   Contains the names and locations for 9,000 airports around the world. Use the data in the World Airports table to execute spatial queries on non-trivial data.
- **Highways**   Contains the paths of two major highways, the US 5 and US 101.
- **CountyBorders**   Contains the outlines of a few counties in California.

One of the table names contains a space, and this table's name must be embedded in square brackets in the corresponding queries. The brackets are not used in the text, just in the queries involving this table. The last two tables will be used later in the chapter with examples that involve lines and polygons. In the course of this chapter, you will see how these tables were populated and how to insert additional data, if you're interested.

To populate the tables, execute the remaining SQL scripts in this chapter's support material. The scripts are presented in the sidebar "The SQL Scripts to Populate the Sample Tables" later in this chapter.

The examples will also work with SQL Server 2008 (including the 2008 Express version) with one exception: The `STContains` method was introduced with SQL Server 2012 and was not supported by earlier versions. If you don't need to select points that lie within specific polygons, all supported versions of SQL Server will do. This method, however, is too convenient to ignore and you should consider switching to version 2012 of SQL Server.

This chapter contains no JavaScript code, or applications. It's an introduction to the topic of handling geospatial data with SQL Server, and all examples are queries that can be executed in SQL Server Management Studio.

Designing the Sample Tables

Let's start with a quick overview of the tables you're going to see in the examples. The `Samples.sql` script will create the GEO database for you and it will add the tables mentioned. Assuming that you have installed one of the versions of SQL Server 2008 or 2012 on your computer, double-click the `Samples.sql` file and it will open in SQL Server's Management Studio in a new Query window. Execute the script, and the database will be set up for you. Then, switch to the GEO database and explore its tables and their structure.

You can also create the tables on your own with the table editor in SQL Server's Management Studio. Just right-click the Tables item under the GEO database and you'll be presented with a nice interface that allows you to specify column names and types. If you want to see, and possibly edit, the tables created by the script, right-click a table name in the left pane of Figure 13-1 and select the Design command. The World Airports table, for example, contains the columns shown in the following table.

Column Name	Data Type
ID	bigint
Code	varchar(5)
Name	varchar(100)
City	varchar(50)
Country	varchar(50)
Location	geography

The ID column is an Identity column (it's assigned a unique value every time a new row is added). The remaining columns store text, except for the last one, which stores spatial data. The Location column is of the `geography` type and stores geography features of any type: points, lines, and polygons.

The Location column of the World Airports table stores points only because all airports are identified by a pair of latitude/longitude values. You usually don't mix features with different geometries in the same column. In other words, you avoid storing points and polygons in the same column because this will complicate your queries. If a column contains both points and polygons, it wouldn't make much sense to request the area or the length of the points. You would have to keep track of each item's `geography` type so it's best to store different geometry types in different columns, or different tables. By the way, SQL Server won't crash if you attempt to calculate the length or the area of a point; it will simply return the value null.

Figure 13-1 shows the results of a query that selects all rows in the World Airports table and displays them as text in the Results pane. The Location column is a binary column, and you will see later in this chapter how to display locations in a human-readable format.

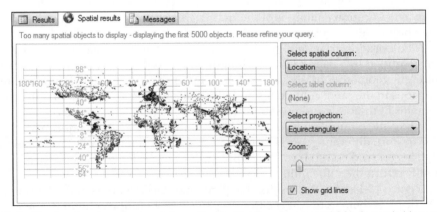

Figure 13-1   The results of a query that selects all the rows from the [World Airports] table in the Results pane

Figure 13-2 shows the distribution of the airports on the latitude/longitude grid, shown in the Spatial Results pane. This grid is basically a map without a background; SQL Server Management Studio populates this grid automatically with points, lines, and polygons, depending on the query.

The remaining sample tables have a similar structure: an ID value that identifies each row, a number of text columns, and a `geography` column to store the geospatial data. In the World Airports table, the Location column stores the location of the corresponding airport. In the Highways table, the `geography` column is called Route and it stores a path

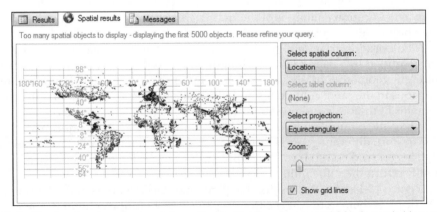

Figure 13-2   Viewing the airports as points on the Spatial Results pane of SQL Server's Management Studio

(the highway's route). This table contains two highways: US 5 and, US 101 and is shown in the following table. The Route column of this table stores a `LineString` object, which is equivalent to the `Polyline` object of the Google Maps API. The CountyBorders table stores the polygons that outline each county; in the Border column.

Column Name	Data Type
ID	bigint
Highway	varchar(20)
Route	geography

Inserting Spatial Data

The first really non-trivial task is to insert geospatial data in your tables. Inserting data into the text columns is straightforward, but how about the geography data? There are several ways to represent geography data and they're explained in the following sections. After you understand how to insert geographical data into a table, you'll see how to perform elaborate queries based on geographical data.

There are three ways to represent spatial data: the Well-Known Text format, the Well-Known Binary format, and the GML (Geography Markup Language) format. All three formats are discussed in the following sections.

Well-Known Text Representation of Geography Data

There are three types of well-known strings to represent the three basic geographical features (points, lines, and polygons), and they have the same form: They start with the name of the entity followed by one or more points in parentheses. Point entities are followed by a single location, while lines and polygons are followed by a series of locations.

```
-- point definition
'POINT(-89.2902 29.44893)'
-- line definition
'LINESTRING(-89.2902 29.44893, -88.7802 29.0328)'
-- polygon definition
'POLYGON((-89.2902 29.44893, -88.7802 29.0328, -89.2902 29.44893))'
```

The coordinates are specified just as with KML files: Longitude and latitude values are separated by spaces, and consecutive points are separated by commas. Lines and polygons are usually followed by a large number of points; the samples here show a line and a polygon with very few vertices. Note that polygon coordinates are embedded in two pairs of parentheses, and you will see why in the following sidebar.

To convert the well-known text representation of the various items into geography data suitable for use by the INSERT statement, pass them as arguments to the methods `STPointFromText()`, `STLineFromText()`, and `STPolyFromText()` of the geography data type. The following expressions are valid values for geography data, and they can be used in an INSERT statement to populate a `geography` column:

```
-- representation of a geography point element
Geography::STPointFromText('POINT(-89.2902 29.44893)', 4326)
--representation of a geography line element
```

```
geography::STLineFromText(
        'LINESTRING(-89.2902 29.44893, -88.7802 29.0328)', 4326)
-- representation of a geography polygon element
geography::STPolyFromText(
        'POLYGON((-89.2902 29.44893,
                -88.7802 29.0328,
                -89.2902 29.44893))', 4326)
```

All three methods accept a second argument, which is a numeric value that identifies the so-called SRID: the *Spatial Reference System Identifier*. This value identifies the projection system in use. The value 4326 identifies the Mercator projection, so if you need a database of geography features to use with Google Maps, just memorize the value 4326 as the SRID of your data.

There are many reference systems in use today, and all major GIS vendors, as well as authorities such as the European Petroleum Survey Group, have their own reference system or have adopted one of them. It's also possible to convert between different reference systems, and you can even store entities in the same table with different SRIDs. Keep in mind, however, that you can't perform any spatial operations with data from different reference systems.

Polygons may contain holes, which are also polygons, and so the proper syntax to specify polygons involves arrays of polygons. This well-known text notation is made up of multiple arrays of points:

```
POLYGON((vertices of outer polygon),
        (vertices of inner polygon))
```

Note that the polygon is made up of one or more exterior rings and one or more interior rings. Even if a polygon has no holes, the coordinates of its vertices must still be enclosed in two pairs of parentheses. To insert a polygon in a geography column, use an expression like the following:

```
INSERT CountyBorders
VALUES('CountyName',
    geography::STPolyFromText('POLYGON((-89.2902 29.4489,
            -88.7802 29.0328, -89.2902 29.44893, ...),
            (-78.2003 31.58384, -77.0932 33.20012, ...)) ', 4326)
```

There's a shorter method, too, namely to skip the call to the STPolyFromText() method. The following statement inserts a new row to the CountyBorders table:

```
INSERT CountyBorders
VALUES('CountyName',
        'POLYGON((-89.2902 29.44893,
                -88.7802 29.0328, ...
                -89.2902 29.44893)'
```

The short method of defining geography features assumes that all features are specified in the 4326 SRID, which is the proper setting for Mercator projections. If you need to specify a different SRID, you must use the STPolyFromText() method.

Polygons with Holes

In Chapter 8, you saw how to create polygons with holes on top of Google Maps. You used the following JavaScript statements to create the outline of the state of Utah and the Utah Lake as a hole in the state's polygon (the ellipses indicate missing vertices).

```
var utah = new Array();
utah = [
      new google.maps.LatLng(42.0083149369298,  -111.039287109375),
      new google.maps.LatLng(41.9838201251284,  -114.0385546875),
      . . .
      new google.maps.LatLng(41.0045986236626,  -111.02830078125)
      ]
var lake = new Array();
lake.push(new google.maps.LatLng(40.3589241562642,-111.898967285156));
lake.push(new google.maps.LatLng(40.3557814813435,-111.849528808594));
. . .
lake.push(new google.maps.LatLng(40.2458126855149,-111.852275390625));
```

The same coordinates can be used to create a POLYGON structure in SQL. The polygon is made up of two segments, one that corresponds to the state of Utah and another nested one that corresponds to the Utah Lake. Here's a SQL statement that creates two nested POLYGON structures and then displays them. The statement doesn't store the shape in any database; it simply assigns the definition of the shape to a variable and then selects this variable.

```
DECLARE @Utah geography
SET @Utah = geography::STGeomFromText(
'POLYGON(( -111.039287109375 42.0083149369298,
          -114.0385546875 41.9838201251284,
          -111.039287109375 42.0083149369298),
        . . .
        (
          -111.898967285156 40.3589241562642,
          -111.849528808594 40.3557814813435,
          -111.767131347656 40.3296171465965,
        . . .
              )',  4326)
SELECT @Utah
```

Figure 13-3 shows the query and the Spatial Results pane of the SQL Server Management Studio, where you can see the outer polygon with the outline of the state and inner polygon rendered as a hole with the shape of the lake. The script shown in the figure is Utah Polygon.sql.

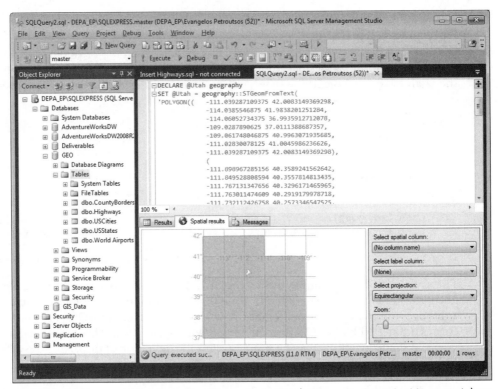

Figure 13-3 A polygon with nested paths. The nested paths (only one is shown in this example) are rendered as holes in the outer polygon.

Point features are inserted a very similar statement, which is much shorter because it contains the coordinates of a single point:

```
INSERT [World Airports]
VALUES('LAX', 'Los Angeles International', 'Los Angeles',
       'United States',
       'POINT (-118.407222 33.9425))')
```

Well-Known Binary Representation of Geography Data

In addition to the well-known text format for specifying geography features, you can use the well-known binary format as well. The various features (points, lines, and polygons) are stored by SQL Server in binary format and this format is well documented by Microsoft. You will not use the binary format in this chapter, but a typical application of this format is to extract data in binary format from one table and insert the same data into another table.

The binary value of a feature is the long string you see in Results pane of SQL Server Management Studio, and it's totally meaningless to humans. You can still store these binary values in variables and use them later as needed.

GML Representation of Geography Data

The last format is GML, which stands for Geography Markup Language. GML is an XML variation for describing geography features, similar to KML. GML is quite verbose and you will use it only to extract data from a database and move it to another one, or another system capable of understanding GML.

To retrieve the outlines of the various California counties in GML format, apply the AsGml() method to the Border column:

```
SELECT County, Border.AsGml() FROM CountyBorders
```

The result is a list of county names and links to GML segments that describe the outline of each county, as shown in Figure 13-4.

If you click one of the links, you will see the GML description of the selected county's outline. This description is something like:

```
<Polygon xmlns="http://www.opengis.net/gml">
  <exterior>
    <LinearRing>
      <posList>37.90397 -122.26822 37.90453 -122.27494 37.89787
              ...
              -122.25876 37.90194 -122.26254 37.90397 -122.26822
      </posList>
    </LinearRing>
  </exterior>
</Polygon>
```

The outlines contain too many points to list here and the ellipses indicate points that have been skipped. The GML format looks very similar to KML. After all, both formats describe geography features and they're both based on XML. The LinearRing element is the same as in KML, but you must replace the <posList> tag under it with the <coordinates> tag.

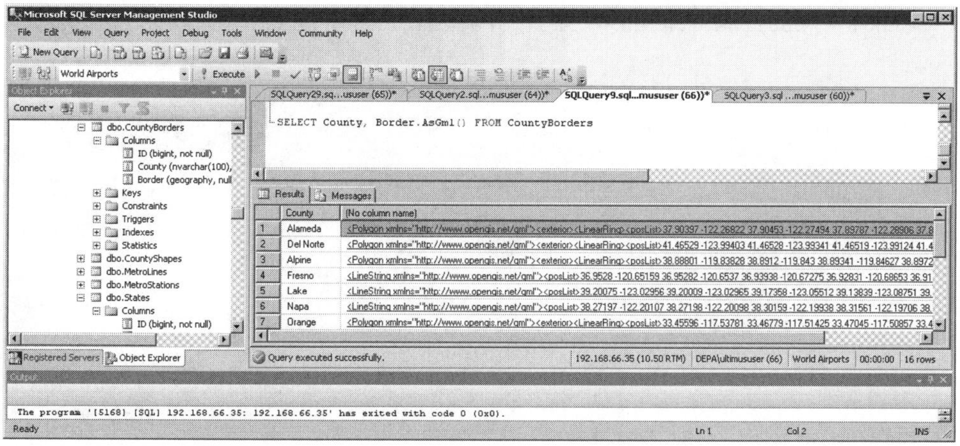

Figure 13-4   Retrieving county outlines in GML notation

Creating the GML description of a feature is certainly the least efficient method to insert data into a `geography` column, but it may come in handy if you already have a collection of geospatial features in GML format. Another detail to keep in mind is that GML uses the space to delimit individual coordinates as well as consecutive points. There are no commas between consecutive points in a `<posList>` element in GML.

Outer and Inner Polygons

Polygons must be specified in a clockwise fashion. A polygon drawn in counterclockwise fashion is a hole. If such a polygon lies within another, then it represents a hole in the outer polygon. On its own, however, it still represents a hole! It's a hole in another polygon that spans the entire globe.

To understand how this works, let's create a polygon that outlines the state of California. If the points are specified in a clockwise fashion, then they will generate a polygon with the shape of California, and this is the "desired" interpretation of the points that make up the polygon. If the points are specified in the opposite direction, they will generate a polygon that spans the entire globe, except for the state of California. Figure 13-5 shows two polygons with the vertices that delimit the state of California.

The small filled polygon that resembles the state of California was created with a POLYGON structure that contains the vertices that make up California's outline in the correct order: in a clockwise direction. The other filled polygon was created with the same POLYGON structure, only this time the coordinates of California's vertices were reversed. This polygon represents a hole the size and shape of California. A hole into what? Because the shape doesn't belong to another one, it will become a hole on the entire globe. The two polygons that represent the state of California are stored in the StateOutlines table and were inserted with two simple statements.

Some simple calculations with two shapes will verify these claims. First, let's calculate the total area of California with the STArea() method. This method is discussed later in the chapter, but here's the statement that uses SQL Server's spatial methods to calculate the area of a polygon:

```
SELECT  outline.STArea() FROM StateOutlines WHERE id=1
```

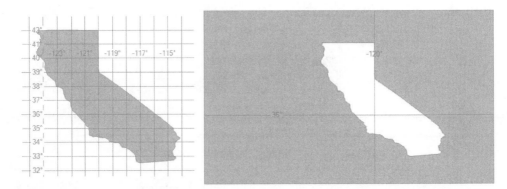

Figure 13-5   The outline of California defined in both directions. When the outline's vertices are specified in the wrong direction, the resulting polygon covers the entire globe and the intended shape becomes a hole.

This statement returned the numeric value 419,366,861,058.543. This is nearly half a million square kilometers. To calculate the area of the other shape that spans the entire globe, apply the same method to the row whose ID is 2. The result is 509,646,254,849,938, which is half a billion square miles. The sum of the two should be earth's total area:

```
SELECT   SUM(outline.STArea()) FROM StateOutlines
```

The SUM() function returns the numeric sum of the column specified as an argument and for the two polygons it returned the value 510,065,621,710,996, or 510,065,621 square kilometers. This value is pretty close to earth's total area as reported by Wikipedia (510,072,000 square kilometers). The difference is less than 1 part in 10,000.

You can also calculate the earth's total area, considering it's a perfect sphere with a radius of 6,371 kilometers. The area of a sphere's surface is given by the following calculation:

```
DECLARE @R int
SET @R = 6371000
PRINT convert(numeric(24,2), 4.0 * PI() * @R * @R)
```

The result is 510,064,471.90, which is even closer to the value returned by the STArea() function. As mentioned in Chapter 1, Google Maps approximate the earth with a perfect sphere, which is not quite accurate. The total area of the earth has no practical meaning because the earth's surface is not smooth. Approximating the earth by a sphere introduces just a marginal error, but the mountains on the surface of the earth can make an enormous difference when you calculate the earth's area.

To experiment with the two polygons of California, use the StateOutlines sample table, which contains two rows with the IDs 1 (the state of California) and 2 (the reversed shape). The two outlines are identical, except for the order of their vertices. Execute the CaliforniaOutlines.sql file to create the table and populate it with the two shapes of California.

Handling Spatial Data with SQL Server Management Studio

Spatial data can be points, lines, and polygons, or collections of these types. SQL Server supports two types of spatial data: geometry and geography data. The difference is that geography data is expressed in terms of latitude and longitude (and optionally altitude) coordinates, while geometry data is arbitrary (any coordinate system will do). The examples in this chapter deal exclusively with spatial data of the geography type.

Just as you create columns of the appropriate type to store simple data (text, numbers, and dates), you can create a column of the geography type and store geospatial data in it. It doesn't matter what type of geography feature you store in this column. SQL Server will recognize points, lines, and polygons in a column of this type. Of course, you usually set up different columns for different entity types.

Figure 13-1 shows the SQL Server Management Studio with some this chapter's sample data. On the left pane is the structure of the World Airports table, and on the right pane is a query that selects all airports and the results of the query. The table contains data for over 9,000 airports all over the world. The data was obtained from www.openflights.org, a site that provides this information for free but will accept your donation. They also maintain a database with airlines and another one with flight routes.

The SQL Scripts to Populate the Sample Tables

The Insert Airports.sql script inserts the airport data in the World Airports table and contains a series of INSERT statements like the following:

```
INSERT [World Airports]
   (Code, Name, City, Country, Location)
   VALUES ('RLA', 'National', 'Rolla', 'United States',
        Geography::STPointFromText('POINT (-91.78333 38.13333)', 4326))
```

The Insert State Cities.sql script, which inserts the cities in the USCities table (and the states in the USStates table), is also a series of INSERT statements, only this time the statements are slightly more complex:

```
INSERT USCities (CityName, StateID, Population, Location)
   VALUES('Dallas', (SELECT TOP 1 ID FROM USStates WHERE State='Texas'),
        1197816,
        Geography::STPointFromText('POINT(-96.7967 32.7757)',4326 ))
```

The list of values contains a subquery, which retrieves the ID of the corresponding state, but this is not related to geospatial data. The city coordinates are specified with the STPointFromText() method, which accepts as an argument a POINT feature.

The county borders are inserted into the CountyBorders table as POLYGON features with the Insert Counties.sql script, which contains statements like the following:

```
INSERT INTO CountyBorders
    VALUES ('Alameda',
        Geography::STGeomFromText(
            'POLYGON((-122.26822 37.90397,
                    -122.27494 37.90453,
                    -122.28906 37.89787,
                    . . .
                    -122.26822 37.90397))', 4326));
```

The last script, Insert Highways.sql, contains two statements that insert two very long paths to the Highways table, one for each of the US 5 and US 101 highways:

```
INSERT Highways (Name, Route)
    VALUES ('US 101',
        geography::STGeomFromText(
                'LINESTRING(-118.218126296997 34.0310739627677,
                        -118.219714164734 34.0322476132612,
                        -118.220958709717 34.0338480195878,
                        . . .
                        -122.406578063965 37.7753281516829
        )', 4326))
```

In Figure 13-1, you saw the result of the following query:

```
SELECT ID, Code, Name, Country, Location
FROM   [World Airports]
```

The airport locations are spatial data (points, to be exact) and are displayed as text-encoded binary data. Regardless of the techniques for inserting spatial data into a SQL Server table, SQL Server stores the spatial data internally in a binary format.

If you want to see the actual coordinates, change the query to apply the STAsText() method to the Location column:

```
SELECT ID, Code, Name, Country, Location.STAsText()
FROM [World Airports]
```

This time, the query returns the coordinates of each airport in a format suitable for humans, as you can see in the table that follows.

CIR	Cairo	United States	POINT (-76.01666 4.66666)
CDW	Caldwell Wright	United States	POINT (-74.28139 40.87527)
CLR	Calipatria	United States	POINT (-115.51666 33.13333)
CWG	Callaway Gardens	United States	POINT (-84.88333 32.83333)

This is the well-known text format, which is suitable for humans. The actual data are maintained by SQL Server as binary values, which are converted by the STAsText() method into text format.

CAUTION While all keywords in T-SQL are case-insensitive, the names of the spatial methods, which are extensions to T-SQL, are case-sensitive. You can actually mix and match case-sensitive with case-insensitive keywords in the same statement, which is a rather odd behavior. T-SQL has always been case-insensitive, but the spatial extensions are case-sensitive.

Viewing Spatial Data on the Map

If the result set contains a spatial column, a new tab is added to the pane with the results, the Spatial Results pane, which is shown in Figure 13-2. The revised query that makes use of the STAsText() method doesn't contain any spatial data because the locations of the airports were retrieved as strings. Remove the STAsText() method from the Location column and execute the following query to see the Spatial Results pane:

```
SELECT  ID, Code, Name, Country, Location  FROM [World Airports]
```

The spatial data are displayed as strings; this format is totally unsuitable for humans, but you can actually see the data points on a grid in the second tab. Switch to the Spatial Results pane to view the locations of the airports. Airport locations are shown as dots on the map. There's no map, of course, just a grid with the coordinates. The density of the airports, however, is such that their locations practically outline all continents. Even though the Spatial Results tab doesn't display more than 5,000 points, that's a lot. Note that you can specify the projection used to display the results in the "Selected projection" combo box. Settings include EquiRectangular, Mercator, Robinson, and Bonne.

> ## OGC vs. Extended Geography Methods
>
> You can request that spatial columns be returned as readable text or as GML, with the methods STAsText() and AsGml(), respectively. You may have noticed an inconsistency in the naming scheme of these methods (and a few others you will read about later). All methods that belong to the OGC (Open Geography Consortium) specification begin with the ST prefix. The other methods are extended methods of the geography data type and are unique to SQL Server. The STAsText() method is an OGC method, while AsGml() is an extension to T-SQL.

Querying Spatial Data

The main function of a database is not the storage of data. Databases are designed to facilitate the selection of the data. The operations for inserting and deleting data are not as efficient as they could be because the database has to maintain additional information that assists the fast retrieval of data. Without the spatial data types, you'd have to write some serious code to query your data. For example, how easy would it be to find out if two polygons intersect, or even select the cities (points) that lie in a specific state (polygon)? Querying such a database would be nearly impossible without advanced calculus.

The geography data type allows developers to write code to perform similar queries very easily. This is the reason why spatial data are represented with their own data type and this is why databases provide special methods for handling spatial data. As you will see shortly, you can write a simple query that allows you to select the airports within a specific range from a location, cities that lie within a specific state or country, and so on. The function STDistance(), for example, returns the distance between two points in meters, which means that you don't have to supply your own code to calculate distances. The spatial features of SQL allow you to query tables based on geography data very efficiently. In this section, you'll read about the basic spatial functions of SQL and how they're used in queries.

All the methods you're going to explore in this and the following sections are extensions to the geography type: They apply to a variable or column of the geography type and they accept as arguments another geography instance. In other words, there's no function that calculates the distance between two points; you can't write the following in T-SQL:

```
SELECT Distance(@p1, @p2)    -- THIS IS WRONG!
```

where @p1 and @p2 are two properly declared and initialized variables that represent points. Instead, there's an STDistance() method, which can be applied to either one of the variables and accepts the other variable as an argument:

```
SELECT @p1.STDistance(@p2)
```

The STDistance() method will return the distance between the points @p1 and @p2. If you reverse the role of the two variables, the method will still return the same result:

```
SELECT @p2.STDistance(@p1)
```

Calculating Distances

You have seen the syntax of the `STDistance()` method in the introduction to this section; let's exercise it by calculating the distance between two airports, the LAX and JFK airports:

```
DECLARE @LAX Geography
SELECT  @LAX = Location
             FROM World_Airports WHERE AirportCode = 'LAX'
DECLARE @JFK Geography
SELECT  @JFK = Location
        FROM World_Airports WHERE AirportCode = 'JFK'
PRINT   CONVERT(numeric(10,0), @LAX.STDistance(@JFK))
```

The distance between the two airports is 3,982,550 meters, or 3,892 kilometers. This is the length of the geodesic path between the two airports and it's the same distance returned by the `calculateLength()` method of the Google Maps API. Let's write a query that calculates the distances of all U.S. airports from the Lambert–St. Louis International airport. Start by declaring a `geography` variable that corresponds to the location of the airport:

```
DECLARE @STLuis
SELECT  @STLuis = Location FROM Airports WHERE Code = 'STL'
```

Now write a `SELECT` statement using the `STDistance()` method to calculate the distances of all other airports from the St. Louis International airport:

```
SELECT   Code, Name, Location.STDistance(@STLuis) AS Distance
WHERE    CODE <> 'STL' AND Country = 'United States'
```

The `WHERE` clause was added to exclude from the result the St. Louis airport. It's not required, but there's no reason to include a pair of airports in the result that are 0 meters apart from one another.

The result of the preceding query is a list of airport codes and names, and their distance from the St. Louis International Airport, as you can see in the table that follows.

ALN	Alton	Alton	23392,7699587697
SUS	Spirit Of St Louis	St Louis	26333,0789283737
CPS	St. Louis Downtown Airport	St Louis, Il	27130,3301629627
VIH	Rolla National	Vichy	62699,0463184338

You can modify the query a little so that it selects all airports that are within a circle of 200 kilometers from the St. Louis airport, or any other location. This time, the `STDistance()` function must also be included in the `WHERE` clause to limit the number of qualifying airports. Listing 13-1 shows the revised query.

Listing 13-1
Selecting airports within range from the World Airports table

```
DECLARE @STLAirport geography
SELECT  @STLAirport = Location FROM [World Airports]
        WHERE Code = 'STL'
SELECT  Code, Name, city,
        Location.STDistance(@STLAirport) AS Distance
```

```
FROM     [World Airports]
WHERE    Code <> 'STL' AND Country = 'United States'
         AND Location.STDistance(@STLAirport) < 200000
```

The result of the query is shown in Figure 13-6. This query doesn't return any spatial data because it does not include the Location column. To see the distribution of the airports on the map, you should include the Location column as the last item in the selection list.

Line Lengths and Polygon Areas

You have seen the calculateLength() and calculateArea() functions of the Google API in Chapter 10. These two methods calculate the length of a line (or path, in terms of the Google API) and the area of a polygon. SQL Server provides the STLength() and STArea() methods, which perform the same calculations. The functions of SQL Server are extremely fast, however, because SQL statements are executed on a powerful server and not at the client. As efficient as JavaScript may be, it's an interpreted language that can't beat a highly optimized and extremely specialized language like T-SQL. Moreover, T-SQL can use the STLength() method to quickly calculate the lengths of hundreds or thousands of lines and return the one with the longest or shortest length and even order a large number of lines according to their lengths.

The CountyBorders table contains California's counties with columns for their names (column Country) and their geography (column Border). To calculate the perimeter of a country, apply the STLength() method to the Border column. Likewise, to calculate the

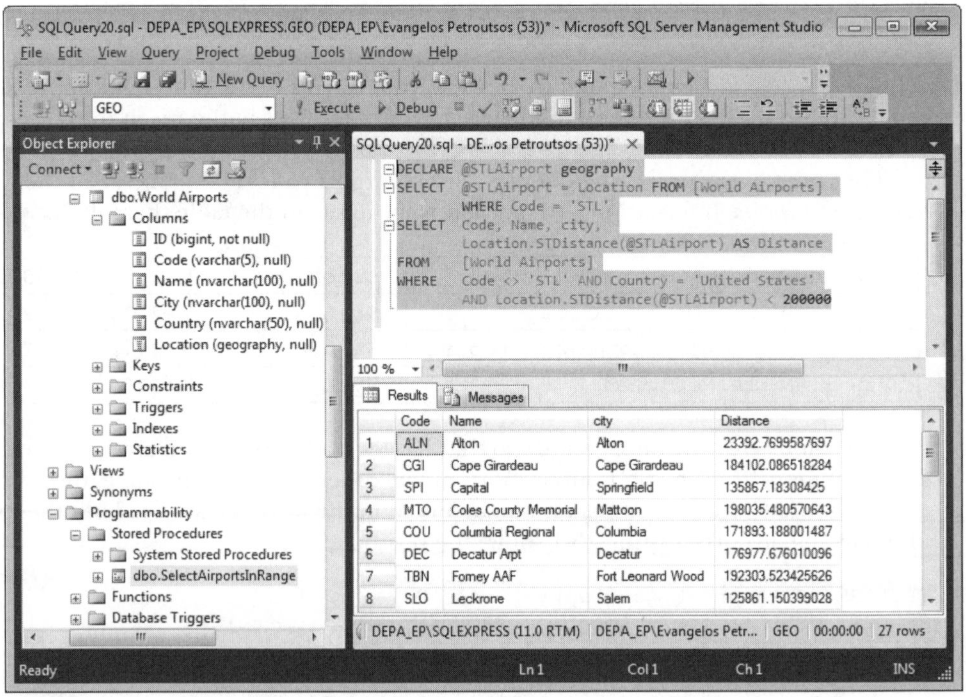

Figure 13-6 Viewing all U.S. airports within 200 kilometers from the St. Louis International Airport and their distance from this airport

area of a county, apply the STArea() method to the same column. The following statement returns the names, perimeters, and areas of all counties in the CountyBorders table:

```
SELECT      CountyBorders.County,
            CountyBorders.Border.STLength() AS Perimeter,
            CountyBorders.Border.STArea() As Area
FROM        CountyBorders
ORDER BY    CountyBrders.Border.County
```

Note that you need not prefix the column names by their table name, because the query involves a single table.

The output of this statement (the first few counties) is shown in the following table.

County	Perimeter	Area
Alameda	233142.983234716	2123865380.32568
Alpine	200888.735852157	1920851873.20043
Del Norte	285486.795128642	3180605155.35546
Los Angeles	715783.980323663	12292409728.6485

To change the order of the results, specify one of the other two expressions in the selection list after the ORDER BY clause. To retrieve the largest county, use the following expression, which calculates the area of all counties, sorts them in descending order, and returns the top row only:

```
SELECT TOP 1    CountyBorders.County,
                CountyBorders.Border.STArea() As Area
FROM            CountyBorders
ORDER BY        CountyBorders.Border.STArea() DESC
```

The largest county is Riverside with an area of 18,892,717,528.5141 square meters, or 18,892.72 square kilometers. According to Wikipedia, the area of Riverside is 18,915 square kilometers; the more points you add along the perimeter of the county, the more closely you will approximate the county. Even with a fairly rough outline, the error is 80 units in 19,000 units, which is less than 0.5 percent.

The STDistance() method accepts as an argument a geography instance, which isn't necessarily a point. You can use this method to calculate the distance between two points, or the distance between a point and a polygon, or even the distance between two polygons. For the latter, the distance is the length of the shortest possible line that can be drawn between the two polygons.

Let's apply the STDistance() method to calculate the distance from all counties to the LAX airport in Santa Monica. Listing 13-2 shows the query.

Listing 13-2
Calculating distances of counties from the LAX airport

```
DECLARE    @LAXlocation Geography
SELECT     @LAXlocation = Location FROM [world Airports]
           WHERE Code = 'LAX'
SELECT     CountyBorders.County ,
           CONVERT(int, @LAXlocation.STDistance(Border)/1000)
FROM       CountyBorders
ORDER BY @LAXlocation.STDistance(Border)
```

Note that the location of LAX is not hard-coded. Instead, it's retrieved from the World Airports table. The rest of the query deals with the CountyBorders table: It passes the geography of each state, the `Border` column, to the `STDistance()` method as an argument to calculate the distances, and then it orders the results based on this distance.

```
Los Angeles 0
Orange      33
Riverside   68
```

LAX airport lies within Los Angeles County, and its distance from Los Angeles County is zero. Any point that lies within a polygon has a distance of 0 from the same polygon.

You can also create a stored procedure to retrieve the airports that lie within a specific range from any given location. The location and the maximum distance are arguments of the stored procedure. The `SelectAirportsInRange()` stored procedure does exactly that, as you can see in Listing 13-3.

Listing 13-3
The definition of the `Select Airports InRange()` stored procedure

```
ALTER PROCEDURE [dbo].[SelectAirportsInRange](
        @userLocation geography,
        @rangeInKM int)
AS
SELECT     Code, Name, City, Country,
           Location.STAsText() AS Location,
           Location.Long AS Longitude, Location.Lat AS Latitude,
           Location.STDistance(@userLocation)/1000 AS DistanceKM
FROM       Airports_GEO
WHERE      Location.STDistance(@userLocation) < @rangeInKM * 1000
ORDER BY   Location.STDistance(@userLocation)
```

The `rangeInKM` argument is the maximum distance expressed in kilometers. To execute this procedure, set up a `geography` variable with the desired location and a maximum distance:

```
DECLARE @loc Geography
SET @loc = Geography::STPointFromText(
                'POINT (-117.183333 32.733333)', 4326)
EXEC SelectAirportsInRange @loc, 40
```

This query will return a list of airports like the one shown in Figure 13-7.

Intersections

Another very useful set of methods in SQL spatial extensions deals with shape intersections. Note that there are no equivalent methods in the Google API. The `STIntersects()` method detects whether two geographies intersect or not and returns a `true/false` value, while the `STIntersection()` method returns the geography of the intersection. If you use the `STIntersection()` method with a line and a polygon, for example, the method will return a line, which is the segment (or segments) of the line that lies within the polygon. If you use it with two lines, the same method will return the point where the two lines meet. To interpret correctly the result of the `STIntersects()` method, you need to know the type of the intersecting geographies.

```
SQLQuery20.sql - DE...os Petroutsos (53))*  ×

 DECLARE @loc Geography
 SET @loc = Geography::STPointFromText(
              'POINT (-117.183333 32.733333)', 4326)
 EXEC SelectAirportsInRange @loc, 40
```

100 %

Results | Messages

	Code	Name	City	Country	Location	Longitude	Latitude	DistanceKM
1	SAN	San Diego International Ai...	San Diego	United States	POINT (-117.183333 32.733333)	-117.183333	32.733333	0
2	NZY	North Island Nas	San Diego	United States	POINT (-117.215278 32.699167)	-117.215278	32.699167	4.82967525476292
3	MYF	Montgomery Field	San Diego	United States	POINT (-117.133333 32.8)	-117.133333	32.8	8.7527546863917
4	NKX	Miramar MCAS	San Diego	United States	POINT (-117.1425 32.868333)	-117.1425	32.868333	15.4523949425358
5	CJN	Gillespie Field	El Cajon	United States	POINT (-116.9725 32.826111)	-116.9725	32.826111	22.2710781230567
6	SDM	Brown Field Municipal	San Diego	United States	POINT (-116.98 32.572222)	-116.98	32.572222	26.1367225531734
7	TIJ	General A. L. Rodriguez Intl	Tijuana	Mexico	POINT (-116.970278 32.541111)	-116.970278	32.541111	29.2247425913731

Figure 13-7   Executing a stored procedure against the World Airports table

Let's find the part of US 101 that lies within Los Angeles County. This is a typical operation that can't be performed with the methods of the Google Maps API. On the other hand, it's practically trivial with SQL Server's spatial methods. The route of US 101 is represented in the Highways table with a `LINESTRING` primitive that contains 1,745 vertices. The locations of these vertices were obtained by tracing the freeway on the map with the Map Traces sample project of Chapter 9. To view the path of US 101 limits, execute the following query against the Highways table in the GEO database.

```
SELECT * FROM Freeways WHERE ID = 1
```

In Figure 13-8, you see that only a segment of US 101 was traced, but it's a fairly lengthy segment starting in Los Angeles and extending all the way to San Francisco (695.584 kilometers in all).

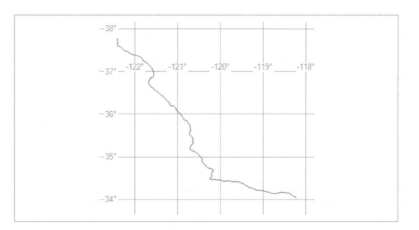

Figure 13-8   The route of US 101 on the Spatial Results tab of SQL Server Management Studio

Create two `geography` instances to store the polygon that outlines Los Angeles County and the line that corresponds to the highway. The following are the two statements that retrieve the desired data from the corresponding tables:

```
DECLARE @geo_shape geography
SELECT  @geo_shape = Border
FROM    CountyBorders
WHERE   County = 'Los Angeles'

DECLARE @geo_line geography
SELECT  @geo_line = route
FROM    Freeways
WHERE   Name = 'US 101'
```

Now you're ready to calculate the intersection of the two instances, which is the part of the freeway that lies in Los Angeles County. The method `STIntersects()` lets you know if the two geographies intersect at all:

```
IF @geo_shape.STIntersects(@geo_line)=1
    PRINT 'The two shapes intersect one another'
ELSE
    PRINT 'The two shapes do not intersect'
```

The `STIntersection()` method goes one step further: It returns the intersection of the instance defined by its argument with the instance to which the method is applied. Replace the `IF` statement of the preceding example with a call to the `STIntersection()` method of the `@geo_shape` variable:

```
SELECT  @geo_shape.STIntersection(@geo_line)
```

Figure 13-9 shows the result of the query in the Spatial Results pane. What you see is the segment of the line that lies within the specified polygon and it's the part of US 101 in Los Angeles County. If you commute on this highway daily, you'll probably recognize it.

To actually get the definition of the segment of US 101 within Los Angeles County, apply the `STAsText()` method to the result:

```
SELECT  @geo_shape.STIntersection(@geo_line).STAsText()
```

This time, the result is a textual description of the same line, and it will appear in the Result pane of the SQL Management Studio as a `LINESTRING` primitive:

```
LINESTRING (-118.81506719099721 34.152540209883071,
            -118.803234100342 34.1487492806211, -118.793449401855
            ...
            -118.218126296997 34.0310739627677)
```

If you need to know the coordinates of the points of the intersection, request the starting and ending points of the intersection with the `STStartPoint()` and `STEndPoint()` methods. Just replace the `SELECT` statement in the preceding example with

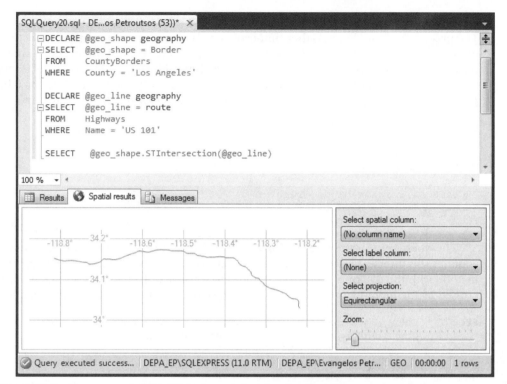

Figure 13-9   The segment of US 101 highway in Los Angeles County

the following statements that create the @line variable to hold the intersection geometry, and then apply the two methods to retrieve the endpoints of this variable:

```
DECLARE   @line geography
SELECT    @line = @geo_shape.STIntersection(@geo_line)
SELECT    @line.STStartPoint().STAsText() AS StartPoint,
          @line.STEndPoint().STAsText() AS EndPoint
```

The preceding statements will generate the following output:

```
POINT (-118.81506719099721 34.152540209883071)
POINT (-118.218126296997 34.0310739627677)
```

Copy the coordinates of the points returned by the query and locate these points on the map. You must also reverse the order of latitude and longitude values when you paste them into Google Maps. To locate the first intersection point, enter the string 34.152540209883071, -118.81506719099721 in the search box of Google Maps. The two endpoints correspond to Thousand Oaks and downtown Los Angeles.

Using Intersections as Selection Criteria

The preceding example was rather simplistic because it requested a single intersection of two specific geography instances. A much more useful type of query is one that retrieves the segments of the highway that fall within each county. This time, let's apply the STIntersection() method to each county's border in the CountyBorders table, passing as an argument the definition of the line that represents the freeway:

```
DECLARE   @geo_line geography
SELECT    @geo_line = route
FROM      HighWays
WHERE     Name = 'US 101'

DECLARE   @lineSegment geography
SELECT    County, Border.STIntersection(@geo_line)
FROM      CountyBorders
```

The query returns the intersection of the highway with all counties, and for most counties this intersection is a null instance. Let's combine the STIntersection() method with the STIntersects() method to retrieve only the counties that are actually crossed by the highway and the corresponding segments of the highway (see Listing 13-4).

Listing 13-4
A query for
retrieving the
intersections of
the two major
highways
with various
California
counties

```
SELECT    CountyBorders.County AS County, Highways.Name AS Highway,
          CountyBorders.Border.STIntersection(Highways.Route) AS
                              RouteInCounty
FROM      CountyBorders, Highways
WHERE     Border.STIntersects(Highways.Route)=1
```

The results of the query of Listing 13-4 are shown on the grid in Figure 13-10. Hover the pointer over a segment to see the row to which it belongs. Each segment of the highway in the Spatial Results pane is identified by the name of the county and the name of the highway. The figure shows the labels on the segments of the two highways that lie in Los Angeles County.

The results of the same query in text format are shown in the table that follows. The RouteInCounty column is the LINESTRING feature that belongs to the highway and is

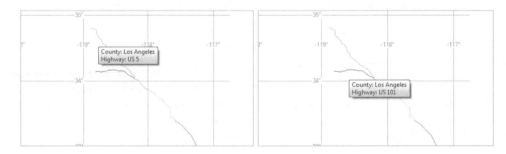

Figure 13-10   Viewing the intersections of US 101 and US 5 with various counties in California

contained within the corresponding county. It's a very long string and only part of it is shown on the printed page; US 101 is made up of 784 vertices and US 5 is made up of 1,745 vertices.

County	Highway	RouteInCounty
Los Angeles	US 101	0xE61000000104C ... 00000002
Orange	US 5	0xE610000001049 ... 00000002
Sacramento	US 5	0xE610000001042 ... 00000002
Los Angeles	US 5	0xE61000000104E ... 00000002
San Diego	US 5	0xE61000000104C ... 00000002
Fresno	US 5	0xE610000001041 ... 00000002

Joining Tables on Geo-Coordinates

The GEO sample database contains a table with geo-coded cities all over the states, the USCities table, but the USCities table contains no county information—just the state each city belongs to through a pointer to the USStates table. The CountyBorders table, on the other hand, contains the county borders in the state of California. Because both tables contain geographical data, you can associate them. To do so, you're going to use the STContains() method of a geography instance, which accepts another geography instance as an argument and returns 1 if the second instance is contained within the first instance. Obviously, the first instance must be a polygon. The second instance can be a line, a polygon, or a point. In the case of polygons and lines, the method will return 1 if the entire feature lies within the polygon to which the method applies.

The STContains() method enables you to retrieve the cities whose geo-coordinates fall within the polygons that outline the various counties. Here's the statement that retrieves the cities and the counties they belong to:

```
SELECT  County, City, Population
FROM    CountyBorders, USCities
WHERE   CountyBorders.Border.STContains(USCities.Location)
ORDER   BY County, City
```

The result of this query is similar to the following, depending on the number of counties and cities you have added to the corresponding tables:

```
Alameda     Oakland     390724
Alameda     Fremont     214089
Orange      Anaheim     336265
Orange      Santa Ana   324528
. . .
Sacramento  Sacramento  466488
Sacramento  Elk Grove   153015
. . .
```

The results are sorted by county and by city name within each county. (The ellipses indicate additional cities in the same county.)

Additional Spatial Features

The methods discussed so far are the core of SQL Server's spatial extensions, and these are the methods you will use to process geo-coded data in the context of preparing datasets for mapping applications. There are additional methods for specialized operations, which you can look up in the documentation. A few of the remaining methods, which seem to be useful in mapping applications, are presented in the section.

Extracting a Line's Vertices

It's quite possible that you have stored a line in a `geography` column but no longer have access to the coordinates of the points you used to construct it. Or, you may have obtained the line definition in binary format. You can always retrieve the line's vertices as text with the `STAsText()` method, but you will have to write some serious parsing code in T-SQL to extract individual points. A better alternative is to use the `STPointN(i)`, which returns the ith vertex of the line or polygon to which it's applied. The method's argument is the index of the vertex you're requesting and the value 1 corresponds to the first vertex. Unlike JavaScript, the first index in SQL Server collections starts at 1, not 0.

Here's a practical application of the `STPointN()` method. As mentioned earlier in this chapter, the order in which vertices are specified in the definition of a polygon makes an enormous difference. Polygon vertices should be listed in a clockwise fashion; otherwise, they're considered holes. If a polygon in your data has been defined backwards, you can reverse the order of its vertices by iterating through its vertices with the `STPointN()` method and create a new Well-Known Text representation for the reverse polygon. Listing 13-5 shows a SQL procedure that reverses the polygon representing the county of Alameda.

Listing 13-5
Reversing the order of vertices in a POLYGON feature

```
DECLARE @border geography
SELECT TOP 1 @border = Border
FROM CountyBorders
WHERE County='Alameda'

DECLARE @index int
SET @index = 1
DECLARE @points int
SET @points = @border.STNumPoints()
DECLARE @reverseBorder varchar(max)
SET @reverseBorder = ''
WHILE (@index <= @points)
BEGIN
  SET @reverseBorder = @reverseBorder +
        CAST(CAST(@border.STPointN(@points - @index + 1).Long
              AS DECIMAL(12,8)) AS varchar(40)) + ' ' +
        CAST(CAST(@border.STPointN(@points - @index + 1).Lat
              AS DECIMAL(12,8)) AS varchar(40)) + ', '
  SET @index = @index + 1
END
-- remove the extra comma at the end of the string
SET @reverseBorder = SUBSTRING(@reverseBorder, 1, LEN(@reverseBorder)-2)
SET @reverseBorder = 'POLYGON ((' + @reverseBorder + '))'
PRINT @border.STAsText()
PRINT @reverseBorder
```

```
-- convert string with the POLYGON definition (the well-known text)
-- to a geography instance and then select it.
SELECT CAST(@reverseBorder AS geography)
```

The last statement in the script selects the reversed polygon as a geography instance. In the Spatial Results tab, you will see that the county of Alameda has become a hole in the global map. You will find the query of Listing 13-5 in the `ReversePolygon.sql` script in the support material of this chapter.

Valid Geography Instances

All instances stored in a `geography` column must be valid; otherwise, you won't be able to process them with the usual spatial methods. However, SQL Server will accept invalid instances, as long as their definition is syntactically correct. If you specify a `POLYGON` primitive made up of points with the correct syntax, SQL Server will accept it and generate a binary representation of it. The polygon may still be invalid for many different reasons. A polygon with two vertices, for example, can be stored in a `geography` column, but it's not a valid polygon. This polygon has no area!

The `IsValid()` method accepts a geography instance as an argument and returns 1 if its argument represents a valid geography, 0 otherwise. Figuring out what's wrong in a polygon with many vertices by examining its definition is practically out of the question. Use the `IsValidDetailed()` method instead, which will give you a clue as to what's wrong with your polygon and then try to fix it. As mentioned, many conditions may result in an invalid geography and they're listed in SQL Server's documentation at http://msdn .microsoft.com/en-us/library/hh710083.aspx.

Another related method is `MakeValid()`, which accepts as an argument the definition of an invalid geography and fixes it. The process of converting an invalid instance into a valid one may "slightly" shift the vertices of the shape. If you can't figure out what's wrong with your instance so that you can fix the raw data, the `MakeValid()` method is your best bet. The following statement was used to fix one of the county borders in the CountyBorders table:

```
UPDATE CountyBorders SET border = border.MakeValid() WHERE ID = 4
```

The `IsValid()` method is an OCG method, while the other two extended methods, `IsValidDetailed()` and `MakeValid()`, are provided by SQL Server.

The Union Operator with Shapes

Another interesting aspect of the spatial data is the union operation. With other data types, the `UNION` operator combines the results of two or more queries, as long as all queries return the same number of columns and the data types of the columns match. The `UNION` operator can't be used with spatial data. Instead, there's an `STUnion()` method that combines spatial data into a single entity.

To explore this `STUnion()` method, let's use the CountyBorders table with the outlines of the counties in California. The shape of California is the union of the shapes of the counties that make up the state. The `STUnion()` method combines the geography feature to which it is applied and another geography feature that's passed as an argument to the method. To combine a few counties, start with the first one and then extend it by adding another county's outline with the STUnion() method. The following statements attempt to reconstruct the state of California as the union of its counties:

```
-- the state of CA as union of its counties
DECLARE @CA geography
DECLARE @c geography
SELECT @CA = Border from CountyBorders WHERE County='Alameda'
SELECT TOP 1 @c = Border FROM CountyBorders WHERE County='Del Norte'
SELECT @CA = @CA.STUnion(@c)
SELECT TOP 1 @c = Border FROM CountyBorders WHERE County='Alpine'
SELECT @CA = @CA.STUnion(@c)
SELECT TOP 1 @c = Border FROM CountyBorders WHERE County='Orange'
SELECT @CA = @CA.STUnion(@c)
SELECT TOP 1 @c = Border FROM CountyBorders WHERE County='Riverside'
SELECT @CA = @CA.STUnion(@c)
SELECT TOP 1 @c = Border FROM CountyBorders WHERE County='Sacramento'
SELECT @CA = @CA.STUnion(@c)
SELECT @CA AS CaliforniaUnion
```

The statements shown here gradually build the outline of California by combining the polygons that correspond to individual counties. The variable @CA represents a multi-polygon structure, as you can see in Figure 13-11, that shows the @CA variable in the Spatial Results pane, and it's made up of the individual county polygons. The figure shows a few of the counties only. Note that most of them are easily distinguishable. The counties of Riverside and Orange at the lower-right corner of the tab, however, are totally joined because they have a common border. Add all counties to the @CA variable and you'll end up with a polygon that has the exact same shape and size as the state of California.

If you request the total area of the *@CA* variable with the statement:

```
SELECT @CA.STArea()
```

T-SQL will return the value 31,161,176,910.9897, which is the sum of the areas of the counties added to the @CA variable. If you include all counties in the query, you'll get the total area of California.

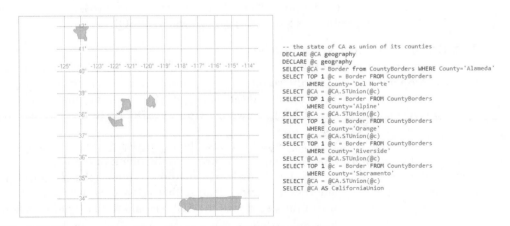

Figure 13-11 The union of the polygons of the California counties

Approximating Lines

As you recall from Chapter 17, the Directions service returns approximate paths. The route from Manhattan to Chicago, for example, includes every turn along the way. When this path is placed on the map, however, and users view the map at a state level, there's no need to render the complete path. The details of the route are not visible at that zoom level. You also learned how to approximate paths with the `Encode()` method of the `google.maps` `.geometry.Poly` library. You used the `Encode()` method in Chapter 10 to reduce the size of a line's representation. SQL Server provides a similar method to approximate both lines and polygons, and it's described in this section.

A path can be approximated with another path made up of fewer points. The approximation is based on a path's vertices, but it doesn't include all of them. Actually, it doesn't include any of the original vertices; it's made up of a smaller number of vertices that approximate the original path. This approximation is achieved with a famous algorithm in computational geometry, the Douglas-Peucker algorithm. The details of the algorithms are quite interesting, and you can easily find them on the Web, if you wish. SQL Server provides a method for approximating lines and shapes with the Douglas-Peucker algorithm, through the `Reduce()` method. As you can see from its name, this method isn't part of the OGC standard; it's a SQL Server extended method, and you may find it quite useful in certain applications. If you want to further explore this algorithm, or implement your favorite language, you can find an interesting article that explains how it works with an animation at http://www.gitta.info/Generalisati/en/html/GenMethods_learningObject3.html.

The `Reduce()` method is applied to a geography feature (line or polygon) and accepts a maximum tolerance as an argument. The smaller the tolerance, the closer to the original shape is the approximation. The tolerance is specified in meters and its value depends on the type of feature you're approximating. Let's perform three different approximations of the polygon that outlines California. Figure 13-12 shows this polygon approximated with the following statement and with three different settings of the tolerance argument.

The following are the statements that produced the shapes shown in Figure 13-12:

```
SELECT StateOutlines.Reduce(100) FROM    States
    WHERE   State = 'California'
SELECT StateOutlines.Reduce(1000) FROM    States
    WHERE   State = 'California'
SELECT StateOutlines.Reduce(10000) FROM    States
    WHERE   State = 'California'
```

Douglas-Peucker Polygon Approximation

Tolerance = 1000   Tolerance = 1000   Tolerance = 10000

Figure 13-12   Approximating the state of California with the `Reduce()` method at three different tolerance settings

As is evident from the figure, the tolerance value depends on the actual size of the shape and the acceptable distortion. You will probably experiment with the value of the argument to the `Reduce()` method to find the most suitable value for the application at hand.

To understand the meaning of tolerance in the Douglas-Peucker algorithm, you need to understand how the algorithm works in broad strokes. The Douglas-Peucker algorithm starts by approximating the path with a straight line, which has the same two endpoints as the path. Then, it locates the point along the path that lies the furthest away from the approximating line. This is the point that will have the most profound effect on the shape, if added to the approximation. If the distance of this point from the approximating line exceeds the tolerance, it's added to the approximating line. Now the original path is approximated with two line segments and the algorithm continues with the two line segments on either side of the point that was added. It finds the two points that would have the most significant effect on the approximation of the two segments and, if they exceed the tolerance, it adds them to the approximating line. The algorithm continues by breaking the approximating line into two segments and adding (if needed) the point that will reduce the approximation error the most.

If you increase the tolerance too much, you'll end up with a very rough sketch of the original line or shape, as you can see in Figure 13-12. Even this extremely rough approximation, though, may be useful in certain situations. It could simplify the first pass of a query that involves too many points or too many shapes. If you look at the last approximation of California's shape, you'll realize that it could be the ideal outline for a PowerPoint presentation, or similar application.

Converting Geography Features into JSON Objects

In this chapter, you learned a lot about SQL Server's spatial features. You know how to store geospatial data into a database and retrieve it as needed, instead of maintaining numerous JSON arrays or KML files. Before ending this chapter, I should make the connection between the knowledge you acquired in this chapter with the scripts you use to create web pages with interactive maps.

In all scripts created so far in the book, the necessary data was embedded into the script. This is neither a JavaScript requirement, nor is it always the best approach. Even so, you should be able to extract the desired data from SQL Server and convert them to a format suitable for processing with JavaScript. To use the data, you should write queries that retrieve the desired data and then convert it to arrays of custom objects. The query in Listing 13-6 creates an array of JSON objects that represent the airports in the World Airports table of the GEO database.

Listing 13-6
A T-SQL script that creates a JSON array of custom objects with the data from the World Airports table

```
DECLARE @crlf varchar(2)
SET @crlf = CHAR(13) + CHAR(10)

DECLARE @json varchar(max)
SET @json = ''
SELECT '{"Country": "' + Country + '", "City":"' + City +
       '", "AirportCode": "' + AirportCode +
       '", "AirportName": "' + AirportName +
       '", "Location":" new google.maps.LatLng(' +
       CAST(Location.Lat AS varchar(30)) + ', ' +
       CAST(Location.Long as varchar(30)) + ') }'
```

```
FROM Airports_GEO

IF LEN(@json)>1
    SET @json = '[' + + @crlf +
                SUBSTRING(@json, 1, LEN(@json)- 3) +
                + @crlf + ']' + + @crlf
ELSE
    SET @json = null
PRINT @json
```

The preceding statements will generate the following output when executed against the World Airports table of the GEO sample database:

```
{ "Country": "United States", "City":"Crows Landing",
  "AirportCode": "NRC",
  "AirportName": "Aux Field",
  "Location":" new google.maps.LatLng(37.4, -121.067) },
{ "Country": "United States", "City":"Catalina Island",
  "AirportCode": "SXC",
  "AirportName": "Avalo Vor/WP",
  "Location":" new google.maps.LatLng(-21.5833, -67.5833) }
{ "Country": "United States", "City":"Catalina Island",
  "AirportCode": "AVX",
  "AirportName": "Avalon Bay",
  "Location":" new google.maps.LatLng(33.3333, -118.35) }
. . .
```

You will find the query of Listing 13-6 in the `Airports2JavaScript.sql` script in the support material of this chapter. This JavaScript array can be used as is in a script. You can embed this array definition in a script, or store it at your server and reference it in the script with a `<script>` directive. The most flexible approach is to download the file at the client as needed, with the `XMLHttpRequest` object. This object allows you to download XML and/or JSON files in your JavaScript code as needed and use them just like any array embedded in the script. The `XMLHttpRequest` object is discussed in detail in Chapter 15.

Listing 13-7 shows another interesting script, which converts the outline of a county from a `POLYGON` structure into a JavaScript array of coordinates. The query starts by extracting from the CountyBorders table the polygon that outlines the county of Alameda. Then, it iterates through the polygon's vertices, reads each vertex's coordinates, and gradually builds a string, which is the definition of the JavaScript array. The script uses the shape's `STNumPoints()` method to extract the number of points in the polygon, and the `STPointN()` method to extract the coordinates of each vertex.

Listing 13-7
A T-SQL script that transforms the coordinates of a POLYGON geography feature into an array of LatLang objects

```
DECLARE @border geography
SELECT TOP 1 @border = Border
FROM CountyBorders
WHERE County='Alameda'

DECLARE @crlf varchar(2)
SET @crlf = CHAR(13) + CHAR(10)
DECLARE @index int
SET @index = 1
DECLARE @points int
```

```
SET @points = @border.STNumPoints()
DECLARE @json varchar(max)
SET @json = ''
WHILE (@index <= @points)
BEGIN
   SET @json = @json + '   new google.maps.LatLng(' +
                  CAST(CAST(@border.STPointN(@index).Lat
                         AS DECIMAL(12,8)) AS varchar(40)) + ', ' +
                  CAST(CAST(@border.STPointN(@index).Long
                         AS DECIMAL(12,8)) AS varchar(40)) +
                         '), ' + @crlf
   SET @index = @index + 1
END
IF LEN(@json)>1
   SET @json = '[' + + @crlf +
                  SUBSTRING(@json, 1, LEN(@json)- 4) +
                  + @crlf + ']' + + @crlf
ELSE
    SET @json = null
PRINT @json
```

A segment of the output of the preceding query is shown next. It's a JavaScript array of LatLng objects that can be used as a line's or polygon's path to render Alameda's polygon on the map.

```
[
   new google.maps.LatLng(37.90397000, -122.26822000),
   new google.maps.LatLng(37.90194000, -122.26254000),
   new google.maps.LatLng(37.89909000, -122.25876000),
   . . .
]
```

The SQL script of Listing 13-7 can be found in the Polygon2JavaScript.sql file in the chapter's support material.

Summary

In the last few chapters, you have seen how to annotate maps with markers and shapes. These items are placed on their own layer on top of the map, and you know how to persist them in KML format, as well how to store them in a database. You also know how to query the database and retrieve the desired data in many different formats, depending on your application requirements. In Chapter 15, you will see how to expose the database data as web services and access these services from within your script.

In the following chapter, you build a Windows application for annotating maps with data that resides in a database. You will do so by selecting the items you want to place on the map, and then the application will generate a stand-alone web page with the appropriate script and data, which can be presented to end users.

CHAPTER

14

Marker Clustering: Handling Many Markers on the Map

In Chapter 7, you learned how to use markers to identify features on the map. You have also seen how to handle the click event on a marker, and you've learned several methods of displaying additional information about the selected marker. The preceding chapters included examples of handling markers on a map, even from within Windows applications.

There's a special, yet rather common, situation that I haven't discussed yet: how to handle maps with too many markers. More often than not, maps contain multiple markers. Displaying a few markers on the map is a simple process, but what if you want to mark a large number of features on the map? Technically, you can add any number of markers to a map. But as the number of markers on the map increases, you'll have to deal with two problems: Your application will become sluggish and the drag operations will make your application less and less responsive. In addition, when users zoom out, the map will be covered with markers. Figure 14-1 shows a map with the locations of 9,000 airports around the world. The data for the airports, which is included in the sample scripts of this chapter, was obtained from http://openflights.org/data.html. The data at this site is free, but if you find it useful, you can give a donation to keep the site going. When you view a large portion of the globe, the markers cover all but the least populated parts of the planet. This chapter explores techniques to handle maps with a very large number of markers; there are several approaches. The first idea that comes to mind is to use smaller icons for the markers, right? Even so, the United States and Europe will be totally covered with markers. For a smaller marker icon, consider the following image (you'll find differently colored versions of the same pin at this location):

```
var smallPin = 'http://labs.google.com/ridefinder/images/mm_20_white.png';
```

Then, in each marker's declaration, assign the smallPin variable to the marker's icon property.

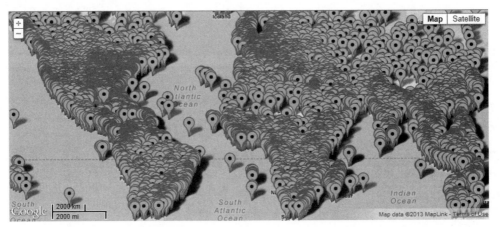

Figure 14-1 Placing too many markers on the map results in crowded maps and sluggish performance.

Handling Maps with Too Many Markers

If there are too many markers to display on your map, you must redesign your application and somehow reduce the number of markers. A functional application shouldn't overwhelm the user with data; it should display only as many markers as can fit comfortably on the map. The markers shouldn't cover the map's features, not to mention that too many markers convey very little information, except perhaps for the density of the points of interest. Handling maps with too many markers is more common than you think and there are a few tools that will help. But before exploring any specialized tools, let's start with design principles based on common sense.

As the number of markers increases, the application becomes less responsive—or quite sluggish, depending on the number of markers on the map. The first rule is to not display the markers that are not visible. It makes absolutely no sense to create markers that lie outside the current viewport. If you have up to a few hundred markers, then go ahead and place them all on the map. As users drag the map, all markers will be in place and will appear instantly. If you have a few thousand markers, however, then the invisible markers will bog down your application. Display only the markers that are visible. You can include the ones just outside the visible part of the map to be prepared for small displacements, but loading thousands of invisible markers on the map is a common mistake.

Another common sense technique to avoid the display of too many markers on the current viewport is to display a subset of the markers at small zoom levels. If possible, assign a detail level to each marker and don't show the markers with a detail level less than the current zoom level. If you're displaying cities, for example, it's reasonable to not display all towns with a population of less than 10,000 at the state level. As users zoom in, then you can display the smaller towns. At that time, the viewport is fairly limited and only a small number of markers will become visible. The two techniques mentioned here require some programming, but nothing special.

Another method of reducing the visible markers on the map is to filter the various features. You can design a page that gives users the option to see only a subset of the markers on the map. If you're displaying the airports in a country, for example, you might want to view the airports near a specific location, airports for international flights, small/large airports, and so on. If you attempt to display all airports in the world, the entire map will be covered with markers with the exception of the deserts and certain countries in central Asia. Sometimes you need to see the density of airports around the world, and there are special graphs, called heatmaps, which map the density of data points to gradients. Heatmaps use color to represent the density of a large number of data points—you will actually see such maps in Chapter 18. Heatmaps represent the density of the data with a color range but no individual data items.

In certain situations, however, you need to display a large number of markers on the map. There are two ways to handle the markers without overloading the map. To make such a map meaningful, you must limit the zoom level. It makes no sense to display 9,000 airports on the map and zoom out to continent level. You can let users view the markers in a small section of the map, but then you need a mechanism to display only the markers that fall within the current viewport. Otherwise, your application will be sluggish because of the large number of markers that are not even visible.

Another interesting approach is to cluster markers together and display a single marker that represents a large number of individual markers over small areas of the map. There's actually a third-party component you can use to perform the clustering, the `MarkerClusterer` component, which is presented a little later in this chapter. The `MarkerClusterer` component clusters a number of markers that are close to each other into a single marker. As you zoom in, the cluster marker breaks up into individual markers, or smaller clusters.

Display Markers as You Go

The first method of handling a large number of markers is demonstrated by the `Map with Many Markers.html` web application, which is shown in Figure 14-2. An array in the script holds the data for 9,000 airports. Listing 14-1 shows the definitions of the first two elements of this array.

Listing 14-1
An array of custom objects representing airports

```
var airports = [
{'Name':'Bamiyan', 'Code':'BIN', 'City': 'Bamiyan', 'Country':
'Afghanistan', 'Location': {'Latitude':34.8, 'Longitude': 67.816667}},
{'Name':'Bost', 'Code':'BST', 'City': 'Bost', 'Country': 'Afghanistan',
'Location': {'Latitude':31.55, 'Longitude': 64.366667}},
...
```

The script selects the airports that fall in the current viewport, creates a marker for each one of them, and then places the markers on the map. This process is repeated every time the user changes the map's viewport, and this may take place either after a zoom operation or after a drag operation. Both actions are captured by the `bounds_changed` event, and this event is associated with a listener that places the visible markers on the map.

If the user zooms out far enough, he or she may end up filling the map with markers. The technique presented in this section doesn't decongest the map; it simply makes the map more manageable by placing on the map only the visible markers. If the user zooms out at continent level, the map will become crowded. Actually, it will become so crowded, that you'll end up seeing only markers and oceans, with the markers outlining the continents.

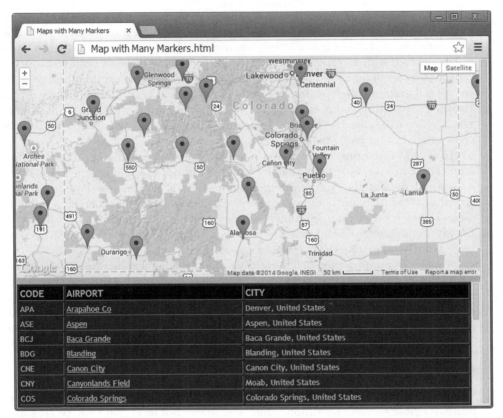

Figure 14-2   The Map with Many Markers application adds only the markers that are visible in the current viewport.

To make this approach a little more functional, you can select a minimum zoom level for each marker. If you had data about the number of passengers arriving at each airport per year, you could skip the "smaller" airports at small zoom levels. As the user zooms in, the less "busy" airports will become visible. It's also reasonable to assume that viewers are interested in exploring airports in a specific part of the world and impose a minimum zoom level. You can set the map's minZoom property to 5 or 6, which corresponds roughly to country level. Sensible users shouldn't even attempt to view all airports at once, but users are known to abuse applications in any way imaginable.

To help readers locate the desired airport, a table with data about the selected airports is placed below the map. This table, which is a navigational tool, contains one row per airport and displays the airport's name and code, as well as its location. If you had more data about the airports, this would be the place to show it. The airport codes are links and when you click them, the corresponding marker on the map is selected. The selected map bounces a couple of times and then an info window is displayed for this marker. Likewise, when you select a marker on the map, the corresponding table row is highlighted.

Designing the `Map with Many Markers` Page

Let's design an application for displaying only the markers in the current viewport—which is the `Map with Many Markers.html` web page. First, the code adds an event listener for the `bounds_changed` event, which occurs when the viewport changes. At that time, the markers on the map must be updated, an action that takes place from within the `showMarkersInViewport()` function. Every time the user changes the viewport, either by dragging the map or by zooming in or out, the `showMarkersInViewport()` function is executed:

```
google.maps.event.addListener(map, 'bounds_changed', function()
                    {showMarkersInViewport()});
```

The `showMarkersInViewport()` function iterates through the `airportsInViewport` array, which contains the airports that belong to the current viewport. For each airport, it creates a new marker and sets its `position` and `title` attributes. In addition, it sets the marker's `objInfo` property to an HTML fragment that will be displayed when the user clicks the marker. To display the info window, the script adds a listener for the marker's `click` event. The event listener is a typical function that creates an `InfoWindow` object with the data that describes the selected airport and opens it. The last few statements generate the `<tr>` element corresponding to the current airport and add it to the table below the map. This is just HTML code, which uses styles to achieve the visual effect shown in Figure 14-2. Listing 14-2 shows the `showMarkersInViewport()` function.

Listing 14-2
The
showMarkers
InViewport()
function

```
function showMarkersInViewport() {
    if (viewportMarkers != null) {
        for (i=0; i<viewportMarkers.length; i++) {
            viewportMarkers[i].setMap(null);
        }
        viewportMarkers = [];
    }
    var markerCount = 0;
    var divTable = '<table id="tbl" width="100%" ' +
        'bgcolor="#202020" border="all"><tr>' +
        '<td width="10%" style="color:white; background-color:black; ' +
        'font-family: Trebuchet MS; font-size:11pt; ' +
        'color: orange; font-weight: bold">CODE</td>' +
        '<td width="40%" style="background-color:black; ' +
        'font-family: Trebuchet MS; font-size:11pt; ' +
        'color: orange; font-weight: bold">AIRPORT</td>' +
        '<td width="50%" style="color:white; background-color:black; ' +
        'font-family: Trebuchet MS; font-size:11pt; ' +
        'color: orange; font-weight: bold">CITY</td></tr>'
    var divText = '<span style="background-color:black; ' +
        'font-family: Trebuchet MS; font-size:12pt; color: white;">' +
        '<b>List of airports in range</b><br/><br/></span>';
    var airportsInViewport = getAirports(map.getBounds());
    for (i=0; i < airportsInViewport.length; i++) {
        var marker = new google.maps.Marker({ position:
            google.maps.LatLng(airportsInViewport[i].Location.Latitude,
            airportsInViewport[i].Location.Longitude),
            title: 'AIRPORT: ' + airportsInViewport[i].Name + ' in ' +
            airportsInViewport[i].City + ', ' +
            airportsInViewport[i].Country});
```

```
                    marker.objInfo = 'AIRPORT: <b>' + airportsInViewport[i].Code +
                             '</b>   ' +
                             airportsInViewport[i].Name + '<br/>' +
                             'CITY: ' + airportsInViewport[i].City +
                             '<br/>COUNTRY: ' + airportsInViewport[i].Country;
     (function(index, selectedMarker)
     {
         google.maps.event.addListener(selectedMarker, 'click', function() {
                     if (infoWindow != null) infoWindow.setMap(null);
                     infoWindow = new google.maps.InfoWindow();
                     infoWindow.setContent(selectedMarker.objInfo);
                     infoWindow.open(map, selectedMarker);
                     selectDataRow(airportsInViewport[index].Code)});
     })(i, marker)
                    marker.setMap(map);
                    viewportMarkers.push(marker);
                    var currentIndex = viewportMarkers.length-1;
                    var linkText =  'AIRPORT: ' + airportsInViewport[i].Name +
                         ' (' + airportsInViewport[i].Code + ')' + '<br/>';
                    var linkInfo = 'CITY: ' + airportsInViewport[i].City +
                               '<br/>COUNTRY: ' + airportsInViewport[i].Country;
                    divText += '<a href="javascript:highlightMarker(' +
                         currentIndex + ')">' + '<b>' + linkText + '</b>' + '</a>' +
                         linkInfo + '<br/><br/>';
                    divTable += '<tr><td
     style="font-family: Trebuchet MS;font-size:10pt;color:#D0D0D0">' +
                         airportsInViewport[i].Code + </td> +
                         '<td style="font-family: Trebuchet MS; font-size:10pt; ' +
                         'color:#D0D0D0">' +
                         '<a href="javascript:highlightMarker(' +
                         currentIndex + ')">' + airportsInViewport[i].Name +
                         '</a></td>' +
                         '<td style="font-family: Trebuchet MS; " +
                                 "font-size:10pt; color:#D0D0D0">' +
                         airportsInViewport[i].City + ', ' +
                         airportsInViewport[i].Country + '</td></tr>'
                    markerCount++;
             }
       }
```

The getAirports() function, shown in Listing 14-3, accepts as an argument a
bounding box, which is a LatLngBound object that delimits the current viewport, and
selects the elements of the airports array that fall within that box. The selected airports
are stored in the selected array, and this array is returned to the caller.

The function very quickly iterates an array of 9,000 airports and selects the ones that
match the spatial criteria. In Chapter 15, you replace the call to a function with a call to a
web service that looks up the same airports in a database and selects some of them based on
the same criteria. Even with the getAirports() function, shown in Listing 14-3, you can
follow the code that displays a small number of markers on the map depending on the
map's zoom level and location.

Listing 14-3
The getAirports()
function

```
function getAirports(B) {
    var selected = [];
    for (i=0; i < airports.length; i++) {
```

```
        var airport = new google.maps.LatLng(
                          airports[i].Location.Latitude,
                          airports[i].Location.Longitude
        if (B.contains(airport)) {
            selected.push(airports[i]);
        }
    }
    return selected;
}
```

Note the in-place function that adds the `click` event listener to the current marker in Listing 14-1. As explained in Chapter 4, when you add event listeners that rely on a variable that changes with each iteration of the loop, you must use closures to make sure that the listener will be called with the appropriate arguments for each marker. For more information on closures, refer to Chapter 4.

The MarkerClusterer Component

The `MarkerCluster`, a third-party tool that's available from Google, allows you to cluster markers together. As users zoom in, clusters break up into smaller ones and finally into individual markers. Figure 14-3 is a typical example of clustered markers. The map shown was generated by the application `Clustered Markers Demo.html` and the markers correspond to U.S. cities. The map shows various clusters of different sizes. The `MarkerClusterer` component uses a grid-based algorithm, which divides the map into a grid and clusters the markers in each square into a single one. The script that implements

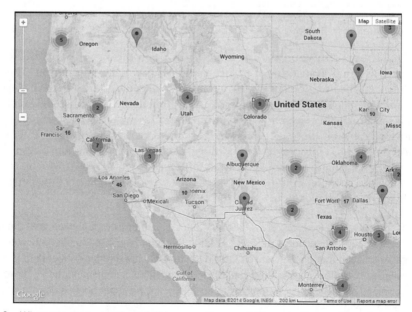

Figure 14-3   When too many markers fall in a small area of the map, the `MarkerClusterer` component clusters them into a single marker with a custom icon.

the Marker Cluster component can be found at http://google-maps-utility-library-v3
.googlecode.com/svn/trunk/markerclusterer/src/markerclusterer.js. You can also
download the file to your own web server and add a reference to it in your project.

Clustering your markers is as simple as creating a new instance of the `MarkerCluster`
object and passing to its constructor an array with the markers. Each cluster stands for a
number of individual markers, and the number of markers in a cluster is indicated by the
cluster icon's color, as well as the number in each cluster icon. The densest clusters, ones
with more than 10,000 markers, are colored with a deep purple color. The next densest
clusters are colored purple, and then red, yellow, and blue for the least dense clusters. A
map with over 10,000 markers in a single cluster is probably too busy no matter how you
look at it. To experiment with the `MarkerClusterer` component, you will find the
`Clustered Airports.html` sample page, which displays a little over 9,000 markers that
correspond to airports and can be used as a test bed for mapping applications with many
markers. Both Chrome and Internet Explorer handle the markers pretty well.

To use the `MarkerClusterer` component, you must reference the following script in
your code (or copy the file at your web server and adjust the `src` attribute of the `<script>`
tag accordingly):

```
<script type="text/javascript" src="http://google-maps-utility-library-
v3.googlecode.com/svn/trunk/markerclusterer/src/markerclusterer.js"></script>
```

The sample application's code is simpler than the code used in the preceding examples.
Here are the statements that generate the overlay on the map:

```
var markers = createMarkers();
var mcOptions = {gridSize: 60, maxZoom: 15};
markerclusterer = new MarkerClusterer(map, markers, mcOptions);
```

The `createMarkers()` function goes through the airports and creates the individual
markers, as usual. It just doesn't place them on the map. This action takes place in the
`MarkerClusterer` object's constructor, which accepts as arguments a `Map` object and the
array with the markers. It also accepts a third argument with options. The `MarkerClusterer`
options are the grid's size and a maximum zoom level, after which all markers are displayed
individually, even if there are multiple markers in the same grid square. The algorithm
breaks up the map into a grid and clusters together all markers that fall in the same cell of
this grid. It may happen that a cell contains a few dozen markers, which are all clustered
together into a single multi-point marker, and one of the neighboring cells contains just a
single marker, which can't be clustered.

NOTE The `CreateMarkers()` function populates an array with markers that are constructed with
data already embedded in the script. Later in this book, you'll see a different implementation of the
same function that doesn't rely on local data. Instead, it will request its data from a web service and
will read only the markers in the current viewport. With this implementation, you won't have to
download a huge dataset to the client and your script won't get bogged down by data that the user
doesn't need.

Open the application and see how the MarkerClusterer component handles the markers. As you zoom in, clusters break up into smaller ones. If a grid square contains a single marker, this marker is displayed without a cluster. Experiment with the grid size setting to understand how the MarkerClusterer handles many markers that fall close to each other at any given zoom level and find out the best grid size for your data.

The MarkerClusterer component provides quite a few methods. The addMarker() and addMarkers() methods add a single marker and an array of markers to a MarkerClusterer object, respectively. Use these methods to update the clusters as more data become available. To remove a marker, call the removeMarker() method passing the marker to be removed as an argument. To remove all markers from the map, just call the removeMarkers() method without any arguments. The getTotalClusters() and getTotalMarkers() methods return the total number of clusters on the map and the total number of markers being clustered. Unfortunately, there's no method to retrieve the number of markers per cluster, or the individual markers that make up a cluster.

Ultimately, you can get as creative as you wish when it comes to handling maps with too many markers. For example, you can create a set of markers that represent clustered markers and display the overview data at certain zoom levels. The overview data could include a single marker for each country or state. When users click one of these markers, you can display the markers in the selected country, even if it's not the only country visible on the map.

Another approach is to use clusters up to a certain zoom level and then switch to individual markers. When the zoom level is less than 5, for example, you can display a set of markers that correspond to states (one marker per state). This marker represents all cities in the state, and you can set their title to the state name and the number of cities grouped by that marker. When users exceed a specific zoom level, you can switch to another set of markers that represent cities.

Summary

Markers are the trademark of Google Maps and being able to create maps with many markers is a technique you need to master. In this chapter, you saw how to handle a large number of markers on the map, either by limiting the number of visible markers, or through the use of an external component for grouping the markers. The downside of the approaches presented in this chapter is that all markers are defined in the script and are immediately available to your script.

A totally different approach is to limit the number of data items downloaded to the client and to write a script that requests only the data items that fall in the map's current viewport. If you can write a web service to retrieve only the markers in the current viewport, then the client application will never have to download nearly 10,000 airports at once. A web service is a special kind of program that exposes methods that can be called from a remote computer. The service is executed on a server and returns the requested dataset. Then, you can use simple techniques in your script to create a marker for each data point and place it on the map.

Even if you don't plan to write your own web service, you can still take advantage of other people's web services and use their data to generate annotated maps, as explained in the following chapter.

CHAPTER

15

Web Services: Updating Maps On the Fly

In the examples of this book so far, the data are embedded in the script so that you can experiment with the sample applications without having to develop server side components or publish your data on a web server. You've built some highly interactive applications using the Google Maps API as stand-alone pages, but no dynamic applications that request data from a remote server on demand. Typical map-driven applications request data from remote servers as needed and process the data at the client. Such data include hotels near a convention center, airports in a specific country, or any feature of interest in the current viewport.

If you're a web developer, you know how to write a web application with a server side component that accepts requests from the client and prepares a new page with the appropriate data. For example, you can allow users to select a country either from a list or by clicking it on the map and then submit the country name to the server, where an application will retrieve the relevant data, create a new page, and send it to the client. This approach is slow, not very elegant, and so '90s. With so much functionality and computing power at the client side, you should be able to request just the data you need from a remote server and update the map from within a script at the client. All you need is a mechanism for requesting data and storing it in a variable at the client. Once the data arrives at the client, you can process it from within your script as if the data were stored in a local array.

This mechanism exists already and it's the XmlHTTPRequest object, which allows you to request data from any server and then use it from within your script to update the interface. The Google Maps API runs at the client and you can embed a whole lot of functionality in your client script, as you have seen in the sample applications so far in the book. In this chapter, you learn how to retrieve the required data, the moment the user requests it, and update the map on the fly.

Web Services

To avoid downloading large datasets to the client along with the script, there has to be a server component from which the client applications can request their data. At the server, you need a mechanism to parse the request, retrieve data from a database or any other data source, and submit the data to the client in the appropriate format. In essence, the client should be able to call a function on a remote server that accepts parameters and returns a set of data. This special kind of function, called a *web method*, must be executed at the server. Web methods are parts of an application known as web service. A web service is an application that runs on a web server and exposes its functionality through methods: It accepts requests like any server-based web application, but instead of a new HTML page, it returns a set of data.

At the client, you need a mechanism to request the data and store it in an array or an XML document. The script will then process the data as if the data was included in the script; viewers will not be aware of the fact that the data was requested from a remote server. The interaction between the client application and the server component takes place over HTTP, so the data must be plain text. Moreover, it has to have a very specific format so that clients can process the response. Web services return data in two formats: XML (eXtensible Markup Language) and JSON (JavaScript Object Notation). Web services were designed for the XML format and for a while they were known as XML web services. JSON is a newer protocol, but it's catching up quickly. You have already seen examples of both data formats in previous chapters. XML and JSON can describe structured data in an unambiguous manner so that all clients can process it.

By the way, web services aren't limited to web clients. All kinds of applications can contact a remote web server and request data through a web service's methods. The web service accepts HTTP requests and returns an HTTP stream with data, and doesn't care about the origin of the request. Most web services are not free and they do authenticate their requests, but they really can't say if the request was made by a Windows .NET application, a Java application, or from within a web page's script.

Web services are used widely in the computer industry, but setting up a web service and configuring it on a web server is not a trivial task. To include readers of all levels, this chapter explores how to use web services posted by third parties on the Web. In this chapter's support material, you will find the WebServices.pdf document, which describes how to build and deploy your own web service that provides spatial data using Visual Studio. The topic of designing and deploying web services is not a trivial one, and if you decide to make use of web services, you will certainly have to explore web services in depth.

Calling an Existing Web Service

Let's start by looking at an existing web service. You will see the data returned by the service, the code for contacting the remote web service from within a script, and how to process the data at the client. Once the data arrives at the client, the script can read it and update the page. In the case of mapping applications, the script will update the map by adding the necessary annotations to it. In the past, web pages were static and updates required trips to the server to get the updated page. Modern web applications, however, can update sections of the page without retrieving a new page. This capability is at the core of AJAX: the ability to make asynchronous requests and display the data returned by the server without having to redraw the entire page. By the way, AJAX stands for *Asynchronous JavaScript and XML* because it's a technology that was originally developed to enable clients to make asynchronous calls from within JavaScript and accept XML data from the server. AJAX is no longer limited to XML (many web services use JSON), and the requests need not be asynchronous. Its name, however, isn't going to change.

You're going to use the same underlying technology to request spatial data from a remote web server. Typical scripts update part of the page, usually `<div>` elements. A map-driven application will use the data returned by the service to annotate the map. In specific, you'll use earthquake data to show locations and magnitudes of major earthquakes around the globe. This time, you will not download data about hundreds or thousands of earthquakes to the client, as you have done with other examples so far in the book; instead, you'll request data regarding the part of the globe that's visible at the time on the map as needed. When users drag the map, the script will request new data from the server. As you will see shortly, the data is obtained from a government agency and the sample page will display the most up-to-date information.

This technique will also enable you to better handle pages with a very large number of features that entail many markers on the map. By requesting only the relevant data, the map won't be overloaded. If users zoom out too far and the application becomes less responsive, they'll know that they need to limit the amount of data to be refreshed on the map by zooming into the map. You can also provide other filters, such as date ranges and minimum/maximum magnitudes to help users find a balance between the information they need and the application workload.

Retrieving Earthquake Data

To demonstrate the process of requesting data from a remote web service, you're going to build a web page that displays earthquake data on the map. You will build the Earthquake Map sample application in this section. Two versions of it are in this chapter's support material: the JSON and XML versions (in the files `Earthquake Map JSON.html` and `Earthquake Map XML.html` files, respectively). Both pages generate the same output, which is shown in Figure 15-1. The page's script requests the earthquakes in the currently visible part of the globe every time the viewport changes and displays the earthquakes as filled semi-transparent circles on the globe. The circles' sizes are proportional to the size of the earthquakes they represent on the map. Moreover, as users select an earthquake with the mouse additional details are displayed in the lower-right corner of the map.

The data is read from the USGS (United States. Geological Survey) site at https://www .usgs.gov, which provides earthquake data for the entire planet.

Information about each earthquake around the world is stored in a database; it's made available to the public with several different methods. You can even download the data and process it with your own tools, but the data will become outdated the moment you download it.

A much more practical approach is to request the data as needed from within your page's script so that you can be sure that your viewers are seeing up-to-date information. To do so, you must use a web service provided by the USGS site to retrieve earthquake data based on multiple criteria (the date of the earthquake, its magnitude, focal depth, and so on). To design the URL that will contact the USGS service and request earthquake data based on various criteria, go to http://earthquake.usgs.gov/earthquakes/feed/v1.0/ urlbuilder.php.

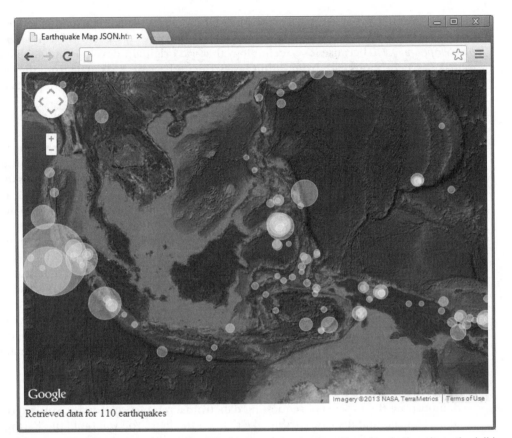

Retrieved data for 110 earthquakes

Figure 15-1 The Earthquake Map web page displays data about earthquakes in the currently visible part of the globe.

Part of this page is shown in Figure 15-2. Here, you specify the selection criteria, and when you're done, you can click the Search button to view the data returned by the service in textual format (the data will be returned in GeoJSON or KML format depending on your selection).

To view the earthquakes of size 6.0 and larger that took place in 2010, set the Start Time field to 2010-01-01, the End Time field to 2010-12-31, and the Minimum Magnitude field to 6. Then, set the Output Format option to GeoJSON. When you click the Search button, you'll be taken to http://comcat.cr.usgs.gov/fdsnws/event/1/query?starttime=2010-01-01&endtime=2010-12-1&minmagnitude=6&format=geojson.

This is the URL of the web method that will return an array of custom objects that describe the selected earthquakes. As you can see, it's quite easy to generate the web service's URL with the desired criteria from within your script. The sample application limits the earthquakes to those with a magnitude of 6.5 or larger. Among the many selection criteria, you can specify the minimum/maximum latitude and longitude values that delimit a rectangular area, and you can make this rectangle equal to the current viewport.

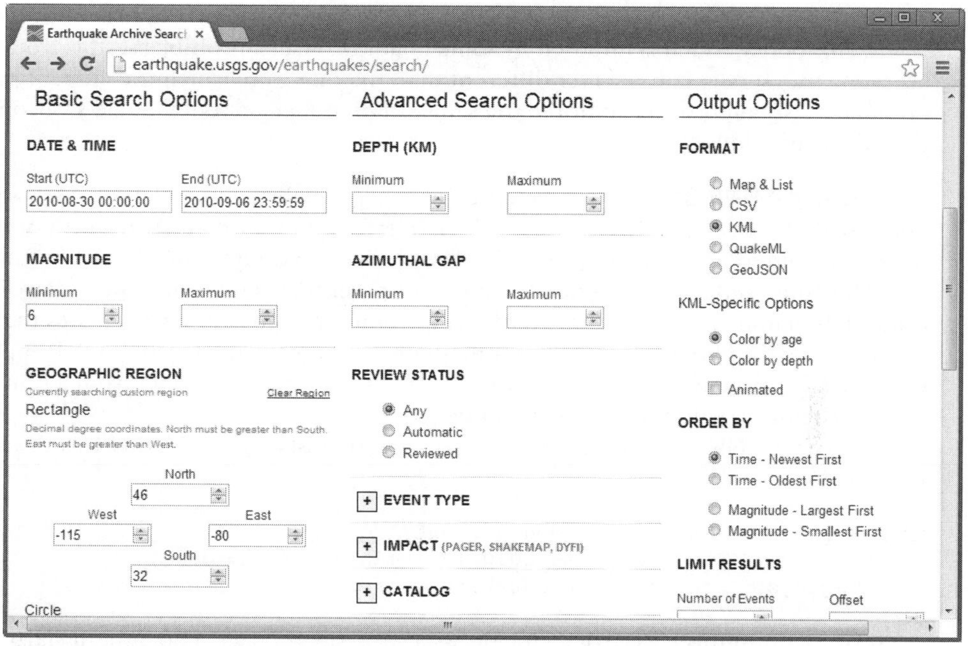

Figure 15-2   Building the URL of a web service that retrieves earthquake data from the USGS site

The WebService's Response

The URL you have designed interactively on the URL Builder page will return a document with the requested data in the selected format. The earthquakes are represented as a collection of custom objects: The collection is called `features` and each earthquake is represented as a `feature` object. The following listing shows the `features` array and its first item in GeoJSON format:

```
"features":[{
    "type":"Feature","properties":{"mag":7.4,
    "place":"282km SW of Vaini, Tonga",
    "time":1369329544000,"updated":1370903475901,"tz":-720,
    "url":"http://comcat.cr.usgs.gov/earthquakes/eventpage/usb000h3k3",
    "detail":"http://comcat.cr.usgs.gov/fdsnws/event/
            1/query?eventid=usb000h3k3&
            format=geojson",
        "code":"b000h3k3","ids":",at00mn9hfs,usb000h3k3,pt13143000,",
        "gap":72,"magType":"Mw","type":"earthquake"},
        "geometry":{"type":"Point",
        "coordinates":[-177.109,-23.025,171.4]},"id":"usb000h3k3"}
```

Each `feature` element contains a lot of information regarding a specific earthquake, including the quake's magnitude (property `mag`), a textual description of its location (property `place`), and its geo-coordinates (property `Point`). By the way, there are many more properties which were left out of the text for the sake of brevity.

This service, however, can't be called as is from within a script, because of the *same-origin policy*. This policy, which is imposed by some major browsers, prohibits scripts from accessing web services on a server different than the one from which the current page originated. Not all browsers enforce the same-origin policy yet, but Google's Chrome does and others may follow.

Requesting JSONP Data   To bypass the same origin policy, a variation of JSON was developed: the *padded* JSON, or JSONP. JSONP is no different than JSON, with one small but crucial difference. The output of the web service is passed to the client as a function call. The entire output is embedded in a pair of parentheses following the name of a callback function. The data arrives at the client as a function call, which means that the author of the script must provide the function to process the data. The JSONP approach isn't risk-free, but currently is the only method of retrieving JSON data from a remote server working around the same-origin policy.

To request JSONP data from the USGS server, you must append the `callback` parameter to the URL:

```
http://comcat.cr.usgs.gov/fdsnws/event/1/query?
starttime=2010-01-01&endtime=2010-12-1&minmagnitude=6&
format=geojson& callback=processEarthquakes
```

If you request this URL from your browser, you will get back a document starting with the following text:

```
processEarthquakes({"type":"FeatureCollection",
"metadata":{"generated":1378119793000," ......
```

Note that this time the response will not be displayed on the browser; instead, you will be prompted as to whether you want to execute the script. The script is a call to the `processEarthquakes()` function with a very long argument. Choose the Save As option to save the response to a local file, and then open it with a text editor to examine it.

No similar workaround exists for XML data. You can still use web services that return XML data, but they must be deployed on the same web server with the application. As far as the sample applications are concerned, you can still test their XML versions as long as you open them with Internet Explorer.

Processing the JSON Response

Obviously, you need to implement the `processEarthquakes()` function in your script to process the array of JSON objects that represent the earthquakes. This function should iterate through the elements of the array, generate a `Marker` object for each `feature` item, and place it on the map. Listing 15-1 shows a possible implementation of the function.

Listing 15-1
The process Earth quakes() function

```
function processEarthquakes(results) {
    var earthquakesArray =
                Array.prototype.slice.call(results.features, 0);
    earthquakesArray.sort(compareMagnitudes);
    clearMarkers();
    for (var i = 0; i < earthquakesArray.length; i++) {
        var feature = earthquakesArray[i];
        var geometry = feature.geometry;
```

```
    var eqLocation = new google.maps.LatLng(geometry.coordinates[1],
                                    geometry.coordinates[0]);
    var eqDepth = geometry.coordinates[0];
    var eqMagnitude = feature.properties.mag;
    var eqPlace = feature.properties.place;
    var eqTime = new Date(feature.properties.time);
    var M = new google.maps.Marker({
        position: eqLocation, zIndex: i,
        icon: { path: google.maps.SymbolPath.CIRCLE,
            scale: Math.pow(Math.E, eqMagnitude)/100,
            fillColor: "yellow", fillOpacity: 0.4,
            strokeColor: "red", strokeWeight: 0.5},
        map: map
    });
    var eqFormattedDate = eqTime.getFullYear() + '-' +
                        eqTime.getMonth() + '-' + eqTime.getDay() +
                        ' ' + eqTime.getUTCHours() + ':' +
                        eqTime.getUTCMinutes();
    var eqDescription =  'Date and time: ' + eqFormattedDate  +
                        '<br/>' + 'Magnitude: ' + eqMagnitude +
                        '<br/>' + 'Depth: ' +  eqDepth + '<br/>' +
                        'Location: ' + eqLocation.lat() + ', ' +
                        eqLocation.lng() + '<br/>' +
                        'Place: ' + eqPlace +  '<br/>' +
                        'Depth: ' + eqDepth + '<br/>' +
                        '<br/>';
    M.objInfo = eqDescription;
    google.maps.event.addListener(M, 'click', function()
                                {showEarthquake(this)});
    }
}
```

You can focus on the statements that iterate through the array's elements and extract the feature item for each earthquake in the beginning of the function. They read the current earthquake's data and store its properties into individual variables, which are used later in the code to build the description of the earthquake and set the properties of the Marker object that represents the earthquake on the map. The description (eqDescription variable) is stored to the objInfo property of the Marker object that represents the current earthquake. When the user clicks a marker on the map, the earthquake's description is readily available and the script prints in the lower-right corner of the map with the showEarthquake() function. The last statement associates the click event of the earthquake's marker with the showEarthquake() function, which displays information about the selected earthquake in a <div> element in the lower-right corner of the page, as shown in Figure 15-1.

The markers are displayed with a custom icon, which is a circle. For more information on using shapes as marker icons, as well as additional map annotation techniques, see Chapter 18.

Sorting the Earthquakes   The circles that identify the earthquakes on the map are sized proportionally to the magnitude of the earthquake. This technique provides immediate feedback to the user and is far more useful than a regular marker. Unless you use different colors or icons for your markers, they are all equal in stature and they don't convey additional information about the event. Even different icons wouldn't convey as much information as the differently sized shapes. In Chapter 18, you will learn how to move beyond traditional markers and use more meaningful symbols, as well as how to display relevant information directly on the map.

The problem with this approach, however, is that a large earthquake may cover the icons of neighboring smaller earthquakes. A large earthquake may "shadow" smaller ones in the same area. In this case, users won't be able to click the markers underneath a larger one. To avoid this overlapping that will render many markers inactive, you must sort the markers according to their size and display the circles that correspond to smaller earthquakes on top (use larger `zIndex` values). This way, the smaller earthquakes (smaller circles) will end up on top of the larger ones and users will be able to click on them. This technique is described in detail in Chapter 18, using an example with the same earthquake data.

Contacting the Web Service from Within Your Script

One last piece of information is needed to complete the Earthquake Map JSON sample application: how to contact the remote web service. This is done with a call to the `getEarthquakes()` function every time the map is dragged or zoomed in/out. You can use the `idle` event listener to call this method when the user has stopped zooming or dragging the map.

The `getEarthquakes()` function accepts as arguments the latitude and longitude ranges of the current viewport. The idea is to retrieve only the data that is visible on the map, and not every earthquake that took place in a single call. Here's how the function is called from within the map's `idle` event listener:

```
google.maps.event.addListener(map, 'idle', function() {
        var bounds = map.getBounds();
        var minLat = bounds.getSouthWest().lat();
        var maxLat = bounds.getNorthEast().lat();
        var minLng = bounds.getSouthWest().lng();
        var maxLng = bounds.getNorthEast().lng();
        getEarthquakes(minLat, maxLat, minLng, maxLng)});
}
```

The statements of the listener's anonymous function set up the arguments of the `getEarthquakes()` function and the last statement contacts the web service with the appropriate URL and retrieves the requested data. But where is the data stored? In a new `<script>` element that's created on the fly. The web method's response contains data, and not an HTML fragment to be displayed on a `<div>` element on the page, so it must be contained in a `<script>` segment. The code creates a new `<script>` element (just as you created `<div>` elements from within your code in other chapters) and inserts the response of the server into the script by assigning the URL of the service to the script's `src` attribute, as you can see in Listing 15-2.

Listing 15-2
Requesting
earthquake
data with a URL
that contains
selection criteria

```
function getEarthquakes(minLat, maxLat, minLon, maxLon) {
    var URL = 'http://comcat.cr.usgs.gov/fdsnws/event/1/query?' +
            'starttime=2010-01-01&' +
            'endtime=2012-12-31&minmagnitude=6.0&' +
            'minlatitude=' + minLat + '&'
            'maxlatitude=' + maxLat + '&' +
```

```
                        'minlongitude=' + minLon +
                        '&maxlongitude=' + maxLon + '&' +
                        'format=geojson&callback=processEarthquakes';
        var script = document.createElement('script');
        script.src = URL;
        document.getElementsByTagName('head')[0].appendChild(script);
    }
```

The first statement, which accounts for more than half of the listing, builds the URL based on the supplied arguments. Then the code creates a new `<script>` element on the fly and appends it to the `<head>` section of the page. In effect, the script modifies itself by adding a call the `processEarthquakes()` function with the appropriate argument. By embedding the data into a new script section, you're modifying the page's script from within itself.

Open the file `Earthquake Map JSON.html` to see how the script requests data from a remote web service and uses it to annotate the map on the same page. The page is updated from within its own script. No trips to the web server are required to fetch a new page; the script updates the map of the current page as soon as the data is downloaded to the client. By requesting the data as needed, you can minimize the number of data values moved to the client. The client script processes only the data it needs to update the page, and your application provides a much richer user experience. If you examine the source of the page when it's rendered at the client, you will not see the definition of your data. This doesn't mean that you can hide your data. There's no technique to totally protect your data on the Web, as you know.

Calling XML Web Services

If you request that the service returns XML instead of JSON, there's no equivalent technique to work around the same-origin policy. XML web services must reside on the same server as the page that contains the script that calls them. Of all modern browsers, Internet Explorer (up to version 11 Preview, so far) allows cross-origin calls. It's also possible to disable the same-origin policy in Firefox, but you don't want to ask users to fiddle with their browser's settings.

The version of the same application that uses the XML format can only be tested with Internet Explorer, but it's included in the chapter's support material to demonstrate how to call an XML web service and how to process its results. The application you'll explore in this section is the `Earthquake Map XML.html` page, and it's very different from the application of the preceding section: It uses a different method to call the web service, and it processes an XML document instead of an array of JSON objects.

Calling an XML web service from within a client script requires the use of the `XMLHttpRequest` object, which is initialized as you can see in Listing 15-3.

Listing 15-3
Setting up an
XMLHttp
Request
object
```
var xmlhttp;
if (window.XMLHttpRequest)
  {// code for IE7+, Firefox, Chrome, Opera, Safari
     xmlhttp=new XMLHttpRequest();
}
else
{// code for IE6, IE5
     xmlhttp=new ActiveXObject("Microsoft.XMLHTTP");
}
```

These statements are pretty standard and you can copy and reuse them in your script. To contact the web service, you must build a URL, as before, and pass it as an argument to the xmlhttp object's open() method, as you can see in Listing 15-4.

Listing 15-4
Contacting
a remote
web service
asynchronously

```
var URL = 'http://comcat.cr.usgs.gov/fdsnws/event/1/query? '+
          'starttime=2010-01-01&endtime=2010-12-31&' +
          'minmagnitude=6.5&minlatitude=' + minLat +
          '&maxlatitude=' + maxLat + '&minlongitude=' + minLon +
          '&maxlongitude=' + maxLon;
xmlhttp.open("GET", URL, true);
xmlhttp.send();
```

The first argument to the open() method specifies that the arguments will be passed with the GET method. The last argument specifies whether the method will be called synchronously (if false) or asynchronously (if true). You set this argument to true for asynchronous operation so that the script won't freeze the interface until the data becomes available. As is always the case with asynchronous requests, you must also supply a callback function that will be invoked automatically upon completion of the asynchronous operation. This function is assigned to the attribute onreadystatechanged of the xmlhttp object, as shown in Listing 15-5.

Listing 15-5
Reading the
response's
XML document
through the
XMLHttp
Request object

```
xmlhttp.onreadystatechange=function() {
   if (xmlhttp.readyState==4 && xmlhttp.status==200)  {
      if (window.DOMParser)
         {
            var parser=new DOMParser();
            xmlDoc=parser.parseFromString(
                             xmlhttp.responseText, "text/xml");
   }
   else {  // Internet Explorer
      xmlDoc=new ActiveXObject("Microsoft.XMLDOM");
      xmlDoc.async=false;
      xmlDoc.loadXML(xmlhttp.responseText);
   }
    // Function body
}
```

The part of the script that processes the response is discussed in the following section. The statements shown here examine the state and status of the response. If you have a valid response from the web service, the code continues by loading the response into the xmlDoc variable, which is an XML document. If not, you must display a message to the user and exit. The xmlDoc variable, which represents the object model of an XML document and provides the basic methods for traversing the elements of the document, is created differently in Internet Explorer than in all other browsers.

The two properties you must examine before processing the data returned by the remote server are readyState and status. The status property returns the status of the request and it can have one of the following values:

```
200:  OK
404:  Page not found
```

The `readystatechange` property reflects the state of the `XMLHttpRequest` object, which can be one of the following:

0:   Request not initialized

1:   Server connection established

2:   Request received

3:   Processing request

4:   Request finished and response is ready

There are no constants for these values, and that's why they're hard coded in the script. Every time the `readystate` property changes, the `readystatechange` event is fired. Your script must examine the values of the two properties and act only when the `XMLHttpRequest` object has returned a valid response.

Processing XML Documents in JavaScript

Now you can look at JavaScript's tools for processing XML documents. The `xmlDoc` variable is initialized differently in different browsers, but it behaves the same way in all browsers. The basic concept in processing an XML document is the current node, or current element. To access any element under the current one, use the `getElementsByTagName()` method, which accepts a string as an argument and returns the elements by that name under the current element. This method returns an array of XML elements; you must either access the first element by its index (which is 0) or iterate through all the elements returned by the method. Even if you know that there's only one element with a specific name, you must still use an index to access it (an index value of 0).

Let's consider that you have read an element of the XML document, and you have stored it in the `itm` variable. This element represents an earthquake, and it looks something like this (many of its elements were left out of the listing):

```
<event>
  <time>
  <value>2010-04-04T22:40:43.100Z</value>
  </time>
  <longitude>
    <value>-115.278</value>
  </longitude>
  <latitude>
    <value>32.297</value>
  </latitude>
  <depth>
    <value>4000</value>
  </depth>
  <magnitude>
    <mag>
      <value>7.2</value>
    </mag>
    <type>mwc</type>
  <magnitude>
</event>
```

The following JavaScript statement reads the magnitude of the earthquake represented by the preceding XML fragment:

```
var mag = itm.getElementsByTagName("magnitude")[0].
  getElementsByTagName("mag")[0].getElementsByTagName("value")[0].text;
```

First, it locates the `<magnitude>` element of the specific XML fragment, then the `<mag>` element, and finally the `<value>` element under the `<mag>` element. There are a few additional properties that allow you to retrieve the siblings of an element (the other elements on the same level), the parent element, and the child elements.

The sample application's code starts by extracting the earthquakes from the response and sorts them, as before:

```
var earthquakes = xmlDoc.getElementsByTagName("event");
var earthquakesArray = [];
for (eq=0; eq<earthquakes.length; eq++) {
    earthquakesArray.push(earthquakes[eq]); }
earthquakesArray.sort(compareMagnitudes);
```

The script requests all `<event>` elements of the document with the `getElementsByTagName()` method. This method returns a list of nodes, not an array. To create an array with the selected elements, the script iterates through them and adds each one to the `earthquakesArray` array and then sorts it. For more information on sorting arrays of custom objects, see Chapter 4.

Then, the script iterates through the elements of the `earthquakesArray` and creates a new marker for each element. The properties of the markers, its location and title, are attributes of the earthquake. The basic loop that displays the earthquakes on the map is shown in Listing 15-6.

Listing 15-6
Processing the
earthquakes in
the array earth
quakes
Array

```
for (i=0; i<earthquakesArray.length; i++) {
    var itm =earthquakesArray[i];
    var lat = itm.getElementsByTagName("origin")[0].
                  getElementsByTagName("latitude")[0].
                  getElementsByTagName("value")[0].textContent;
     var lon = itm.getElementsByTagName("origin")[0].
                  getElementsByTagName("longitude")[0].
                  getElementsByTagName("value")[0].textContent;

    var mag = itm.getElementsByTagName("magnitude")[0].
                  getElementsByTagName("mag")[0].
                  getElementsByTagName("value")[0].text;
    var depth =  itm.getElementsByTagName("origin")[0].
                  getElementsByTagName("depth")[0].
                  getElementsByTagName("value")[0].text;
    var eqDescription = 'Magnitude: ' +
                          mag + '<br/>' +
                          'Depth: ' +
                          depth + '<br/>' +
                          ...   // more data
      var lat = itm.getElementsByTagName("origin")[0].
```

```
                        getElementsByTagName("latitude")[0].
                        getElementsByTagName("value")[0].text;
    var lon = itm.getElementsByTagName("origin")[0].
                        getElementsByTagName("longitude")[0].
                        getElementsByTagName("value")[0].text
    var magnitude =  itm.getElementsByTagName("magnitude")[0].
                        getElementsByTagName("mag")[0].
                        getElementsByTagName("value")[0].text
    var depth = ...
    var M = new google.maps.Marker({
                        zIndex: i,
                        position: new google.maps.LatLng(lat, lon),
                        title: 'MAG: ' + magnitude +
                        ' AT: (' + lat + ', ' + lon + ')', map: map,
                        icon: { path: google.maps.SymbolPath.CIRCLE,
                        scale: Math.pow(Math.E, mag)/100,
                        fillColor: "yellow", fillOpacity: 0.4,
                        strokeColor: "red", strokeWeight: 0.5}
    });
```

The listing is fairly lengthy and the trivial parts of it were skipped and replaced by an ellipsis. Note the `scale` attribute of the `Marker` object: it's the exponential of the earthquake's magnitude. Magnitudes can't be used as they are to scale the marker's shape, because sizes of 6, 7, and even 8 pixels are practically the same on the map. Even if scaled by a factor of 10, they wouldn't reflect the earthquake's size because the Richter scale is an exponential one. The expression $(e^{mag}) / 100$ is a good scaling factor for representing earthquake magnitudes.

You can examine the code of the two applications presented in the first half of this chapter to see how you process JSON and XML data from within a script, which is a prerequisite for designing web pages that consume web services. Contacting a web service from within your script allows you to download the data requested by the user on the fly, without having to download large datasets along with the script. Neither you need to develop a server component that will process each request and generate a new page with every request. However, you do need a server component that implements the web service.

Assuming that you have a database that includes entities with a spatial component, you will most likely develop your own web service to allow applications to retrieve the desired set of data based on various criteria. The most flexible method of supplying the requested information to multiple clients of all types is to expose this information through a web service. You will shortly see how to create a web service of your own, but first you must explore another related topic: how to convert the spatial data into formats suitable for consumption on the Web. These formats are JSON and KML, which you have explored in previous chapters. You have also seen how to store and query data in a SQL Server database. In the following section, you will combine these topics, and you'll learn how to get spatial data out of SQL Server and package it in a format appropriate for displaying on a Google map.

Preparing Spatial Data for the Web

If you want to provide spatial data through a web service, you will need to understand how to extract data from a database and convert it to a format that can be easily consumed by a web client. Even if the web service is going to be consumed by a Windows application, the response must be plain text because it will be transmitted over HTTP. The KML and JSON formats are pretty much universal because they are firewall-friendly (they will never be blocked by a firewall), and they describe structured data in an unambiguous manner.

All major databases (including SQL Server, Oracle, and MySQL) support spatial data, and all major programming languages can be used to retrieve and process spatial data from a database. For the purposes of this book, we're going to look at SQL Server and how to access its spatial data from within a .NET application. In Chapter 13, you learned about SQL Server's spatial features and how to write T-SQL queries to manipulate spatial data. In this section, you will see how to use queries similar to the ones presented in Chapter 13 to extract data from the GEO sample database, and also how to convert the data in JSON and KML formats using .NET languages. Figure 15-3 shows the SQL Spatial application, which reads the data from three tables of the GEO database and stores it in three different

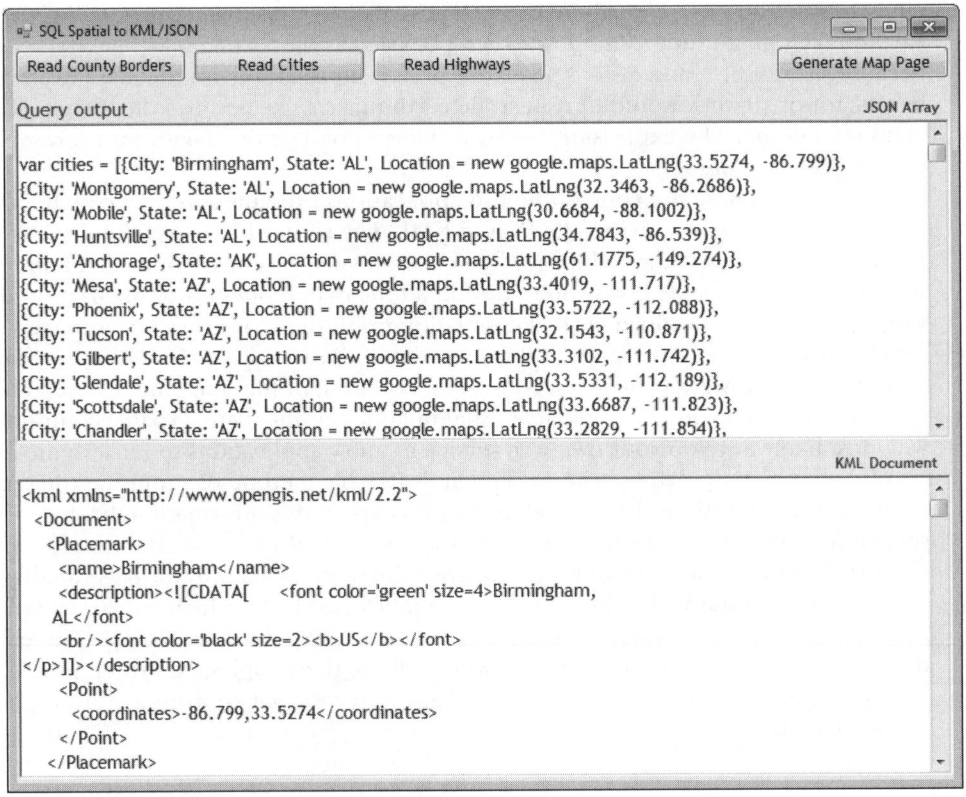

Figure 15-3 The SQL Spatial application retrieves spatial data from SQL Server and converts it in JSON and KML formats.

collections. After populating the collections with the data, you can click the Generate Map button to place the data on a map displayed on an auxiliary form, as shown in Figure 15-4. The code uses the JSON array to place the data on the map: It generates a new web page in code using the JSON array and then opens the page on a `WebBrowser` control. It actually saves the auto-generated page in a HTML file, which you can open in your browser by double-clicking the filename.

The KML description can be placed on the map with the techniques discussed in Chapter 11. You must copy the data, store it to a file with the extension KML, and then generate a new KML layer on top of the map using the file as the layer's data source. As explained in Chapter 11, the KML file must reside on a public server. If you don't have access to a public facing web server, upload the file to a web drive such as Google Drive.

The files `CACities.kml`, `CACounties.kml`, and `CAHighways.kml` were generated with the SQL Spatial application and published on https://sites.google.com/site/samplekmlfiles/.

You can open these files on top of a Google map, as described in Chapter 11. Grab the URL of one of the files (right-click the Download link under the filename and select Copy Shortcut from the context menu). Then create a URL for the Google Maps site using the shortcut you copied as a parameter: https://maps.google.com/?q=https://sites.google.com/site/samplekmlfiles/home/CACounties.kml.

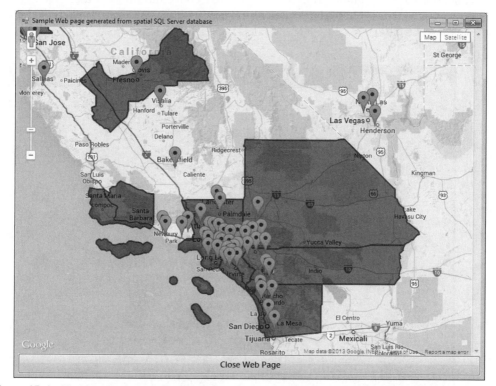

Figure 15-4 Viewing the output of the SQL Spatial application on the map

If you open this URL, you will see the map of California with the outlines of several counties on top of it. In this chapter's support material, you will find the KML Demo CA Data.html sample page, which overlays all three KML files on top of the map, as shown in Figure 15-5.

The key statements in the sample page's script are the ones that create three layers, one for each file:

```
var countyLayer = new google.maps.KmlLayer(
    'https://sites.google.com/site/samplekmlfiles/home/CACounties.kml',
    { suppressInfoWindows: false});
var HWYLayer = new google.maps.KmlLayer(
    'https://sites.google.com/site/samplekmlfiles/home/CAHighways.kml',
    { suppressInfoWindows: false});
var CityLayer = new google.maps.KmlLayer(
    'https://sites.google.com/site/samplekmlfiles/home/CACities.kml',
    { suppressInfoWindows: false});
```

The SQL Spatial application reads the rows from the various tables of the GEO database and stores them in three collections: the cities collection, which contains the rows of the Cities table; the counties collection, which contains the rows of the CountyBorders table; and the highways collection, which contains the rows of the Highways table. The three collections are implemented as lists in the .NET code, and they contain objects of three custom data types. These data types represent the entities stored in each of the GEO database's tables.

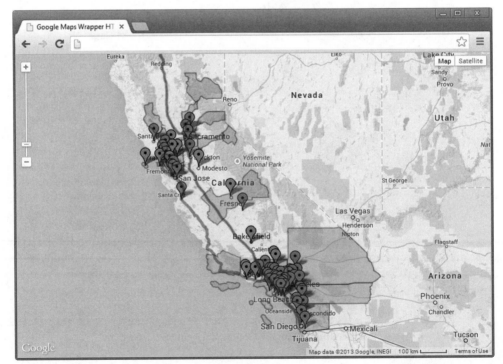

Figure 15-5 Viewing the KML files generated by the SQL Spatial application on top of the map

Reading the County Borders

You'll look at the most complicated operation—the handling of county outlines. The other routines that read cities (locations) and highways (polylines) are similar, but substantially simpler. County outlines are sometimes made up of multiple polygons and this adds a level of complexity to the code that handles the county borders. Santa Barbara County, for example, includes the San Miguel, Santa Cruz, and Santa Rosa islands in addition to the mainland. The code handles such shapes by generating a path with multiple polygons. In JSON notation, these polygons are arrays of `Polygon` objects, and each polygon is an array of points. In KML, they're represented by a `<MultiGeometry>` element that includes multiple `<Polygon>` elements.

Let's look at the outline of Santa Barbara County as represented in both JSON and KML. Here's the JSON custom object that represents the specific county:

```
{county: 'Santa Barbara',
   outline: [  // the outer array
           [  // the uotline of the first polygon
             new google.maps.LatLng(34.37449, -119.47654),
             new google.maps.LatLng(34.37452, -119.4766),
             ...
             new google.maps.LatLng(34.37449, -119.47654)],
           [  // the outline of the second polygon
             new google.maps.LatLng(33.87515, -120.01541),
             new google.maps.LatLng(33.87884, -120.00862),
             ...
             new google.maps.LatLng(33.87515, -120.01541)]
   ]}
```

The `county` property is the name of the county, and the `outline` property is an array of polygons. Each polygon, in turn, is an array of `LatLng` objects with the vertices of the polygon's path. Most counties are represented by a single polygon, but some of them are made up of multiple polygons.

The KML notation uses a `<Placemark>` for each county. Under the `<Placemark>` element, there's a `<MultiGeometry>` element which contains multiple `<Polygon>` tags. The definition of each polygon is straight KML: Under each `<Polygon>` tag, there's an outer boundary (element `<outerBoundaryIs>`) that contains a `<LinearRing>` element. There are no holes in the county outlines, so the `<innerBoundayIs>` element will never be used with this application. For the states that are made up of a single polygon, you need not create the `<MultiGeometry>` element; you can place the `<Polygon>` element directly under the `<Placemark>` element. Listing 15-7 shows the KML description of Santa Barbara County.

Listing 15-7
The outlines of the polygons that make up Santa Barbara and its neighboring islands in KML format

```
<Document>
  ...
  <Placemark>
     <name>Santa Barbara</name>
     <MultiGeometry>
       <Polygon>
         <outerBoundaryIs>
           <LinearRing>
             <coordinates>-119.47654,34.37449 -119.4766,34.37452
```

```
                        ... -119.5108,34.33085 -119.47654,34.37449
              </coordinates>
            </LinearRing>
          </outerBoundaryIs>
       </Polygon>
       <Polygon>
         <outerBoundaryIs>
           <LinearRing>
             <coordinates>-120.01541,33.87515 -120.00862,33.87884
                        ... -120.02781,33.86651 -120.01541,33.87515
             </coordinates>
           </LinearRing>
         </outerBoundaryIs>
       </Polygon>
       <Polygon>
         <outerBoundaryIs>
           <LinearRing>
             <coordinates>-119.00093,33.53589 -119.00807,33.53755
                        ... -119.00093,33.53582 -119.00093,33.53589
             </coordinates>
           </LinearRing>
         </outerBoundaryIs>
       </Polygon>
     </MultiGeometry>
   </Placemark>
</Document>
```

To create the two documents, you must first read the raw data from the GEO database and, as you know, there are no tools for reading data in JSON or KML notation directly off of SQL Server. The application stores the data it reads from SQL Server into collections of custom objects and then iterates through these collections to generate the JSON and KML documents.

The Project's Custom Data Types

The application uses three custom data types to store the data read from the database. Each data type is defined as a class and exposes a few simple properties. The properties that store spatial data are of the `SqlGeography` data type, regardless of whether the data describes a point or a polygon. This is the same data type that implements the `SqlGeography` data type in SQL Server.

To use the `SqlGeography` data type in a .NET application, you must add to the application a reference to the file `Microsoft.SqlServer.Types.dll`. To do so, right-click the project's name in Visual Studio and from the context menu select Add Reference. In the Reference Manager dialog box that will appear, select the Browse tab and click the Browse button. The file you're looking for will be in the Assembly folder under Microsoft SQL Server in the Program Files (86) folder, or in the global cache (Windows\ Assembly\GAC_MSIL). Check the box in front of the component's name and click OK to add a reference to it. Then, insert the following statement at the beginning of the code file:

```
Imports System.Data.SqlTypes
```

Without this statement, you would have to fully qualify the `SqlGeography` data type in your code.

Now you can use the `SqlGeography` data type in your .NET application to create a class that represents the entities you wish to read from the database:

```
Public Class County
    Public Property CountyName As String
    Public Property CountyBorder As SqlGeography
End Class

Public Class Highway
    Public Property HWYName As String
    Public Property HWYRoute As SqlGeography
End Class

Public Class StateData
    Public Property StateName As String
    Public Property StateAbbr As String
End Class

Public Class City
    Public Property CityName As String
    Public Property CountryName As String
    Public Property CityPopulation As Integer
    Public Property CityState As StateData
    Public Property CityLocation As SqlGeography
End Class
```

To create the collections for storing items of each type, insert the following declarations:

```
Dim cities As New List(Of City)
Dim borders As New List(Of County)
Dim highways As New List(Of Highway)
```

These three collections are the core of the sample application: They're populated with data read from the database and then they're used to generate the items on the map.

Reading the Spatial Data

To read the data from the database, create objects of the appropriate data type in your code, and populate the three lists. The code behind the three buttons that read the different entities from the three tables of the GEO database establishes a connection to the database, executes a query that returns all rows of each table, and then iterates through the rows and creates the appropriate object for each row.

Here are the statements that read the rows of the CountyBorders table. The RDR variable is a `DataReader` object, and it's the channel between the application and the database: It furnishes the results of the query to the .NET application. The program iterates through the rows of the CountyBorders table and for each county it creates a County object and populates its properties. Then, the newly created object is added to the borders list. Listing 15-8 shows the code behind the Read Country Border button.

```
CMD.CommandText = "SELECT * FROM CountyBorders"
Dim RDR = CMD.ExecuteReader
While RDR.Read()
    Dim G As SqlGeography
    G = RDR.GetValue(rdr.GetOrdinal("Border"))
    Dim Name As String
    Name = RDR.GetString(rdr.GetOrdinal("County"))
    borders.Add(New County With {.CountyName = Name,
                                 .CountyBorder = G})
End While
```

Once the list with the county data has been populated, the script goes through the list and generates the JSON and KML versions of the same list. The program builds two variables, the jsonPoly and xDoc variables. The jsonPoly variable is a string with the definition of an array with JSON custom objects, and the xDoc variable is an XDocument object with the XML description of the same data.

Transforming `SqlGeography` Data into KML   Let's start with the code that transforms the data into KML format. KML is straight XML with a specific schema, which you must respect in your code. The following statement initializes the xDoc variable:

```
Dim ns As XNamespace = "http://www.opengis.net/kml/2.2"
Dim xDoc = New XDocument(
                New XDeclaration("1.0", "utf-8", Nothing),
                New XElement(ns + "kml", New XElement(ns + "Document")))
```

The preceding statements generate the header of the XML document. The ns variable represents the namespace for the KML specification and it's the same for all KML documents. Then the code enters a loop that iterates through the counties and creates a new `<Placemark>` element for each county. This loop contains a nested loop that iterates through the polygons that make up each state. Only a few states are made of multiple polygons, but the application handles the general case; the states with a single polygon are a special case. Finally, a third nested loop iterates through the vertices of the current polygon and builds the `<coordinates>` element by appending the coordinates of the current vertex to a string variable. Listing 15-9 shows the three loops.

```
For Each border In borders
    kmlPolygons = New XElement(ns + "Placemark",
                    New XElement(ns + "name", border.CountyName))
    Dim kmlPartialPolyline As XElement
    Dim kmlGeometry = New XElement(ns + "MultiGeometry")
    For i = 1 To border.CountyBorder.STNumGeometries
        kmlPolygon = New XElement(ns + "Polygon")
        Dim kmlouterBoundary = New XElement(ns + "outerBoundaryIs")
        kmlPartialPolyline = New XElement(ns + "LinearRing")
        Dim strCoordinates = New System.Text.StringBuilder
```

```
    Dim poly = border.CountyBorder.STGeometryN(i)
    For vertex = 1 To poly.STNumPoints
        strCoordinates.Append(
                poly.STPointN(vertex).Long.ToString & "," &
                poly.STPointN(vertex).Lat.ToString & " ")
    Next
    kmlPartialPolyline.Add(
            New XElement(ns + "coordinates",
                            strCoordinates.ToString))
    kmlouterBoundary.Add(kmlPartialPolyline)
    kmlPolygon.Add(kmlouterBoundary)
    If border.CountyBorder.STNumGeometries > 1 Then
        kmlGeometry.Add(kmlPolygon)
        If i = border.CountyBorder.STNumGeometries Then
                    kmlPolygons.Add(kmlGeometry)
    Else
        kmlPolygons.Add(kmlPolygon)
    End If
Next
xDoc.Element(ns + "kml").Element(
            ns + "Document").Add(kmlPolygons)
Next
```

Listing 15-8 is straightforward Visual Basic code for manipulating an XML document. The .NET Framework provides native support for generating and processing XML documents and the preceding listing demonstrates how to build an XML document with the desired structure. In the chapter's support material, you will find a C# version of the SQL Spatial application.

The variable kmlPolygons represents a <Placemark> element, while the kmlGeometry variable represents a <Multigeometry> element. The current polygon, represented by the kmlPolygon variable, is built gradually in the inner loop. If the current county is made up of a single polygon, in which case the property STNumGeometries has a value of 1, the kmlPolygon variable is added to the kmlPolygons variable (that is, it's added directly under the <Placemark> element). If the current county is made up of multiple polygons, the kmlPolygon variable is added to the kmlGeometry variable, which is then added to the kmlPolygons variable. In other words, multiple polygons are added first under the <MultiGeometry> element and then the <MultiGeometry> element is added under the <Placemark> element.

Transforming SqlGeography Data into JSON   The jsonPoly variable that holds a long string with the JSON array definition is easier to generate as it's a string variable. The variable is initialized with the following statement:

```
jsonPolygon.Append("CountyBorders=[" & vbLf)
```

The vbLf constant represents the line feed character and is included to make the output easier to read; it's not really required.

Listing 15-10 shows the nested loops that iterate through the county borders, the polygons that make up each border, and the vertices of each polygon. This time, you see only the statements that build the `jsonPoly` variable:

Listing 15-10
Building a
polygon for each
county's border

```
For Each border In borders
    jsonPolygon.Append("{country: '" &
                       border.CountyName & "', outline: [")
    For i = 1 To border.CountyBorder.STNumGeometries
        Dim strCoordinates = New System.Text.StringBuilder
        jsonPolygon.Append("[")
        For vertex = 1 To poly.STNumPoints
            jsonPolygon.Append("new google.maps.LatLng(" &
                poly.STPointN(vertex).Lat.ToString + ", " &
                poly.STPointN(vertex).Long.ToString & ")," & vbLf)
            strCoordinates.Append(
                poly.STPointN(vertex).Long.ToString & "," &
                poly.STPointN(vertex).Lat.ToString & " ")
        Next
        jsonPolygon.Remove(jsonPolygon.Length - 2, 2)
        jsonPolygon.Append("]" & vbLf & "}," & vbLf)
    Next
Next
```

The code behind the other two buttons on the SQL Spatial application's main form is similar. Each button executes a different query against the database, and then reads the results through a `DataReader` object, creates the custom object for each entity, and adds the newly created object to the appropriate collection. The last button that generates an HTML page with a map and the features reads from the database. The code that generates the HTML page and places the various entities as annotations on the map is discussed in detail in the following chapter.

Building a Web Service

Consuming third-party web services from within your script is straightforward: First, you must understand the structure of the data returned by the web service so that you can write the necessary JavaScript statements to process the response. To call a web method on the remote server, use the `XmlHttpRequest` object for methods that return XML data, or embed the response of the remote server in your script for methods that return JSONP data. How about custom web services that expose your own data? You can create web services to use with your web applications, or make them available to the public.

You will follow a different procedure depending on the tools you use to build the web service. A web method is nothing more than a function that returns custom objects either in XML or JSON format. It's a special type of function that must be deployed on a web server, of course, but the core of a function that implements a web method is no different than a function that implements the same operation: accepts the same arguments and returns the same result. Because this process is not related to the Google Maps API in any way, it's described in a separate document, the `WebServices.pdf` document, included in this chapter's support material. The document describes how to build a web service using

Visual Studio, post it on a web server, and test it from within a client's application script. If you're interested in building a web service with Visual Studio, follow the instructions in the WebServices.pdf document. The sample service exposes the data of the GEO database of Chapter 13.

Summary

The topic of web services is not directly related to Google Maps, but web services will help you write better mapping applications. Web services allow you to request the data you need in your script at the moment you need it so that you won't have to embed large sets of data in your script. What makes web services highly useful in the context of interactive mapping applications is that JavaScript can access web services through the XMLHttpRequest object, and it also provides the tools for parsing XML documents.

A very important issue in accessing web methods is that the web server on which the service resides should allow cross-domain requests. If not, the service must reside on the same server as the application. If this is out of the question, then the web service should return its data in JSONP format.

CHAPTER
16
Map Annotation and Map Generation Techniques

One of the most common features of a GIS package is the generation and publication of annotated maps. You have seen in this book so far how to annotate maps with markers, labels, and shapes, and you have developed applications to place items on the map interactively. Now that you have the tools to manipulate maps, it's time to look at applications that allow you to generate annotated maps and embed them in stand-alone web pages for end users. End users will be able to view the information you place on the map, and even interact to some extent with the items on the map. The web pages you generate, however, are not editable. Users can click a feature to view its properties, even jump to another map, but they won't be able to edit the items on the map. The applications that enable users to annotate maps with data from various sources are usually desktop applications, as they need not be shared by a large number of users. As such, they run behind a firewall, are highly interactive, and incorporate functionality that can't be easily achieved with a web application. Let me remind you again that if you plan to use Google Maps with desktop applications, even web applications that are not posted on a public server, you need to purchase a business license from Google. For more information about licensing the Google Maps API, visit https://developers.google.com/maps/licensing.

Map annotation applications are best implemented as Windows applications. You can use high level languages to access databases with spatial data, process XML files, and, when done, generate custom web pages with the data you want to present to end users. You can add as much interactivity to these pages as you wish, but you shouldn't allow users to edit the maps or directly access your backend data store.

This chapter examines how to generate maps that display very specific information to qualified users. You may have access to the IATA database, with all airports and data about each airport. Or you may own a database with the network of a utility company (oil and gas pipes, electricity cables, and so on). Depending on who is requesting information, you may present different data to different users and even in different formats. This chapter is about preparing the annotations, placing them on the map, and presenting them to end users who can view, but not edit, the annotated map.

This chapter isn't about any new components or libraries of the Google Maps API. Instead, you'll put together many of the topics you have learned so far to build some practical and fairly advanced applications. The applications discussed in this chapter are meant to run behind a firewall, so you will need a business license from Google for their API. Even if you only care about web applications, a map annotation application isn't usually posted at a public URL because you don't want to let users create their own annotations. Typical map annotation application is used within the boundaries of a corporation to prepare annotated maps for specific categories of users, including the general public. The final product, which is a web page with the annotated map, is then posted to a web server and is made available either to the public, or to authenticated users.

The Process of Preparing Annotated Maps

Let's start by looking at the overall process of generating annotated maps and then drill into the details. The first task is to specify the information you want to display on your map, locate the information, and then determine how it will be extracted. This information may reside in XML files or a database, or it may be available to you through a third party's web service, as discussed in Chapter 15. The web service need not be a public one; it could be a web service deployed on an internal web server accessible by employees only, or a public server that requires authentication. Depending on the source of the data, you will take a different approach, and you will most likely use different tools. One of the tools discussed briefly in this chapter is the Visual Studio's `SqlGeography` data type, which maps to SQL Server's data type by the same name. This data type provides the same functionality as SQL Server's `SqlGeography` data type, and you can use the techniques presented in Chapter 13 from within a .NET application. You also know how to read data from XML and JSON documents and how to use it as the data source for your annotations.

The variety of data sources is an important factor in the process. The recommended technique is to design your own web service to provide the data. The web service will encapsulate much of the complexity as it will provide the required data as a well-structured XML or JSON document. On the back end, the web service may contact all kinds of data sources; its role is the isolation of the web application from the raw data. You have already seen in the preceding chapter how to retrieve data from a SQL Server database and convert it into a KML document.

The second task is the generation of an HTML page that displays the selected data on a map. You can write an application that generates a web page with a map and the appropriate script to place your data on the map, or you can create a general web page that acts as a framework and retrieves the desired data as needed. The second approach requires careful design and a substantial amount of non-trivial code. In this chapter, you'll follow the modest approach of generating the necessary HTML code for a map-enabled web page, and then running the script that will place the desired items on the map. The annotation data are the basic items you place on maps, such as markers and labels, images and shapes.

To get an idea of the type of applications you'll learn to design in this chapter, take a look at Figure 16-1, which is the SQL Spatial application. This application uses the database you created in Chapter 11 to store spatial data in SQL Server's GEO database. The SQL Spatial application is a .NET application that allows you to read spatial data regarding cities, county borders, and highways from the database and places it on a map. You have seen in

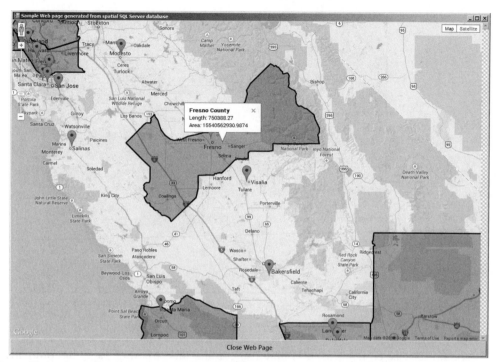

Figure 16-1   A map page generated automatically with spatial data from the GEO database

the preceding chapter how to extract the spatial data from the GEO database and store it into collections of custom objects, as well as how to convert it to KML/JSON format. In this chapter, you're going to explore the code behind the button that generates a stand-alone web page with an embedded map that contains annotation items.

An Alternate Approach to InfoWindows

You'll begin this chapter by looking at a web application that demonstrates how to use legends on the map. The same application also demonstrates an approach for handling maps with a large number of markers. The manipulation of a large number of markers on the map is a non-trivial topic discussed in detail in Chapter 14. Identifying locations on the map with markers and displaying additional information on info windows and RichLabels are not your only options. You can display the relevant data on a section of the page that hosts the map. Or, you can display the additional data on a floating window, like the one shown in Figure 16-2. This window is usually implemented as a `<div>` element displayed on top of the map. Users can drag this window out of the way when they explore the data on the map; they can also minimize and restore it as needed. The floating window on top of the map is the map's legend and it may contain all kinds of information—from symbol explanations to detailed information about the selected feature. Legends on printed maps contain descriptions of the symbols and/or colors used on the map, but legends of electronic maps are extremely flexible and interactive. In addition to displaying details

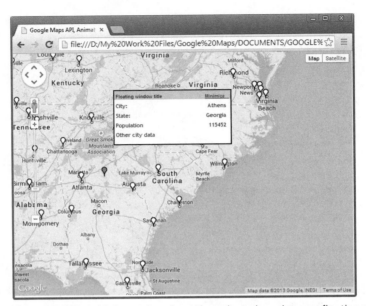

Figure 16-2 Displaying additional information about the selected markers on floating windows on top of the map

about the selected features, they may also contain links to other pages or commands for manipulating the map itself or the features on top of the map. Figure 16-2 shows a map with a legend for presenting additional data about the marker that was clicked. Unlike legends on printed maps, the legends for electronic maps are quite flexible, and their form and contents can change depending on the current selection.

The window with the additional data is a plain `<div>` element and it's not as elegant in appearance. There are jQuery components that you can use in your HTML pages to achieve this functionality, but this book isn't about third-party components or HTML design. Moreover, the `<div>` element that implements the floating window was designed manually, to avoid long listings. Actually, the page uses a jQuery component to make the window draggable, but this component is easy to use (not to mention that it's not required for the proper operation of the sample application).

Designing the Legend Window

The sample page of Figure 16-2 is the Map with data window.html application, included in this chapter's support material, and the data window on top of the map is implemented with the following `<div>` element:

```
<div id='window'>
    <div id='top'><table width=100%><tr><td align="left">
            Floating window title</td><td align="right">
            <a href='#' onclick='minimizeDataWindow()'>
            Minimize   </a></td></tr></table></div>
    <div id='main'><div>
</div>
```

The floating window is implemented with two <div> elements, one that contains the window title and the Minimize/Restore link, and another one with the contents of the window. Both elements are nested within an outer <div> element, which is made draggable. The container element (the one with the id attribute "window") is made draggable with the following statement, which must appear at the script level and be executed as soon as the page is loaded:

```
$(function() {
  $( "#window" ).draggable({containment: "parent", zIndex:999});
});
```

This statement applies a jQuery method to the container <div> element, so you must also insert the following jQuery scripts to your page:

```
<script src="http://code.jquery.com/jquery-1.9.1.js"></script>
<script src="http://code.jquery.com/ui/1.10.3/jquery-ui.js"></script>
```

These few lines turn an element on the page into a draggable element. As each marker is created in code, you must also generate the corresponding entry for the main section in the floating window. To do so, attach the following listener to the marker's click event:

```
google.maps.event.addListener(marker, 'click', function()
                              {showInfo(this)});
```

In the sample page, the showInfoWindow() function populates the custom floating window with data about the selected city. The function accepts as an argument a Marker object whose objInfo property stores a custom object with additional data about the marker. You have only a few data items for each city, but formatting them for presentation may take quite a bit of HTML code. Listing 16-1 shows the sample page's showInfoWindow() function's implementation.

Listing 16-1
The showInfo Window() function generates the legend item for the selected marker on the map.

```
function showInfoWindow(m) {
    document.getElementById("main").innerHTML="<html><body>" +
        "<table width='100%'>" + "<tr>" +
        "<tr><td>City:</td><td align='right'>" + m.objInfo.City +
        "<td/></tr>" + "<tr><td>State:</td><td align='right'>"+
        m.objInfo.State + "</td></td>" +
        "<tr><td>Population</td><td align='right'>" +
        m.objInfo.Population + " </td></tr>" +
        "<tr><td>Other city data</td></tr>" +
        "</table>" +
        "</body></html>"
    if (currentMarker != null) {
       currentMarker.setOptions({icon: whitepin})}
    currentMarker=m;
    m.setOptions({icon: redpin});
}
```

In addition to setting the main section of the floating window, this function also highlights the selected marker by assigning the icon of a white pin to the marker. The selected marker is stored in the currentMarker script variable so that it can be reset to a red pin when another marker is selected. This highlighting technique will work if you're using differently colored pins to indicate another property, such as the population of each city.

The top section of the window contains a hyperlink, which is initially set to "Minimize" and minimizes the window by hiding its main section when clicked. The window is reduced to a narrow bar and the title of the link becomes "Restore." Clicking the link again makes the entire window visible and resets the caption of the link to "Minimize" again. The function minimizeDataWindow() is shown here:

```
function minimizeDataWindow() {
    document.getElementById('main').style.height = '0px';
    document.getElementById('main').style.overflow = 'hidden';
    document.getElementById('window').style.height = '18px';
    document.getElementById('window').style.overflow = 'hidden';
    document.getElementById('top').innerHTML = '<a href="#"
                  onclick="maximizeDataWindow()">Restore </a>';
}
```

The listing of the function is shown here to complete the presentation of the application, but it's not related to mapping features. It's typical JavaScript code that manipulates the contents of the page.

As mentioned already, the floating data window is implemented with straight HTML code. If you think this technique can enhance your application's interface, you will probably go for a much more elegant jQuery component with a distinct look. The floating window isn't limited to displaying HTML fragments; you can actually embed a small form and interact with the user. For example, you can include checkboxes and react to their onchange event. Use this technique to allow your application's users to filter the markers on the map based on certain attributes. Such attributes could be the population of a city, the category of an airport (international, military, and so on), or any classification scheme appropriate for your application.

The ability to easily filter items on floating windows that can be moved out of the way, or minimized, and restored as needed, is a great aid to users viewing maps with a large number of complex annotations. This type of in-place filtering provides immediate feedback (even if it takes a few extra moments to update the map) and users can see the effects of their changes. Of course, you can combine the ideas discussed here with multiple panes on top of the map.

Annotating Maps with Labels

You have already seen examples of applications that allow you to draw shapes and place markers on a map. These are highly interactive applications that are not always suitable for end users. You probably don't want to dump all the airports on a map and let users find their way in an endless collection of makers. Chances are that you want to display airports in a specific part of the world, or specific types of airports (international/military airports), and so on.

The Labeled Airports.html page allows you to place data on maps as labels. The application's form is shown in Figure 16-3 and, as you can see, there are no markers. I have used markers to identify locations of interest on the map in most of the previous chapters, but it's time to move beyond markers. Even with the fanciest icons you can design, a map

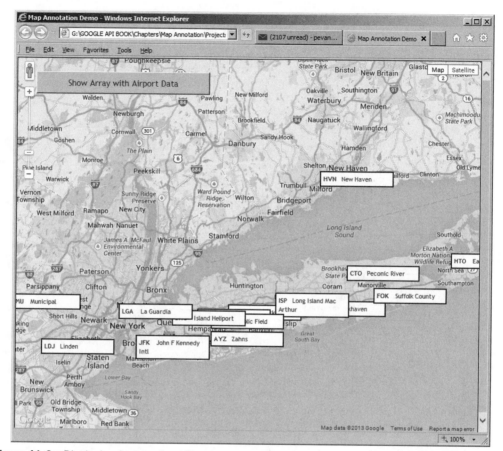

Figure 16-3   Displaying feature data directly on the map

filled with markers isn't terribly useful because users need to locate the point they're interested in. Alternatively, you can provide search features to make your application easier to use. Labels allow you to present the basic information right on the map, as long as you're working at a zoom level that doesn't overload the map with labels.

The labels shown on the map react to the `mouseover` and `mouseout` events by changing the appearance of the label under the mouse pointer. Just hover the mouse over a label on the map and it will expand to display more data about the selected feature, which in the case of the sample application are airports. Figure 16-4 shows the expanded airport label in the Labeled Airports sample page.

To annotate the map, click anywhere you want to place a label, and a pop-up window will appear where you can enter the new feature's data. After closing the pop-up window, a new label will be placed on the map. You can edit the label by moving it to another location with the mouse, or click the label to edit its data on the same popup, as shown in Figure 16-5. The `Labeled Airports.html` application contains a number of labels that correspond to airports located at the two coasts of the United States so that you can experiment with it

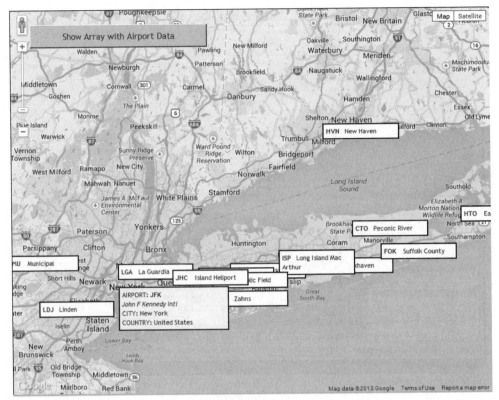

Figure 16-4 Expand a label to view more details by hovering the mouse over it.

right away. If you need to annotate the map with different features, just delete the array with the airport data, which is the `airports` array, and replace it with your own array of custom objects. You can see the structure of the custom objects describing airports by examining one of the elements of the airports array:

```
{Name: 'Clear Lake', 'Code':'CKE', 'City': 'Clear Lake',
 'Country': 'United States',
 'Location': {'Latitude':39.033333, 'Longitude': -122.833333}}
```

You must also change the pop-up window where users enter each feature's data by replacing the fields that describe an airport with the fields that describe the features you're presenting on the map.

The `Labeled Airports.html` Web Page

In this section, you'll examine the code of a web application that allows you to identify features with labels instead of markers. The Labeled Airports sample application is based on the `Maps with Many Markers` sample application you developed in Chapter 7.

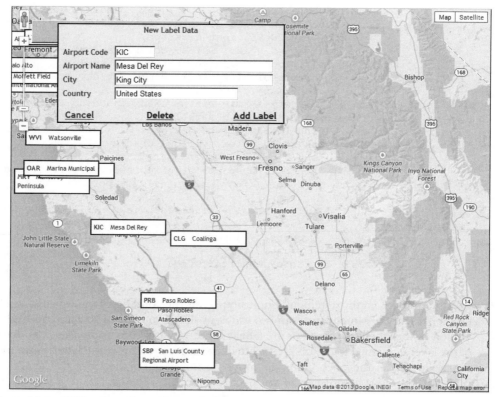

Figure 16-5　Editing the selected feature's data

In Chapter 7, you designed an application that identifies each airport with a marker and displays a table of all airports on the current viewport below the map. The revised application shows a label with the airport's basic data right on the map, so there's no need to display the auxiliary table.

When the user drags the map, the script selects the airports that fall within the map's viewport and stores them in the airportsInViewport array. Then, it iterates through the elements of the array with the selected airports, creates a new RichMarker control for each airport, and places it at the appropriate location on the map. Listing 16-2 shows the outline of the loop that generates a RichMarker control for each airport and places it on the map.

Listing 16-2
Placing a label for each of the selected airports on the map

```
for (i=0; i < airportsInViewport.length; i++) {
    // create a new RichLabel
    var location = new google.maps.LatLng(
                    airportsInViewport[i].Location.Latitude,
                    airportsInViewport[i].Location.Longitude);
    var label = new RichMarker({
        position: location,
        anchor: RichMarkerPosition.MIDDLE,
```

```
        content: '<div style="min-width: 120px; padding: 4px;
                border:2px solid darkblue; font-family: Trebuchet MS;
                opacity: 0.75; font-size:8pt;
                background-color: white; color: maroon"><b>' +
    airportsInViewport[i].Code + '</b>   ' +
                airportsInViewport[i].Name + '</div>',
                map: map});
    label.objInfo = '<div style="min-width: 180px; padding: 4px;
                border:2px solid darkblue;
                font-family: Trebuchet MS;
                bakground-color: yellow; opacity: 1;
                font-size:8pt; color: maroon">' +
                'AIRPORT: <b>' + airportsInViewport[i].Code +
                '</b><br/><i>' + airportsInViewport[i].Name +
                '</i><br/>' +
                'CITY: ' + airportsInViewport[i].City +
                <br/>COUNTRY: ' +
                airportsInViewport[i].Country + '</div>';
        label.setDraggable(true);
    viewportLabels[airportsInViewport[i].Code] = label;
}
```

It's a rather lengthy statement, but it simply sets the contents of the two `<div>` elements that represent the same features in two states, as shown in Figures 16-3 and 16-4. The short version of the label is assigned to the label's `content` attribute, while the extended version of the label is assigned to the `objInfo` attribute and is used to set the labels contents when the mouse is over the label. When the mouse is moved out of the label, the label's content is reset to the short description of the airport.

Attaching the Event Listeners

The challenging parts of the script are the statements that associate the event listeners with each label. Because the event listeners are added from within a loop when the labels are created, the script uses closures to pass the correct arguments to each listener when it's executed. As you recall from Chapter 4, each event listener is added with an anonymous function that's executed without being called.

The events you're interested in are the following:

- **click** When the label is clicked, the script prepares it for editing by displaying the pop-up data window with the label's data.
- **position_changed** When the label is dragged with the mouse, the script updates its position in the array with the label data. The dragging of the label is a limited edit operation that affects the label's position only.
- **mouseover** When the mouse pointer enters the label, the script displays the extended version of the label.
- **mouseout** When the mouse pointer leaves the label, the script displays the short version of the label.

Let's start with the `click` event, which is really simple. To add a listener for the `click` event to the current label, which is represented by the `label` variable, insert the following statement in the loop:

```
(function (airportCode) {
    google.maps.event.addListener(label, 'click',
                        function () { editLabel(airportCode)});
    })(airportsInViewport[i].Code);
```

The array `airportsInViewport` holds the airports (or any other feature you choose to display in your customized version of the application) that fall within the current viewport. This technique was demonstrated in Chapter 7; it displays only the airports that are visible at the time so that the application remains responsive even with a very large number of labels (as long as you don't zoom out too much, of course, in which case you may end up with hundreds, or thousands, of airports in the viewport).

The preceding statement associates the `editLabel()` function with the `click` event of the current label, which is represented by the `label` variable. The airport's code must be passed to the function as an argument when the function is invoked. The `editLabel()` function is straightforward: It copies the values of the feature that was clicked on the floating data window's fields and then displays the `<div>` element that implements this window by setting its `visibility` property, as shown in Listing 16-3.

Listing 16-3
The editLabel()
function

```
function editLabel(code) {
    for (var i = 0; i < airports.length &&
                        airports[i].Code != code; i++);
    labelLocation = airports[i].Location;
    selectedAirportCode = code;
    document.getElementById("txtCode").value = code;
    document.getElementById("txtName").value = airports[i].Name;
    document.getElementById("txtCity").value = airports[i].City;
    document.getElementById("txtCountry").value = airports[i].Country;
    document.getElementById("LabelData").style.visibility='visible';
    document.getElementById("lnkDelete").style.visibility='visible';
}
```

The element names shown in the listing are the names of the various elements in the `<div>` element that implements the pop-up window. You can find the HTML code that implements this element in the application's HTML section. Whether the user is adding a new label to the map or editing an existing one, he or she must end the operation by clicking one of the Add Label or Cancel buttons. The Add Label button creates a new object and adds it to the `airports` array, or updates the selected airport data with the function shown in Listing 16-4.

Listing 16-4
The addNew
Label() creates a
new label on the
map, or updates
an existing one

```
function addNewLabel() {
    var newCode = document.getElementById("txtCode").value;
    var newName = document.getElementById("txtName").value;
    var newCity = document.getElementById("txtCity").value;
    var newCountry = document.getElementById("txtCountry").value;
    if (selectedAirportCode == -1) {
        airports.push(
```

```
                    {Code: newCode, Name: newName,
                     City: newCity, Country: newCountry,
                     Location: {Latitude: labelLocation.lat(),
                                Longitude: labelLocation.lng()}
                });
        }
        else {
            for (var idx = 0; i < airports.length &&
                            airports[idx].Code != selectedAirportCode; i++);
            airports[idx].Name = newName;
            airports[idx].City = newCity;
            airports[idx].Country = newCountry;
        }
        hideDataWindow();
        showMarkersInViewport();
        selectedAirportCode = -1;
}
```

Note the use of the `selectedAirport` variable: If the user has selected an airport label to edit, this variable holds the code of the selected airport and the program uses it to update the appropriate row in the array: the `airports[idx]` element. If the `selectedAirport` variable's value is –1, then the user is entering a new label's data and, in this case, the code appends a new custom object to the `airports` array. The values of the custom object's properties are read from the fields of the popup window. Note the one-line loop that iterates through the `airports` array to locate the index of the selected airport based on its code. The desired index is stored in the `idx` variable, which is then used to access the appropriate element in the array and update its value.

The code doesn't contain any validation code, which you can add if you feel like exercising your HTML and JavaScript skills. You can make sure that all airports have a unique code, and that users aren't allowed to edit the airport code. The script doesn't update the airport code in the array, even if the user has modified it. You should either make the code's field read-only, or remove the custom object with the old code (the airport's key in the collection) and insert a new custom object to the `airports` array. You could simplify the script a little by using a collection to store the airports (an associative array that uses the airport code as the key for its elements).

Deleting Labels

To delete an airport, the script calls the `deleteSelected()` method, which removes the selected airport's label from the `airports` array and also from the map. To find out the selected airport, the code iterates through the array's elements and locates the row whose Code field matches the value stored in the `selectedAirportCode`. Then it removes this row from the array with a call to the `splice()` method. Removing an airport's data from the array doesn't remove it from the map; to remove the corresponding element from the map, the script goes through the items of the `viewportLabels` array, finds the label with the same code, and removes it from the map by calling its `setMap` method, passing the value

null as an argument. Listing 16-5 shows the implementation of the deleteSelected()
function.

Listing 16-5
Removing an
airport label from
the map

```
function deleteSelected() {
    for (var i = 0; i < airports.length &&
                        airports[i].Code != selectedAirportCode; i++);
        airports.splice(i, 1);
    for (cd in viewportLabels) {
        if (cd == selectedAirportCode) {
            viewportLabels[cd].setMap(null);
            hideDataWindow();
        }
    }
}
```

The hideDataWindow() function, which is called after each editing operation,
hides the data window with the selected airport's data. The deletion operation removes the
label from the map and keeps it up to date. The insertion and edit operations do not add
a new label or update the selected label on the map, respectively; instead, they call the
showMarkersInViewport() method to redraw the current viewport. This operation
may take a couple of seconds to (unnecessarily) redraw all labels on the map, but there's
an advantage to updating the window based on the raw data: If an operation fails for any
reason, users will notice that their changes have not taken effect as they should. You should
use an exception handler to handle all errors in your code, but going to the source of your
data from time to time is a good practice.

After editing the labels on the map, you can click the button at the top of the map to
generate the listing of the airports array with its current data. The array is displayed on
a <div> element, and you can copy its definition and reuse it as needed. For example, you
can replace the original contents of the airports array in the sample page, or create a
new page that uses this array to display the updated labels on the map.

If you thought about it even for a moment, no, you can't modify the file that contains
the HTML document from within the script! It's possible for the script that has been loaded
to update itself, but not the file in which it resides.

You can also create more elaborate labels that contain formatted text and even images.
All labels need not have the same structure. For example, you can use different labels for
different types of airports. Because the labels will overlap heavily if you zoom out, you should
add a parameter that determines the minimum zoom level for each label to prevent users
from cluttering their maps with symbols.

When too many labels are visible on the map, some of the mouseout events are missed
and you may see multiple selected labels. You can simply move the pointer slowly over these
same labels to reset them back to their summary view.

The Labeled Airports.html page is lengthy, but it's well documented and you can
follow it easily. You should try to combine the functionality of the Labeled Airports application
with the Simple Drawing application so that you can annotate your maps with all kinds of
items: markers, lines, circles, shapes, and labels.

Map Generation Techniques

The ultimate technique for generating maps is a web application that allows users to specify the information they want to view on a web page and then transmits to the client a web page with the map as usual, with the desired data laid over the map. This type of application requires server components tied to a specific environment. In this section, you'll see how to generate annotated web pages from within a .NET language. These pages can be placed in a directory under your web server, where people can request and view them.

To generate an HTML page from within an application, you create a string variable with the page's contents. You can use your favorite programming language to streamline the generation of an HTML with a script, including JavaScript. It's very simple as long as you pay attention to the use of single and double quotes. In .NET languages, strings are delimited with double quotes. If you want to embed double quotes in a string with a VB statement, you insert two double quotes in succession. To assign the string

```
<script type="text/javascript" src="http://maps.google.com/maps/api/js?
        libraries=geometry&sensor=false"></script>
```

to a VB variable, you must replace each instance of the double quote character with two double quotes, as shown here:

```
HTMLMapPage &= "<script type=""text/javascript"" " &
       "src=""http://maps.google.com/maps/api/js?libraries=geometry& " &
       "sensor=false&language=en""></script>" & vbLf
```

This is a VB statement and the vbLf constant indicates a new line character. The & symbol is an operator that concatenates strings (in JavaScript and C# you use the addition symbol). Note that this symbol is used as part of the embedded string to separate the arguments to the URL as well as to combine the fragments of a long string in Visual Basic. To produce the same result in C#, use the addition operation and escape the double quote symbol as you would do with JavaScript:

```
HTMLMapPage += "<script type=\"text/javascript\" " +
       "src=""http://maps.google.com/maps/api/js?libraries=geometry&" +
       "sensor=false&language=en""></script>" & "\n";
```

One of the sample applications you will find in this chapter's support material is the SQL Spatial application, which is a .NET application that generates stand-alone HTML pages that contain embedded maps with spatial data. The data is read from the GEO sample database, discussed in Chapter 13. It's a .NET application, and if you're interested in it, please open the SQL_Spatial.pdf file, where the application is discussed in detail. As you will see, once the data have been read from the GEO database into the client application, the code iterates through the data items and generates a new HTML page as a string. The first figure of this chapter shows a map generated by the SQL Spatial application using the data of the GEO sample database.

Summary

You have covered a lot of ground so far. You know how to exploit Google Maps API with both web and Windows applications, how to draw on maps, and how to annotate maps with labels, markers, and shapes interactively. You also know how to persist spatial data in KML files and databases and how to query spatial data from database tables. You have also learned how to request data from web services to place the items you're interested in on a map, and how to generate annotated maps from within your code. You have seen all of Google Maps API in action, and you can build highly customized map-enabled applications.

The following chapter deviates from the Google Maps API and looks at a few related APIs from Google: the Directions API, which allows you to retrieve instructions for getting one place to another, and the Geocoding API, which allows you to discover the geo-location of any physical address or the physical address nearest to any location. You will learn how to use the Geocoding API to find out the country or state that was clicked and react accordingly.

The two APIs discussed in the following chapter are also available as web services, which you can access through a URL from within your browser, or call them directly from within an application written in any language that supports web services.

17 More Google Services: The Geocoding and Directions APIs

Google offers several smaller APIs related to the Google Maps API. The most commonly used ones are the Geocoding and the Directions APIs, which you're going to explore in this chapter. *Geocoding* is the process of converting physical addresses to geo-coded locations (longitude/latitude pairs). You can use the Geocoding API to request your house's coordinates by specifying its address. The reverse process, known as *Reverse Geocoding*, does the opposite: You request the physical address at a specific location. The Directions API is the single most popular tool based on Google Maps. The Directions API provides driving/cycling or walking directions between any two points, as long as there's a "ridable" path between them (it doesn't work over oceans and tropical forests, for example).

   Google provides a few more APIs that are not covered in this book. The Earth API was designed for Google Earth, and it could be the topic of another book. The Elevation API provides altitude information about locations, and the Time Zone API is another web service for finding the time zone at any location. Finally, the Places API allows you to find information about places other people have added to Google Maps.

Geocoding API Usage Limit

Use of the Google Geocoding API is subject to a query limit of 2,500 requests per day. If you exceed the 24-hour limit or otherwise abuse the service, the Geocoding API may stop working for you temporarily (a 24-hour period initially). If you continue to exceed this limit habitually, your access to the Geocoding API may be blocked.

   Twenty-five hundred requests may sound like a lot, but if you have an application that requests the address at the center of the map every time you drag the map around, you can easily hit this limit in a few hours (especially if you are debugging your application!). If you do, your requests will not be honored for a 24-hour period, so be sure you don't keep hitting this limit constantly. Or get a Business license from Google to have unlimited access to its services.

The Geocoding API

The Geocoding API is a library like the other APIs, and you can access its services not only through the appropriate object (an object of the `google.maps.geocoder` type) in your script, but also through a URL from within your browser. Because this API is implemented as a web service, you can access it from within any application, not just a script. However, please pay attention to the following note.

Correct Usage of the Geocoding and Directions APIs

Calling the Geocoding and/or the Directions API from within applications running behind a firewall is not allowed by Google unless you have a Business license—or your application is hosted at a public site and is free. If it's a web application, you can still limit access to your application by requiring users to log in, but the application must still be hosted as a public site. For more information on using the APIs described in this chapter, please read the license (https://developers.google.com/maps/licensing), or contact Google's sales department (you will find the link at the same site). By using any of the Google APIs, you implicitly agree to comply with Google's license agreement—which certainly isn't a trivial document you can accept without reading.

The easiest method to geocode an address is to make an HTTP request to a specific application at Google, passing a physical address as parameter. The application returns the results in either XML or JSON format. To geocode an address and retrieve the results in XML format, use a URL like the following: http://maps.googleapis.com/maps/api/geocode/xml?address=1029 Palm Ave, S. Pasadena, CA&sensor=false.

The `sensor` parameter is set to `false` as usual, while the `address` parameter is the physical address whose geo-location you want to retrieve. It could be a mailing address such as the one shown in the example, a city name like "South Pasadena," or even a monument or building name such as "Space Needle" or "Christ Redeemer."

The Geocoding Response

Open your browser, paste the preceding URL in the address bar, and press ENTER. Google will respond with the XML file shown in Listing 17-1 (it's a trivial, but fairly lengthy, listing, included here in its entirety for your convenience). The response is an XML document, because in the request you specified the **xml** application. It's also possible to retrieve the results in JSON format (see the section "JSON Response" later in this chapter).

Listing 17-1
A typical geocoding XML response for an address in the United States

```
<?xml version="1.0" encoding="UTF-8"?>
    <GeocodeResponse>
        <status>OK</status>
        <result>
            <type>street_address</type>
            <formatted_address>1029 Palm Ave, South Pasadena, CA 91030,
                    USA</formatted_address>
            <address_component>
                <long_name>1029</long_name>
                <short_name>1029</short_name>
```

```
            <type>street_number</type>
        </address_component>
        <address_component>
            <long_name>Palm Ave</long_name>
            <short_name>Palm Ave</short_name>
            <type>route</type>
        </address_component>
        <address_component>
        <long_name>South Pasadena</long_name>
        <short_name>South Pasadena</short_name>
        <type>locality</type>
        <type>political</type>
    </address_component>
    <address_component>
        <long_name>Los Angeles</long_name>
        <short_name>Los Angeles</short_name>
        <type>administrative_area_level_2</type>
        <type>political</type>
    </address_component>
    <address_component>
        <long_name>California</long_name>
        <short_name>CA</short_name>
        <type>administrative_area_level_1</type>
        <type>political</type>
        </address_component>
        <address_component>
            <long_name>United States</long_name>
            <short_name>US</short_name>
            <type>country</type>
            <type>political</type>
        </address_component>
        <address_component>
            <long_name>91030</long_name>
            <short_name>91030</short_name>
            <type>postal_code</type>
        </address_component>
    <geometry>
        <location>
            <lat>34.1129570</lat>
            <lng>-118.1638010</lng>
        </location>
        <location_type>ROOFTOP</location_type>
        <viewport>
            <southwest>
                <lat>34.1116080</lat>
                <lng>-118.1651500</lng>
            </southwest>
            <northeast>
                <lat>34.1143060</lat>
                <lng>-118.1624520</lng>
            </northeast>
        </viewport>
    </geometry>
    </result>
</GeocodeResponse>
```

The XML document with the response will be displayed right in your browser, as shown in Figure 17-1. It's a lengthy response that contains the correct address, which may not be exactly the same as the one you typed. Note that the "Ave" abbreviation became "Avenue" and "S. Pasadena" became "South Pasadena." The location's geo-coordinates are stored in the `<location>` element under the `<geometry>` element. The location's geo-coordinates are the values of the `<lat>` and `<lng>` elements. You can process this file either in your script, using JavaScript, or in any high level language, such as Visual Basic or C#, that can parse XML. You will see examples of VB/C# and JavaScript code shortly.

Grab the geo-coordinates from the response to the Geocoding request and form a new URL, which is a request for a reverse geocoding operation: http://maps.googleapis.com/maps/api/geocode/xml? address=34.1143060,-118.1624520&sensor=false.

The URL is the same as before, but now the value of the `address` parameter is a geocoded location and not a physical address. You will get an identical document, which describes the same physical address as before. In effect, both requests refer to the same location on the globe, regardless of whether the location was specified as a physical address or as a pair of geo-coordinates. It's possible that you may not get the exact same address, but one very near the original.

The Response Status

Note that the first element in the response is the `<status>` element, and its value is OK for successful requests. If the URL you specified contains errors, or if Google can't geocode the specified address, then the response will contain a different `<status>` element and no additional information:

```
<?xml version="1.0" encoding="UTF-8"?>
<GeocodeResponse>
<status>ZERO_RESULTS</status>
</GeocodeResponse>
```

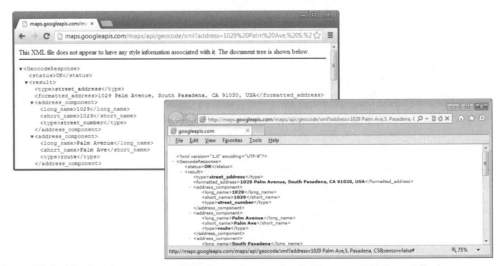

Figure 17-1 Viewing the response of the Geocoding service in Chrome and Internet Explorer

Finally, if the coordinates you specified are in the middle of the ocean, you will get back a valid, but very generic, response, like the one shown in Listing 17-2.

Listing 17-2
The XML
response of
a geocoding
request in an
uninhabited area

```xml
<?xml version="1.0" encoding="UTF-8"?>
<GeocodeResponse>
    <status>OK</status>
    <result>
        <formatted_address></formatted_address>
        <geometry>
            <location>
                <lat>34.1129570</lat>
                <lng>-131.1638010</lng>
            </location>
            <location_type>APPROXIMATE</location_type>
            <viewport>
                <southwest>
                    <lat>29.2540704</lat>
                    <lng>-139.3596020</lng>
                </southwest>
                <northeast>
                    <lat>38.7080323</lat>
                    <lng>-122.9680000</lng>
                </northeast>
            </viewport>
        </geometry>
        <partial_match>true</partial_match>
    </result>
</GeocodeResponse>
```

This response contains a new element, the `<partial_match>` element. If you receive a response that contains this element, you should probably ignore it. It means that the address you specified does not correspond to a known feature, such as a building or landmark, but is an approximate location. When this happens, the `<partial_match>` element will be set to `true`.

JSON Response

If you prefer the JSON format, which is better suited for processing the results in a JavaScript client script, use the following URL (note that only the application name changes; the parameter names are the same): http://maps.googleapis.com/maps/api/geocode/json?address=1029 Palm Ave, S. Pasadena, CA&sensor=false.

Listing 17-3 shows the same response in JSON format. As you can see, the JSON response is an array with many custom objects, equivalent to the XML elements of Listing 17-1. The listing was condensed a little by moving the curly brackets on the same line as the objects they delimit to conserve space on the printed page.

Listing 17-3
The JSON
response to a
typical geocoding
request

```json
{
    "results" : [
        { "address_components" : [
            { "long_name" : "1029",
              "short_name" : "1029",
              "types" : [ "street_number" ] },
```

```
              { "long_name" : "Palm Avenue", "short_name" : "Palm Ave",
                "types" : [ "route" ] },
              { "long_name" : "South Pasadena", "short_name" : "South Pasadena",
                "types" : [ "locality", "political" ] },
              { "long_name" : "Los Angeles", "short_name" : "Los Angeles",
                "types" : [ "administrative_area_level_2",
                            "political"},
              { "long_name" : "California",
                "short_name" : "CA",
                "types" : [ "administrative_area_level_1",
                            "political" ] },
              { "long_name" : "United States", "short_name" : "US",
                "types" : [ "country", "political" ] },
              { "long_name" : "91030", "short_name" : "91030",
                "types" : [ "postal_code" ] }
          ],
          "formatted_address" :
              "1029 Palm Avenue, South Pasadena, CA 91030, USA",
          "geometry" : { "location" : {
                          "lat" : 34.1129570, "lng" : -118.1638010 },
          "location_type" : "ROOFTOP",
          "viewport" : {
              "northeast" : {
                  "lat" : 34.1143059802915, "lng" : -118.1624520197085
              },
              "southwest" : {
                  "lat" : 34.1116080197085, "lng" : -118.16514998029
              }
          }
        },
        "types" : [ "street_address" ] }
    ],
    "status" : "OK"
}
```

Both the JSON and XML fragments of the two listings describe the same document. The format is syntactically different, but the data is identical in both responses. The structure of the two documents is also identical.

The Response's Elements

The query returns a custom object, the `results` custom object, which has five items (one of them is a string and the remaining four are objects):

- The `address_components` object, which is an array with the components of the address. The address is specified in more detail than you'll ever need.

- The `formatted_address` object, which is a string with the properly formatted address. This is not always the same as the address you passed to the method, but it's the nearest address to the one you specified and it's absolutely valid (according to Google, of course).

- The geometry object, which has three properties: the location, location_ type, and viewport properties.

- The types object, which is an array of address types. For residential addresses, this array holds a single element, the street_address type.

There's a fifth object at the end, the status object, which stores the status of the response. You should attempt to process the response only if the status of the response is "OK." In the JSON response, the address components are property names, while in the XML response, the same components are element names. As you recall from Chapter 11, there's a correspondence between XML elements and JSON properties, as both formats describe the same data.

Each item in the address_components has a type property and two descriptive properties: the short_name and long_name properties. The type denotes a part of the address: whether the item represents the address's street or number, the city, and so on. Not all addresses will contain the same number of address components, especially if you're working with suburban locations outside the United States.

If you look up the Space Needle monument in Seattle (the address argument being "Space Needle, Seattle"), the types array in the response will have the following two values:

```
"types" : [ "point_of_interest", "establishment" ]
```

The Space Needle has two different descriptions because they both fit this type of landmark. Other landmarks may have even more types, and new landmark types may be added in the future as Google Maps is a project in progress.

Using the Geocoding API from Within JavaScript

To use the Geocoding services from within your script, you must create an object of the Geocoder type like this:

```
var geocoder = new google.maps.Geocoder();
```

This object will enable your script to contact the Geocoding service by calling its geocode() method. The geocode() method is executed asynchronously and it expects two arguments: an address or a geo-location (as with the HTTP request) and a function that will be executed when the result of the web service becomes available. The following is a typical call to the geocode() method:

```
geocoder.geocode({'address': pt}, function(result, status) {
if (status == google.maps.GeocoderStatus.OK) {
        // JavaScript statements to process the result
    });
```

The two arguments of the callback function are the service's response to the request and the status of the response. The pt variable in the preceding code segment is a LatLng object, declared with a statement like the following:

```
var pt = new google.maps.LatLng(38.125, -105.510);
```

or

```
var pt = map.getCenter();    // extract the map's center location
```

If you want to pass a physical address to the method, set the `address` parameter to the physical address you're trying to reverse geocode, as shown here:

```
geocoder.geocode({'address':'1029 Palm Ave, S. Pasadena, CA'},
                      function(results, status) {
                          // function statements
                      });
```

The `geocode()` method returns its result always in JSON format. To retrieve the `formatted_address` attribute of the first result, use the following expression:

```
result[0].formatted_address
```

When you specify an address as the argument, you're probably interested in the location's geo-location, so you must retrieve the `location` attribute of the `geometry` object from the response:

```
var location = results[0].geometry.location
```

The complete physical address with all its details is still available in the response, of course. Typical scripts use the `formatted_address` property of the first result:

```
var strAddress = results[0].formatted_address
```

In the section "An Enhanced Map" later in this chapter, you'll see how to display not only the coordinates of the map's center point, but also the physical address of that location (if available). The contents of the status bar of the enhanced mapping page, shown in Figure 17-3, were generated by the `updateStatusBar()` function, which is shown in Listing 17-4.

Listing 17-4
The update
Status()
function displays
the map's center
coordinates and
address.

```
function updateStatusBar() {
    var pt = map.getCenter();
    geocoder.geocode({'latLng': pt}, function(result, status) {
        varstrAddress = 'GEOCODING OPERATION FAILED';
        if (status == google.maps.GeocoderStatus.OK) {
            if (result[0])    strAddress = result[0].formatted_address;|
        }
        else
            strAddress=status;
        document.getElementById('statusbar').innerText="Lat: " +
            pt.lat().toFixed(6) + "\t " + "     Lon: " +
            pt.lng().toFixed(6) + "\t " + strAddress;
    });
}
```

The code extracts the `formatted_address` property from the response and displays this string, along with the current coordinates, on the status bar. This is a rather simplistic approach; it assumes that the desired location is the first one. It uses the first element of the result array and ignores the rest. In the following section, you'll see how to handle all results and let the user select the most appropriate address.

The `updateStatusBar()` function is attached to the `dragend` event of the map and is invoked every time the user drags the map to a new location. The following statement associates the function with the `dragend` event:

```
google.maps.event.addListener(map, 'dragend',
        function (event) {
            updateStatusBar();
        });
```

You can also use the `bounds_changed` event, which is fired when the user drags the map, but the `bounds_changed` event is fired on zooming operations as well, and there's no reason to update the status bar when the map is zoomed in or out because its center remains the same.

Note that there's a limit on the geocoding requests you can make, and Google will stop responding to your request if you exceed the 2,500 requests per day—unless, of course, you have a business license, in which case you can make as many requests as you wish. A business license is required if you make your application public and too many users hit the geocoding services through your site. If you keep hitting this limit for several days, Google will ban requests from your site permanently.

CAUTION A last word of caution: You should never, absolutely never, call the geocoding services from within a `drag` event's handler! Google will detect the frequency of the requests (several requests per second) and refuse to service them, even if you have a business license. If you get back the `ACCESS DENIED` status code, make sure your application is not calling the geocoding services too often and that it doesn't exceed the maximum number of requests on a daily basis. As shocking as it may be, even Google's servers *do* have limits.

Responses with Multiple Matches

The geocoding response may contain multiple results if the address included in the request is not specific enough. In this case, each location is stored in its own `result` object (in JSON) or `<result>` element (in XML). If you specify "Rushmore Mountain" as the address without any other qualification, the response will contain four different results:

- *Green Mountain, Mount Rushmore, SD 57702, USA*, a natural feature in SD

- *Rushmore Place, Forest Park, GA 30297, USA*, a route in GA

- *Ford Mountain, West Pennington, SD 57730, US*, a natural feature in SD

- *Mountain Meadow, Rapid City, SD 57702, USA*, a route in SD

You will get even more results, and over a much broader area, if you specify "Athens" as the address. You'll get back one "Athens" in Greece, obviously, and five more in Georgia, Alabama, Ohio, Texas, and Tennessee.

If you get multiple results, you should process them all and present a list of options to the user so that she can select the desired one. The Geocoding.html application, shown in Figure 17-2, is a simple web page that demonstrates how to handle multiple results returned by the geocode() method. Users can enter an address in the text box and press ENTER. The script calls the Geocoding service with the user-supplied string as an argument. If the service returns a single location, the map is centered at that location. If the service returns multiple results, they're all displayed as hyperlinks on a <div> element on top of the map, and the user can jump to any one of them by clicking the appropriate link, or the user can click the Close Dialog link to dismiss the window without changing location.

The sample application uses a simple technique to display the results of the query on a floating window—a technique based on the <div> element, which is populated as needed, and its visibility is turned on or off depending on the service's response and the user's actions. For more information on displaying a floating window on top of a web page, see Chapter 7. You will probably use a third-party tool for a more elegant auxiliary window, but no such tools are used in this book.

To detect the pressing of the ENTER key, the application uses the following event listener:

```
document.getElementById("address").addEventListener("keydown",
        function(e) {
            if (e.keyCode == 13) { locateAddress(); }
        },     false);
```

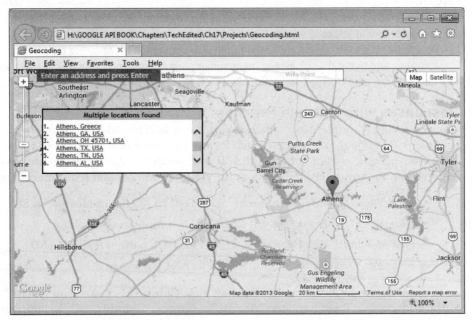

Figure 17-2 The address specification "Athens" resulted in six different locations, of which the user is prompted to select one.

The locateAddress() function does all the work: It builds the proper URL for the Geocoding API, calls the service, and either pans the map to the specified location (if the service returns a single location) or displays all the matches on a floating window. Listing 17-5 shows the locateAddress() function.

Listing 17-5
The function
locate
Address()
processes
the results of
a geocoding
request.

```
function locateAddress() {
    geocoder = new google.maps.Geocoder();
    geocoder.geocode( {
        'address':document.getElementById("address").value },
        function(results, status) {
            if (status == google.maps.GeocoderStatus.OK) {
                var msg = '<b>Found ' + results.length +
                    ' addresses</b><br/><br/>';
                if (results.length > 1) {
                    for (i=0; i < results.length;i++) {
                        msg += (i+1).toString() +
                '.    ' + '<a href="javascript:goto' +
                results[i].geometry.location.toString() + '">' +
                results[i].formatted_address + '</a><br/>';
                    }
                msg += '<br/><div style="text-align:right; width:70%">
                        <a href="javascript:hideMain()"><b>
                        Close this dialog</b></a></div>';
                document.getElementById("main").innerHTML = msg;
                document.getElementById("window").
                        style.visibility='visible';
            }
            else {
                map.setCenter(results[0].geometry.location);
                map.setZoom(15);
            }
        }
    });
}
```

The indentation of the code is rather whacky, but this listing contains long nested statements that can't be broken clearly on the printed page; you may wish to open the GeoCoding.html file with a text editor and view the code in its original format.

The function calls the geocode() method of the API passing as an argument the string entered by the user on the page, and processes the results with a custom function, which is specified in-line. This anonymous function is activated automatically as soon as the results of the method are in.

If the status of the response is "OK" , the function proceeds by counting the number of items in the results array in the response. If there's more than one element in the array, the function builds the string with the addresses to be displayed. It does so by iterating through the results array and reads each element's geometry.location and formatted_address properties, which it then uses to build the contents to be displayed on the auxiliary window. Each item on this window is formatted as a hyperlink that users can click to pan the map to the desired location. To go to a specific location, the hyperlink calls the goto() function, passing as an argument the geolocation of the selected address:

```
function goto(lat, lon) {
            hideMain();
            map.setCenter(new google.maps.LatLng(lat, lon));
            map.setZoom(15);
}
```

Note how the script builds the URL of the anchor that calls the goto() function; it builds a string that contains the coordinates of the location without parentheses:

```
'javascript:goto' + results[i].geometry.location.toString()
```

The geometry.location object's toString() method returns the coordinates in parentheses already, so there's no reason to embed them in another pair of parentheses. In effect, this would cause a run-time error.

The "Longitudes Latitudes" project presented in Chapter 1 uses the Geocoding service to retrieve the address of the point that was clicked on the map. This application, however, displays the address as a label directly on the map. The label is an instance of the RichMarker object, and the script displays the coordinates of the point that was clicked, the name of the nearest city, and the corresponding country. Locations in the ocean return only the geo-coordinates and no address information. For your convenience, Listing 17-6 shows the statement that creates the label with the appropriate content and places it on the map (the entire listing is a single statement):

Listing 17-6
Displaying geographical data on a RichMarker object

```
var label = new RichMarker({
            position: location, anchor: RichMarkerPosition.MIDDLE,
            content:  '<div style="min-width: 180px; padding: 4px; ' +
                      'border:2px solid darkblue; font-family: ' +
                      'Trebuchet MS; opacity: 0.75; ' +
                      'font-size:8pt; background-color: white; ' +
                      'color: maroon"><b>Current Location:</b><br/>' +
                      '     ' +
                      location.lat().toFixed(6) + ', ' +
                      location.lng().toFixed(6) + '<br/>' +
                      '<b>Nearest City:</b>   ' +
                      city + '<br/><b>Country:  </b>' +
                      country + '</div>',
            map: map});
```

Localizing the Geocoding Service

The result returned by the geocoding API is in English, but this is an option you can overwrite by specifying the region attribute. The parameter region=el will return the results in Greek, while the argument region=zh-cn will display the results in Chinese. The actual location names (street, city, and county names) will appear in the default language of the client computer.

Figure 17-3   Displaying useful information regarding the map's current location in the status bar

The region parameter can also affect (or *bias*) the result. If the region is el (for Greece) and you're searching for "Athens," the first result will be Athens, Greece. If the region is US and you perform the same request, the first result will be Athens, Texas or Athens, Ohio.

An Enhanced Map

The web page shown in Figure 17-3 is the Basic Map with Status Bar.html sample page. In the black status bar below the map, this page displays the map's current location as well as this location's address. The status bar is another <div> element and not the browser's status bar; browsers do not allow scripts to control their status bar.

The Directions API

Another related API from Google is the Directions API, which provides instructions for getting from one location to another, as well as driving or walking distances. There's an abundance of sites on the Internet that can calculate the distance between any two points and provide directions for getting from one point to another. The vast majority of these sites use Google's Directions API and Google Maps.

You can access the functionality of the Directions API from within any application, regardless of whether the application is based on Google Maps. The map will make it easier for the user to specify the two points and visualize the suggested route, but this isn't always true. If you know the address of the origin and the destination of your trip, you can use the Directions API to retrieve all the information you need. If you're working for a delivery company, for example, you can incorporate this functionality in your applications and print the driving instructions automatically for each order to be delivered. No user interaction is required as long as you have a complete delivery address. Most drivers aren't interested in seeing the route on the map; a few simple instructions will suffice. This is especially true for local drivers, who are familiar with the major avenues in their area and only need to know which exit to take to get to their destination, which is usually a small, less-known street.

Another advantage of using the Directions API in the context of a Windows application is that you're in control of the printing process. While in the browser you're limited to the printing capabilities of the browser (a notoriously cumbersome process), printing from within your application's code is a breeze. You can also assign deliveries to drivers based on the drive's duration, track distances travelled, charge by the distance, and so on. These operations are handled more easily in the context of a rich client application. On the other end of the spectrum, however, it's much more practical to pass the instructions to a text-to-speech synthesis application running on a mobile device.

Using the Directions Web Service

You'll certainly come up with original ways to use the Directions API and add value to your applications, so let's see how it works. Like the Geocoding API, the Directions API can be accessed outside the context of a map through a URL (as a web service), or from within a script. To see the web service in action, enter the following URL in your browser:

```
http://maps.googleapis.com/maps/api/directions/xml?origin=Storke
Tower, UCSB, Santa Barbara&destination=Beckman Auditorium,
Caltech,Pasadena&mode=driving&units=metric&sensor=false
```

and you will see an XML document with the directions for driving from the first address (specified with the `origin` parameter) to the second address (specified by the `destination` parameter). Figure 17-4 shows the response to the preceding request, displayed in a browser window.

The Directions Request and Response

The URL to contact the Directions service is made up of the address of the Directions service on Google's server and four arguments: the two locations (specified as physical addresses or geo-locations), the driving mode, and the `sensor` parameter. The driving mode, specified with the `mode` parameter, can have one of the following values: `driving`, `walking`, or `bicycling`. You are free to specify the two addresses as best as you can. The specific locations used in the preceding example are landmarks of two universities in Southern California. You can include the state if you wish, but the two university names are unique in the country and Google didn't require any additional information.

The document returned by the service contains the instructions in XML format and is shown in Listing 17-7 (I've skipped most of the document, which contains a `<step>` element for each segment of the trip):

Listing 17-7
The response of
a typical request
to the Directions
API

```
<?xml version="1.0" encoding="UTF-8"?>
<DirectionsResponse>
    <status>OK</status>
    <route>
        <summary>I-35 S and US-160 E</summary>
        <leg>
        <step>
            <travel_mode>DRIVING</travel_mode>
            <start_location>
                <lat>37.6931300</lat>
```

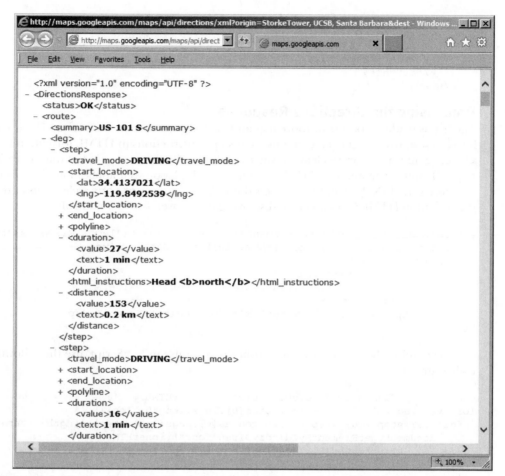

Figure 17-4   Viewing the driving instructions returned by a request to Google's Directions API

```
            <lng>-97.3833200</lng>
        </start_location>
        <end_location>
            <lat>37.6931800</lat>
                <lng>-97.3838900</lng>
        </end_location>
    <polyline>
        <points>a}`eFvdkqQAzAGT</points>
        </polyline>
    <duration>
        <value>7</value>
        <text>1 min</text>
    </duration>
    <html_instructions>Head <b>west</b> on <b>
                    N Newell St</b> toward <b>
```

```
                                        N WestridgeDr</b></html_instructions>
    <distance>
        <value>51</value>
        <text>51 m</text>
    </distance>
</step>
```

Processing the Directions Response

The trip is made up of one or more legs and each leg has one or more steps. The document is self-descriptive and it even contains each step's instructions in HTML format, in the <html_instructions> element. You can't display the response as is, but you can easily parse the XML and create your own HTML document to display on your application's interface.

Here's the LINQ query that extracts the <html_instructions> elements and creates the output in HTML format before displaying it on a web browser control:

```
For Each stp In directions.Element("route").Element("leg").Elements("step")
    instructions&= stp.Element("html_instructions").Value
    instructions&= "<br/>"
    instructions&= "Duration: " &
        stp.Element("duration").Element("text").Value &
        ", Distance: " &
        stp.Element("distance").Element("text").Value & "<p/>"
Next
```

To combine the step instructions from the response in JavaScript, use the following code segment:

```
document.getElementById("divDirections").innerHTML = '';
for (var leg = 0; leg < trip.routes[0].legs.length; leg++) {
  for (var step = 0; step < trip.routes[0].legs[leg].steps.length; step++) {
      document.getElementById("divDirections").innerHTML +=
          trip.routes[0].legs[leg].steps[step].instructions + '<br/>';
   }
 }
```

Each leg is made up of steps, and each step has its own duration/distance and description. The <overview_polyline> element outlines the entire trip on the map. This element's value is a path, and you will see in the section "Displaying the Route on the Map" how to display the suggested route on the map.

Each step of the trip has an <html_instructions> element that contains instructions. To generate a textual representation of the trip's directions, you must combine the <html_instructions> elements of the response. Listing 17-8, which shows the HTML code of a web page that, was created by combining the <html_instructions> elements Directions service's response.

Listing 17-8
Displaying the instructions as a HTML fragment

```
<html>
<body style='font-family:tahoma;color:black;font-size:12px;
background-color:mintcream;'>
<div style='font-weight: bold; color:green; font-size:13px'>
        3301 N Newell St, Wichita, KS 67203, USA
```

```
</div>
<div style='font-weight: bold; color:red; font-size:13px'>
        811 E 6th Ave, Winfield, KS 67156, USA
</div>
<br/>
<div style='font-weight: bold; color:black; font-size:12px'>
        Distance: 87.5 km Duration: 1 hour 1 min
</div>
<hr/>
        Head <b>west</b> on <b>N Newell St</b> toward
        <b>N WestridgeDr</b><br/>
        Duration: 1 min, Distance: 51 m<p/>
        <b>N Newell St</b> turns <b>right</b>
        and becomes <b>N WestridgeDr</b><br/>
        Duration: 1 min, Distance: 0.2 km<p/>
        Turn <b>left</b> onto <b>W Central Ave</b><br/>
        Duration: 4 mins, Distance: 2.3 km<p/>
        Turn <b>left</b> onto <b>N Gilda St</b><br/>
        Duration: 1 min, Distance: 0.2 km<p/>
        Turn <b>left</b> to merge onto <b>I-235 S</b><br/>
        Duration: 8 mins, Distance: 12.9 km<p/>
        Keep <b>right</b> at the fork, follow signs for
        <b>I-135 S/I-35</b>
and merge onto <b>I-135 S</b>
<div style="font-size:0.9em">Partial toll road</div><br/>
        Duration: 1 min, Distance: 1.7 km<p/>
        Keep <b>right</b> at the fork, follow signs for <b>
        I-35 S/Oklahoma City/Kansas Turnpike</b> and merge onto <b>
        I-35 S/Kansas Turnpike</b>
<div style="font-size:0.9em">Toll road</div><br/>
        Duration: 20 mins, Distance: 36.4 km<p/>
        Take exit <b>19</b> for <b>US-160</b> toward <b>Wellington/Winfield</b>
<div style="font-size:0.9em">Toll road</div><br/>
        Duration: 1 min, Distance: 1.0 km<p/>
        Turn <b>left</b> onto <b>US-160 E/E 10th Ave</b>
<div style="font-size:0.9em">Continue to follow US-160 E</div><br/>
        Duration: 22 mins, Distance: 32.3 km<p/>
        Turn <b>left</b> onto <b>Maris St</b><br/>
        Duration: 2 mins, Distance: 0.3 km<p/>
        Take the 3rd <b>right</b> onto <b>E 6th Ave</b>
<div style="font-size:0.9em">Destination will
        be on the right</div><br/>
        Duration: 1 min, Distance: 62 m<p/>
```

The Google Directions API, whose main form is shown in Figure 17-5, is a Windows application that demonstrates the use of the Directions API from within a .NET language. The driving directions are displayed on a second WebBrowser control docked to the right-hand side of the form.

The Google Directions API sample application is a .NET application designed with Visual Studio 2010—you can open it with any later version of Visual Studio. The interface provides four boxes to specify either the physical addresses or the geo-coordinates of the trip's origin and destination, and you can either type in these boxes or click on the map to set the trip's origin and destination. The code will do the necessary reverse geocoding to translate geo-locations to addresses, if available. Even if you click in a forest, the application will attempt

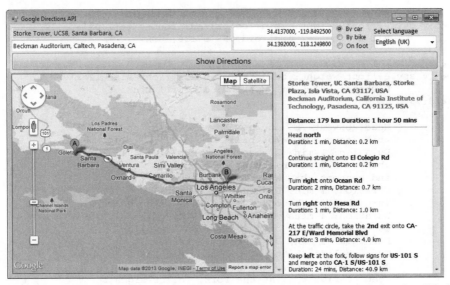

Figure 17-5 Requesting driving/cycling/walking directions between any two locations in a Windows application

to retrieve the driving instructions from the Directions service. However, it will start and end the trip on a road, which may be quite far from the points you clicked.

The Google Directions API application combines both JavaScript and .NET components to demonstrate how you can exploit the best of both environments. When the Show Directions button is clicked, it calls the `calculateRoute()` method in the script to display the route on the map with the following statement:

```
WebBrowser1.Document.InvokeScript("calculateRoute",
            New String() {origin, destination, mode})
```

where the arguments are the user-supplied data about the trip's origin and destination and the selected travel mode. The `calculateRoute()` function is discussed in the section "Requesting Directions from a Script," a little later in this chapter. Then, it calls the same service to retrieve the actual driving instructions, which are displayed in the application's window. The process of requesting the Directions service from within a .NET application is explained in the section "Requesting Directions from a Windows Application."

Trips with Multiple Legs

Simple trips with an origin and a destination have a single leg. If you want to go through specific interim destinations during the trip, you can define one or more so-called *waypoints*. A trip with waypoints has multiple legs: the first leg from the origin to the first waypoint, the second leg from the first waypoint to the second, and so on until the destination is reached. To specify one or more waypoints in your request, use the `waypoints` argument and separate successive waypoints with a pipe symbol (|). The following URL describes a trip from Los Angeles to San Francisco with stops at Ventura, Lompoc, and Solvang.

```
http://maps.googleapis.com/maps/api/directions/xml?
origin=Los Angeles,CA&destination=San Francisco,CA&
waypoints=Ventura,CA|Lomboc, CA|Solvang, CA&sensor=false
```

This trip has four legs and the response contains four `<leg>` elements (or four `leg` objects in the case of JSON). Figure 17-6 shows the XML response to a query with a multi-leg trip. The response is too long to repeat here, but you can navigate to the preceding URL and see it in your browser.

The Trip's Paths
Each step in the response contains a `<polyline>` element, which in turn contains a `<points>` element with a rather odd value. The `<points>` element contains the points that define the step's path, in text format. Google uses a special technique to convert geo-coordinates into text, which is well documented, but you'll hardly ever need to decode this information on your own. You can request that the path described by the `<polyline>` element be rendered on the map, but this option is available only when you call the web

Figure 17-6   The structure of the Directions response when the trip contains multiple legs

service from within a script. The encoded version of the path was discussed in Chapter 10, where you saw how to decode the path into a series of `LatLng` objects. You won't have to decode the path on your own, because you can use the encoded form of the path to display the route on the map.

Requesting Directions from a Windows Application

To make a request from within a Windows application, you must first create the URL of the service, including the parameters. The following VB statement builds the URL of the Geocode request:

```
Dim DirectionsURL = "http://maps.googleapis.com/maps/api/directions/xml?" &
    "origin=" & origin & "&destination=" & destination &
    "&mode=" & mode & "&units=metric" &
    "&sensor=false&language=" & language
```

The variables `origin`, `destination`, `mode`, and `language` have been declared and populated with the content of the appropriate controls before the call. To request the driving instructions in Russian from a UCSB landmark to a Caltech building, use the following URL; it's identical to the one used in the first example of this section, except for the insertion of the `language` parameter.

```
http://maps.googleapis.com/maps/api/directions/xml?
origin=Storke Tower, UCSB, Santa Barbara, CA&
destination=Beckman Auditorium, Caltech, Pasadena,CA&
mode=driving&units=metric&sensor=false&language=ru
```

In case you're wondering what the result looks like, here's the beginning of the instructions. Everything is in Russian, except for the street names and the captions "Duration" and "Distance," which are part of the code.

```
Storke Tower, Калифорнийскийуниверситет, СторкПлаза, АйлаВиста,

Калифорния 93117, СоединённыеШтатыАмерики

Beckman Auditorium, Калтех, Пасадина, Калифорния 91125, СоединённыеШтатыАмерики

Distance: 179 км Duration: 1 час. 50 мин.

-----------------------------------------------------------------

Направляйтесьнасевер

Duration: 1 мин., Distance: 0,2 км

Продолжайтедвижениепо El Colegio Rd

Duration: 1 мин., Distance: 0,2 км

Повернитенаправона Ocean Rd

Duration: 2 мин., Distance: 0,7 км

Повернитенаправона Mesa Rd

Duration: 1 мин., Distance: 1,0 км
```

The code that extracts the instructions from the service's response is also simple and is shown in Listing 17-9.

Listing 17-9
Extracting the
instructions from
the response of
the Directions
service

```
Dim instructions As String
instructions = "<html><body style='font-family:tahoma;color:black'>"
instructions&= "</div><hr/>"
For Each stp In directions.Element("route").Element("leg").Elements("step")
    instructions&= stp.Element("html_instructions").Value
    instructions&= "<br/>"
    instructions&= "Duration: " &
    stp.Element("duration").Element("text").Value &", Distance: " &
    stp.Element("distance").Element("text").Value & "<p/>"
Next
instructions&= "</body></html>"
WebBrowser2.DocumentText = instructions
```

Requesting Directions from a Script

In this section, you're going to see the code of the `Directions Service.html` web page, which prompts the user for the addresses of two locations and displays the driving directions for getting from the origin to the destination. The web page is shown in Figure 17-7, and you can enter the origin and destination of the trip in the two boxes at the top of the page. Alternatively, you can center the map at a location and click the Origin or Destination link to copy the coordinates of the map's center point to the two boxes. The two locations can be specified either as physical addresses or as geo-coordinates.

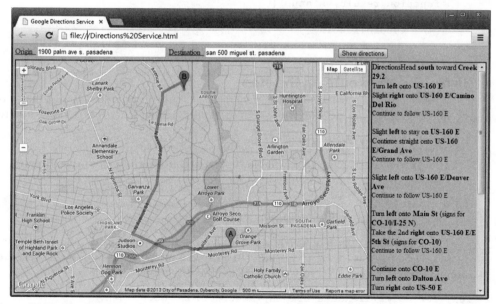

Figure 17-7   The Directions Service page demonstrates how to use the Directions service from within a client script.

To contact the Directions API from within your script, you must create an object of the DirectionsService type:

```
var directionsService = new google.maps.DirectionsService();
```

Then, you can call its route() method to request instructions and distances. The route() method is executed asynchronously and you must specify two arguments when you call it: the request and the name of a function that will be called as soon as the result is available at the client.

The request object has three attributes: origin, destination, and mode.

```
var request =
    {
       origin:originAddress
       destination:destinationAddress
       travelMode: mode
    };
```

In the preceding code, travelMode is a member of the google.maps .DirectionsTravelMode enumeration: DRIVING, WALKING, or BICYCLING. The origin and destination arguments are the addresses of the two endpoints of the trips and they're strings. You use the values entered by the user on the appropriate controls.

To request driving directions for a specific request object, like the one just shown, call the route() method as follows:

```
directionsService.route(request,
       function(result, status){
          if (status == google.maps.DirectionsStatus.OK){
             return(result);
          }
       });
```

Displaying the Route on the Map

The callback function usually returns the response, but you can also request that it renders the suggested path on the map with the setDirections() method, as shown here:

```
directionsDisplay.setDirections(result);
```

The directionsDisplay variable represents another object of the Directions API and must be declared and initialized as follows:

```
directionsDisplay = new google.maps.DirectionsRenderer();
directionsDisplay.setMap(map);
```

The setDirections() method can only be called from within a scrip that resides in the same web page as the map. Listing 17-10 shows a JavaScript function that retrieves the directions between two locations and displays the directions on a pane:

Listing 17-10
The claculate
Route()
function

```
function calculateRoute(origin, destination, mode)
{
      var travelMode = google.maps.DirectionsTravelMode.DRIVING;
      if (mode == 'walking') travelMode =
                google.maps.DirectionsTravelMode.WALKING;
```

```
    if (mode == 'bicycling') travelMode =
            google.maps.DirectionsTravelMode.BICYCLING;
    var request = {
        origin: origin,
        destination: destination,
        travelMode: travelMode
    };
    directionsService.route(request, function (result, status)
    {
        if (status == google.maps.DirectionsStatus.OK)
        {
            directionsDisplay.setDirections(result);
        }
    });
}
```

The `directionsService` variable represents the Directions web service and it must be declared at the script level as follows:

```
var directionsService = new google.maps.DirectionsService();
```

The `route()` method of the `DirectionsService` object contacts the remote service and retrieves the result. The method is executed asynchronously and its second argument is a *callback function*, a function that will be called as soon as the result becomes available. This function is usually defined inline and it processes its two arguments, the `result` and `status` arguments. The `result` argument contains the service's response and the `status` argument contains a status code. If the status is OK, you can process the result; otherwise, you should display an error message. Fortunately, the processing of the result is trivial, thanks to the `directionsDisplay` component.

The `directionsDisplay` variable represents a component that renders the route returned by the Directions service object onto the map. First, you must initialize the variable as follows:

```
directionsDisplay = new google.maps.DirectionsRenderer();
```

and then you must associate it with the Map object on which it will render the trip's path:

```
directionsDisplay.setMap(map);
```

Finally, when the Direction service's response becomes available, you can call the `setDirections` method of the `directionsDisplay` variable to render the trip's path on the map:

```
directionsDisplay.setDirections(result);
```

So far, you have made a request to the Directions web service, retrieved the result with the driving (or biking or walking) directions, and rendered the route on the map. How about displaying the text on your page? Well, `directionsDisplay` to the rescue. The same object that rendered the trip's path on the map can also display the textual directions on a `<div>` or `<span>` element, if you associate it with the appropriate element. Just as you associated the `directionsDisplay` component with the Map object to render the path automatically, you can associate it with a `<div>` element using the `setPanel()` method:

```
directionsDisplay.setPanel(document.getElementById("directionsPanel"));
```

The `directionsDisplay` is a very handy component because it completely automates the processing of the response of the Directions service. If you need more information on using the `directionsDisplay` component from within a web page, you can look up the `Directions Service.html` sample page included with this chapter's support material.

Summary

You have seen practically all aspects of the Google Maps API, including the geometry library, as well as two related APIs: the Geocoding and Directions APIs. The two related APIs can be used outside the context of a map, and you can exploit them from within Windows applications.

There are a few more things you can do with Google maps. One of them is to display a really large set of data as a special type of graph. When you want to display many locations on the map, sometimes it makes no sense to display individual locations. A graph that depicts the distribution of the locations with varying colors conveys very important information. This type of graph is called heatmap, and it's the main topic of the following chapter.

CHAPTER 18

Visualizing Large Datasets

So far, this book has covered ways to represent data with a spatial component on the map. Any type of data nowadays has a spatial component, which makes it suitable for viewing on the map. Actually, most data have an implied spatial component, and now we have tools to exploit this component. A typical business application handles customers, and customers have an address. This field is the spatial component of any data related to customers. Sales can be grouped by city, ZIP code, or state and presented on the map.

New tools to exploit the spatial characteristics of data are already in use today. SQL Server Reporting Services supports the display of data on a map, and Google has introduced a service called Fusion Tables to facilitate the binding of data of all types with geographical data. I'm not going to discuss Fusion Tables in this book because it's not a programmable environment; instead, I discuss techniques for placing spatial data on the map.

There are types of data that are inherently tied to a location, and you have seen a few examples in previous chapters. The earthquakes occur at specific locations and any analysis of seismic data involves the earthquake's location. Earthquakes have a temporal component too, and you will learn how to exploit both the temporal and spatial components of your data in the last two chapters of this book. Cities and airports are simpler examples of data with a prominent spatial component. This chapter doesn't introduce a new dataset; you will use sample data from previous chapters to create interesting presentations of earthquake data, U.S. city populations, and world airports.

Beyond Markers

In Chapter 5. you learned how to place markers on the map to identify points of interest, and in Chapter 14, you learned how to handle large numbers of markers on a map. The basic idea was to display a summary at small magnification levels and wait for the user to zoom deeply into the map before showing all the markers. You can control which markers are displayed at each magnification level from within your script or use the Marker Clusterer component to cluster individual markers into groups. Even so, the task of handling too many features on a map is not a trivial one, and there are situations where it's preferable to move away from markers and explore other techniques for visualizing large datasets.

In this chapter, you will see two new techniques for visualizing data with a spatial component. The first technique uses shapes to represent the data points instead of markers. The advantage of the shapes (circles in particular) is that their size can indicate an attribute of the data value being displayed. Figure 18-1 shows on the map the earthquakes that exceed a certain magnitude. Each circle represents an earthquake and it's centered at the earthquake's epicenter. The size of the circle is proportional to the magnitude of the earthquake.

This type of visualization offers a whole lot of information at a glance compared to the marker approach you used to present the earthquake data in preceding chapters. Moreover, users can view data about each earthquake by clicking the circle that represents a specific earthquake. The relevant data is displayed in a section at the map's lower-right corner. The practical aspect of this technique is that it conveys very useful information at a glance; the size of the earthquake is evident while multiple earthquakes of different magnitudes are visible on the map at once. Contrast this type of visualization with a map filled with markers. Figure 18-2 shows the same area of the globe with the same earthquakes marked with markers (left) and circles (right).

The other approach is to place a color map, known as a *heatmap*, over the map. The colors of the heatmap represent the density or intensity of the data. A heatmap of the airports or U.S. cities represents the density of the data points. Figure 18-3 shows a heatmap

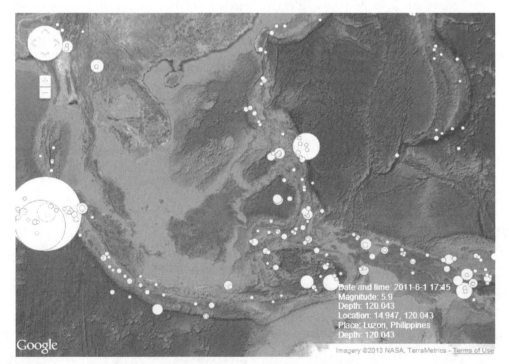

Figure 18-1 Viewing individual features on the map without markers

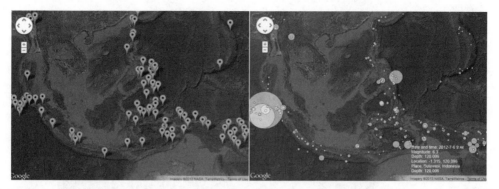

Figure 18-2   Using the appropriate visualization technique for different types of data makes a world of difference

generated by the list of world airports. The more airports in an area, the "warmer" the color over this area of the map. Incidentally, the heatmap of the airports shows the distribution of the most populated areas on the planet. Notice that sub-Saharan areas in Africa have very few airports. The same is true for the steppes in northern China. You will probably be surprised to find out that the country with the largest density of airports is New Zealand!

Figure 18-3 was generated by the sample page `Density Heatmap - World Airports.html`, which is included in this chapter's support material. The heatmap's colors may not be easily distinguishable on the printed page, but you can open the original application to view the gradient that represents the density of the airports.

The heatmap of the U.S. cities in Figure 18-4 shows not only density, but also intensity. The data points have an additional attribute, which is their population. Unlike the distribution of the airports in Figure 18-3, the heatmap shown in Figure 18-4 takes into consideration not only the density of the cities, but their populations as well. Notice that the two most populated areas in the United States are the Los Angeles basin in California and New York City in the east.

Figure 18-3   A heatmap with the distribution of airports all over the globe

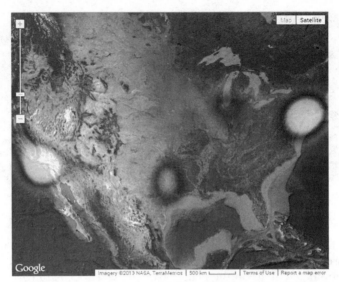

Figure 18-4 A heatmap with the density and populations of various cities across the US

This happens not only because of the population of Los Angeles and New York City, but also because there are many cities with substantial populations around them. The shape in red follows the coastal line in both sides of the country! With a relatively small number of cities in the United States, I was able to generate a fairly accurate map of the population distribution. Figure 18-4 was generated by the `Density Heatmap - US Cities.html` sample web page, also discussed later in this chapter.

Visualizing the Earthquakes

In Chapter 15, you saw how to contact a web service at the U.S. Geological Survey (http://comcat.cr.usgs.gov/fdsnws/event/1) and retrieve data about earthquakes worldwide. This service accepts several arguments, the most important of them being a range of dates, the rectangle on the earth's surface you're interested in, and the minimum/maximum earthquake magnitudes. USGS also provides a visual interface for building the appropriate URL, which is located at http://earthquake.usgs.gov/earthquakes/feed/v1.0/urlbuilder.php.

The URL Builder page is shown in Figure 18-5 (you see part of this page in the figure). On this page, you specify the parameters that determine the earthquakes you want to retrieve, and the application builds the appropriate URL, which you can view by clicking the Search button at the bottom of the page.

The following URL retrieves all earthquakes that occurred from 2010 through 2012 and exceed 7.5 points on the Richter scale:

```
http://comcat.cr.usgs.gov/fdsnws/event/1/query?
starttime=2010-01-01&endtime=2012-120-31&minmagnitude=7.5
```

As you can see, it's easy to build the URL in your code by allowing users to specify, or select, the parameter values on a custom form.

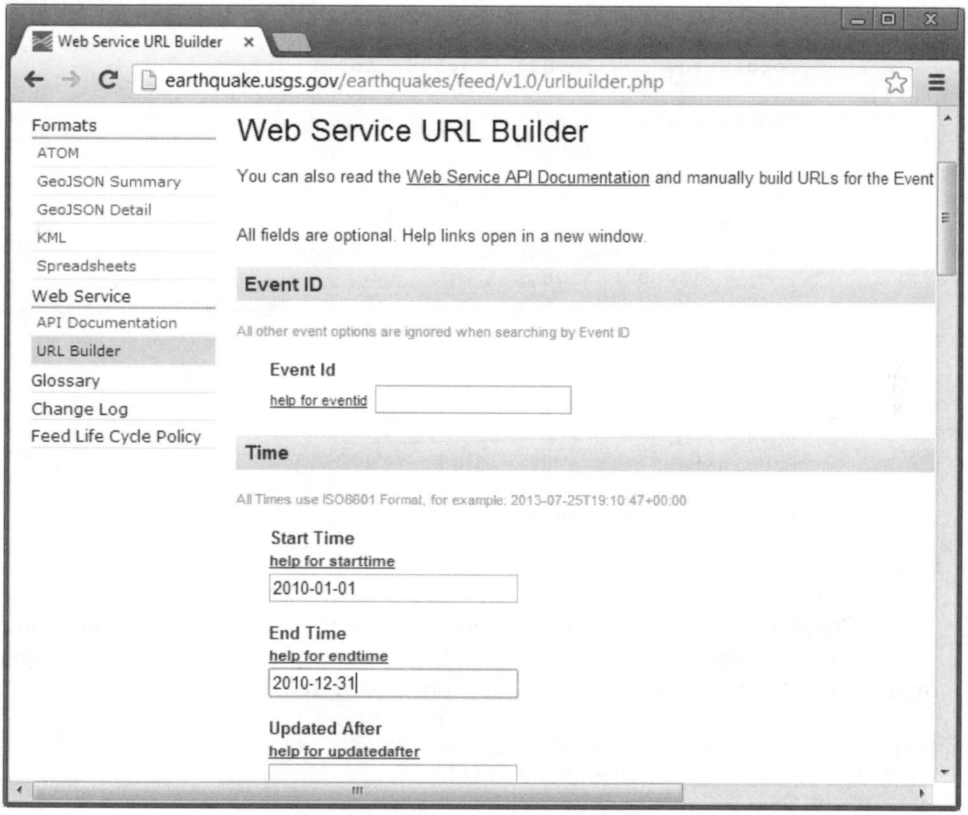

Figure 18-5   Building the URL for the USGS earthquakes web service

Parsing the Earthquake Data

Once you have the appropriate URL, you can request the data in JSON format from within your script and get back an array of custom objects that represent the selected earthquakes. Listing 18-1 shows the structure of the document returned by the earthquakes service at USGS (just click the URL displayed at the bottom of the URL Builder page to see the GeoJSON document returned by the service):

Listing 18-1
The GeoJSON
description of
two earthquakes

```
"features": [{
    "type": "Feature",
    "properties": {
        "mag": 7.1,
        "place": "Banda Sea",
        "time": 1355158388770,
        "url": "http://comcat.cr.usgs.gov/earthquakes/
                eventpage/pde20121210165308770_155",
        "type": "earthquake"
    },
```

```
        "geometry": {
            "type": "Point",
            "coordinates": [129.825, -6.533, 155]
        },
        "id": "pde20121210165308770_155"
}, {
        "type": "Feature",
        "properties": {
            "mag": 6.6,
            "place": "near the south coast of Papua, Indonesia",
            "time": 1350001888270,
            "url": "http://comcat.cr.usgs.gov/earthquakes/
                    eventpage/pde20121012003128270_13",
            "type": "earthquake"
        },
        "geometry": {
            "type": "Point",
            "coordinates": [134.03, -4.892, 13]
        },
        "id": "pde20121012003128270_13"
}, ...
}];
```

In Chapter 15, you wrote an application to parse the array of earthquakes and place a marker on the map for each earthquake. The JavaScript code that iterates through the items of the earthquakesArray is shown in Listing 18-2.

```
for (var i = 0; i < earthquakesArray.length; i++) {
    var feature = earthquakesArray[i];
    var geometry = feature.geometry;
    var eqLocation = new google.maps.LatLng(
                        geometry.coordinates[1], geometry.coordinates[0]);
    var eqDepth = geometry.coordinates[0];
    var eqMagnitude = feature.properties.mag;
    var eqPlace = feature.properties.place;
    var eqTime = new Date(feature.properties.time);
    var M = new google.maps.Marker({
                position: eqLocation,
                map: map
        });
    var eqFormattedDate = eqTime.getFullYear() + '-' +
                    eqTime.getMonth() + '-' + eqTime.getDay() + ' ' +
                    eqTime.getUTCHours() + ':' + eqTime.getUTCMinutes();
    var eqDescription =  'Date and time: ' + eqFormattedDate  + '<br/>' +
                    'Magnitude: ' + eqMagnitude + <br/>' +
                    'Depth: ' +  eqDepth + '<br/>' +
                    'Location: ' + eqLocation.lat() + ', ' +
                    qLocation.lng() + '<br/>' + 'Place: ' + eqPlace +
                    '<br/>' + 'Depth: ' + eqDepth + '<br/>' + '<br/>';
    M.objInfo = eqDescription;
    }
```

The variables `eqFormattedDate` and `eqDescription` are used to display the earthquake description later in the code. The actual code that places the marker on the map is quite simple. The `earthquakesArray` variable is an array of custom objects, one for each earthquake, and the structure of these objects is determined by the web service.

Using the Circle Symbol as Marker Icon

To generate a map annotated with shapes, you must replace the marker's default icon with the symbol of a filled circle. The circle's radius should be proportional to the size of the earthquake to help users visualize seismic activity at a glance. Symbols don't have specific sizes; the circle symbol, for example, doesn't expose a radius property that you can set in your code. Instead, symbols provide the `scale` property. For the example of the earthquakes, the scale property can be set to the following expression:

```
scale: Math.pow(Math.E, eqMagnitude)/100
```

The scale is equal to the natural logarithm base raised to the value that corresponds to the earthquake's magnitude. The earthquake scale is a logarithmic one and you can't use a linear function of the magnitude. An earthquake of size 7 is 10 times larger (and more than 10 times more catastrophic) than an earthquake of magnitude 6. If you set the scales of the two circles that represent two such earthquakes to 6 and 7, respectively, their difference will be hardly noticeable on the map. The proposed function yields circles that indicate the relative sizes of the earthquakes, yet they don't allow a few very large earthquakes that occurred in the Pacific to cover an entire hemisphere. If you have an interest in seismology, you will come up with a better function to map the earthquake magnitudes into scaling factors.

The icon that represents the current earthquake in the loop that generates the markers must be declared as follows:

```
icon: { path: google.maps.SymbolPath.CIRCLE,
        scale: Math.pow(Math.E, eqMagnitude)/100,
        fillColor: "yellow", fillOpacity: 0.4,
        strokeColor: "red", strokeWeight: 0.5 }
```

You should use constants for the various colors and the opacity in your script, but we can tolerate a few hard-coded values in the sample application.

Interacting with the Symbols

Your next step is to add some user interaction to the map. When users click an earthquake's icon, additional data about the selected earthquake should appear somewhere. To display the additional data, you must add a listener to each marker's `click` event with a statement like the following:

```
google.maps.event.addListener(M, 'click',
                function(){ showEarthquake(this)});
```

The *M* variable in Listing 18-2 is the current marker and `showEarthquake()` is a simple function that displays the M variable's `objInfo` property on a `<div>` element. The `objInfo` property is set to a lengthy description of the earthquake data (the `eqDescription` variable in Listing 18-2) and the task of the `showEarthquake()` function is implemented with a single statement:

```
function showEarthquake(m) {
    document.getElementById('eqData').innerHTML = m.objInfo;
}
```

Less trivial is the placement of the `eqData` element on the page, as it overlaps the map. This element is declared in the page's body with the following simple HTML statement:

```
<div id='eqData'></div>
```

However, to place this element on the map, the following style definition is required:

```
<style>
  #eqData {
      position: absolute;  float:none;  width: 220px;  top:400px;
      left:480px;  z-index:100;
      font-family: Tebuchet, Arial; font-size: 11px;
      font-weight: regular; color:white;
  }
</style>
```

The `<div>` element is transparent because the `background-color` property isn't set. It's also positioned absolutely on the page and it has a large `zIndex` value to remain on top of the map. The downside of this approach is that the map isn't resizable. You can either use JQuery code to make the `<div>` element follow the changes in the map's size, or display the relevant data on another element of the page, outside the map. If you decide to redesign the page, you should include controls to allow users to specify the basic selection criteria for the earthquakes and build the URL in your code. The data for a specific earthquake, as returned by the USGS web service, is shown here:

```
Date and time: 2010-3-3 22:15
Magnitude: 7.8
Depth: 97.048
Location: 2.383, 97.048
Place: northern Sumatra, Indonesia
Depth: 97.048
```

Sorting the Earthquake Data

Some earthquakes occur near other ones—after all, most earthquakes occur along some well-known faults. If one of them is large, the circle that represents this earthquake may completely overlap the circles that correspond to multiple smaller earthquakes in the same area. And here we have a problem: The circles that are covered by a larger one can't be clicked. The larger circle will receive all the clicks and users won't be able to select one of the underlying circles.

The solution to this problem is to display the circles that correspond to smaller earthquakes on top of the larger ones. In other words, smaller circles should have larger `zIndex` values. For this to happen, you must sort the array of earthquakes according to their magnitudes in descending order. Then, as each circle symbol is placed on the map, the script should assign a larger zIndex value to it. The following two statements sort the earthquakes according to their magnitude:

```
var earthquakesArray = Array.prototype.slice.call(results.features, 0);
earthquakesArray.sort(compareMagnitudes);
```

The first statement converts the features collection of the web service's response into an array. The results variable represents a collection of nodes, which can't be sorted directly. By converting it to an array, you can then apply the sort() method to sort the array. And this is what the second statement does. However, because the earthquakesArray array contains custom objects, you must supply your own function to compare two elements of the array. For more information on the syntax of the sort() method, see the discussion of arrays in Chapter 4.

The compareMagnitudes() function accepts as arguments two feature objects and compares their magnitudes. If the first one is larger, it should return 1, and if the first one is smaller, it should return –1. If both arguments have the same magnitude, the comparer should return 0. The compareMagnitudes() function, shown in Listing 18-3, reverses the two results so that the sort is ascending: You place the larger circles on the map first (using a smaller zIndex value) and the smaller ones on top.

Listing 18-3
Comparing earthquakes based on their magnitudes

```
function compareMagnitudes(event1, event2) {
    var m1 = event1.properties.mag;
    var m2 = event2.properties.mag;
    m1 = parseFloat(m1);
    m2 = parseFloat(m2);
    return (m2-m1);
}
```

Representing earthquakes with circles leads to another improvement in the interface; namely, to display the data of the earthquake as the user moves the pointer over the cirlces on the map. Let's add the necessary listeners for the mouseover and mouseout events:

```
google.maps.event.addListener(M, 'mouseover',
                    function() {showEarthquake(this)});
google.maps.event.addListener(M, 'mouseout', function()
                    document.getElementById('eqData').innerHTML = ""});
```

Heatmaps

When you have to display too many features on the map, like the 9,000 world airports, you may find out that none of the techniques presented so far works to your satisfaction. You can't place so many markers on the map, not even with the MarkerClusterer component. When you deal with a very large set of data points, you visualize it better as a continuous distribution, rather than individual data points. After all, individual data lose their meaning in the crowd.

Let's consider for a moment the requirements of a user viewing the airports on the map. If you want to look at the airports in a specific country, or a specific state/county, you can simply zoom into the area you're interested in and view the airports as markers. Or, place a label for each airport on the map, as you have seen in Chapter 14. If you want to see the distribution of the airports on the map, however, a heatmap graph like the one shown in Figure 18-3 earlier in this chapter conveys a lot of information about the distribution and density of airports. The same is true for city populations. At large magnification levels, you may wish to see individual symbols for each city and request additional information. As you zoom out, you probably want to see the distribution of the population over the country, rather than individual cities.

The heatmap is a unique type of graph that conveys information like no other chart. It translates the density, or intensity, of the data into a color gradient and blends the individual data points into a colorful surface that covers the relevant areas of the globe. This surface is constructed with a gradient, where areas with fewer points are mapped to the gradient's beginning color, and areas with the most points are mapped to the gradient's ending color. Areas between the two extremes are mapped to the middle colors of the gradient.

Note that the gradient need not extend between two colors only. You can specify any color sequence and the API will generate an elaborate gradient that goes smoothly through all colors.

Constructing the Heatmap

You don't really need to understand how the heatmap is constructed, but here's a simple explanation. Imagine that data points are represented by pegs. Then, you throw a flexible sheet over the pegs. The sheet will take a shape dictated by the pegs it covers. Instead of rendering a three-dimensional surface over the map, you assign a different color to each point, depending on its altitude. The points that lie on the earth's surface are transparent while the points with the highest altitude are colored with the gradient's ending color.

If the sheet is very flexible, each peg will affect a small area around it. In areas with many pegs, the sheet will flow smoothly over the pegs and will not touch the ground. In areas with isolated pegs, the sheet will make a peak and then it will fall quickly on the ground. You can control the "stiffness" of the sheet by adjusting the `radius` property of the heatmap. Using larger values for the heatmap's radius is equivalent to covering the pegs with a stiffer sheet that can't change its shape easily. In other words, the radius determines the area that will be affected by each peg's height.

To generate a density or intensity heatmap, you need a set of data with a spatial component (geo-coordinates) and a value. Each data item may have any number of attributes, but only the geo-coordinates are required.

The list of cities you used in a couple of chapters contains locations as well as populations. The locations are adequate for producing a distribution heatmap, as long as all data points are equal in stature. You can also include the population, in which case the script will generate an intensity heatmap. Cities with a larger population will be colored differently from cities with a smaller population.

To produce a heatmap, you must first create an array of geo-locations like the following:

```
var points = [new google.maps.LatLng(33.5274, -86.799),
              new google.maps.LatLng(34.7843, -86.539),
          ...
];
```

The `points` array holds all the information required to build a density heatmap. If you add a third column to the array, this column will be used to weigh the location. A value with a weight of 2 will affect the heatmap twice as much as a point at the same location with a weight of 1. Adding a weight is like adding some points more than once. The same array with weights will look like this:

```
var points = [new google.maps.LatLng(33.5274, -86.799), 212237
              new google.maps.LatLng(34.7843, -86.539), 180105
              ...
];
```

The last value in each row is the population of the corresponding city. These values are heavy weights, but it doesn't really matter; all locations are weighted proportionally.

The Heatmap Layer

To generate the heatmap, you must create a new variable that represents the heatmap layer with the following statement:

```
var heatmap = new google.maps.visualization.HeatmapLayer({data: points});
```

The HeatmapLayer object isn't included in the script with the basic Google Maps functionality. To include this functionality in your script, you must include the visualization library. Change the <script> tag that imports the Google Maps API script by adding the libraries=visualization parameter:

```
<script type="text/javascript"
        src="https://maps.googleapis.com/maps/api/js?" +
            "libraries=visualization&sensor=false"></script>
```

Besides the array with the data points, the HeatmapLayer object's constructor accepts a number of optional parameters:

- **map**   The Map object to which the heatmap will be applied.
- **radius**   This parameter specifies the area of influence for each data point, in pixels. The area is a circle centered at any given point with radius equal to this property.
- **dissipating**   This parameter is a true/false value that determines whether the heatmap's colors will dissipate on zoom. When it's false, which is the default value, the radius of influence is adjusted to the current zoom level to ensure that the color intensity is preserved. When this property is set to false, the heatmap doesn't change as users zoom in or out.
- **gradient**   This parameter is an array of colors that specify the progression of colors in the heatmap. You usually start the gradient with cold colors and move on to warmer colors for areas with greater density and/or intensity.
- **maxIntensity**   The maximum intensity of the heatmap. By default, the points are colored according to their intensity with one of the colors in the gradient, and the entire range of colors is used. If your data includes points with unusually high weights, use the maxIntensity attribute to clip their values. All points whose weights exceed the maxIntensity value are colored with the last color in the gradient. These points are considered outliers, and they usually distort the heatmap by forcing all other points to be colored with colors from a relatively small range of the gradient.
- **opacity**   The opacity of the heatmap (a numeric value between 0 and 1).

You should experiment with the settings of the dissipating and radius attributes of the heatmap to get an idea of how they affect the heatmap and how they interfere with one another. When dissipating is set to true, you will most likely need to increase the radius. Figure 18-6 shows how the same data is rendered on the heatmap using the two settings of the dissipating property. As you zoom in and out, you will realize what the dissipating property really does: It causes the heatmap to be redrawn when the magnification level is changed. When the dissipating property is set to false, the heatmap isn't recalculated; it's blown up along with the map.

By adjusting the radius, you can force a data point to affect a larger area and you can practically fill the map with a heatmap based on a relatively small number of data points.

The gradient Property   The value of the gradient property is defined as an array of colors. The HeatmapLayer object will generate automatically the transitions from one color to the next and the final gradient will be very smooth. The colors can be specified in many different notations, but the most common method of specifying colors is the rgb() and the rgba() functions. Both functions describe a color based on its three basic components: the red, green, and blue components. The rgba() function accepts an additional argument, the opacity of the color. Here's the definition of a typical array of colors, which you can pass as an argument to the constructor of the HeatmapLayer object:

```
gradient: [
        'rgba(0,      0,      0, 0.20)',
        'rgba(0,    255,    255, 0.40)',
        'rgba(0,    255,      0, 0.60)',
        'rgba(255,  255,      0, 0.80)',
        'rgba(255,    0,      0, 1.00)']
});
```

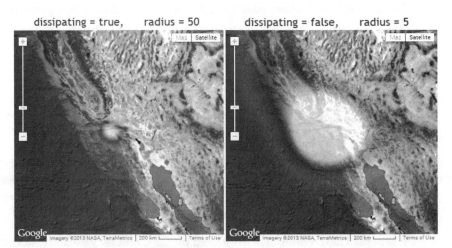

Figure 18-6   Adjusting the heatmap's appearance through the radius and dissipating parameters

The rgb() and rgba() Functions

The `rgba()` function generates a color value given its four components: the red, green, and blue intensities, and the opacity of the color. Thus, `rgba` stands for "Red Green Blue and Alpha," alpha being the opacity. The three intensities are integers in the range from 0 to 255. The minimum value indicates the lack of the corresponding color component, and the maximum value indicates the presence of the corresponding color with full intensity. The opacity (alpha) value goes from 0 (completely transparent) to 1 (completely opaque). The color values can also be specified as percentages: The value 50% means that the intensity of the corresponding color is at 50 percent of the full intensity. The following color value corresponds to a bright red color:

```
rgba(255, 0, 0, 1)
```

A dark red color can be specified as `rgba(128, 0, 0, 1)` or as `rgba(50%, 0, 0, 1)`. The following expression combines red and green in full intensities to produce a bright yellow color: `rgba(255, 255, 0, 1)`. If you wish to work with opaque colors and you don't care about the transparency, use the `rgb()` function. The `rgb()` function is identical to the `rgba()` function except that it doesn't require the last argument. It's possible to produce any color by combining the three basic color components and there are tools you can use to create colors interactively. This site allows users to construct colors interactively: http://www.calculatorcat.com/free_calculators/color_slider/rgb_hex_color_slider.phtml.

For more information on constructing colors based on their three primary components, look up "color cube" in Wikipedia.

This specific gradient starts with a black color that is mostly transparent. The next color is cyan with a higher opacity. Then comes a green color (only the green component of the color has a non-zero value), and the gradient ends with a red color that is totally opaque.

Exploiting the Heatmap's Opacity   Figure 18-7 demonstrates an interesting effect you can achieve by manipulating the opacity values in the definition of the gradient. The map shown in the figure is an intensity heatmap of the populations of major U.S. cities. It looks as if the most populated cities are illuminated with spotlights. The printed image may not convey actual contrast, so open the sample page `Dark Heatmap.html` to see the full effect.

The map shown in Figure 18-7 is based on the city population data, and the heatmap layer was defined with the following statement:

```
heatmap = new google.maps.visualization.HeatmapLayer({
            map: map, data: data,
            radius: 75,  dissipating: true,
            maxIntensity: 7000000,
            gradient: [
               'rgba(0,      0,    0, 0.95)',
               'rgba(255,    255, 255, 0.95)']
            });
```

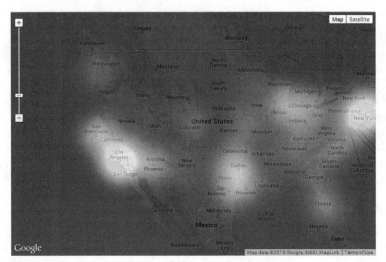

Figure 18-7   Illuminating the map with spotlights through a heatmap layer

The colors that make up the gradient are practically opaque, leaving the areas of the country without major cities in the dark. The largest cities are illuminated with a spotlight whose light circle is proportional to the city population.

For a similar effect, which doesn't blur the text on the map, use the following color definitions for the gradient:

```
gradient: [
        'rgba(0,     0,     0,     0.95)',
        'rgba(0,     0,     0,     0.05)']
});
```

To see the alternate spotlight effect in action, open the `Dark Heatmap 2.html` sample page, included in this chapter's support material. A few cities (New York and Los Angeles) dominate the effect. You can achieve a better result by experimenting with the setting of the `maxIntensity` attribute, which limits the effect of the very large cities.

Summary

In this chapter, you learned how to represent spatial data on the map using symbols and a unique type of chart, the heatmap. Heatmaps are colored graphs that summarize a lot of data, and they represent the density and/or intensity of the data, rather than individual data. When you're faced with an application that calls for displaying too many markers on the map, forget the marker and related tools and use the techniques discussed in this chapter. The two techniques described in this chapter squeeze a large dataset into a picture and convey a lot of information to the user.

I have pretty much exhausted the presentation of the Google Maps API, and you have seen examples of many types of applications you can build on top of Google Maps. There's one more interesting feature to explore in the last two chapters of this book: how to animate items on a map. The topic of animating items on a map with JavaScript is discussed in detail in the last two chapters of this book.

CHAPTER

19

Animating Items on the Map

If you have read the book so far, you're ready to tackle all types of mapping projects. You can annotate maps with markers and shapes and enable users to edit these items interactively. You can also publish your finished maps and save the annotations to KML files. In the last two chapters of this book, you will learn about another exciting feature of mapping applications: namely, how to animate items on the map. This chapter isn't about bouncing a few happy faces on your map, or making a label drop in place. I'm talking about real animation of map items, such as moving the symbol of a train on its track in real time, or the symbol of an airplane along its flight path.

The techniques for animating items on the map are not part of the Google Maps API. As you will see shortly, it's a feature of the JavaScript language and it's implemented with a few functions. The sample applications you're going to build in this chapter demonstrate the use of JavaScript's animation functions and apply them to Google Maps objects, mostly for animating symbols along fixed paths, but also for animating attributes such as the transparency of a circle, the density of a heatmap, and any quantity that has a temporal component. The preceding chapters focused on the spatial aspect of data, so now we'll combine the spatial and temporal dimensions of data. A list of cities and their populations or their temperature is a dataset with a spatial component and you know how to present this component on the map. The same list with data for several years has a temporal dimension too, and the only way to visualize this dimension is to generate an animation that evolves with time.

Animating Items on a Map

The most interesting samples you'll examine in this chapter are based on symbol animation, such as moving the symbol of an airplane along its flight path, or the symbol of a train along its track. As you recall from Chapter 8, it is possible to place one or more instances of a symbol along a `Polyline` object. You know how to repeat a symbol along the line to indicate the flow of movement or other relevant information. The symbols can be placed at specific intervals along the line and these intervals can be expressed either in pixels or as percentages of the path's total length. Figure 19-1 shows the geodesic path between two airports that are far away from one another. The symbol of an airplane is repeated along the line to indicate that the line is a flight path. The symbols of this specific figure (which is a repeat of Figure 10-2 from Chapter 10) are repeated every 50 pixels along the underlying path. Note that the path on which the symbols are placed is made transparent, and only the airplane symbols are visible on the map. The figure was generated by the `Geodesics with Symbols.html` sample page, included in the chapter's support material.

The idea behind animating a symbol is to place a single symbol at the beginning of a path and change its relative position every so often. For example, you can animate an airplane symbol along its flight path by setting its initial position to 0 percent of the path's length and increasing the percentage by 100/60, or 1.66 percent, every second. The symbol will move from the departure airport to the destination airport in 60 seconds. If that's too slow for your animation's purposes, shorten the animation cycle (move the symbol every half a second, or less) or double the increment (advance its position by 3.3 percent of the total length at a time). In general, you should use a shorter animation cycle to speed up the animation. If things move by leaps, then the animation becomes "bumpy" and "jerky."

There are other types of items you can animate on a map. It's also common to animate object attributes, such as the size, color, or transparency of a Circle object. You can make a filled circle appear gradually on a map by changing its opacity in small steps. You will see an example of attribute animation in the following chapter.

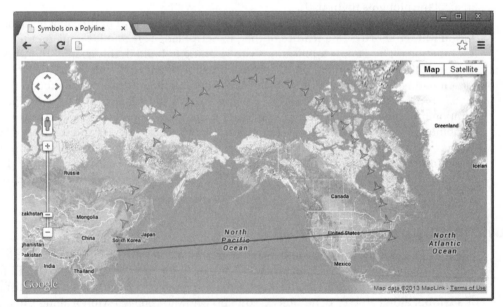

Figure 19-1   Using symbols to create alternative paths on a map

Basic Animation Concepts

The two basic components of the animation are (a) a function that implements the animation, known as the *animation function*, by changing the position of an item, or one of its attributes and (b) the interval between successive invocations of the animation function. The animation function contains a block of statements that update the contents of the web page to produce the animation. The interval between successive invocations of the animation function is known as the *animation cycle*. It goes without saying that the animation function should complete in a single animation cycle. Otherwise, some animation steps will be skipped and the animation will not be as smooth as you'd expect.

The statements that are executed in every cycle handle the animation itself: They redraw the items on the map at their new locations. To produce any type of animation, you redraw the same image with small changes many times per second. When the changes are played back in rapid succession, the human eye can't distinguish the various frames, and animation appears to evolve smoothly.

Animating in JavaScript is performed in real time: The animation function does all the calculations in real time and redraws the animated items on the map in rapid succession. You don't have the luxury to create animation frames offline and play them back later. Instead, you must produce optimized code that can be executed many times per second. Today's fast processors and GPUs (Graphics Processing Unit) support are a big help, but it's of the utmost importance that your code is very efficient.

JavaScript Animation

To animate items on a Google Map, you need a single and surprisingly simple method, the `setInterval()` method. This method, which belongs to the `window` object, accepts two arguments: the name of the animation function and the animation cycle in milliseconds. Every time this interval elapses, the animation function is executed. The following call to the `setInterval()` function call will cause whatever function you specify with the first argument to repeat every 500 milliseconds.

```
var id = window.setInterval(animation_function, 500)
```

The `setInterval()` function returns an integer, which identifies the specific animation. You use this integer for a single purpose: namely, to end the animation with the `clearInterval()` method, which accepts as argument the identifier of an animation started with a call to the `setInterval()` function. `animation_function` is the name of the animation function. You can also define this function inline, in which case the call to the `setInterval()` method looks like this:

```
var id = window.setInterval(function {
// animation function statements
        }, 500)
```

The `setInterval()` method is called once, but the function you specify as its argument will be executed indefinitely, unless you stop it with a call to the `clearInterval()` method. The two functions are not used exclusively for animation; in fact, they weren't even included in the language for this purpose. The `setInterval()` method enables a script running at the client to repeat a task every so often, and this task is usually to contact a remote server to retrieve data such as stock prices, real-time measurements, and other timely information. The web page can be updated automatically from within the script when changes in the remote data occur, without any user interaction.

Figure 19-2 shows a very simple fiddle that demonstrates how the `setInterval()` function is used. The page's script displays the value of a variable, `count`, which is increased every 1.5 seconds. When the variable reaches its maximum value, 10, the script stops calling the function specified in the call to the `setInterval()` function. The script shown in Figure 19-1 is shown next:

```
var count = 0;
var id = window.setInterval(function(){
document.getElementById("caption").innerText =
    'Counter = ' + count++;
        if (count == 10) {clearInterval(id)}
        }, 1500);
```

Using the `setInterval()` method to perform animation is practically just as simple: Instead updating the contents of a `<div>` element, you change the position (or the shape) of an item on the page. You can change the location of a marker or label on the map, the radius of a circle, and so on. In the examples of this chapter, you will change the position of a symbol along a path on the map.

Figure 19-2 A simple script that demonstrates the use of the `setInterval()` and `clearInterval()` methods

The Paris Metro Animated

In the remainder of this chapter, and in the following one, you will build some interesting animation applications. This section's sample application involves one of the largest subway systems in the world, the Paris Metro. You're going to develop a web page that displays the lines of the Paris Metro, along with their stations, and animates a train on each track. You will actually see a number of trains (depicted with small discs) move back and forth on their tracks.

The `Paris Metro.html` web page is shown in Figure 19-3. The colored discs along each line are the line's stations and the white discs (only one per line) are the moving trains. Each line in the Paris metro map has its own color, in addition to a name, and the actual colors were used for the lines and their stations—the saturation may be wrong, but you get the idea. Open the application and click the Animate Trains buttons to see the animation in action. The map is a bit dark because I've overlaid a semitransparent layer to smooth out the sharper features of the map and help the viewer focus on the metro lines, instead of the map elements, street names, and so on. You can remove this layer, if you wish, or experiment with custom map styles to simplify the background and bring forth the items of interest, which are the metro lines and their stations. For information on styling your maps, see Appendix C available online.

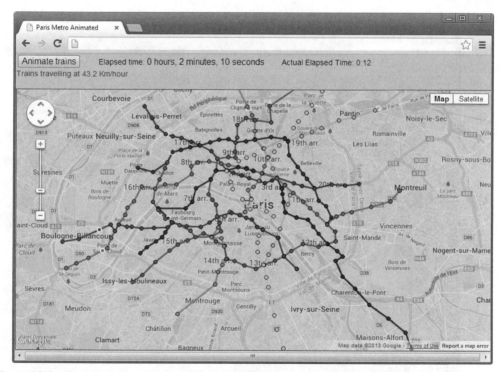

Figure 19-3   Each line of the Paris Metro is represented by a colored line. The metro stations are shown as solid circles, while the moving trains are shown as white circles.

The trains start all at once and travel at the same speed toward their destinations. As each train reaches its terminal station, it reverses its direction and starts traveling toward the terminal station at the other end of the line, and so on. The application uses an average speed, which includes the time at the stations. You can experiment with different train speeds, and you can even include a stop time at each station. This last feature, however, requires a bit of extra code and, although far from trivial, it would make a very interesting project.

Figure 19-4 is a detail of the Paris Metro web application and it shows the names of the stations along the blue line. To view the stations along a line, just pick the line on the map with the mouse. The selected line is rendered in white color to stand out and the names of the stations are shown as labels on the map. As you have probably recognized, the labels are implemented with RichMarker objects, an object that was discussed in detail in Chapter 7. Another useful feature you can add to the application is the ability to display the name of the next station of the selected line on a separate element of the page. Each time the train of the selected line reaches a station, you could display the name of the next station on the form. Short of zooming and dragging the map, the selection of a line is the only custom user interaction feature of the application. No action takes place when the user clicks a metro station, or the station's label.

The image was captured 27 minutes and 45 seconds after the animation was started. This time interval corresponds to 1 hour and 59 minutes of actual travel time. In other words,

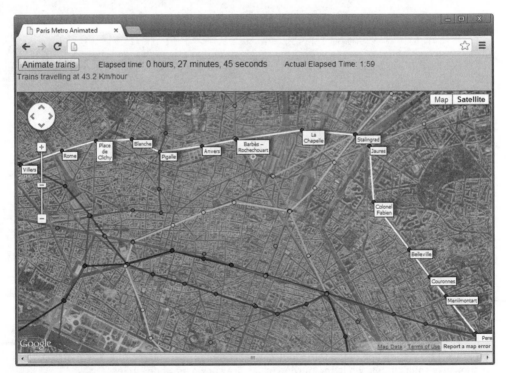

Figure 19-4 When you select a Metro line, the application displays the names of the stations along the selected line.

7,140 seconds of actual travel time ($1 \times 3600 + 59 \times 60$) were scaled down to 1665 seconds, which is equivalent to a scaling factor of approximately 4.3. In other words, 1 minute of real time is condensed into 14 seconds of animation time (scaled time), which is a reasonable scaling factor for this type of application. As you will see, an important aspect of any practical animation is to scale the speed of moving objects and keep track of the elapsed time. In the following sections, you learn how to design animations that simulate real-world scenarios, like the movement of trains and airplanes.

The Application's Data

Before you explore the application's code, you should take a look at the structure of the data used for the metro lines and how the data was obtained. Because I didn't have access to the actual coordinates of the Paris Metro's tracks, I used the Map Traces application of Chapter 9 to generate a list of named locations (the stations) and their coordinates. If you live in Paris, you will probably spot some errors in the data; even so, bear with us through the code's explanation. If you come up with a more accurate or more elegant application, please share it. The names of each line's stations came from Wikipedia; then the stations were located on the map by their names and used as guides to trace the metro lines. As you can see, the tracks take very sharp turns at the stations, making it rather obvious that each path was constructed with consecutive line segments.

As you recall from Chapter 9, the Map Traces application is a map-driven Windows application. Its interface is repeated in Figure 19-5 for your convenience. This application

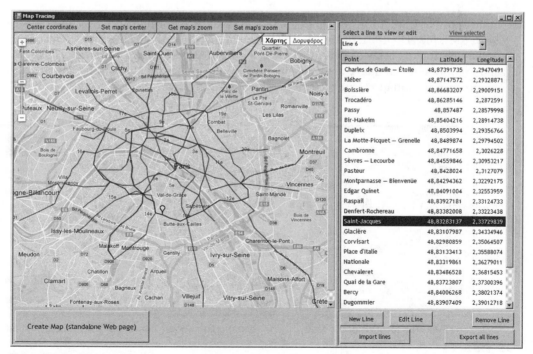

Figure 19-5   Tracing the routes of the metro line on the map with the map tracing application. The figure shows the trace of Line 6 with the Saint-Jacques station selected both in the list and on the map.

The "Floating" Stations

Some rather unexpected problems were encountered during the tracing of the paths of the Paris Metro lines, as demonstrated in Figure 19-6. I mention it here because it can totally confuse you and make you think you're not using the application correctly, or that the application behaves strangely. The problem is demonstrated with Google Maps and not by the application itself. Both maps shown in the figure are centered near the Mabillon metro station. The map on the left was captured at a zoom level of 16 and the station is shown between Rue du Four and Boulevard Saint-Germain. The map on the right was captured at zoom level 17, and this time the same station is south of Rue du Four! This is a side effect of the tile mechanism used by Google to serve sections of the map. The titles are different at different zoom levels, as they contain different levels of detail. This is an extreme example of things that can go wrong. You should trace the features you're interested in at the deepest possible zoom level, even if they are not in total agreement with the map at other zoom levels. If you examine the image carefully, or if you look up this part of the world in Google Maps, you will also notice that the other metro station (Saint-Germain-des-Pres) is not at the same location at all zoom levels. The metro lines that stop at these stations will not always appear to go through the station; at some zoom levels, the lines will appear to go near the stations, but not right over the stations.

allows you to trace any route on the map and saves the coordinates and names of its vertices to a KML file. The KML file generated by the Map Traces application was then converted manually into an array of JSON objects and embedded into the application's script. If you're interested in this or any other metro system, you can use this application and other sources of information, such as Wikipedia, to trace any path based on map features.

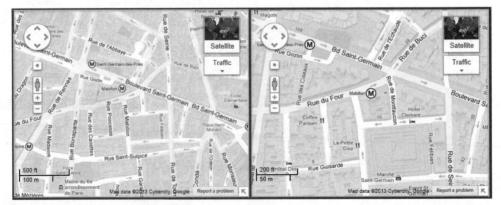

Figure 19-6 The location of the Mabillon metro station on Google Maps is slightly different at different zoom levels.

The Array with the Metro Data   The application's data are the locations of the stations that make up the paths of the metro lines; this data must be downloaded to the client as part of the script. You can request the data from a remote server as needed with a web service, but this specific application needs the data at the client at the same time. Because the script requires all data at the client, and because the paths of the metro lines aren't likely to change, you can include the data in your script or store it to a JavaScript file at the server and include this file in your script. The application uses an array of custom objects to embed the metro lines and their stations into the script. The metro lines and their stations are stored in an array of custom objects with the following structure:

```
{line, color, stations[]}
```

where *line* is the name of the metro line, *color* is the color of the metro line, and stations is an array of custom objects, one for each station. Each station is stored in a custom object with the following structure:

```
{name, coords}
```

where name is the station's name and coords is a LatLng object with the station's geo-coordinates. Here's an object that represents a station:

```
{'name':'Porte Dauphine', 'coords':
        new google.maps.LatLng(48.871687, 2.276144)}
```

The data is stored in the Paris_Metro array, whose contents are shown in Listing 19-1 (just a small section of the lines and their stations; you can open the Paris Metro.html page to examine the entire contents of the Paris_Metro array).

Listing 19-1
The structure and contents of the Paris_ Metro array

```
var Paris_Metro = [
    {'line': 'Line 2', 'color': 'blue', 'stations': [
        { 'name':'Porte Dauphine', 'coords':
            new google.maps.LatLng(48.87168743, 2.27614403)},
        { 'name':'Victor Hugo', 'coords':
            new google.maps.LatLng(48.86990907, 2.28592873)},
        { 'name':'Charles de Gaulle - Etoile', 'coords':
            new google.maps.LatLng(48.87395969, 2.29474783)},
        . . .
    },
    {'line': 'Line 7', 'color': 'pink', 'stations': [
        . . .
    },
    {'line': 'Line 8', 'color': 'maroon', 'stations': [
        . . .
    },
        . . .
    {'line': 'Line 12', 'color': 'green', 'stations': [
        { 'name':'La Courneuve - Aubervilliers',  'coords':
            new google.maps.LatLng(48.92075091, 2.41046906)},
        . . .
        { 'name':'Mairie d\'Issy',  'coords':
            new google.maps.LatLng(48.82408742,2.2732687) }]
    }
];
```

Embedding the JSON formatted data into your script is straightforward. Just make sure you escape any special characters such as the single quote (see the last station's name in the preceding listing). The `Paris_Metro` array contains custom objects, and each custom object has a property—the `stations` property—which is also an array of custom objects with a different structure.

TIP Some of the stations may end up being stored in multiple arrays. These are the stations where multiple metro lines merge. A more elegant approach would be to store all stations in a single array and associate an `id` value with each station. Each metro line then would be a sequence of `id`s that correspond to the stations along the line. With this technique, you wouldn't have to store the same station more than once, even if it's shared by multiple metro lines. This approach would complicate the code and would have made it more difficult to follow.

Designing the Metro Map

With the data in place, you can examine the code that draws the metro lines on the map and animates the trains. Each metro line is rendered on the map with a `Polyline` object, which is defined by a path. The vertices of the path are the locations of the stations of the corresponding metro line. By the way, the actual subway rails are not straight-line segments between the stations, but unless you have access to more detailed data, there's not much you can do. If the rails were on the surface of the city, you would be able to trace them more accurately by using many more points along each line. The animation techniques explained in this chapter, however, can be easily applied to any other path.

To draw each metro line on the map, you must set up two nested loops: one that iterates through the lines of the `Paris_Metro` array and another one that iterates through the current line's stations. For each line, you must construct an array of coordinates and then use it as the path for a `Polyline` object that represents the current metro line. In the inner loop, you must also create a `Circle` object for each station and place it on the map at the station's location. Listing 19-2 shows the two nested loops.

Listing 19-2
Laying out the metro lines and their stations on the map

```
for (iLine = 0; iLine < Paris_Metro.length; iLine++) {
    lineLengths.push(google.maps.geometry.spherical.computeLength(
        [Paris_Metro[iLine].stations[0].coords,
         Paris_Metro[iLine].stations[
                    Paris_Metro[iLine].stations.length - 1].coords]));
    var path = [];
    for (iStation = 0;
         iStation < Paris_Metro[iLine].stations.length; iStation++) {
        path.push(Paris_Metro[iLine].stations[iStation].coords);
        var stationSymbol = {
            path: google.maps.SymbolPath.CIRCLE, offset: "0%",
            scale: 3.5, fillColor: Paris_Metro[iLine].color,
            strokeColor: "black", strokeWeight: 1, strokeOpacity: 1,
            fillColor: Paris_Metro[iLine].color, fillOpacity: 1
        };
        var station = new google.maps.Marker({
            position: Paris_Metro[iLine].stations[iStation].coords,
            icon: stationSymbol,
            title: Paris_Metro[iLine].stations[iStation].name,
            map: map
```

```
    });
    google.maps.event.addListener(station, 'mouseover', function () {
                  this.setOptions({ zIndex: 99 }) });
    google.maps.event.addListener(station, 'mouseout', function () {
                    this.setOptions({ zIndex: 1 }) });
  }
  // Create a PolyLine for each metro line,
  // set the line's symbol to the appropriate train symbol
  // and finally place the Polyline object onto the map
  var pLine = new google.maps.Polyline({
      path: path,  geodesic: false,  strokeOpacity: 1,
      strokeWeight: 3, strokeColor: Paris_Metro[iLine].color,
      icons: [{ icon: trainSymbols[iLine], offset: '0%'
      }]
  });
  pLine.setMap(map);
  lines.push(pLine);
  // the directions array holds the direction of each train.
  directions.push(1);
  // add an event listener to allow user to select a line by clicking it.
  google.maps.event.addListener(
          lines[iLine], 'click', function () {selectLine(this)});
}
```

The code stores the coordinates of the current line's stations in the path array—a local variable—and uses this array to specify the path of the Polyline object that represents the current metro line on the map. The following statement adds to the path array the location of the current station of the current line:

```
path.push(Paris_Metro[iLine].stations[iStation].coords);
```

The path array is used later by the statement that creates the Polyline object corresponding to the current metro line:

```
var pLine = new google.maps.Polyline({
    path: path,  geodesic: false,  strokeOpacity: 1,
    // other attributes . . .
  });
```

The Polyline objects that represent the metro lines are stored in the lines array so that they can be reused later during the animation. The last statement in the listing associates each line's click event with the selectLine() function, which highlights the line that was clicked.

Designing the Animation

The trains travel on their paths at a constant speed and the application assumes the same speed for all trains, which is a reasonable assumption, but in a different type of application you could use a different speed for each moving object. Once you know the speed of the train and the length of the line, you can calculate the percentage of the line's length covered at each animation cycle. Let's say that the animation cycle specified in the setInterval() function is 1000 milliseconds, which is 1 second, and the line's length is 18 kilometers.

The position of the train is updated once every second. If the speed is 36 kilometers per hour, it will take 30 minutes for the train to travel the distance. This will result in a very slow animation so you must speed things up by varying the animation time.

Let's do the math. The speed of the train is 36,000 meters per hour, or 36,000/60 = 600 meters per minute, or 600/60 = 10 meters per second. The entire distance is 18,000 meters and it will be covered in 18,000/10 = 1,800 steps. Between successive animation steps, you must advance the train's symbol by 1/1,800 of the total distance, which is 18,000/1,800 = 10 meters. In real time, the entire length of the line will be covered after 1,800 seconds, or 30 minutes. Initially, the train's position will be at the starting position, or 0 percent of the total length away from its starting position. After the first animation cycle, the train's position will be at 10/18,000 or 1/1,800, which is 0.055 percent, of the total length away from its starting position, and so on. After 1,800 animation cycles, the train will be at its destination, which is 100 percent of the length away from the starting position.

Scaling the Animation Time   Using an animation cycle of 1 second will result in animation that lasts 30 minutes: a very slow animation. You realize that no one wants to watch this animation in real time. To produce an interesting animation, you could scale the animation time so that the train covers the line's length in, say, 30 seconds. Going from 30 minutes to 30 seconds is equivalent to scaling the time by a factor of 60. So instead of updating the animation every second, you can update it 60 times per second. To use round numbers, let's scale the animation time by a factor of 50. Instead of updating the animation once a second, you can update it every 20 milliseconds to scale the animation time by a factor of 50. The relative distances and times will remain proportional, but the entire animation will end in just over 30 seconds, instead of 30 minutes. And this is a reasonable animation length—you will actually see the trains move.

The `Paris Metro.html` application updates the animation every 50 milliseconds, or 20 times per second. The animation looks pretty smooth in Google's Chrome and Firefox browsers. I'm afraid I can't say the same for Internet Explorer; with IE, it's rather "jerky." It seems IE is optimized for Flash-type animation but not for JavaScript animation. I don't think there are any tricks to make the animation smoother with Internet Explorer, but I may be wrong. Just make sure that you have enabled the GPU rendering option on the Advanced tab of Internet Explorer's Options dialog box.

The code calculates the distance traveled every second given the speed of the train. A train traveling at the speed of 43.2 kilometers per hour covers 12 meters every second. This is 12 × 60 = 720 meters per minute, or 720 × 60 = 43,200 meters per hour. If the animation is updated every second by advancing the train's position by 12 meters, the train will appear to travel in real time—that is, very slowly on the computer screen.

Because the animation is updated every 50 milliseconds, the train appears to travel 20 times faster. The animation function moves the train at each animation cycle by the same distance, which is the variable `step` in the code, not once, but 20 times per second. The blue line of the metro has a length of 12,121.7 meters and a train traveling at 43.2 kilometers/hour covers it in 1,010 seconds of real time. Because the animation is updated 20 times per second, the travel time is scaled by a factor of 20, and the animation lasts 1010/20 = 50.5 seconds. It takes the train just over 50 seconds of animation (scaled) time to travel the total length of the blue line.

The animation cycle, the `animationCycle` variable in the code, determines the time scaling factor; the `step` variable is the distance in meters traveled between successive animation updates. The clock that displays the scaled time is updated 20 times per second to show the elapsed time, and it runs very fast. When you scale the speed of a moving item, you are implicitly changing its time scale as well so you need a mechanism to present the real elapsed time, which goes much faster than actual time.

The variables `step` and `animationCycle` determine the train's speed and the scaling of the animation time. The `step` variable is the distance covered every second when the `animationCycle` variable is set to 1000 (1 second). In effect, the `animationCycle` variable determines the scaling factor for the animation: Set it to 500 to make things move twice as fast, to 100 to make things move 10 times as fast, and so on.

The values of these two variables in the sample application are 12 (meters) and 50 (milliseconds), respectively. You can set them to 6 and 50 to get a smooth animation of a train traveling at half speed because the scaling factor remains the same, but the distance covered between successive animation cycles is half of the original value. If you set these variables to `step=48` and `animationCycle=200`, you'll get a jumpy animation, which will also last 50 seconds since you bumped up both values by a factor of 4. This time the animation is updated only 5 times per second. This value of the `step` variable corresponds to an actual distance of 48 × 5, or 240 meters per second between successive animation cycles, which explains the jumpy appearance of the animation. If you zoom out far enough, however, even this animation will look smooth because consecutive pixels on the monitor will eventually correspond to distances of a few hundred meters on the surface of the earth! This indicates that a set of values that may result in a smooth train animation is totally inappropriate for a flight animation, where the speeds and distances are drastically different, and vice versa.

The Paris Metro Simple Page

The page `Paris Metro Simple.html` shows an animated train traveling the blue line of the Paris metro. It's a simplified version of the `Paris Metro.html` page that animates a single train and doesn't display the actual or elapsed time. Use this simple version of the application to understand the animation logic and experiment with the settings discussed in the preceding paragraphs. The complete Paris Metro application contains additional features that are discussed in the following section.

Here's the complete listing of the simple version of the application. The majority of the stations in the *Metro_Line* array are not shown in the listing because the exact number of stations isn't of any importance for the purposes of this tutorial. The *Metro_Line* array is a reduced version of the *Paris_Metro* array, since it holds the stations of a single line. The page's script is shown in its entirety in Listing 19-3 for your convenience and it's discussed in detail in the following sections.

Listing 19-3
The Paris
Metro Simple
html web page

```
<script type="text/javascript">
var Metro_Line =
    {'line': 'Line 2', 'color': 'blue', 'stations': [
        { 'name':'Porte Dauphine',
          'coords': new google.maps.LatLng(48.87168, 2.276144)},
        { 'name':'Victor Hugo',
```

```
                    'coords': new google.maps.LatLng(48.8699, 2.2859233)},
            { 'name':'Charles de Gaulle - Etoile',
                    'coords': new google.maps.LatLng(48.87396, 2.29474783)},
            { 'name':'Nation',
                    'coords': new google.maps.LatLng(48.84839, 2.3958134)}]
        }
var map;
var trainSymbol;
var pLine;
var lineLength;

function initialize() {
// set up a symbol for the train
    var trainSymbol = { path: google.maps.SymbolPath.CIRCLE, offset: "0%",
        scale: 4, strokeColor: "red", strokeWeight: 2, strokeOpacity: 1,
        fillColor: "blue", fillOpacity:1, zIndex:999 };
    var myLatLng = new google.maps.LatLng(48.870, 2.350);
    var mapOptions = { zoom: 13,  center: myLatLng,  minZoom: 8,
        streetViewControl: false,
        navigationControlOptions:
                {style: google.maps.NavigationControlStyle.ANDROID},
          mapTypeId: google.maps.MapTypeId.ROADMAP
        };
    map = new google.maps.Map(document.getElementById('map_canvas'),
                            mapOptions);
// calculate the length of the metro line
    lineLength = google.maps.geometry.spherical.computeLength(
            [[Metro_Line.stations[0].coords,
            Metro_Line.stations[
                        Metro_Line.stations.length - 1].coords]);
    var path = [];
    var stationSymbol = { path: google.maps.SymbolPath.CIRCLE,
                        offset: "0%", scale: 3.5,
                        fillColor: Metro_Line.color,
                        strokeColor: "black", strokeWeight: 1,
                        strokeOpacity: 1,
                        fillColor: Metro_Line.color, fillOpacity:1};
    for (iStation = 0; iStation < Metro_Line.stations.length; iStation++) {
            path.push(Metro_Line.stations[iStation].coords);
              var station = new google.maps.Marker(
                      {position:Metro_Line.stations[iStation].coords,
                        icon: stationSymbol,
                        title: Metro_Line.stations[iStation].name,
                      map: map});
                }
// Create a PolyLine for the metro line
    pLine = new google.maps.Polyline({
                      path: path, geodesic: false,
                      strokeOpacity: 1, strokeWeight: 3,
                      strokeColor: "blue", icons: [{
                              icon: trainSymbol, offset: '0%'}]
            });
    pLine.setMap(map);
```

```
        }
        var offsetId;
        // the train's speed is 12*3600 (43.2 km/h),
        // including time at the stations!
        var step = 12;
        var animationCycle = 50;
        function animateTrain() {
            var tStart = (new Date()).getTime()
            var distance = 0;
            var timeCount = 0;
            var direction =1;
            initialize();
            offsetId = window.setInterval(function () {
                distance += step;
                var icons = pLine.get('icons');
                var currentPercent = ( distance % lineLength) / lineLength;
                    if (currentPercent > 1 - step/lineLength) currentPercent =1;
                    if (currentPercent < step/lineLength) currentPercent =0;
                    if (direction == -1) currentPercent = 1 - currentPercent;
                    if (currentPercent < 1 && currentPercent > 0) {
                        icons[0].offset = (currentPercent * 100) + '%';
                        pLine.set('icons', icons);
                    }
                    else {
                        if (pLine != null) {
                            direction = -direction;
                            // increase distance to avoid double direction
                            // change in two successive steps!
                            // if you omit the following statement
                            // the train will start its next route from
                            // its initial starting point and
                            // will not reverse its direction.
                            distance += step;
                        }
                    }
            }, animationCycle);
        }
        </script>
        </head>
            <body bgcolor="#b0DDb0" onload="initialize();">
            <input type='button'
                    style="font-family: Tebuchet, Arial; font-size: 16px;"
                    onclick='animateTrain()' value='Animate train'/>
                                    
            <span style="font-family: Tebuchet, Arial; font-size: 14px;" >
            Click the button to animate the blue line</span>
            <br/><br/>
            <div id="map_canvas" style='height: 480px; width: 100%'></div>
          </body>
        </html>
```

Setting Up the Animation Path

The code starts by parsing the `Metro_Line` array to extract the coordinates of the stations along the metro line and use them to create the appropriate markers. The code is fairly easy. Listing 19-4 shows the loop that iterates through the stations of the metro line, creates a new `Marker` object for each station using the coordinates and the name of the current station, and places the `Marker` object on the map by setting its `map` attribute:

Listing 19-4
The loop that generates the markers to identify stations along the metro line.

```
for (iStation = 0; iStation < Metro_Line.stations.length; iStation++) {
        path.push(Metro_Line.stations[iStation].coords);
        var station = new google.maps.Marker({
                        position:Metro_Line.stations[iStation].coords,
                        icon: stationSymbol,
                        title: Metro_Line.stations[iStation].name,
                        map: map});
}
```

The `stationSymbol` variable is a circle, one of the predefined symbols of the API, and it's declared with the following statement:

```
var stationSymbol = {
        path: google.maps.SymbolPath.CIRCLE, offset: "0%",
        scale: 3.5, fillColor: Metro_Line.color, strokeColor: "black",
        strokeWeight: 1, strokeOpacity: 1,
        fillColor: Metro_Line.color, fillOpacity: 1
};
```

The `path` array is filled with the coordinates of each station and is used later as the path of the `Polyline` object that represents the metro line. After that, the code creates a `Polyline` object, the `pLine` local variable, which is the line's path. The `pLine` variable is defined by the points already stored in the `path` array. The statement that creates the `pLine` variable is trivial, except for the `icons` property, which specifies the symbol of the train that represents the train on the line. This symbol is just a circle in this example, but you can design a nicer SVG graphic for the train's symbol. Moreover, the symbol is placed initially at the beginning of the path (at 0 percent of its length) with the `offset` property of the `icon` object. Note that you can associate multiple symbols with the same line, and the related property is called `icons`. The `icons` property is an array of `icon` objects and in most cases, as in our example, it contains a single symbol. Listing 19-5 shows the statement that creates a `Polyline` object for the current metro line, based on the locations of the `path` array.

Listing 19-5
Generating a polyline with a symbol at its end

```
pLine = new google.maps.Polyline({
        path: path, geodesic: false, strokeOpacity: 1,
        strokeWeight: 3, strokeColor: "blue",
        icons: [{
            icon: trainSymbol, offset: '0%'
        }]
});
pLine.setMap(map);
```

Finally, the length of the path is calculated with the help of the `computeLength()` method of Google's `geometry` library:

```
lineLength = google.maps.geometry.spherical.computeLength(path);
```

The argument to the `computeLength()` method is an array of `LatLng` objects, which is exactly what the `path` array is: an array with the geo-coordinates of the line's stations in their proper order. You just finished setting up the scene for the animation, and now you're ready to explore the code of the animation function, which moves the trains.

The Animation Function   Instead of creating a function and passing its name as an argument to the `setInterval()` function, the script uses an anonymous function definition in the `setInterval()` method's code. It's a very common approach among JavaScript developers, so you should see an example of a lengthy inline function definition. Listing 19-6 shows the call to the `setInterval()` function.

Listing 19-6
The statements that animate the train along its path

```
offsetId = window.setInterval(function () {
        distance += step;
        var icons = pLine.get('icons');
        var currentPercent = (distance % lineLength) / lineLength;
        if (currentPercent > 1 - step / lineLength) currentPercent = 1;
        if (currentPercent < step / lineLength) currentPercent = 0;
        if (direction == -1) { currentPercent = 1 - currentPercent; }
        if (currentPercent < 1 && currentPercent > 0) {
            icons[0].offset = (currentPercent * 100) + '%';
            pLine.set('icons', icons);
            }
        else {
            if (pLine != null) {
                    direction = -direction;
                    distance += step;
                }
            }
        }
}, animationCycle);
```

The `distance` variable is the actual distance covered so far and it's increased by `step` meters at every cycle of the animation. The variable `lineLength` is calculated once outside the animation function because it doesn't change during the animation. Because the animation function's code is executed many times per second, it's imperative that it's optimized. The `step` variable is set to 12 meters and the animation cycle to 50 milliseconds with the following statements, which also appear outside the animation function:

```
var step = 12;
var animationCycle = 50;
```

The train moves 12 meters every 50 milliseconds, or $12 \times 20 = 240$ meters per second, or 14,400 meters per minute. Assuming that the train moves at 45 kilometers per hour, which corresponds to 750 meters per minute, the animation progresses approximately 14,400/750 or approximately 20 times faster than the actual speed of the train.

Notice the statement that changes the sign of the direction variable:

```
direction = -direction;
```

The statement is executed only when the train's location is at 0 percent or at 100 percent of its path. In other words, when the train reaches either one of its terminal stations, the `direction` variable is toggled. This, in turn, toggles the direction of the train. When the train moves back, the `currentPercent` variable, which is the percentage of the length traveled so far, is calculated as usual. Then it's adjusted by the following statement, should the `direction` variable indicate reverse movement:

```
if (direction == -1) { currentPercent = 1 - currentPercent; }
```

This statement says simply that the train's location can be either 3 percent of the total length away from one end, or 97 percent of the same length away from the other end station. The first two `if` statements in the code compare the percentage of the total length traveled so far to the values 0 and 1 (the two terminal stations). If the train is less than `step` meters away from either station, the program considers that the train has reached its destination. Because the trains will never reach the terminal stations exactly, the code toggles the direction of the train when the train is less than `step` meters away from the terminal station.

Another statement that may not be obvious at first glance is the statement that calculates the current percentage of the route traveled:

```
var currentPercent = (distance % lineLength) / lineLength;
```

The `%` operator is the modulus operator, which returns the remainder of the division. The distance `variable` isn't reset every time the train changes direction. Its value may become 64,500 meters after a while. The `%` operator in essence subtracts the number of integer lengths of the line and the result is the actual distance covered since the last direction change. The length of the blue line is 12,121.7 meters, and the operation

```
64,500 % 12,121.7
```

yields the value 3,891.5. The train has traveled the entire line five times, and on its sixth route it has covered the first 3,891.5 meters. This is the value you must divide by *lineLength* to figure out the percentage of the current route that has been covered already and place the symbol on the path accordingly. Note that changing the `offset` attribute of the symbol isn't enough; you must also set the `icon` attribute of the polyline to force a redraw of the symbol:

```
icons[0].offset = (currentPercent * 100) + '%';
pLine.set('icons', icons);
```

Open the `Paris Metro Simple.html` page to examine the code and experiment with the various settings. Familiarize yourself with the program's logic and then open the Paris Metro application, which animates all 14 metro lines. The following section points out the key differences between the two applications and how the animation technique applied to a single line is extended to handle all trains.

Animating All Metro Lines

The Paris Metro.html page is a web application that animates a train on every line of the Paris metro. The metro lines and their stations are stored in the Paris_Metro array, as discussed in the earlier section "The Application's Data." The script draws a different colored line on the map for every metro track and places the stations along each one of them. The stations are small filled circles with the same color as the corresponding line, and they're placed on the map with the code shown in Listing 19-2. The animation function is a bit more complicated this time, as it must iterate through all the items in the lines array and animate a symbol on each one of them. It must also keep track of the lengths of all lines and reverse the direction of each train when it reaches the end of its line.

To animate multiple trains, the script uses the animation function shown in Listing 19-7. It's a lengthy listing printed here in its entirety to help you understand the animation logic.

Listing 19-7
The statements
that animate
multiple trains

```
function animateTrains() {
    var tStart = (new Date()).getTime()
    var distance = 0;
    var timeCount = 0;
    var speed = step * 3600 / 1000 + ' Km/hour';
    document.getElementById('trainSpeed').innerHTML =
            'Trains travelling at ' + speed;
    initialize();
    offsetId = window.setInterval(function () {
        distance += step;
        timeCount += 1;
        document.getElementById('txtElapsedTime').innerHTML =
            Math.floor(timeCount/3600) + ' hours, ' +
            Math.floor((timeCount/3600.0 - parseInt(timeCount/3600.0)) *
            60) + ' minutes, ' +
            (Math.floor(timeCount % 60)) + ' seconds';
        var currentTime = new Date()
        var hours = currentTime.getHours()
        var minutes = currentTime.getMinutes()
        var seconds = currentTime.getSeconds()
        document.getElementById('txtTime').innerHTML =
                parseInt((currentTime - tStart) / 60000) + ':' +
                        parseInt((currentTime - tStart) / 1000 % 60);
        for (i = 0; i < lines.length; i++) {
            if (lines[i] != null) {
                var icons = lines[i].get('icons');
                var currentPercent =
                        (distance % lineLengths[i]) / lineLengths[i];
                if (currentPercent > 1 - step / lineLengths[i])
                    currentPercent = 1;
                if (currentPercent < step / lineLengths[i])
                    currentPercent = 0;
                if (directions[i] == -1)
                    currentPercent = 1 - currentPercent;
                if (currentPercent < 1 && currentPercent > 0) {
                    icons[0].offset = (currentPercent * 100) + '%';
                    lines[i].set('icons', icons);
                }
            }
            else {
```

```
            if (lines[i] != null) {
                    directions[i] = -directions[i];
// increase distance to avoid double
// direction change in two successive steps!
// if you omit the following statement
// the train will start its next route from
// its initial starting point and will not reverse its direction.
                    distance += step;
            }
        }
    }
}
}, animationCycle);
}
```

The code that animates the train symbols is the same as before, but instead of the lineLength variable (which was the length of the blue line), it uses the lineLengths array, which holds the lengths of the individual metro tracks. The symbols are animated in a loop that goes through each item in the lines array. In addition to the lineLengths array, this time the code uses the lines array. Where as in the simple version of the application you used the pLine object to represent the blue line, you now use the lines array to store a Polyline object for each metro line.

Different trains change direction at different times because each line has a different length, and you need to store the direction of each train. Instead of the variable direction, the script uses the directions array with a separate item for each metro line. The logic of the animation code is the same, only a bit lengthier.

A very important aspect of an application that animates real-world entities is the elapsed time: how much actual time corresponds to the animation time. Let's take a look at the statements that display the two times at the top of the page. To display the actual animation time, the code calculates the difference between the current time (variable currentTime) and the time when the animation started (variable tStart) and formats it as hours:minutes:seconds. The calculation of the elapsed time involves the variable timeCount, which is increased by one every animation cycle. This time flies faster than real time by the specified scaling factor. The scaling factor of the animation time, in turn, depends on the animation cycle. If the animation cycle is 50, the animation time is scaled by a factor of 20 because the timeCount variable is increased 20 times per second. If the animation cycle is 1000, the scaling factor is 1, and the train appears to travel on the map at its real speed.

Summary

This example concludes the first chapter on animating items on Google maps. I discussed in detail the animation of symbols along paths with data that has both a spatial and a temporal component. A moving object changes its position (the spatial component) with time (the temporal component). In the following chapter, I discuss another type of data: data that remains in place, but evolves with time. You've learned how to produce heatmaps; it's now time to produce animated heatmaps that show how the intensity of the quantity they represent changes over time.

You will also see an application that animates an airplane over a geodesic path and the equivalent rhumb line on the map. You will actually "see" why geodesic paths are actually shorter than the equivalent rhumb lines, even though they appear to be longer on the map.

20 Advanced JavaScript Animation

In the last chapter of this book, you're going to examine a few more animation techniques and build a couple of interesting and visually appealing applications. You have read about geodesic lines in several chapters of this book and you already know that geodesics lines are the shortest paths between any two given points on the globe, even though they appear very long on the map. On the map, the shortest path is a straight one, not a curve. Yet when the shortest path between two points on the globe is subject to a Mercator projection, it becomes a lengthy curve. In this chapter, you will see why geodesic lines are shorter than rhumb lines using animation. You will actually see two airplanes flying on a geodesic and a rhumb line at constant speed, and, surprisingly, the airplane following a geodesic path will cover a seemingly longer distance, but it will arrive at its destination sooner.

You will also explore an animation technique that involves heatmaps. Heatmaps represent density or intensity of a data items over areas of the globe, as you saw in the previous chapter. The data can be anything from precipitation to population density, and from crime scenes to visitors at specific locations. The data explored in this chapter is tied to geographic locations—as opposed to moving items—and it evolves with time. You will actually see an animation of the precipitation in various parts of the eastern United States and how the precipitation changes in the course of a year.

Scalable Vector Graphics

In the examples in preceding chapters, you used the built-in symbols to represent items on the map as alternatives to the default marker symbol. For the examples in this chapter, you need more elaborate icons, which you must design on your own. The airplane symbols shown in Figure 20-1 are vector graphics generated with a few simple commands. Figure 20-1 is a detail of two airplanes flying on their paths, shown as gray lines: It's taken from one of the examples you will develop later in this chapter.

The simplest technique for overlaying symbols on a map is to use small images as icons, but images have two major drawbacks. First, they don't scale very well. Moreover, images can't be aligned with the path. If you look carefully at the airplane icons in Figure 20-1,

Figure 20-1   The airplane symbol is a vector graphic described with SVG commands.

you will see that the airplane icon follows the orientation of its path. Your other option is to use vector graphics, which can be scaled infinitely and rotated at will. A scalable symbol is defined with geometric operators so that it's rendered perfectly at any resolution. Every time the page is refreshed, vector graphics are recalculated and rendered at the current zoom factor. Images are just copied—and you know how easy it is to distort an image when you zoom in or out too much.

The most common type of vector graphics in web applications are the Scaled Vector Graphics (SVG), which are created with simple commands embedded in a string. There are tools for generating SVG graphics interactively, but my goal is to explain the structure of an SVG file and not to discuss the details of creating SVG symbols.

Creating SVG Icons

No special software was used to generate the symbol of the airplane. The outline of an airplane was drawn on an engineering pad (a very simple outline), and then the coordinates of each line segment were estimated and written down. The entire drawing is contained in a box with dimensions 400 by 400. The units don't really matter; the graphic will be scaled when used on a web page. Here's the result:

```
M -100 200 L 100 200 L 020 150 L 10 40 L 0 20 L -10 40 L -20 150 z
```

This is a declaration of a shape that (kind of) resembles an airplane. The M command stands for moveto and it moves the pen by the specified units horizontally and vertically, without leaving any trace. The L command stands for lineto, and it moves the pen by the specified units horizontally and vertically, this time leaving a trace. The L and M are the two most basic SVG commands, and they're followed by two numbers, which are the displacements in the horizontal and vertical directions. The z command at the end of the path closes the shape. That's why it doesn't accept any arguments. There are other commands for drawing smooth curves, arcs, and so on.

The origin is always the upper-left corner of the drawing area, so negative *X* units point to the left. Positive *X* units point to the right and positive *Y* units point downward. As you can see, the SVG commands allow you to create a path, which will be rendered on the map as needed. To test your SVG description, you must place it in an XML file and open it with your browser. Start Notepad and insert the preceding SVG command in the necessary headers, as shown in Listing 20-1.

Listing 20-1
The SVG
description of the
airplane symbol

```
<svg>
    <path
        d= "M -100 200 L 100 200
        L 020 150 L 10 40 L 0 20
        L -10 40 L -20 150 Z"
        fill = "red" stroke = "blue"
        stroke-width="2"
        transform="translate(100,0)" />
</svg>
```

Save this text with the SVG symbol description to a file with the extension SVG and then open it in your browser (just double-click the file's icon). Alternatively, enter the SVG commands in a new fiddle and run it to see how the shape will be rendered, as shown in Figure 20-2. Note that the SVG description of the shape must be entered in the HTML pane, not the JavaScript pane.

The SVG file contains a few commands needed to scale and move the shape into position. These commands are only necessary for viewing the symbol in the browser. If you omit the command:

```
transform="translate(100,0)"
```

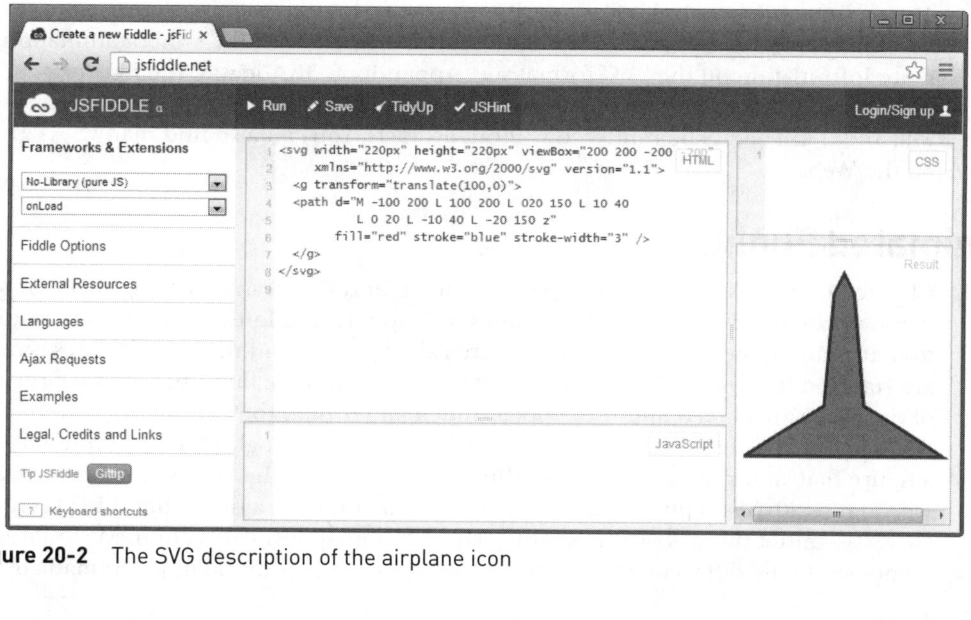

Figure 20-2   The SVG description of the airplane icon

from the `<svg>` element, the symbol's vertical axis will be aligned with the left side of the browser: You will see only one-half of the airplane in the browser. The origin is the point (0, 0) and the first horizontal displacement is –100, so everything to the left of the origin will end up to the left of the window.

Using the SVG Icon

To use the airplane shape as a symbol in your script, you only need the commands that describe the outline of the symbol. The following statement creates an icon that resembles the outline of an airplane:

```
icon: {
    path: 'M -100 200 L 100 200 L 020 150
          L 10 40 L 0 20 L -10 40 L -20 150 z',
    scale: 0.090,
    strokeColor: '#3333FF',
    fillColor: '#AA00AA',
    fillOpacity: 1
    }
```

All you really need from the SVG file is the command that outlines the shape's path. If you use a third-party tool to design SVG graphics, just extract the description of the path and use it in your script. As you can see, the actual size of the symbol doesn't matter either because the entire symbol is scaled with the `scale` attribute. The value of the `scale` attribute used in this example was the result of some experimentation; the airplane symbol has a reasonable size regardless of the current zoom factor for a scale value of 0.090. The remaining attributes of the icon object shouldn't be new to you.

An SVG graphic is basically a path that's defined with SVG commands. The symbol's outline and fill colors can be specified in the constructor of the `icon` object in the script. The scaling of the symbol is also specified in the script. For the time being, you can use the definition of the `airplane.svg` symbol to experiment with the symbol animation. For more information on the SVG format see, Appendix B. By the way, the figure of the globe with the parallels and meridians shown in Chapter 1 is an SVG graphic. You can resize it at will, and it will always be rendered without artifacts. You can also find many SVG graphics on the Web.

Animated Flights

Chapter 10 discussed the topic of geodesic lines, and you designed an application to demonstrate the difference between lines on a sphere and lines on a flat map. As discussed in that chapter, the lines on the sphere are called *geodesic* and the straight lines on the map are referred to as *rhumb* lines. On the flat map, the geodesic lines that span a large portion of the globe are curved and they appear much larger than the equivalent rhumb lines, but this is just a side effect of the Mercator projection used by Google Maps. For your convenience, a figure that shows the geodesic and rhumb lines between the Dallas and Beijing airports (see Figure 20-3) is repeated here. It's doubtful that there's a direct flight between the two airports—and if there is one, it might even go in the opposite direction. My intention is to demonstrate the difference between the two types of paths in the most dramatic manner.

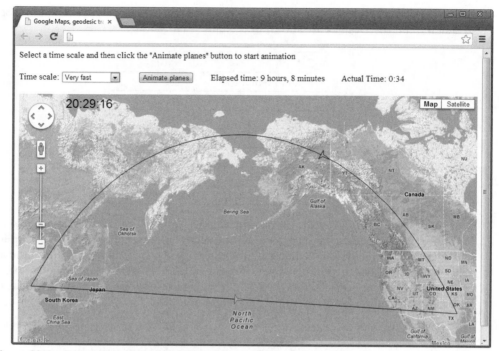

Figure 20-3   Two ways to fly from Beijing, China to Dallas, Texas

The two airplane symbols are a dead giveaway of my intentions, aren't they? Indeed, you're about to actually see why one of the two planes flying at the same speed over the two paths is covering the distance in a shorter time interval. The animation will actually help you understand why the path that appears to be longer is actually shorter. As mentioned in Chapter 10, a geodesic line is the shortest distance between two locations on the globe. Because the planes are cruising at the same speed, the one on the shorter path will get there sooner, no matter what its path looks like! And this is the airplane flying on the geodesic path.

You probably know that there's no straight line in the universe either, but for a very different reason. There's no way to travel to a distant star following a straight line path (in the sense of the Euclidean geometry) because gravity affects everything. Even light itself cannot escape gravity, so straight lines in the universe are hugely distorted. Assuming that light takes the shortest possible route, its path is as straight as it can get in the vastness of our universe.

Scaling the Flight Animation Time

Let's now return to our earthly flight animation. The Geodesic Flight Path.html web application, shown in Figure 20-3, uses a different technique to control the animation than the example of the Paris Metro animation. This application keeps the animation cycle constant at 20 updates per second; the animation cycle is always 50 milliseconds and this value yields a fairly smooth animation. The distance covered at each cycle varies depending on the user's selection in the Time Scale drop-down list. The settings for the Time Scale parameter and their values are shown in the table that follows.

Setting	Value
Real-time flight	1
Slower	50
Slow	100
Normal	250
Fast	500
Faster	750
Very fast	1000

The setting Fast causes the animation time to run 500 times faster than actual time; it condenses 500 seconds of actual time into one second of animation time. This application uses a constant animation cycle because it's crucial for the smooth movement of the airplane symbol, and it adjusts the animated speed of the airplane. The airplane speed is 200 meters per second, but more on this shortly. The percentage of the distance traveled so far in the animation is calculated with the following statement:

```
var currentPercent = 200 * scaledCount/lengths[i];
```

where the scaledCount variable is the number of animation seconds:

```
var scaledCount = count * 50 / 1000;
```

The lengths[i] variable is the length of the equivalent path, and count is an auxiliary variable that's increased at each animation cycle by the factor of the time scale. The scaledCount variable is actual time in seconds: It's the number of animation cycles that have occurred so far, multiplied by 50 milliseconds. The count variable is not increased by 1; it's increased by the factor that corresponds to the item selected in the Time Scale list with the statement

```
count += timeScale;
```

When the time scale is set to 1, the airplane flies in real time: very, very slowly. This is because the count variable corresponds to actual seconds. Larger values for the timescale variable correspond to faster animation times. If you change the Time Scale setting during the flight, the airplane's speed will be increased from that point on. In other words, the calculations will affect the rest of the animation without any complication.

If the current setting is Slow, the currentPercentage will be increased by 200 x 100 x 50 / 1000 = 1,000 meters every 50 milliseconds or 1000 * 20 = 20,000 meters per second. This is the animated speed of the airplane. The actual speed of the airplane is 720 kilometers per hour (or 12,000 meters per minute, or 200 meters per second) and the scaling factor is 20,000 / 200 = 100. When the time is scaled by a factor of 100, each second of animation corresponds to 1 minute and 40 seconds of flying time. A flight that lasts 15 hours, for example, will take 15 x 3,600 / 100 = 540 seconds, or 9 minutes of animation time, when using the Slow setting. Conversely, one hour of animation will be played back in 3,600 / 100 = 36 seconds with this specific setting.

Using the `Faster` setting, which has a factor of 750, the percentage is increased by 200 x 750 x 50 / 1000 = 7,500 meters every 50 milliseconds, or 7,500 x 20 = 150,000 meters per second. This time the scaling factor is 150,000/200 = 750 and each second of animation corresponds to 12 minutes and 30 seconds of flying time. The same 15-hour flight will take 15 x 3,600 / 750 = 72 seconds, or 1 minute and 12 seconds on your monitor. These are the exact numbers you will see at the top of the page if you execute the animation for the two settings discussed here.

The actual flying time's calculation is based on the premise that the planes fly at 200 meters per second, or 720 kilometers per hour. To be fair, commercial airplanes are a bit faster than that, averaging close to 900 kilometers per hour. The specific speed of 720 kilometers per hour was selected because it yields integers and simplifies the numeric example. Change the factor 200 in the statement that calculates the value of the `currentPercent` variable to experiment with different airplane types. You can even add a second drop-down list with the speeds of various airplane types and calculate the speed in meters per second in your code (add choices like Cessna, 747, supersonic, and so on).

The actual flying time is reported by the `scaledCount` variable. The following statement formats the flying time as hours and minutes, as you can see in Figure 20-3, and assigns it to the `txtElapsedTime` element of the page:

```
document.getElementById('txtElapsedTime').innerHTML =
        parseInt(scaledCount / 3600) + ' hours,  ' +
        (((scaledCount / 3600) -
        parseInt(scaledCount / 3600)) * 60).toFixed(0) + ' minutes' ;
```

NOTE The code rounds flying times to minutes and animation times to seconds, so don't be surprised if you run the animation twice with the exact same settings and the values of the times displayed at the top of the page differ by one minute or one second respectively.

The Animation Function

The application's animation function, `animatePlanes()`, is shown in Listing 20-2.

Listing 20-2
The animate
Planes()
function
animates the
two planes along
their paths.

```
function animatePlanes() {
  var scaledCount = count * 50 / 1000;
  document.getElementById('txtElapsedTime').innerHTML =
              parseInt(scaledCount / 3600) + ' hours,  ' +
              (((scaledCount / 3600) - parseInt(scaledCount /
              3600))*59.999).toFixed(0) +' minutes' ;
// the count variable is increased by the value of timeScale,
// which is set every time the user selects a different animation speed
  count +=  timeScale;
  var currentTime = new Date()
  var hours = currentTime.getHours()
  var minutes = currentTime.getMinutes()
  var seconds = currentTime.getSeconds()
  document.getElementById('txtActualTime').innerHTML =
              parseInt((currentTime - tStart) / 60000) + ':' +
              parseInt((currentTime - tStart) / 1000 % 60);
  for (i = 0; i < 2; i++) {
      if (lines[i] != null) {
      var icons = lines[i].get('icons');
```

```
// The distance covered is speed (200 meters per second) * time.
    var currentPercent = 200 * scaledCount / lengths[i];
    if (currentPercent < 1.0 ) {
        icons[0].offset = (currentPercent * 100) + '%';
        lines[i].set('icons', icons);
    }
    else {
        if (lines[i] != null) {
            lines[i].setMap(null);
            lines[i] = null;
            landed++;
            if (i == 0)
                geodesicTime =
                    document.getElementById('txtElapsedTime').innerHTML;
            else
                rhumbTime =
                    document.getElementById('txtElapsedTime').innerHTML;
        }
    }
}
if (landed == 2) {
    window.clearInterval(offsetId);
    alert('All flights have landed!\n' + 'FLIGHT TIMES: \n   ' +
        geodesicTime + ' for the geodesic path and \n   ' + rhumbTime +
        ' for the rhumb path.\n\n' +
        '    The plane on the geodesic route covered ' +
        (lengths[0] / 1000).toFixed(0) +
        ' kms,\n    and the one on the rhumb route covered ' +
        (lengths[1] / 1000).toFixed(0) + ' kms');
    }
}
```

Other than calculating the value of the current Percent variable and moving the symbol on each path accordingly, the animation function is fairly straightforward. The actual animation is performed by the statement that sets the offset attribute of the polyline's first icon. It requests the line's icon with the statement

```
var icons = lines[i].get('icons');
```

then it sets the offset of the first icon (there's only one symbol anyway):

```
icons[0].offset = (currentPercent * 100) + '%';
```

and finally assigns this icon back to its line with this statement:

```
lines[i].set('icons', icons);
```

The script resets the icons attribute to force a redraw of the symbol on the line. These actions take place while the current Percent variable is less than 1. Once the percentage of the distance traveled reaches or exceeds 100 percent, the code removes the airplane's path from the map and displays a different symbol at the end of the path to indicate that the airplane has landed.

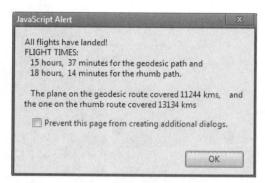

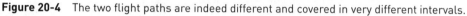

Figure 20-4   The two flight paths are indeed different and covered in very different intervals.

At the end of the animation, a message showing times and distances traveled is displayed in a popup box, like the one shown in Figure 20-4.

Are the Two Airplanes Racing One Another?

Run the animation at the fastest rate and watch the relative positions of the two airplanes. You will notice that the airplane flying on the rhumb route is getting ahead initially, but the other one catches up as it approaches the Arctic Circle, as you can see in Figure 20-5. The airplane flying on the geodesic route appears to move faster when it's near the Arctic Circle. This is when it gets ahead of the other plane and maintains this lead to the end of the flight.

But aren't both planes flying at the same speed? This isn't a glitch in the code. The geodesic route is distorted when projected on a flat surface, and while both airplanes fly at the same constant speed at all times, one of them appears to fly faster when it reaches higher latitudes. The reason for this is that distances near the poles are shorter than they appear. For the very same reason, Alaska appears to be comparable in size to Brazil, while in reality it's only one fifth the size of Brazil. This is a well-known side effect of the Mercator projection. For the airplane to maintain the same speed over an area that "appears" to be larger, when in reality it is smaller, it must move faster. In other words, it's the projection of the airplane on the flat map that appears to move faster, not the airplane flying around the globe. For more information on geodesic paths and the side effects of the Mercator projection, see Chapter 10.

Another way to look at the varying speed of the airplane on the geodesic path is that the poles are the two locations where all meridians merge together and the distance between consecutive meridians is much smaller than the distance between the same two meridians near the equator. In a sense, if you were standing on the North Pole, you could traverse the world on foot because you could walk a very small circle that intersects all meridians. If you chose to traverse the world by crossing all parallels, then there's no shortcut; you would have to go from one pole to the other.

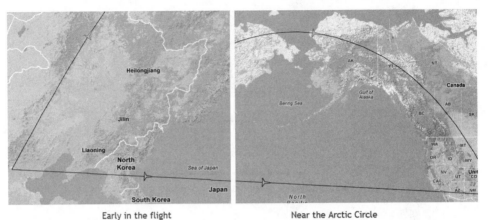

Early in the flight   Near the Arctic Circle

Figure 20-5   The lower airplane seems to get ahead of the upper one early in the flight, at least in the direction of the final destination (left image). Near the Arctic Circle, however, the upper airplane catches up and gets ahead of the other one, and maintains this lead to the end of the trip.

The `Geodesic Flight Path.html` page contains a fairly lengthy script, and I've discussed the key points of this listing. Open the file in your favorite JavaScript editor to go through the details. The source is well documented, so you should have no problem following it through.

Animating Multiple Airplanes

In this chapter's support material, you will find the `Multiple Planes.html` application (shown in Figure 20-6), which demonstrates how to animate multiple airplanes on the map. The application's code is discussed in detail in the `MultiplePlanes.pdf` document.

Animated Heatmaps

Creating a heatmap based on static data tied to specific coordinates is a straightforward process, as you recall from Chapter 19, but you can create far more compelling presentations by animating the heatmaps. In the animation examples so far, you exploited the spatial dimension of the data: The data points move in space, but their remaining attributes don't change. If the data changes over time, you can create animated heatmaps to visualize both the spatial and temporal component of the data at once. The more data you have, the smoother the animation will be. You will find a few interesting examples of animated heatmaps on the Internet, including an animation of the growth of the WalMart stores at http://gmaps-samples-v3.googlecode.com/svn/trunk/heatmaps/walmart.html (the script is included in the page and you can easily view it). This page was published by Google to demonstrate advanced animation techniques, and it uses basic animation techniques very creatively.

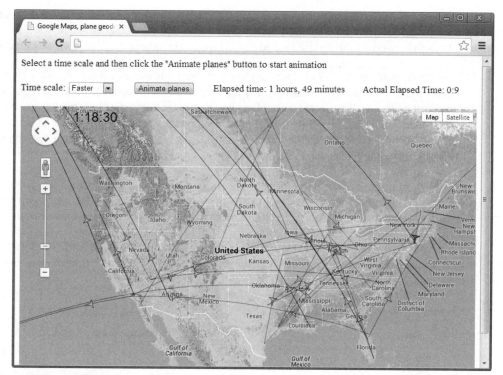

Figure 20-6   Animating multiple airplanes in their flight paths

To demonstrate the techniques for animating a heatmap layer, you're going to build the `Precipitation.html` and `Precipitation Aggregate.html` pages, which are self-contained, and you can open them in your browser by double-clicking them. The precipitation examples show rainfall data per month in a number of different states. The script contains data for the 12 months of 2012 and for 12 eastern states, one value per state per month. Each measurement is a state total (inches of rainfall per month), and the geo-location associated with each data point is the location of the state capital.

The data is stored in an array of custom objects with the following structure:

```
var precipitationData = [
    {'name': 'Florida', 'coords': [26.25, -80.43],
     'precipitation': [2.90,3.16,3.65,2.92,3.86,7.10,7.49,
                       7.38,6.70,3.80,2.31,2.72,53.95/12.0]
    },
    {'name': 'Georgia', 'coords': [33.76, -84.42],
     'precipitation': [4.27,4.46,5.05,3.75,3.58,4.51,5.55,4.98,
                       3.98,2.82,2.89,4.06,49.94/12.0]
    },
    ...
]
```

The last element in each site's `precipitation` array is the average rainfall height (the sum of the 12 month values divided by 12). Note that the geo-location is encoded as a pair of numbers that correspond to the latitude and longitude values, and not as a `LatLng` object.

TIP The heatmap of Figure 20-7 contains very few sites, but if you can obtain data for many metropolitan areas, you can create very interesting animations, not only with precipitation data, but temperatures, humidity, and so on. The richest source of weather data is the NOAA site (National Oceanic and Atmospheric Administration). The site's data can also be accessed with a web service to obtain relevant data in JSON/XML format, as explained in Chapter 15. Visit http://www.ncdc.noaa.gov/cdo-web/ webservices/v1 for more information on using the NOAA's web services.

The `Precipitation.html` page is shown in Figure 20-7 after several frames. Load the page and then click the Animate button to start the animation. The speed of the animation is controlled from within the page's code, and you can easily provide an interface element to let the user control the animation's play back rate.

To create the heatmap, declare a `HeatmapLayer` object as usual and set its data source to the `data` array, which will be initially empty. Here's the statement that creates the layer and associates it with the map:

```
heatmap = new google.maps.visualization.HeatmapLayer({
        map: map,   data: data,
        radius: 40,  dissipate: true,   maxIntensity: 700,
        opacity: 1,
```

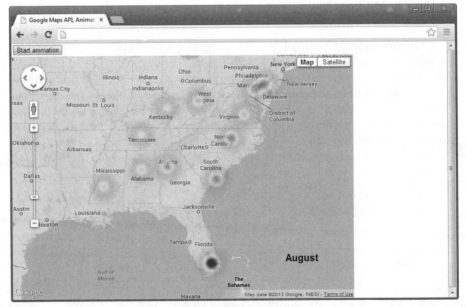

Figure 20-7 The `Precipitation.html` page displays monthly rainfall data at different locations for a period of one year.

```
        gradient: [
          'rgba(0, 0, 0, 0)',
          'rgba(255, 255, 0, 0.50)',
          'rgba(0, 0, 255, 1.0)'
        ]
    });
```

The heatmap's gradient goes from a totally transparent black color to a semitransparent yellow tone and then to an opaque blue color. The point of the initial color is that areas with small precipitations will be colored with light grayish/yellowish color. Note also that the `rgba()` function used to specify each color is embedded in quotes so that it's evaluated as needed. The value of the `radius` property was the result of some experimentation, and the value of the `maxIntensity` property is approximately equal to the largest data value (the original values have two decimal digits and they're multiplied by 100 before being appended to the `data` array so that all data values are integers).

The `data` array is initialized to an empty array:

```
data = [];
```

The idea is to fill the array with another month's data every second or so, so that the heatmap will be updated accordingly. If you had daily data, you could animate the heatmap every one-tenth of a second. The current animation cycle gives users a chance to actually see the month name displayed on top of the map and spot the areas with the heaviest rainfall in each month.

The `data` array's elements are objects with two properties: `location` and `weight`. The `location` property is a geo-location and `weight` is the precipitation value at the location. Here's a statement that adds an element to the `data` array:

```
data.push({location: new google.maps.LatLng(38.5, -119.2),
          weight: 8.5}
```

The Animation Function

To generate the graph, you need a function that populates the `data` array and assigns it to the `data` property of the `Heatmap` object. This function will be called from within the animation function every so often to populate the same array with another month's data. Let's start with the basic function, the `animate()` function, whose task is to populate the `data` array with the precipitation data of the current month (one data point per location). The definition of the `animate()` function is shown in Listing 20-3.

Listing 20-3
The `animate()` function populates the data array associated with the heatmap.

```
function animate() {
  data = [];
  for (site=0; site<12; site++) {
    if (month == 0)
        data.push({location: new
          google.maps.LatLng(precipitationData[site].coords[0],
                          precipitationData[site].coords[1]),
          weight: 100 * parseFloat(
                  precipitationData[site].precipitation[month])});
```

```
            else
                data[site]={location: new
                    google.maps.LatLng(precipitationData[site].coords[0],
                                    precipitationData[site].coords[1]),
                        weight: 100 * parseFloat(
                            precipitationData[site].precipitation[month])};
        }
    heatmap.setData(data);
    month++;
}
```

The function populates the data array with rainfall data for each of the 12 sites (states). The month variable, which represents the current month, is incremented by one at each iteration of the animation function, and it's declared outside the function because it must maintain its value between successive calls of the function. The code starts by clearing the data array, and then it iterates through the elements of the precipitationData array; each element of this array is an object that holds the coordinates of a specific city as a LatLng object and the precipitation of this city for each month in an array of 13 elements (the 12 values and their total). The animate() function iterates the elements of the precipitationData array and extracts the city location and the current month's rainfall value. This value is then multiplied by 100 to end up with integer values, but this is not a requirement of the Heatmap layer or the code.

After populating the data array, the code sets the heatmap object's data to the data array by calling the setData() method and passing the array with the current values as an argument. The last statement increases the month variable by one, to point to the next month's data. As you can guess, the application's animation function will call this function once for each month, as explained next.

Calling the Animation Function

To initiate the animation, create the startAnimation() function to update the heatmap every second:

```
function startAnimation() {
    month = 0;
    int=setInterval(function(){animate()},1000);
}
```

If you had daily data, you could update the heatmap every few milliseconds for a fluid animation, but with 12 frames you can't produce real animation. The function initializes the month variable and then calls the setInterval() method. The startAnimation() function must be called from within a button's click event. When all frames are exhausted, you must end the effect of the setInterval() method. This must take place in the animate() function when the month variable's value exceeds 12. Insert the following statement in the animate() function (it's the very first statement in the function):

```
if (month > 12) {clearInterval(int); return;}
```

To complete the page, you must add to your form the map and a button that will initiate the animation. Here's the complete listing of the page's <body> section:

```
<body onload="initialize()">
  <button onclick="startAnimation()">Start animation</button>
  <div id="map_canvas" style="height: 500px; width: 700px;"></div>
  <div id='monthDisplay'></div>
</body>
```

The name of the current month is displayed on a <div> element that is placed on the map with the appropriate style. This is the monthDisplay element, and it's updated from within the animate() function with the following statement:

```
document.getElementById('monthDisplay').innerHTML = monthNames[month];
```

The monthNames array is initialized in the JavaScript code, along with the percipitationData array—you can open the Percipitation.html page to view the complete code. In addition to the monthly data, there's a yearly average value for each site in the precipitation data, which is displayed after the animation has gone through all 12 months. The last value is treated like another monthly value that corresponds to an extra month with the caption "Year Average." The definition of the monthNames array is the following:

```
var monthNames = ["January", "February", "March", "April", "May", "June",
                  "July", "August", "September", "October", "November",
                  "December", "Year Average"];
```

Aggregating the Rainfall Values

Another similar page is the Precipitation Aggregate.html page, which displays a heatmap of the same data, but instead of showing one month's data at a time, it displays the total rainfall so far. The difference between the two pages is that the new one aggregates the precipitation values by adding the new precipitation to the current total in the data array. Figure 20-8 shows the final heatmap of the yearly aggregate precipitation.

At the end of the animation, the heatmap displays the yearly total precipitation at each location, and not the yearly average. Both the average and the total are useful metrics and each one is better suited for specific requirements. You should open both pages to see how they differ and the type of information each one conveys. You will notice, for example, that the heatmap over Florida turns blue for certain months. This indicates heavy rainfall during the summer months in Florida, and especially during July. In the aggregate version of the page, the map over Florida never becomes blue because the total rainfall over Florida isn't nearly as much as it is over other areas, such as Alabama. If you're wondering why the color over Florida becomes blue for the monthly data and never for the aggregate precipitation, you should take into consideration the fact that the heatmap's color range is determined by the minimum and maximum values of the entire data set, and not by the absolute values. As you can see, both presentations are meaningful and each has its own merits.

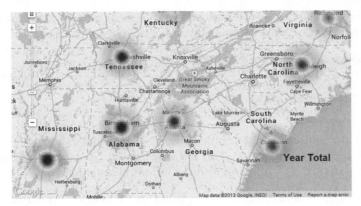

Figure 20-8   The yearly total precipitation of eastern states

The two pages differ in the way they update the data array. While the first page assigns a new precipitation value to each element of the array, the Precipitation Aggregate .html page adds the new precipitation value to the array element, and the values of the array passed to the heatmap layer are aggregates. Here's the complete listing of the animate() function of the new page:

```
function animate() {
  if (month > 11) {clearInterval(int); return;}
  document.getElementById('monthDisplay').innerHTML = monthNames[month];
  for (site = 0; site < 12; site++) {
    if (month == 0)
        data.push({location:
                     new google.maps.LatLng(
                             precipitationData[site].coords[0],
                             precipitationData[site].coords[1]),
                   weight: 100 * parseFloat(
                             precipitationData[site].precipitation[month])});
    else {
        data[site] = {location:
                       new google.maps.LatLng(
                             precipitationData[site].coords[0],
                             precipitationData[site].coords[1]),
                     weight: data[site].weight +
                             100 * parseFloat(precipitationData[site].
                             precipitation[month])};
    }
  }
  heatmap.setData(data);
  month++;
}
```

The rest of the code remains the same. It still displays the map of the United States, populates the data array, and initiates the animation when the button Start Animation is clicked. After that, the animation function takes over and updates the heatmap every second.

That's All Folks, Thank You!

Thank you for reading this book. You have a solid understanding of the Google Maps API by now and in the course of reading this book, you have probably found some interesting or useful topics and techniques that you can apply to your projects. I hope you liked reading it, because I certainly enjoyed writing it.

If you come up with corrections and/or ideas to improve this book, or an interesting idea in the general area of mapping and GIS that you would like to share, please contact me at pevangelos@yahoo.com.

Index